ST. JOHN'S SCHOOL
LIBRARY

WEALTH AND SOCIETY IN EARLY SIXTEENTH CENTURY ENGLAND

WEALTH AND SOCIETY IN EARLY SIXTEENTH CENTURY ENGLAND

J.C.K. CORNWALL

Routledge & Kegan Paul

LONDON

First published in 1988 by
Routledge & Kegan Paul Ltd
11 New Fetter Lane, London EC4P 4EE

Set in 10/12 Erhardt
by Columns of Reading
and printed in Great Britain
by Butler & Tanner Ltd, Frome & London

British Library Cataloguing in Publication Data
Cornwall, J.C.K.
Wealth and society in early sixteenth
century England.
1. England—Social conditions—16th
century   2. Great Britain—History—
Henry VIII, 1509–1547
I. Title
942.05   HN385

ISBN 0–7100–9637–2

To W.G. Hoskins

CONTENTS

TABLES

PREFACE

A STAGE has been reached at which further contributions to the now formidable volume of work on Tudor England risk retracing already well-trodden paths unless they break fresh ground. 'Recent years', as Messrs Wilson and Parker have observed,[1] 'have seen a growing volume of criticism of the older "institutional" type of economic history which consisted to a large extent of the description of economic institutions and supposed systems, *dirigiste* or *non-dirigiste*', in place of which today's socio-economic historians demand 'a type of history more securely, precisely and dynamically based on quantitative material'.

With the new course charted, the records of Cardinal Wolsey's ingenious experiment in fiscal reform in the 1520s affords the requisite material. Although far from unknown or unused, this source has not hitherto been exploited to the full. Now, explored without the constraints of institutions and systems, these extraordinary records prove capable of adding little short of a whole new dimension to the social history of England in the sixteenth century.

ACKNOWLEDGMENTS

IN THE COURSE of this work I have become greatly indebted for the invaluable advice and assistance of friends and colleagues, as well as many others with whom I have not the pleasure of being personally acquainted. Its inception owes much to the example of Professor W.G. Hoskins, and his encouragement and wise counsel in the early stages of research.

Although the subject lies outside his own area of specialisation, my old friend Walter L. Arnstein, Professor of History at the University of Illinois, gallantly undertook the duties of *ad hoc* literary adviser, offering invaluable guidance on presentation. As Series Editor, Eric Evans, of whose well-earned promotion last year to the University of Lancaster Chair of Social History I was glad to learn, has been an unfailing source of sound common sense. Dr A.L. Beier, also of Lancaster, kindly read and commented on Chapter 5, and John Pound, University of East Anglia, generously made available an unpublished study of the Norfolk clergy. Paul Rutledge, Mrs E.M. Elvey and Professor B.P. Wolffe kindly supplied information on specific points. I am most grateful to Alan D. Dyer for permission to reproduce his statistics of Worcester city, as well as to those who have kindly permitted me to cite their unpublished theses: Jeremy Goring, Felix Hull, Eric Kerridge, Roger Schofield and John Sheail; the Goldsmiths' Librarian of the University of London sanctioned citation of Mr J. Spratt's thesis when the author could not be traced. My thanks to Mrs R.J. Hammond of West Hartford, Connecticut, in respect of her late husband's work must be coupled with deep regret that my enquiry should have been made in all innocence shortly after his recent decease.

Besides, as is her wont, taking responsibility for the index, my wife made the numerical analysis of the Essex subsidy, a great saving of time, made possible by the kindness of Vic. Gray, County Archivist, in lending me the transcripts belonging to the Record Office. Last, but by no means least, my former colleague Andrew Phillips has done yeoman service in proof reading.

Any merits the ensuing pages may possess are due to these and numerous kindnesses; any defects are my exclusive responsibility.

J.C.

Copford Green, Essex

INTRODUCTION

THE FORCEFUL personalities and towering creative geniuses that give Tudor England a perennial fascination as much for the general reader as for the professional historian also make it easy to overlook the millions of less distinguished contemporaries who were too involved in the problems of living to leave any mark on history. If there are no masterpieces by some forgotten Shakespeare still awaiting discovery, it was not simply for lack of talent but for the more prosaic reason that the vast majority of sixteenth-century Englishmen were either illiterate or very nearly so. Nor were their personal papers, if any, thought worth preserving; intimate details of the life of King Edward IV's illegitimate son Arthur Plantagenet, Viscount Lisle, whom Henry VIII appointed deputy of Calais in 1533, have become familiar to us only because one day in 1540 he was arrested on (groundless) suspicion of treason, and his papers confiscated by the government and filed with the state papers.[1]

For most of the Tudor age this 'silent majority' appears to us as an anonymous, undifferentiated mass whose members were hardly ever recorded as individuals. Social surveys were never even contemplated, much less attempted, but the elements of one can be extracted, as an unintentional, though none the less welcome by-product, from the comprehensive survey of people and their wealth included in the extraordinary muster held in 1522. In March of that year the commissioners for the county of Essex directed the bailiff and chief constable of Waltham half hundred[2] to order

> all Constables of euery towne, hamlet, Parish and village within the said hundred, personally to appeare before vs ... the said

1

commissioners on Monday next coming, the last day of the month of March at Waltham holy crosse, and there to bring with them a certificate in writing of the names of all manner of men aboue the age of 16 yeeres, dwelling within . . . the said hundred . . . [And] also give commandment to all manner of temporall men dwelling . . . within . . . the same halfe hundred personally to appeare before vs . . . the said Monday next coming, furnished and apparelled in their best array for the war . . .

and in addition to

certifie vs in writing . . . of all their names and whom they belong vnto. Also who is Lord of euery towne or hamlet . . . and who bee Stewardes. Item who be parsons of the same townes, and what the benefices be worth by yeere. Also who be owners of euery parcell of land within any towne . . . with the yeerely value of euery mans land within the same townes . . . And of euery stocke and stocks of Cattell, or other things that be occupied vpon any ferme . . . and who be owners of them. Also what aliants or strangers dwell in anytowne . . . and where they were borne, and vnder whose dominion. Item, what occupation, mystery or substance they be of. Item, the value and substance of euery person being 16 yeeres and aboue . . . as well spirituall as temporall. Also what pensions goeth out of any lands there to any religious or spirituall men.

Implementation in full of these specifications was certain to create an unparallelled record of people actually living at the time. For one little, but not untypical, village in Rutland[3] it reads:

TIXOVER

The Warden of Tattershall is Chieff lord of the Town	in land £10		nonresident
Robert Whalley, gent. steward	fees	6s. 8d.	„
Edward Darby, Clerk, parson	parsonage goes with Ketton (where he lives)		
John Smyth, yoman	land £3	goods £26	
William Brettyn, husbandman, tenant to the Warden	„	24s.	£20
John Plattis, husbandman & tenant to the Warden		nil	£16
Richard Johnson, ditto		nil	£15
John Euerton, ditto		nil	£10

2

Robert Strawker, ditto	nil	£4	
Henry Fairman, ditto	nil	40s.	
William Hochyn, laborer & tenant to the Warden	nil	20s.	
3 laborers (names)	nil	nil	old men & pore
6 servants (to men above)	nil	nil	yong men & pore

The Church Stoke £3

Although he could hardly have seen any of this material for himself, an eighteenth-century Huguenot historian did not hesitate to rate it as comparable to Domesday Book,[4] though, in detailing individuals, it surpassed William the Conqueror's survey of 1086, which, except for the king's tenants-in-chief, dealt exclusively with categories. Not all the certificates have been preserved – some were never returned – and inevitably the quality of those that have been preserved is variable. Nonetheless, augmented by some of the loan books for 1522–3 and the subsidy rolls for 1524–5, they add up to a unique record of the economic standing of almost 70,000 of Henry VIII's subjects, down to the very poorest, who owned nothing at all – a clear 10 per cent of the adult male population at the time[5] – living in six complete counties, with sizeable portions of three more, and two leading provincial cities.[6]

Executed in strict secrecy, this project was a thinly disguised preliminary to taxation,[7] a necessary step towards the reform of the obsolete system. Cardinal Wolsey's plan was to obtain by subterfuge the new and realistic assessments that were essential for effective taxation and could not be got openly. Everybody was required to declare on oath the full value of his assets, the commissioners being instructed to counter the surprise this caused by explaining that the purpose was solely to ascertain the rate at which each man should contribute to the furnishing of arms and harness for the war with France which was in fact declared in May. Employing any and every means, foul as well as fair, the commissioners, hand picked for the occasion, pressed everyone to make a full and frank statement of his wealth; indeed, the tale went that 'some avaunced themselfes more than they were worth of pride, not remembryng [realising] what was comyng . . .'[8]

First of all, as soon as the assessments were complete, came a swingeing forced loan levied on the better-off people at the rates of 10 per cent on £20–£300, 13⅓ per cent on £300–£1,000, and at the commissioners' discretion on higher assessments; in 1523 also the 10 per cent was extended to assessments down to £5, catching people who in the ordinary way escaped taxation, and netting in all upwards of £260,000.[9] Next Wolsey demanded from Parliament a subsidy of £800,000, levied at the rate of 4s. in the pound (20 per cent) on the new assessments. A hostile House received this coolly and, after lengthy haggling, granted 1s. in the pound for two years on all income from land and the value of moveables worth £20 and over, 6d. in the pound on goods less than £20 down to £2, also a poll tax of 4d. on those owning less than 40s. in goods but taking wages of at least 20s. a year; a third payment of 1s. was added on assessments upwards of £50, making 3s. in all; all rates were doubled for aliens. No one was to be taxed on more than one form of wealth, but was taxed on whichever would yield the largest amount.[10]

Although it was tacitly understood that assessment should revert to earlier, somewhat lower levels, this subsidy produced a total – unprecedented for a parliamentary grant – of nearly £156,000;[11] the lords temporal were privileged to assess themselves independently, and the clergy taxed themselves separately in their convocations. In some respects the most interesting feature of this exceptionally comprehensive subsidy is the fleeting glimpse it affords of labourers whose only assets were their wages; since they only paid 4d. they cannot have contributed very much to the sum total – at any rate the experiment was not considered worth repeating.

The purpose of the work now in hand is for the first time fully to exploit these unique sources in order to take a broad cross-section of the nation towards the mid-point of the reign of Henry VIII and bring into sharper focus certain rather elusive aspects of the society and economy of Tudor England.

As in any social survey the point of departure is a review of the types of people comprised by society in the sixteenth century, taking the opportunity to extend the familiar definitions of status with economic parameters. The core of this essay consists of an analysis of the distribution of wealth socially, noting also the many regional variants, firstly of personality, and secondly the more complex question of landed property. This establishes the basis of an examination of the complex of social relationships which at that time was epitomised as the Common Weal, taking advantage of the nature of the evidence to probe further that much-discussed subject the peasantry. After this, indeed, as an extension of the same topic, we may proceed to clarify the novel phenomena wage labour, unemployment and vagrancy, and, in conclusion, attempt a reassessment of the critical rural and urban problems of the era.

4

It is no accident that the available records produce a bias towards the southern and eastern counties, and no disadvantage, for it was there that the majority of the population lived and that most wealth was produced, which may well account for the failure of some of the more remote and backward shires to make their returns.

Most history, as some people are apparently never weary of complaining, ignores ordinary people. The sense of this hackneyed expression seems largely a matter of taste; the question of its validity, if any, is best left to those who are inclined to ponder abstract concepts. It is immeasurably less rewarding than getting to know Henry VIII's people as individuals in their own right irrespective of their relationship to institutions and their place in 'supposed systems'.

CHAPTER ONE

STATUS AND WEALTH

IN THEIR most rudimentary state the returns which form the basis of this study amount to nothing more exciting than parallel columns of names and sums of money flanked, in the musters, by notes of military particulars. The occasional person is classed as a gentleman, and very infrequently mention is made of the occupation of some humbler mortal, usually (one suspects) to distinguish him from a neighbour of the same name. It is only too evident that the scribes considered gentility the only status worth recording, and even in this they were not consistent; civic dignity was almost invariably ignored. Consequently the first problem in tackling this mass of data, comprehending nearly 70,000 names, is to devise a taxonomy capable of transcending the obvious fact that some were richer (or poorer) than others – one, moreover, which bears some tangible relationship to the structure of society at the time, and preferably is verifiable in terms of contemporary theory.

THEORIES OF SOCIETY

Interest in the nature of society was not lacking in the sixteenth century, and in one way or another commentators found a good deal to say about it. Granted, many of their observations are fragmentary, confined to particular social groups, most commonly the gentry and clergy, vagabonds and beggars, and directed more to their conduct (or rather misconduct) than to anything else. Where anything resembling an analytic survey was attempted the outcome is prone to reveal more about the background and interests of the author than the matter in hand, describing the aristocracy and gentry in detail while displaying markedly less understanding of the composition and characteristics of the lower orders.

Edmund Dudley, Henry VII's minister, composed *The Tree of Commonwealth* in the Tower while awaiting execution for treason. Primarily a political tract, it can in no sense be regarded as an empirical analysis of society. The concept of the social order is schematic, a simplistic division into three estates, the chivalry, the church and the commonalty. The first of these was the landowning class, the nobility and gentry; the leaders of the community, whose duty it was to set a good example to the rest, to be 'the helpers and releuers of poore tenantes, and also be the maynteynors and supporters of all poore folkes'. The commonalty embraced the remainder of the laity inclusive of 'merchants, craftsmen (or artificers), franklains and husbandmen' as well as 'serving men'. But where, on the one hand, the hierarchy of the chivalry is systematically catalogued, from dukes to mere gentlemen, the commonalty is differentiated only to the extent that a passing reference to 'the chief of theis folkes, as the substantiall marchauntes, the welthie grasiers and farmers' acknowledges the existence of sub-species. Unconcerned with the affairs of such people, the author does not attempt to do more than define their essentially subordinate role: they should not 'presume aboue ther own degre, nor conterfete the state of his Better, nor excede in their apparell or diet'. It was the duty of merchants and craftsmen to trade honestly with one another, of husbandmen and artificers to apply themselves diligently to their labours and take pleasure in them, eschewing ostentation as well as hunting and hawking, which were the privileges of the gentry, nor wasting their time and substance in alehouses or playing unlawful games. 'And how well content will men be from the highest degre to the lowest, to encrease ther howshold seruantes and laborers, whereby all idle people and vagaboundes shalbe sett a worke.' Servants too ought to be diligent and refrain from gaming and other dissolute pursuits, although at the same time they were fully entitled to 'competent wages and clothing with trew paymentes of the same'.[1]

Surveying the state of England in 1551, Sir Thomas Smith dealt more circumstantially with the question of social status.[2] He identified four 'sorts' of people – gentlemen, citizens or burgesses, yeomen, and artificers or labourers. The clergy no longer formed a discrete estate, the religious having disappeared while the secular establishment had been deprived of its privileges. Gentlemen corresponded to Dudley's 'chivalry', with peers defined as being 'the greater sort'. 'No man', he adds, 'is created baron excepte he maye dispend of yearly reuenue one thousand poundes, or one thousand markes at the least', figures that were normally exceeded by the estates of earls. Legally an income of £40 a year rendered a freeholder liable to take up knighthood, but as a result of inflation £120 was now desirable to support the dignity. Esquires are described simply as men who bear arms. The definition of gentleman is explored in some detail. The rank was either conferred by birth or else acquired by practice of the law, medicine or the liberal sciences, membership of a university, or serving as a 'captain in war'. But the qualifications were elastic; anyone who could 'live without manuell labour, and thereto is able and will beare the port, charge, and countenance of a gentleman, he shall for monie haue a cote and armes bestowed vpon him by heralds and therevnto being made so good cheape be called master and reputed for a gentleman euer after'.

What Dudley had dismissed as the faceless commonalty Smith perceived as three distinct status groups, and accordingly found space to comment on each. By citizens and burgesses he meant the freemen of corporate towns, taking it for granted that his readers would understand that this privilege had in practice come to be restricted to the richer inhabitants – merchants, not working craftsmen. Unlike Dudley he was well aware that merchants, a fast growing class, were not segregated from the gentry by an unbridgeable gulf, but 'often change estate with gentlemen, as gentlemen doo with them by a mutuall conuersion of the one with the other'.

The definition of yeomen was complex, a matter of subtle distinctions.[3] Freeborn men and small landowners, they were in theory able to 'dispend of their owne land in yearlie reuenue, to the summe of fortie shillings sterling, or six pounds as monie goeth in our time & commonlie liue wealthilie, keepe good houses and travell to get riches'. Within the community they made no attempt to ape the gentry, were accorded no special title, and yet enjoyed 'a certeine preheminence, and more estimation than labourers & the common sort of artificers'. Nonetheless, having surveyed the yeomanry at length, Smith too reached the point beyond which he possessed little specific knowledge of the people under discussion, unless he felt that there was little that could usefully be said about those who had 'neither voice nor authority in the commonwealth, and no account is made of them but onelie to be ruled, not to rule others'. This 'fourth sort of people' did not own land in freehold, but comprised poor husbandmen, day labourers and copyholders, with some retailers and all artificers. There were also 'great swarms of idle servingmen', whom he seems to have regarded as

9

peripheral to ordered society, if not actually outside it, quoting a proverb, 'Young servingmen, old beggars'.

In the *Discourse of the Common Weal*[4] Smith (to whom it is now attributed) did not set out to delineate the structure of society, but rather to present and analyse the responses of the four main economic interests in the community to the crisis of the late 1540s. Freed thus from the constraint of traditional sterotypes, he was able to develop a dynamic model of society, although the four sorts of people are still present. The knight speaks for the landed interest, the merchant for international trade, and the capper for the working master craftsman. Agriculture is here represented not by the glamorous (and faintly mythical) yeoman but by the workaday husbandman, or small peasant farmer, counterpart of the craftsman. To the extent that it preserves the concept of *De Republica* the scheme would appear designed to mirror an ideal that was ordinarily taken for granted. But the author, assuming in the guise of the Doctor the role of moderator, reminds his interlocutors of the existence of an additional element, a large class of landless peasants who were almost entirely dependent on wages for their livelihood. In effect it is conceded that society was in a state of flux, consisting not of four but of five estates, subject nevertheless to fundamental reservations, for the labouring poor are not adjudged worthy of an independent voice. Almost a hundred years later the Levellers, in the Putney debates, were to reach deadlock over the problem whether men without an assured livelihood could be admitted to the political nation.[5]

The common feature of all these interpretations is, however, that, the gentry apart, they define rank and degree in none but the most general terms. At best they furnish little more than an outline guide to the interpretation of the numerical data, a hint of the kind of hypothesis that needs to be tested.

THE SUMPTUARY ACTS

The official definition of social status found expression in sumptuary regulation which, between 1510 and 1533, was embodied in several statutes.[6] Apart from any need to counter persistent infringement of the rules of dress and display, the number of enactments is indicative of considerable uncertainty, for not only did the legislature feel impelled to extend the terminology of rank with monetary equivalents, these latter were made the subject of continual amendment within the broad permanent framework. Here again it was the nobility and gentry who got the most attention, but at the same time the inferior ranks of society were defined with some rigour.

Peers, naturally, posed no problem. Knights too were readily identifiable, but it had become imperative to make provision also for the many untitled men whose wealth was as great or even greater. Consequently in 1510 these were bracketed with squires of the body and other court officers, while the 1533 act specifies in addition esquires or gentlemen eligible for knighthood or to serve as knights of the shire. Even this proved insufficient to cover all cases, and so the class was enlarged to embrace 'other men' possessing incomes from land of 200 marks a year (1510) or £200 (1533); these might have been merchants or any other persons whose wealth was of recent acquisition.

Taken as a whole the acts envisage several grades of gentleman. The highest rating was £100 a year, the next 100 marks, which was equated with 'other' landowners of £100, the implication perhaps being that the latter had not yet got as far as quartering their arms. Next came gentlemen on incomes of £40 and £20, respectively. The second amount bore a twofold significance, since a statute of the previous century stipulated a minimum of £20 per annum for justices of the peace,[7] while two of the sumptuary acts evidently assumed this to have been the minimum for any gentleman by defining a class 'under the degree of gentlemen', including university graduates, having £10 a year in lands or £100 in goods – a clear reference, it would seem, to merchants. Room was also found in one act for men of £5 per annum plus yeomen, or servants, who were 40s. freeholders. Finally came men who did not own freehold land: husbandmen, servants in husbandry and the servants of artificers – anyone whose estate in goods and chattels did not exceed £10. By process of elimination a further group intermediate between these and the smaller freeholders can be inferred, men owning personal estate worth £10–£99, such as larger tenant farmers, provincial merchants and so forth. Last of all there were wage labourers.

These categories reveal an intricate relationship between social rank and economic standing, so much so as to invite the conclusion that by this date, if not much earlier, it had come to be acknowledged that status was a function of source and level of income, subject to the proviso that land took precedence over personal property. Yet since the facts have to be assembled from statutes passed at different dates without any discernible attempt at harmonisation, it is not easy to formulate an exact statement. In approximate terms the picture may be sketched as shown in Table 1.1.

Table 1.1   Social structure from sumptuary acts

| | Specified categories | | Equivalent men | |
	Land £	Goods £	Land £	Goods £
Peers (5 degrees)				
Knights and court officials			133/200	
Gentlemen	67		100	
Gentlemen	40		40	
Gentlemen	20		10/20	100[*]
Other landowners	5			
Yeomen and servants	2			10–99
Husbandmen, servants, artificers		10 (max.)		

[*]Graduates, etc., below the rank of gentleman

In the process of definition the subdivisions of the gentry are shown to have been as numerous as those of the peerage (which for the present purpose need not be set out in detail), and noticeably more complex. Knights naturally took precedence as the leading members of the class, and there is no difficulty about demonstrating that they were also the richest despite the existence of a good many whose incomes fell far short of £200. The clear inference must be that the average knight was expected to have at least the £120 a year postulated by Smith, and indeed the median of twenty-three in Buckinghamshire, Suffolk and Sussex in 1524–5 lay between £120 and £160, while nationally the median of eighteen feodary surveys works out at £204. In the same counties, with the addition of Cornwall and Rutland, the median for eighty-five esquires was about £60 compared with £80 from 124 feodary surveys; several men were worth upwards of £200[8] and clearly correspond with the first group of gentlemen in the table. As the law requiring £40 landowners to take up knighthood was seldom observed, the sumptuary acts conceded that it was reasonable for the many men who did not choose to do so to adopt the dress appropriate to the standard of living they must certainly have enjoyed. Indeed, the specification of grades of untitled gentlemen of £40 or more amounted to an admission that the qualification was obsolete, that this level of income was totally inadequate to support the 'port and charge' of the dignity of knighthood.

The borderland between gentlemen and others occurred in the region below £20 a year. Only one of the statutes accords the title of gentleman to landowners of this magnitude, yet it is clear that a great many, if not most of them, laid claim to the style even at the risk of carrying a bigger sail than they could bear. Among them must have been many new men pushing up from below. Graduates, whom Smith classed as gentlemen, and men of £10 a year were privileged to dress like their betters; it is also reasonable to infer that a sizeable proportion of those who feature in the various returns as minor landowners were in effect *ex-officio* gentlemen, qualified by tenure of lesser public appointments.

The elliptical phraseology of the law, amounting in places to ambiguity, obscures the cut-off point for gentility, if indeed there was one in view of the presence in the musters and subsidy rolls of a not inconsiderable number of gentlemen of extremely limited means. Already as early as 1436 the word had lost its original connotation of nobleman, and been extended to cover merchants and yeomen who had got rich, together with some landowners of as little as £5 a year claiming the title.[9] The statistical confirmation of the reality of so many gentlemen 'made good cheape'[10] may have been what prompted Garter King of Arms' decision in 1530 to set a minimum qualification of £10 per annum for sporting a coat of arms.[11] Dr R.B. Smith adopts this criterion in his study of West Riding society in the 1530s,[12] but for the 1520s, albeit the genuinely hard cases (including one assessment as low as £1 per annum) were few and far between, men of £5 or more per annum tended on the whole either to be designated gentlemen or else can be linked with gentry families. Accordingly a minimum of £5 will be preferred in the present work, not so much as an arbitrary demarcation, but rather as one which should prompt us to seek further evidence to confirm the holder's status. Certainly the intermediate standing of many of these men is plain to see; the alternating qualifications of £10 in lands and £100 in goods seem specifically designed to cater for small-town merchants and the less affluent London ones, conceding statutory confirmation of the observation that they 'often change estate with gentlemen'.

The category yeomen or servants of £2 a year underlines not only their theoretical status as 40s. freeholders but also a much older meaning of the word 'yeoman'. The drafters of the 1533 act can readily be imagined looking up the statute of Richard II which referred to 'varlets called yeomen' in the service of lords[13] – the Canon's Yeoman no less. Several yeomen in Rutland were described as servants, while the *Discourse of the Common Weal* comments 'xl^s a yeare was good honeste wages for a yeoman afore this time, and xx^d a wekes borde wages was sufficient'.[14] Conservative in aim, it was natural for this legislation to emphasise an obsolescent, legalistic definition, and evade contemporary reality.

The two final categories call for no comment at this stage beyond the fact that the fiscal evidence shows that the overwhelming majority of husbandmen did actually have less than £10 worth of personal estate; the £10–£99 group looks like an intrapolation to accommodate a broad spectrum of well-to-do peasants (including yeomen), master craftsmen and small-time merchants. The term 'wage earner' sums up what the acts list as servants in husbandry, shepherds (some of whom were recorded in Rutland) – common labourers, and servants to artificers in the towns. To be precise it should be remarked that this catalogue concludes with husbandmen worth less than £10, and as such corresponding almost exactly with Smith's fourth sort of people. In the eyes of their betters the rank and file of the peasantry formed a single class with the labouring poor, the customary epithet 'the poor commons' covering them all.

OCCUPATIONAL WEALTH

Only three of the muster books provide the information necessary to relate assessed wealth to status and occupational groups. Fortunately the areas to which they refer represent sharply contrasted types. Coventry was a provincial capital, one of the half-dozen largest provincial cities and the fourth richest.[15] Babergh hundred in Suffolk was possibly the most intensively industrialised district at the time; while Rutland can with confidence be accepted as representative of the rural East Midlands, a region of mainly traditional farming, innocent of any industrial growth. In quality the evidence varies somewhat. The survey of Rutland not only covers a complete, if miniature, county, but also records the status of virtually every inhabitant in all but three townships; although the subsidy rolls contribute useful supplementary material we will, for the present purpose, restrict ourselves to the muster book. The other two returns, the Coventry one especially, are much less comprehensive though none the less indispensable.

With a few exceptions labourers and servants in Rutland were men whose assessments were below £2, which in turn were virtually identical with subsidy assessments based on wages. The overlap with husbandmen can be attributed in large measure to uncertainty as to the precise status of a minority whom one return called labourers (or servants) while the other described them differently. George Rogerson of Stretton was a servant who owned goods valued at £4 and was reclassed as a husbandman in the subsidy.[16] Some must have been employed as supervisors. In 1549 the ironworks at Sheffield and Worth in Sussex were each managed by 'one man, hyred by the year, to attend upon the works and workmen, all the tyme, and wey the iron ffrom the workman to the merchaunte, and hath for his wages, by the yeare, iiij^{li}, a liuerie or x^s, mete and and drinke'. Two waggoners were also employed at Sheffield at £2 a year each, the rest of the hands at both sites being 'hyred after a rate of taske work'.[17] Although the Rutland subsidy rated 38 out of 270 labourers at £2 on goods, and one as high as £3, all £1 assessments were made on wages or 'profet of wages'.

Husbandmen, as was to be expected with the most numerous class – and as the typical countrymen – comprehended a broad spectrum. Below the £10 mark identification is a simple matter, thanks not least to the corroboration of the sumptuary acts. The £10–£19 group also consisted predominantly of husbandmen, as often as not occupying the position of leading members of the village community, 'commonly made churchwardens, sidesmen, aleconners, now and then constables, and many times enjoy the name of headboroughs'.[18] In fourteen out of fifty-one Rutland townships there was no one who was better off. Many of those at the foot of the scale, whose substance was equalled by that of superior labourers, must have occupied very small holdings, and had to eke out a livelihood with occasional labouring or working at some by-employment; they have aptly been termed 'cottage farmers'.[19] No wonder the muster takers and subsidy collectors sometimes experienced difficulty in classifying them. In the nature of things a leavening of the poorer husbandmen (and yeomen, for that matter) may be presumed to have been elderly and retired from active farming.[20] The top end of the range is confusing. In view of the fact that £20 constituted the base line for richer taxpayers, it is difficult to explain why mere husbandmen, who typically were small farmers, should have formed three-quarters of the £20–£39 class, far outnumbering yeomen, businessmen, and even gentlemen. The tiny minority worth as much as £40 should almost certainly be counted as yeomen.

Table 1.2 Distribution of personal wealth by occupation

Occupation	Nil	£1	£2	£3–4	£5–9	£10–19	£20–39	£40–99	£100+	Total
				Number of assessments						
Rutland										
Esquire							4	2	2	8
Gentleman				2	3	8	3	3	6	25
Yeoman			1	1	4	7	8	5	1	27
Husbandman	2	16	107	146	178	136	64	9		658
Labourer	158	168	26	4	4					360
Servant	76	18	8	4						106
Tradesmen	4	15	5	5	13	4	5	1		52
Laity total	240	217	147	162	202	155	84	20	9	1,236
Clergy		10	9	5	11	9	4	1		49
Suffolk										
Knight									2	2
Esquire								3	2	5
Gentleman							4	4	3	11
Yeoman			1	1	5	16	15	14	2	54
Husbandman	3	1	14	31	54	56	34	3		196
Labourer	168	171	105	63	17	3	1			528
Servant	25	–	1	–	1					27
Cloth trader	2	–	4	4	8	30	31	29	28	136
Cloth artificer	65	56	39	24	27	19	5			235
Leather trades	12	9	5	3	4	5	2	1		41
Victualling	5	4	13	4	13	9	8	3	1	60

Building Trades	9	12	18	4	9	4	3	1	60
Metal trades	11	5	3	7	3	9	1	2	41
Services and misc.	1	8	5	8	3	6	6		37
Trades total	105	94	87	54	67	82	56	36	29	610
Grand total	301	266	208	149	144	157	110	60	38	1,433

Coventry

Cloth trader	8	–	2	1	9	6	11	12	9	58
Cloth artificer	118	40	37	12	18	6	7	3	241
Leather trades	44	8	10	5	11	3	6	2	89
Victualling	17	7	20	3	12	14	5	1	3	82
Building trades	31	3	5	2	2	4	1	48
Metal trades	29	7	8	9	2	2	2	1	60
Services and misc.	11	4	5	3	6	4	2	1	36
Laity total	258	69	87	35	60	39	34	20	12	614
Clergy	2	11	12	8	6	6	2	1	2	50

NOTES

Cloth traders: mostly clothiers in Suffolk, drapers and mercers in Coventry; one haberdasher in each return. Two Merchants of the Staple in Coventry.

Cloth artificers included garment makers, with cappers, plus a few hatmakers, forming the largest single trade in Coventry. Finishing crafts outnumbered weavers in Coventry.

Leather trades: primarily tanners and shoemakers, with numerous skinners and corvisors in Coventry; sprinklings of other trades such as tawyers, glovers, saddlers, etc.

Victualling trades: food processors such as butchers, millers, bakers, cooks, brewers; merchants such as grocers, vintners, fishmongers; retailers, e.g. innkeepers, winesellers.

Building trades: construction workers, as carpenters, masons, tilers; carvers and painters, glaziers; woodworkers including sawyers, turners and coopers.

Metal trades included wrights and armament makers who employed mixed materials. Mostly smiths, also pewterers, goldsmiths, plumbers, braziers, wiredrawers, spurriers, cutlers, pinners, etc.

Services: chiefly barbers; small numbers of physicians, surgeons, scriveners, horse-leeches, musicians, parish clerks, pardoners.

Miscellaneous: chandler, tallowchandler, gardener, woodseller, woodburner, bottlemakers (in Coventry), gardeners, colourmakers, pedlars, merchants overseas – not more than one or two of each.

As regards yeomen the statistics serve chiefly to emphasise the difficulty of pinning them down to a precise definition. In Leicestershire their probate inventories show them to have been essentially large-scale farmers, generally working 100 acres or more, sometimes occupying two or more farms extending into more than one parish, renting additional pastures, and with few exceptions distinguished from plain husbandmen by superior wealth.[21] Half the yeomen of Rutland were also freeholders, unlike the majority of husbandmen, though few had as much as 40s. a year. The median value of their personal property was £15, but £20 was the most typical assessment, well above the £6 of the average husbandman.

Men of this stature were offset by others whose status, if not questionable, shows that the meaning of yeoman was passing through a transitional stage. With some of the poorer ones the possibility of misunderstandings cannot be ruled out. The village of Belton was singular in containing several of decidedly slender means. Thomas A. Leycester, worth £2 in goods, was styled yeoman only by the subsidy; he at least had 6s. a year from land, but two husbandmen rated at £4 and £6 owned real property worth 13s. 4d. and 8s., respectively. Several Oakham yeomen plied trades, including a pewterer called William Plavis who would appear to have employed at least two journeymen or apprentices and was one of the two or three richest men in the shire with £200 in goods besides a 40s. freehold. Some, like Robert Fishlock of Thistleton, were taxed on wages; perhaps he was somebody's chief servant, and in any case the muster described him more realistically as a labourer and valued his goods at 30s. Fifteen yeomen were stated to be in the service of some lord or other, four being 'reteyned' by them; six acted as bailiffs of townships, and the remainder were simply 'servants', like Christopher Lacy of Riddlington, 'Seruant in the Howsehold w^t the Lord Hastings', who had £15 in goods, reduced to £8 in the subsidy, where he was described as husbandman. The earl of Huntingdon's household, in 1564, included two yeomen who received the same wages as gentlemen, i.e. 26s. 8d. per annum, and twenty-two more at £1. The exact nature of some of these relationships is not stated, and is consequently rather baffling. John Parker of Belton was a servant of Lord Hastings though retained to Lord Mountjoy. The bailiff of Teigh, servant to Thomas Sherrard, Esq., was styled husbandman despite owning personal estate to the tune of £30, while a retainer of Sir John Digby worked as a barber in Oakham. However, the keepers of Whaddon Chase, Bucks., employed by Mrs Pigott, can be traced in the muster book, and of these the head keeper, Robert Wyllyott (Willett), would certainly have ranked as yeoman with 40s. in land and £20 in goods; his salary was 40s. with 6s. 8d. for livery. Richard Cocks, one of several on 20s. with 6s. 8d. livery, had 3s. 4d. in land and £5 in goods, though all John Sewster of Mursley owned was 20s. in goods; if the identification is correct he would appear to have been of lower status.[22]

Behind these miscellaneous qualifications a residual military function can be detected. Smith devoted some space to explaining how, imbued with martial spirit, yeomen followed the lords of whom they held their land to war, serving on foot as archers. This, it seems, was a widely held assumption: 'If the yeomanry of England were not, in time of war we should be in shrood case; for in them standeth the chief defence of England.'[23] No fewer than half the yeomen in Rutland owned arms and armour; eleven had a 'whole harness for a man', while six had two or more outfits. We can imagine them standing by for orders to levy and equip soldiers from among their lords' tenants when the king summoned his tenants-in-chief to furnish them.[24] The bailiffs of Sir Thomas Lovell at Ryhall, wealthy men worth £80 apiece, each owned three harnesses which might have been the property of their master. Nevertheless, if men such as these were in fact the local recruiting agents, not all were equipped for the job; Nicholas Hill of Oakham, though servant to no less a figure than the king, possessed neither arms nor armour.[25]

In time 'yeoman' came to mean primarily a farmer who had raised himself out of the ruck of common husbandman, 'such as be exempted out of the rascalitie of the popular bee called and written yeomen, as in the degree next vnto gentlemen'; and while careful to avoid making wealth appear the sole criterion, Smith adds that 'these tende their owne businesse, come not to meddle in publike matters and iudgements but when they are called and glad when they are deliuered thereof'. A sound recipe for getting rich! But again the accent was on seniority: 'Commonly wee do not call any a yeoman till he be married, and have children, and as it were some authoritie among his neighbours'.[26] Different records might call the same man husbandman and yeoman, but as he progressed, the latter description would be used with increasing consistency.[27] The final word may lie with the distribution of wealth. In view of the abrupt falling off in the numbers of husbandmen above £20, plus the fact that this figure coincides roughly with the wealth of the average yeoman, farmers assessed at and above it can pragmatically be counted as yeomen.

With the gentry this overlap in personal wealth counted for far less since, as a class, their hallmark was ownership of land. Esquires were straightforward, men of position whose broad acres produced incomes in the range of £30–£80 per annum. Their relatively smaller personal estates reflect perhaps more than anything else a generally modest standard of living in the shires, for while the greater apparent wealth of some yeomen consisted mainly of farming stock, a big landowner, burdened with a large family and heavily encumbered estates, might find himself compelled to endure a spartan existence; unlike a yeomen, moreover, he might have to support a train of unproductive servants.[28] The wide range covered by 'mere' gentlemen could be the product of a variety of factors. Among the 'poor' ones John Digby was farmer of the parsonage of Preston, and the low value of £4 assigned to his moveables may well have been the result of indebtedness: liabilities reduced the estate of John Ranson of Bicker, Lincs., from £57 to slightly less than £16 in 1542. Another man who lived in modest circumstances was Thomas Harington of Ridlington, a non-landowner with only £7 in goods; yet he must have been related to the squire, John Harington the younger, whose servant he was. Some men of this type cannot have been anything but gentlemen farmers. Many could well be taken as illustrations of Sir Thomas Smith's tart comment on those self-styled gentlemen whose pretensions outran their resources. Two men of Yardley, Worcs., who died early in 1554 (by which date inflation was distorting values) exemplify the lower stratum. John Praty's inventory totalled £23, of which two-thirds were accounted for by livestock, implements, etc., making him a farmer in all but name: he also held the lease of a mill in Birmingham. Three-fifths of Daniel Bentford's estate of nearly £20 represented the contents of his house, such as they were. Beds, bedding and linen formed the largest single item; clothing, pots and pans (some of them pewter) and kitchen stuff made up most of the remainder, and apart from a couple of coffers, a table board, two 'chairstools' and a few small boards and forms, totalling 7s., the house was almost bare of furnishings. Outdoors there were two horses, eleven head of cattle and five store pigs. He also owned ten bushels of wheat, and fourteen of barley, and had sown three dayworks (roods) of winter wheat, but no husbandry implements were listed. Finally his estate was reduced by debts to £4 net.[29]

As in the case of yeomen, terminology tended to obey certain rules. 'Gentleman' was applied to, for example, the cadets of eminent families: thus four of the £100 assessments in Rutland belonged to the younger brothers and sisters of Francis Brown, Esq., of Little Casterton.

Again there might be uncertainty when a man was rising in the world; Edward Watson of Lyddington had a personal estate of £200, and as a justice of the peace[30] should be reckoned as esquire; but in Rutland, at any rate, his income was small, a mere £8 per annum. JPs were for the most part recruited from the greatest landowners in a county, although commissions of the peace often included a few of the humbler type, possibly men with a legal background who were appointed to do the chores. In Sussex William Earnley was the son of the Chief Justice of the Common Pleas; in contrast to most of his colleagues, who had at least £40 a year with an average of £100, he had only £26 produced by a medley of very small properties, in addition to which he leased Cakehan manor from the bishop of Chichester.[31]

As the returns normally distinguish them the wealth of the gentry can be surveyed more generally, as shown in Table 1.3. To these can be added rough figures from Staincliffe wapentake in Yorkshire, where status had to be inferred as it was not recorded.[32] There, out of nineteen possible examples, the minimum was as low as 6s. 8d., the maximum £200, and the median £6. 13s. 4d. As many as three owned less than a pound's worth of personal property, and only four more than

Table 1.3 Personal wealth of the gentry

	County	Number	Minimum £	Maximum £	Median £
Knights	Buckingham	3	40	300	200
	Suffolk	7	40	500	133⅓
	Sussex	2	40	66⅓	–
Esquires	Buckingham	18	20	200	73
	Cornwall (part)	24	30	200	66⅔
	Rutland	8	20	100	36
	Suffolk	26	18	333⅓	100
	Sussex	13	24	300	110
Gentlemen	Buckingham	51	4	500	26⅔
	Cornwall	51	6⅔	100	26⅔
	Rutland	27	3	200	13⅓
	Suffolk	75	1	466⅔	60
	Sussex	62	2	200	40

£20. The only knight there, Sir Henry Clifford of Carleton, was assessed at a wretched £8 in moveables, although his income was given as £80 a year. In nearly every respect the wealth of the gentry matched the poverty of the district, and Dr Smith, moreover, has concluded that Yorkshire knights and esquires as a whole were less affluent than their counterparts in the south.[33] As to Rutland, if at first glance its gentry look significantly less prosperous than similar men in other Midland and southern counties, the impression may well be a by-product of the very completeness of the survey, resulting in virtually everyone answering the description being accounted for, whereas with Suffolk and Sussex in particular the subsidy returns, which provide the sole evidence, highlight gentlemen whose goods exceeded their lands in value, and on which in consequence they were taxed. Landed income was the true measure of the gentry, and will be discussed in due course.[34]

As regards trades and crafts, the Rutland material lists too few for generalisation. In fact tradesmen were part-timers, for one from one return is sure to be represented as a farmer or labourer by the other. It will suffice to observe that those on higher assessments were mostly merchants, and the poorer ones manual workers, and to conclude that a tiny farming community was incapable of generating more than a limited demand for their services.

The much ampler statistics for Suffolk and Coventry bear out this superficial impression, besides underlining the primacy of the woollen textile industry. Although chance dictates that the evidence relates to two major centres, the situation thereby depicted does not necessarily misrepresent the economy as a whole, inasmuch as clothing was the only really large-scale manufacture, ranking high even in towns like Leicester and Northampton which had leather wares for their principal products.[35] Coventry, moreover, differed fundamentally from the Stour Valley. Its prosperity was on the wane,[36] weavers were outnumbered two to one by operatives in the finishing processes, while cap making was easily the biggest trade.

The entrepreneurs who organised the cloth trade and marketed its products were sharply differentiated from the operatives employed at the various manufacturing processes. Two-thirds of the Coventry artificers were valued at less than £2, in Babergh hundred, Suffolk, a clear half, many to re-appear in the subsidy lists as wage earners. Better-heeled artificers must almost certainly have been master craftsmen employing labour themselves. If £5 be taken as the minimum above which there can be no question as to their status, it is noteworthy that half the Babergh men in this category worked in the skilled finishing trades. The sole Coventry man stated to have kept a journeyman was assessed at £5, the master of two apprentices was worth £30; on the other hand, a third, who also had an apprentice, owned no property that could be valued.[37] In passing it may be observed that journeymen and apprentices were seldom specified, although this must have been the status of many of the servants that were listed. Two 'servants and apprentices to Richard Coke' were registered at Exeter among a total of nearly thirty, but the listing was arbitrary, nearly all of them being certified in just two parishes. William Cosyn, servant to William Browne (who was worth no more than 20s.), may very well have been a journeyman, for he is followed in the list by Stephen Martyn, 'apprentice to the same William'.[38] For practical purposes £10 was the minimum assessment of clothiers and men of similar standing; the high proportion in Suffolk worth upwards of £100 is not matched by any other extant muster book, and is unlikely to have been equalled anywhere else outside London.[39] Apart from one draper and one mercer all were clothiers, some of them worth several hundreds, and one, Thomas Spring of Lavenham, ranked among the richest men in the land with no less than £3,200. Only one Coventry man was returned as a clothier, but an exceptional weaver valued at £40 must have qualified as one in all essentials. Most of the top men there were mercers and drapers, but one was a dyer and two were Merchants of the Staple, or wool exporters. Association with the cloth trade was a necessary step towards getting to the top in Coventry, and when wealthy baker Thomas Astelen became mayor in 1529 he was described as a clothier.[40]

The wealth of other trades was on a much smaller scale, one that cannot have been untypical of most provincial communities. Except in the various branches of victualling the effective upper limit was just about £40 – indeed, only a tiny minority of assessments exceeded £20. In the manual occupations it is difficult to determine a man's actual position: a smith, for example, was a smith regardless of whether he was assessed at £2 or £20. Superficially the safe solution is to assume that nil and £1 assessments indicate journeymen and apprentices, while from about £5 most must have been master craftsmen. But although this might be tenable for booming Babergh, it will not do for depressed Coventry where many masters were quite poor, and John Langwood (craft unstated) was not the only employer – in this case of an apprentice – who owned no goods worth assessing.[41] Predictably the solitary three-figure assessment in Babergh belonged to a Sudbury grocer, an importer of costly spices; in Coventry there were two, plus a vintner (or importer of wines) and a baker in this bracket. Innkeepers (in Suffolk) and

butchers – both districts specialised in cattle raising – were prominent
among the next highest classes; in general, distribution, exchange, and
service occupations were consistently more remunerative than production. If the highly developed woollen textile industry be disregarded, the
structure of crafts and trades of Babergh may not have been in any way
unrepresentative of the shires at that time. Large mercantile fortunes
were largely concentrated in regional capitals. At Exeter twenty citizens
(3 per cent of the total) were rated at £100–£300, and there was a
flourishing overseas trade.[42] Coventry had an equal number of men of
the top rank, the two richest being a mercer and a draper worth 2,000
marks and £1,000 respectively. Next to these came a Merchant of the
Staple, or wool exporter (one of two), assessed at £666. 13s. 4d.[43]
Another Stapler lived in the tiny Buckinghamshire village of Hogshaw,
but his assets, totalling £300, were exceptional for a country district; he
ranked as a gentleman and was a justice of the peace.[44]

Finally it may be noted that the gentry of Babergh hundred were
more sharply differentiated from the remainder of the community than
their fellows in Rutland. The lesser ones probably opted to seek their
fortune in the clothing trade. Spring, the greatest of the clothiers, owned
land there valued at £105. 10s.; his ancestors had been gentlemen, and
his son John, in 1522 a gentleman in the household of Sir William
Waldegrave at Smallbridge, Bures, dissolved the business on succeeding
his father in 1523.[45] Here again is found a degree of confusion as
between yeomen and husbandmen, although it is easier to appreciate.
Towards the top of the scale the relatively large number of prosperous
husbandmen must be taken as reflecting the high overall level of wealth
reinforced by the demand of the manufacturing population for food; at
the lower end the paucity of £2 assessments can almost certainly be
attributed to the cottage farmers having turned over to weaving and
kindred trades. At the same time it must be remembered that the
occupations of a quarter of the inhabitants were not stated; some of
them must have been farmers, and it is quite conceivable that many of
the omissions were the result of uncertainty as to whether or not to class
the persons in question as agricultural or industrial. Precisely four-fifths
of the yeomen owned land, but even though this was far more widely
diffused than in Rutland there remained a marked contrast between
them and the husbandmen, of whom rather less than half were
freeholders. As everywhere, labourers (and of course many artificers)
virtually accounted for the two lowest levels of assessment. Nevertheless,
they were not unaffected by the general prosperity of the district: more
than one in three owned goods valued at 40s. or more, suggesting (over

and above the usual affluence) a wider, more varied range of jobs and responsibilities created by a more developed economy.

The absence of descriptions of status and occupations from most other certificates is not really an omission. In Essex at least they would have been required for aliens only. Nevertheless, the wording is not entirely free from ambiguity, and no doubt some officials decided to play it safe. Strictly speaking this information was superfluous; at Coventry it was inserted perhaps with a view to recording guild affiliations. So most certificates distinguish only the clergy, as was required, and the gentry were bound to be noticed as landowners and the lords of many other men. Having dealt with these it was safe to lump everyone else together as what Smith dismissed as 'the fourth sort of men which do not rule', i.e. day labourers, poor husbandmen, merchants and retailers, copyholders and artificers. If Rutland was typical of agrarian society it would have been understood as a matter of course that most men were peasant farmers and smallholders; indeed, husbandman was the commonest description there, followed by labourers and servants whose status was one of dependence, and landless peasants who did not conform to the stereotype of a society composed of small independent producers. The very few designated as tradesmen and craftsmen in the musters were almost without exception represented as farmers or labourers in the subsidy (and vice versa), implying that their trades were subsidiary. There was also the practical reason to provide convincing reasons why so many men were possessed of so little or no assessable 'substance', and in the subsidy to justify the assessments of wages which only became effective in the absence of taxable goods, and, moreover, masters were responsible for the payment of their servants' taxes.

Desirable as these descriptions may be, they are not indispensable, for in the light of what has been noted above the assessments themselves are self-explanatory. In fact, in cobbling together what turned out to be a crudely progressive scheme of taxation, government and parliament cannot have been unaware that they were evolving a fiscal taxonomy which corresponded to the main divisions of society.

FISCAL CLASSIFICATION

Pragmatically the key figure was £20. This was set as the minimum for contributions to the first loan, in 1522, men of less substance being let off until, perhaps, the yield had proved disappointing. In the subsidy goods of this value were taxed at 10 per cent for the first two years, the same rate as for land, the owners of which were mostly drawn from the wealthier strata, and double what was levied on smaller assessments. In the range £20–£39 a clear majority of people were taxed on goods, many not owning any land at all, and since personal property at this level was insufficient to confer gentry status, members of the group occupied an intermediate position, lacking on the one hand the landed property necessary for gentlemen; they were, on the other hand, judged competent to pay tax at the same rate as gentlemen, making them men of undeniable substance in comparison with the rank and file of country folk.

The consensus of opinion, nevertheless, was that the fundamental demarcation occurred at £40. Fiscally it signified little, for the total tax liability (inclusive of the loan payment) remained unaltered at 20 per cent, though there is the important social difference that from this point the proportion of subsidy assessments on landed incomes increases sharply. Some instinctive appreciation of this fact may have given rise to the mystique which surrounded £40 a year in contemporary culture. In addition to the theoretical nexus between this and knightly status, the sumptuary act of 1533 bracketed men in general worth that much with some of the knights who took precedence as esquires. As a conventional yardstick of unchallengeable gentility, it featured prominently in the semi-egalitarian manifesto of the Norfolk rebels in 1549 which, although hostile to the gentry at large in important respects, was directed primarily against those whose pretensions rested on no very sure foundation of landed property, and the position of £40-a-year men was expressly reserved throughout.[46] It cannot have been only in relation to land that £40 had a special significance. For the purpose of the Anticipation – the advance payment of the first instalment of the subsidy on assessments of £40 – both lands and goods were treated alike, their owners being considered equally capable of paying sooner than anyone else. Furthermore, the prominent courtier Sir John Hussey's sycophantic resolution, moved in the midst of haggling over the subsidy bill, burdened landed estates of £50 with an additional shilling in the pound, making a total of 15 per cent compared with the general 10. When the gentlemen in the Commons realised what they had committed themselves to, they quickly extended this surcharge to the goods of merchants (and others) of like value.[47] The choice of this figure suggests a well-judged ploy to restrict the highest rate to the truly rich, for it is noticeable that the majority of assessments between £40 and £100 were bunched around the minimum figure.[48] In Rutland there were very few assessments at £50 in 1522, and all were prudently reduced to £40 (more or less) for the subsidy; men on £60 or more could not so plausibly shed their surtax liability. The incidence of this higher rate of tax – totalling, inclusive of the loan, 25 per cent – is therefore misleading; in effect it acknowledged the superior position of £40 men while seeking to evade the full implications.

Many rural taxpayers at £40 and upwards on goods were yeomen who made up in substance what they lacked in status. Some were actually poised on the threshold of gentility, a state they could well afford to maintain, and to which they very frequently attained through the acquisition of real wealth. In contrast, a good many mere country gentlemen possessed very limited personal estates, arguably because their fortunes were declining or, at best, were static,[49] while the wealth of leading yeomen consisted mainly of flourishing, well-stocked farms. It is not altogether improbable that the moveables of the gentry were often undervalued thanks to some lingering influence of fourteenth-century tax rules, which exempted articles such as jewellery and armour which dignified their rank.[50] It was not necessarily that the rich were more adroit at tax avoidance. The owner of large, complex estates, who did not manage them personally, might never have a clear idea of his full income.[51] Moreover, the upper classes lived habitually, indeed ruthlessly, in debt, putting off paying their bills for years until desperate creditors were driven to offer to accept a fraction of their due and forget the rest.[52] So certain privileged persons would place society under tribute, and since no doubt prices tended to be adjusted in compensation, the effect was comparable with that of shop-lifting at the present time.

The range £40–£99 embraced the main body of the gentry, the more successful yeomen and provincial merchants. A hundred pounds and above covered knights and other leading gentry as well as merchants in overseas trade. Consistency suggests placing assessments of upwards of £300, comprising the very rich, in a separate category, as the base point for the higher rate of $13\frac{1}{3}$ per cent in the loan of 1522, making a total liability of $28\frac{5}{8}$ per cent. Men worth £1,000 indeed were supposed to pay the loan at an even higher rate, determined by the commissioners. However, most county returns contain very few at £300, let alone £1,000; except in the unique circumstances of industrial Suffolk they would form but a tiny group. Even in the biggest cities their numbers were extremely limited; while Coventry contained six, including two worth upwards of £1,000, there were no more than four in Norwich, the second city in the kingdom, and just one at Exeter.[53]

As already indicated, £20–£39 embraced an assortment of yeomen, minor gentry, and lesser merchants and manufacturers who in towns, other than the biggest and most important, might well have formed the ruling elite.

Below the £20 mark were to be found the mass of people, 90 per cent and more of the population. Although very much the 'poor commons' paying for the most part a 5 per cent tax on their goods, they were anything but an undifferentiated whole. Those worth £5–£19 were roped in for the second loan, in 1523, so paying a total of 15 per cent, not so very much less than what was expected of the £20 men, and of course a proportionately heavier burden. The difference is that not only was their subsidy rate half that of wealthier people, but evidently it was not originally planned to levy the loan on them. As a rule non-parliamentary taxation fell on the shoulders of those who were better able to bear it, and hence was not exactly unpopular. Resentment of Wolsey's experiment must have been due largely to its extension to the relatively (though far from inarticulate) poor of the burden normally confined to the rich. The category £10–£19 covered middling or larger peasant farmers, tenants for the most part, though sometimes owner-occupiers, as well as highly skilled craftsmen; in the village community they might well hold positions of responsibility. At £5–9 were the main body of peasant farmers and the less-skilled craftsmen. Men with £3–£4 were probably smallholders, but, although £2 attracted the same rate of tax, men at this level tended to overlap with those beneath, their assessments being reduced to £1 on some occasions. As likely as not they were cottagers partially dependent on casual labouring, while not infrequently assessment on wages gives practical expression to the class of servants mentioned by the act of 1533. Typically they were small-holders or cottagers, village craftsmen and superior servants.

It is not improbable that men worth £1 or less did not begin to attract attention until the later stages of the subsidy bill, as a result of the Commons' determination to shift the burden of taxation downwards, for if the intention was to rope in labourers and servants as a makeweight, it could not have been seriously supposed that any substantial amount could be wrung from them. The rule devised was that if a man's goods could be valued at £1, but less than £2, or alternatively if he owned nothing but received wages of £1 a year, he should pay 4*d*. These were mostly artificers, labourers or servants, many of course being taxed only on wages, as were many of those assessed at nil in the musters; the status of any who were later taxed on wages is obvious, while those never assessed at all almost certainly included the unemployed and, probably, vagabonds and beggars.

It was in the nature of things that the trading-manufacturing element should tend to cluster in towns and industrialised villages, although cottage industry was widely dispersed, especially in the north and west, where population was dense and common land extensive.[54] The rich clothiers of Suffolk were unique, not matched even in the contiguous parts of Essex. There were indeed three men of £200 at Cirencester, a major centre of the West of England wool trade, but they had few peers locally; Newbury had four big clothiers, including the son of the legendary John Winchcombe, who was worth £630, but here too there was no concentration of wealth comparable with that of Suffolk.[55]

Although persistent overlapping and the resultant anomalies means that none of these economic groupings were exclusive, the character of each is governed by the bias of its composition; the minor gentlemen comprehended in the £10–£19 range for instance, were too heavily outnumbered to be in any real sense typical of it.

A WORKING MODEL

Although any clear-cut classification is too much to expect,[56] application of common sense to the broad outlines of the numerical data enables us to pick our way through this statistical minefield with tolerable assurance. Logic suggests that in most circumstances the £100 man is most likely to be the squire of a village, a merchant in a town; while men from £3 to £10 will almost all be small farmers and craftsmen. To disentangle the yeomanry from the middling and lower gentry – and indeed from the richest peasants – is more difficult, but this is in the nature of things since yeomen emerged from the ranks of the husbandmen, while the gentry did not form a closed caste, and in many cases there was little to choose between their respective scales of wealth.

To sum up, personal wealth can be used as a broad guide to status as follows:

£100 and upwards	Knights and other leading gentry, merchants in overseas trade
£40–£99	Gentry, higher yeomen, provincial merchants
£20–£39	Minor gentry, yeomen, lesser merchants
£10–£19	Larger peasant farmers, highly skilled craftsmen
£3–£9	Peasant farmers, less skilled craftsmen
£2	Smallholders, village craftsmen, senior servants
£1 and under	Artificers, labourers, servants

Two reservations must be made. Firstly it would seem logical that the nil group must have included paupers, a challenging question that will be considered in due course. Secondly, assessments of the gentry can be misleading, insofar as large personal estates result in mere gentlemen with relatively little land being classed with major landowners, some of whom had only modest net personalty.

CHAPTER TWO

THE STRUCTURE OF PERSONAL WEALTH

THE DISTRIBUTION of personal property gives the most comprehensive overview of the wealth of the English people in the sixteenth century, because almost everybody must have owned a certain amount of goods and chattels, and, as required, a value was assigned to 'every man's substance', if only a few shillings – commonly reduced to a curt 'nil' – representing the clothes on their backs and other personal effects. Of course, in a predominantly agrarian economy land constituted by far the most important capital asset. Almost certainly Thomas Cromwell was thinking of the data assembled in 1522 when he estimated the nation's wealth at £4 million, one-quarter of which was annual income from land,[1] which should be multiplied by twenty – the customary rate of capitalisation – to effect a valid comparison with the three million comprised by the capital value of moveables. Ownership of this asset accordingly conferred unchallengeable power and influence on a comparative minority, while at the same time working it gave the overwhelming majority of the population their livelihood.

According to this record landowners were rather thin on the ground, a little more than one in ten of all persons listed in Rutland, and fewer than one-quarter in Buckinghamshire, a county of contrasts.[2] Nor was every man assessed on landed income an owner, for some used to take leases so as to be able to sublet them for profit.

In due course we shall see that people's standard of living hinged broadly on their position in the landholding hierarchy, and it will be necessary to examine this after reviewing the material conditions it enabled them to enjoy.

Assessments of less than £1 were not made in the subsidy, and nearly all below £2 were based on wages, except for a few based on income

31

from land; and since the statutory proviso, doubtless intended to allay fears raised by the inquest of 1522, restricted taxation to one form of wealth only, any personal property belonging to persons so taxed was ignored. As earnings rank as personalty in any case and they must have had something in the way of moveables, especially those taxed on land, it is reasonable to treat all assessments as though made on goods. In fact one Sussex gentleman was taxed at £66. 13s. 4d. on goods in 1524 and £40 on land in 1525;[3] at the lowest level some returns used goods and wages almost indiscriminately, the tax payable not being affected.

RURAL SOCIETY

Social structure was closely related to farming systems. Everywhere in lowland England peasant husbandmen and smallholders, worth £2–£10, occasionally £15 or more, in personal estate, formed the solid core. Their farms were rarely large, the ordinary Norfolk peasant having 20 sown acres on average.[4] Officially 20 acres of arable land was regarded as standard,[5] but with some of it left fallow each year, many people must have got by with much less in practice, for in East Anglia, c. 1600, average tilled acreage was less than 10, compared with about 15 in Sussex.[6] Since arable farming was labour-intensive and its efficiency proportionate to scale, this peasant nucleus was flanked in major corn-growing regions, such as Norfolk and the Berkshire Downs, by wealthy yeomen and swarms of poor labouring people (see Table 2.1). The subsidy rolls show much the same profile on the Sussex Downs and coastal plain, though, with trifling exceptions, assessments below £1 were not made, and most below £2 were on wages.

Neither big farmers nor labourers were conspicuous in most pastoral regions, where livestock, principally cattle, formed, as always, the standby of the smallholder; indeed, in some of these districts the minimum, and commonest, assessment was £2 on goods.

At a time when water formed the only practicable means of bulk transportation, the cultivation of grain was profitable in Norfolk and Sussex, where the arable districts were next to the coast, wheat and malt being the chief commodities clearing the ports there, much of it bound for London, though some went farther afield, including victuals for armies operating against Scotland.[7] Berkshire's outlet was Reading, situated on the Kennet just above its confluence with the Thames, and on the way to becoming a major river-port, forwarding malt and meal to

Table 2.1 Arable farming wealth, Norfolk and Berkshire

Assessments £	Persons	Group wealth £	%
100 and over	45	8,218	16.0
40–99	183	10,842	21.1
20–39	339	7,902	15.4
10–19	639	7,509	14.6
5–9	1,100	6,930	13.5
3–4	1,247	4,334	8.5
2	1,303	3,117	6.1
Under 2	2,046	2,195	4.3
Under 1	2,613	246	0.5
Total	9,515	51,293	100.0

London, to which Great Marlow shipped Chiltern corn brought down from High Wycombe.[8] Easy access to the markets of the capital for its corn, dairy produce and fatstock brought the marshland of southern Essex great wealth, of which almost two-fifths belonged to a fairly large class of rich men; smallholders also prospered, the number of £2 assessments more than offsetting the relatively few £1 ones.[9]

The overall impression of similarity cannot entirely mask significant differences between these districts. At the western end of the Vale of the White Horse in Berkshire dairy farming afforded greater opportunities to smallholders,[10] and poor labouring folk were far fewer than on the Downs. Though the proportion of such people on the Sussex Downs and coastal plain looks small by comparison, in fact it varied greatly from one administrative division to another, reaching almost three-fifths in the Liberty of the archbishop of Canterbury where, as on many ecclesiastical estates, the condition of the people tended to backwardness, with villeinage lingering on.[11] At the same time a good many Sussex, and indeed Essex, wage earners were comparatively well paid, not least in the households of magnates like Lord La Warr at Offington and Lord Marney at Layer Marney; the structure of wealth in the little town of Arundel attests to the prosperity generated by the great Fitzalan family, whose seat was the castle there, whilst Chichester city contained not only skilled artisans but also men employed in various capacities in and around the cathedral.[12] Since also the percentage of assessments below £3 was much the same in Sussex as in Norfolk and Berkshire, a good many farm workers there might have been cottagers who had their own plots of land. On the heathland of north-west Norfolk many poor men of no military value were ignored until taxed on wages in the subsidy; above the £1-level people there resembled those who lived farther to the east, except that the outstanding men were great landowners and yeomen, in contrast to the north-eastern district, where peasants were firmly entrenched, usually taking the initiative over enclosure, which had made more progress there.[13] At the top of the scale, landlords and big yeomen farmers owned not much less than one-third of the wealth of Norfolk and Sussex. In Berkshire the Newbury clothiers were the richest men, although it looks as if the decline of the local broadcloth and kerseys had already begun, leaving a trail of poverty.[14] The Norfolk worsted manufacture, unique in having spread from Norwich to an arable farming district, had always remained dispersed in small units without great clothiers and had never recovered from its recession in the previous century.[15] Although the thin soils of the South Downs were less productive than some – Lambourn hundred atop the Berkshire Downs was very similar – rich men were few, mainly because two leading landowners, the earl of Arundel and Lord Bergavenny, were assessed separately as peers, and a third, Sir John Gage, was taxed in the royal household as Comptroller of Calais.[16]

The Chiltern hundreds of Buckinghamshire broadly resembled the Berkshire Downs, though there was no cloth industry and the hills were 'well woodyd and full of enclosures'. The corn-and-sheep husbandry was varied by pig fattening in the beechwoods, where arable fields generally occupied the sunny slopes, pastures the shaded ones, and there was a well-defined local method of improving the lighter soils.[17] Well situated to serve the London market, the district supported numbers of thriving yeomen and husbandmen, those worth £20–£99 forming the most prominent group. However, the most distinctive part was not the chalk uplands but the little Thames-side hundred of Stoke, lying on the richest soil and closest to London, where little short of half the aggregate wealth belonged to just a dozen men – 2½ per cent of the listed inhabitants – rated at £40 and upwards, indeed practically one-third belonged to the five rated at £100 or more. Already perhaps it was commuter country, where the richest man, worth £500 in personalty, had no land at all within the shire: for courtier, and future Master of the Mint, Edmund Peckham, Denham made an admirable rural retreat, an easy ride from either Richmond, Hampton Court or Windsor.

Lacking comparable communications, the northern division of Buckinghamshire could not match the wealth of the Chilterns and other arable regions. Barley, supplemented towards the east by legumes, was the ubiquitous cereal; with investment in crops and livestock evenly balanced on the smaller holdings, mixed farming for subsistence was probably the norm.[18] In contrast to the Chilterns, the top people were sharply divided from the great mass of poor peasants who doubtless thought a combination of the two safer than exclusive reliance on either crops or livestock, just as many customarily sowed mixed seeds, such as maslin (wheat and rye) counting on one at least to come up. The meagre returns from tillage stimulated the conversion of arable land to pasture for sheep, which was proceeding actively in the early decades of the century. This region was one of those most affected by the depopulation of villages and hamlets, several having recently been enclosed;[19] large numbers of poor in parts point to consequent loss of employment, although it is not clear whether people had actually been turned off the land or the townships had gradually contracted.

Although most peasants preferred self-sufficient, family-sized holdings, agricultural labourers were common enough in this and similar regions of thoroughgoing mixed husbandry. Doubtless many a canny husbandman claimed an allowance for wages paid notionally to his sons, who of course would then be taxed on them. Against all odds, too, smallholders persisted in trying to grow corn, for ploughing and reaping, rather than minding sheep, was held to be a man's proper work; the argument that the cornfield was the nursery of archers, who still formed the backbone of English armies,[20] looks like a rationalisation of this instinct. In some conditions the task was beyond them. At the western end of Suffolk, which was 'eether wholly champion or neer, the feilding abounding by tillage and flockes of sheep doe from thence emprove their greatest commodities', the soil was not naturally productive, so that 'the husbandman before he can test the fruits of his labour endureth much travell'.[21] The demands of the barren Breckland effectively squeezed the more affluent sort of peasant out of Lackford hundred, where nine out of ten taxpayers were worth less than £5, and with scarcely anybody in the £5–£19 range, it was almost entirely peopled by big farmers and swarms of poor labourers.[22] The nearby open-field country around Saffron Walden in Essex was comparable, though the absence of extremes of wealth made peasant husbandmen the most conspicuous group.

These extremes of wealth and poverty apparently inseparable from corn-and-sheep husbandry did not exist in most pastoral regions, where, as a rule, little more than a tenth of all wealth belonged to men worth £50 or more. Even in industrial Babergh hundred, Suffolk, stripping the surface layer from the record exposes the original economy of the wood-pasture country – specialised dairying, pig fattening and horse breeding;[23] in almost half its villages, which preserved this traditional system, the top people accounted for not more than 14 per cent of the wealth, a solitary £100 man for just 4½ per cent. In prosperous districts too – most strikingly in central Suffolk – the labouring element was minimal, few assessments falling below £2, and many people had their own smallholdings which, even if not always big enough to afford a really adequate livelihood, at least restricted working for wages to a subsidiary role. Crop husbandry was limited to basic subsistence and animal feed. Large numbers of low assessments in certain districts, like the Forest of Dean, were generally the mark of a lower overall scale of wealth.

Away from the coastal marshes, the grasslands of lowland England consisted of clay vales, and heaths and forests, which differed radically in wealth and social structure. In Gloucestershire the average man in the vale, situated between the Cotswold Edge and the river Severn, was half as much again better off as in the Forest of Dean across the river (see

Table 2.2 Gloucestershire: percentage distribution of wealth, 1522[24]

Assessments £	The Vale		The Forest	
	Persons	Group wealth	Persons	Group wealth
100 and up	0.3	8.3	0.2	9.0
40–99	1.4	11.7	0.5	5.8
20–39	4.9	16.9	2.8	15.0
10–9	12.6	23.3	7.4	21.2
5–9	22.2	22.2	13.3	21.0
3–4	16.4	9.2	14.5	12.8
2	17.9	5.9	18.3	9.7
1, under 2	14.7	2.5	18.8	5.2
Under 1	9.6	–	24.2	0.4
Total	100.0	100.0	100.0	100.1

Table 2.2). Again subsidy rolls show very much the same situation in other comparable areas. The true proportion of people worth less than £2 in the vale was probably closer to the 32.7 per cent in Barton near Bristol hundred than to the 14.8 per cent in Whitstone, just south of Gloucester.[25] Due perhaps to changing conditions, however, a good many men of substance were finally taxed at 20s. on wages, including, no doubt, independent craftsmen who still dominated the local manufacture of fine cloth which, except in the Stroudwater Valley, had not yet come under the control of capitalist clothiers, as prominent in the West Country generally as in East Anglia; pending this development earnings were evidently high and the really poor not numerous. Over much of this county the effective minimum valuation of personal property in 1522 was £2, the trifling possessions of some mere cottagers being disregarded, before each village list concluded with a string of nil assessments; strictly, dependent members of peasant families owned nothing individually; persons of both types reappear in the subsidy rolls taxed on wages.[26]

The economy of the vale was founded on livestock. At the northern tip, where it merges with the Vale of Evesham, some grain was also grown, but the Vale of Berkeley, towards the south, was an area of small dairy holdings where arable farming was restricted in scale.[27] Employment for agricultural labourers was correspondingly limited, and by no means all holdings were too small for subsistence.

The prosperity of the wood-pasture region of Suffolk was fully comparable; with minimal arable it did not require the same great numbers of labourers as the cornfields farther west, a feature that clearly marks the boundary between the chalk soils and the clay loams. An anonymous seventeenth-century chorographer remarked:

> the Woodland and high Suffolk is exceeding fruitfull, comparable to any p't of England for oxen and kine, not so good for sheep. In this p't of the countrye are made butter & cheese in exceeding great quantitie of wonderfull goodnesse comparable to any in the Realme. The comoditie therof is unspeakable unto the inhabitants of the same amongst which are very many yeomen of good credit & great liberalitie, good housekeepers[28]

Robert Reyce described High Suffolk as 'Parts inclining to the east' where pasture ruled, the people 'contenting themselves onely with so much tillage as will satisfie their own expences'. In the belt extending from Hoxne to the Orwell estuary the percentage of assessments below £2 hardly exceeded twenty, save in a few places, and overall more were on goods than on earnings. The 40s. men formed the biggest group, many in Hoxne hundred being described as craftsmen or labourers. 'The middle,' Reyce continues, 'although enjoying much meddow and pasture, yett far more tillage doe from thence raise their cheifest maintenance.'[29] Between Ipswich and Bury St Edmunds the percentage of sub-£2 assessments was at least 35–40, rising towards the west as the proportion of arable increased.

On the coastal sandlings the scene changed again. The chorographer (though not Reyce) points out: 'That p't of the countrye that is nere unto the sea is nothing so fruitfull neyther so comodious for cattell as the other but more fitte for sheepe and corne,'[30] and so contained many more 20s. men – upwards of 43 per cent in Blything hundred, and more than twice as many as in townships situated wholly on the clay.[31] In Colneis hundred, between the Deben and Orwell estuaries, the percentage was only 14½, much the lowest in the shire. The exceptionally rich soil here was producing carrots for London by the end of the century when, perhaps, the trade was already long-established. Cattle fattening on the coastal marshes supported a prosperous peasantry as in Lincolnshire.[32]

The district with the most poor people was virtually the ancient Liberty of St Edmund, later to become the county of West Suffolk, which has always possessed a unity of its own centring on the town of Bury.[33] East of this, £1 assessments topped the 45 per cent mark only in Samford hundred, which was practically coterminous with the 'rich loam' area, identified by Arthur Young, and in the north-eastern corner of the county, which he was 'much inclined to class' with it,[34] and was almost a part of Norfolk. The southern half of the western division was, nonetheless, situated on the central clays, Babergh and Cosford hundreds forming the nucleus of the clothing trade which extended from Clare (Risbridge hundred) down the river Stour to East Bergholt, in Samford hundred. Here the density of the labouring population speaks for itself, though while in the Cosford villages it reached almost 55 per cent, in the rising centre Hadleigh it amounted to less than a third.[35]

On the northern fringe of the wood-pasture belt fewer than a quarter of the people of Blofield, East Flegg and Walsham hundreds in Norfolk had less than £2, almost as many having £5–£9. To the south, Mid-Essex was more varied, interspersed with arable tracts, while the farmers and smallholders of the Thames-side marshes prospered on meat and dairy produce for the London market; doubtless too the proximity of the metropolis affected earnings in Becontree hundred, where many labourers were taxed at 40s.[36]

On average (£5.44 per capita) the Wealden vale was fully comparable with the corn-sheep region (£5–£5.55) and far more affluent than the forest ridge to the east (£4.64), where, in contrast to the rest of Sussex, the scarcity of truly rich people placed the biggest concentration of wealth in the range £10–£19 instead of £20–£39. The Wealden clays supported a richer, more diverse agriculture than the Hastings Beds formation, where impoverished sandy soils combined with abrupt contours largely restricted farming to stock keeping, and grain often had to be brought from elsewhere.[37]

Broad tracts of woodland and common wastes along the ridge attracted squatters irresistibly, and with the whole Weald teeming with people many obscure forest dwellers might easily have contrived to elude the taxman altogether. In arable districts most usable land must already have been taken up, and with the commons jealously guarded by farmers to whom they were essential for keeping the animals on which cultivation depended, the landless man stood a better chance of carving a niche for himself by drifting to a less-developed, mainly pastoral terrain. Nevertheless, in the long run the prospect was apt to prove illusory, poverty being the enduring characteristic of this and similar regions, which, in consequence, attracted by-employments of many kinds.[38]

Although in fact *ultra vires*, taxing many men worth less than £2 on goods[39] must have been considered justified by circumstances, for their numbers alone made them an important element in the local community. Legally those having less than the minimum of 40s. in goods should have been assessed on wages or 'profits *for* wages', which were often treated as interchangeable, though sometimes carefully distinguished: in Goldspur hundred on the Kentish border assessments on profits were specified in 1524, but in the next year the assessments roped in more small taxpayers and divided them into fifty-one on wages, forty-six on profits and seven on goods. Implying the piece rates paid to nominally independent cottage craftsmen by the capitalists who controlled most rural industry, 'profits' looks like an elliptical term for 'wages'. In the Weald they probably embraced the earnings of woodcutters, colliers and other forest workmen; a form of share cropping, which was not unknown,[40] need not be ruled out. In eastern Sussex most sub-£2 assessments were on earnings, but in central districts goods were the rule; in the vale, in common with most of West

Sussex, almost all were on wages, and, with much land under the plough, probably those of farm workers. In pastoral Suffolk fewer than half this class were dependent on wages,[41] presumably younger men who were not yet cottagers. In both regions petty landowners were fairly common, though still only a tiny minority.

If Leland had gone there, he might well have described the eastern Weald as he did the Forest of Dean: 'more fruitful of wood and grass than corn' with 'many iron mines and forges';[42] yet although he judged it self-sufficient in corn, Dean was very much poorer than the Weald.

The north-east corner of Worcestershire escaped the extremes of heathland poverty, though the spacious commons of the ancient Feckenham Forest, which was still not completely cleared, attracted landless squatters. Down towards the river Severn, the Kidderminster area[43] was relatively more prosperous, more like the clay vales, but in some villages near Worcester,[44] the average per person was little more than £4, even though fewer than 30 per cent of assessments were under £2. Having no really rich men, the community enjoyed a measure of equality, similar to Arden – the name of the forest in Warwickshire – where farms averaged just over 30 acres, with less than one in five exceeding 50, and three-quarters of the land under grass; farmers raised beef cattle for profit, and crops – rye, oats, barley and drage – for subsistence, some growing none at all. Sheep flocks were small; diversification and improvement began only towards the turn of the century in response to the challenge of population growth. Almost one-fifth of the assessments in Yardley, a poor parish, were of £5–£9, the highest only £11, yet though nearly half were under 40s., only one man in seven was taxed on wages.[45] Various by-employments foreshadowed subsequent industrial development; indeed, Droitwich salt already enjoyed wide repute, although fifty-four nil-assessments among seventy-five listed townsmen underlines Leland's description of its poverty.[46]

Certain parts of southern England also do not slot neatly into any regular classification. Essex displayed strong individual characteristics, not even the forested western fringe being markedly differentiated from the adjacent parts. The primary division was between the southern saltings and the rest, though stock keeping was general.[47] The mixed-farming central area differed from the north-west corner mainly in having rather fewer poor, even on the prime wheatlands of Chelmsford and Ongar hundreds, but, with few men of the richest sort, average wealth was lower, especially towards the north. Despite its maritime location, Lincolnshire stagnated economically.[48] Louthesk and Ludburgh wapentakes formed a rather poor district; even the most affluent resident, who was taxed on £60 a year and whose family estates were worth double, owned personal estate of only £43, more than half of which comprised a none-too-prosperous farm; whether he was unlucky or incompetent, no one outside the thriving little market town Louth was doing much better.[49]Almost all the people of the wold villages were small husbandmen and labourers, showing no sign of the gulf between rich and poor usual there.[50] The coastal villages were a little bigger, containing many landless peasants, represented by numerous 20s. assessments, who lived by grazing stock on the common saltmarshes.[51]

A scarcity of poor people sharply differentiates the Cotswold Hills in Gloucestershire from other corn-sheep husbandry regions. Although a good 30 per cent of assessments in Kiftsgate hundred were nils, the other hundreds returned none at all. Nonetheless, the absence of labourers is more apparent than real: the local practice of not assessing goods of less value than £2 did not mean that any personal property owned by people of the labouring sort was generally ignored, for a good many men later taxed on wages owned goods worth anything up to £10 in 1522, which (unless perhaps having disposed of, say, a beast or two) they managed to conceal from the taxman and convince him that they had nothing but the minimum in wages. Though not exclusive to the Cotswolds, this scaling down is regular enough to give labourers there the appearence of modest prosperity,[52] with sub-£2 assessments hardly rising above 35 per cent anywhere;[53] Brightwells Barrow hundred closely resembled the contiguous (and mainly pastoral) Berkshire hundred of Shrivenham, which contrasted strongly with the arable parts of Berkshire situated to the east of it. Too steep for tillage, the higher slopes of the hills carried innumerable sheep, and the mild, damp climate made the land less suitable than chalk downlands for the sheep fold and wheat growing.[54]

As the Cotswolds specialised in the production of fine wool, and Cirencester was one of the greatest marts in the land, strategically sited to serve both the Gloucestershire and Wiltshire manufacturing districts, with lesser centres at Chipping Campden and Northleach,[55] the balance might have become decisively tilted towards sheep. The condition of many villages points to depopulation, but, although Sezincote had been enclosed as early as 1486, the region as a whole was 'remarkably free' of depopulating enclosure. The abbot of Hailes, who kept a flock of 900 head at Longborough, was accused at one point of harassing his tenants there preparatory to enclosure, though he never went through with it. Locally depopulation was a wasting process to which enclosure contributed little.[56] Although the land was largely champaign, some demesnes had never lain in common field, or had long ceased to do so.

With few exceptions, villages were tiny, shrinking communities with the irreducible minimum of the poorest people: at Hawling, where the population was well short of a hundred, only three of the twenty different men recorded in the combined muster and subsidy were assessed at less than £2, and none out of eleven at tiny Batsford.[57]

Almost unknown in the region at this time were the tiny freeholds conventionally linked with the proliferation of paupers, whether cottagers clinging to a precarious independence, or young men waiting to come into their patrimony.[58] This perhaps was a feature of the Forest of Dean, where four holdings out of five could have been occupied by their owners (who lived in the same townships) and many belonged to men worth less than £2. Conversely, in the Cotswolds not one property in five – big estates included – could have been owner-occupied. Unless there had been a general exodus of small proprietors, a good deal of land had been acquired by outsiders, possibly with a view to letting it to graziers. Also numerous parcels now belonged to the great religious foundations of the region as a result of pious donations;[59] if many of these were tenanted in conjunction with other, larger holdings, they were unavailable for small men, while there were not enough of the big farmers, who did occupy them, to employ more than a very limited number of servants.

Looking beyond purely local peculiarities, if, as seems likely, the true strength formed by the two lowest groups in the Cotswolds was approximately 35 per cent, this is suggestively similar to Rutland's 37.6, and moreover, the general distribution of wealth was very much the same.[60] This was no mere coincidence, for the oolitic limestone of the Cotswold Hills continues north-eastwards across Northamptonshire and Rutland and into Lincolnshire, taking in, on the way, Towcester hundred, which shows similar characteristics, and skirting the three hundreds of Buckingham, where people were marginally more prosperous than in the rest of north Buckinghamshire. In Rutland at least demand for wage labour was curtailed by restrictions on corn growing imposed by the lack of means of shipment, as in Leicestershire, where labourers seem to have been even thinner on the ground;[61] much effort went into stock rearing, many farmers kept above-average flocks of sheep, and there was abundant fatting pasture in the Vale of Catmose.[62] Great numbers of labouring poor were more characteristic of regions where the soil was chalk-based.

Neither in distribution of wealth nor in social structure was Rutland in any way anomalous. At the same time the general level of wealth in this unremarkable corner of the East Midlands, peopled entirely by peasant farmers, with a leavening of yeomen and only a handful of rich squires, was lower only than on the fertile cornlands of Norfolk and in the opulent Stour Valley manufacturing district – higher not only than in other, similar regions but also Berkshire, which the yield of the loans, 1522–3, placed fifth jointly with Suffolk, and Gloucestershire which shared fourteenth place with Rutland itself.[63] On other occasions Rutland ranked 22nd–24th of English counties, well below not only Berkshire and Gloucestershire but even Buckinghamshire.[64] Evidently the unique thoroughness of its muster book was complemented by a more rigorous standard of assessment than in most shires, since in 1522 personal wealth there averaged £97 per thousand acres, compared with as little as £61.7 in 1515 and £64 in 1524, and, mostly having less than average wealth, the sixty-nine additional men roped in in 1522 cannot account for this difference. The Buckinghamshire ratios were £71 per thousand in 1515, £68 in 1524 and £79 in 1522 when the average for just about half of Berkshire was only marginally higher than the £88 for the complete county in 1515.

The best explanation is that assessment was more realistic in Rutland than anywhere else. The chronicler Hall emphasised the consternation produced by the government's success in establishing a basis for swingeing taxation, and although wealth can seldom or never have been overstated for fiscal purposes, the Rutland muster book could perhaps be the exception that bears out his claim that 'some avaunced them selfes more than they were worth of pride, not remembryng [realising/suspecting] what was coming', naively succumbing to the blandishments of the commissioners, who 'did what they could to set the people to the vttermoste'. The reckoning came with a vengeance when 'The kynge out of hand sent commissions to gather ye loane, this was called practisyng of the loane, which sore emptied men's purses.'[65] Improbable though it may sound, Rutland men found themselves having, with 'much heauiness', to fork out on the basis of the full value of their property which they had unguardedly divulged. No doubt when the subsidy commissioners came on the scene they were prevailed on to restore assessments to approximately the levels of 1515.

The Buckinghamshire assessments seem, on the contrary, to illustrate the other side of the story, of commissioners having to be directed by the Council to commence their labours afresh, employing any and every 'practice' to ferret out the truth.[66] The signs are that some people there were more sophisticated and succeeded in bilking the revenue. Five times the size of Rutland, Buckinghamshire shows every symptom of several standards of assessment: numerous reductions in the Chiltern hundreds in 1524 reduced aggregate wealth from £97 to £67 per thousand acres, while in Buckingham hundreds it only dropped from £84 to £59, but throughout the northern half of the shire many of the 1522 assessments were retained substantially unaltered, conceivably because the people concerned deemed it prudent to keep their mouths shut and pay up; a significant number were actually uprated, perhaps penalised for having the gall to seek abatements, so attracting a further, more searching investigation of their means. Overall the level of wealth was slightly raised in the subsidy, indeed by more than 25 per cent – from £57 to £71 – in the Newport hundreds where many more men were swept into the net. The returns for Lothingland and Mutford hundreds, Suffolk, permit a rare glimpse of the mechanics by which many assessments were revalued, under the heading 'The namys of those personys forgotyn and not charged at the last subsidie which are to be charged now'.[67]

THE HIGHLAND ZONE

Far from the fertile cornfields and lush pastures of the southern counties, the poverty of North Country hill farmers had no parallel. Up in the Pennines, nine out of ten people of Staincliffe wapentake in the West Riding of Yorkshire owned less than a pound's worth of moveables. Arncliff folk were so poor – the meagre belongings of all twenty-seven totalling no more than £9. 7s. 4d. – that when the subsidy came to be levied, Robert Selson and William Prysche, with 20s. apiece, John Knolles (26s. 8d.), and Thomas and Leonard Atkynson (10s. each) were selected as if at random and assessed at £2 each; although the first two also enjoyed tiny incomes from land, it is to be hoped that some at least of their neighbours chipped in to make up the shilling due from each. This was the regular practice in the North, especially in south Lancashire and on the barren North York Moors around Whitby where, typically, at Hutton Bonville only squire George Conyers was taxed – on lands worth £40 a year.[68] Fylingdales parish returned only ten taxpayers even though its biggest settlement was the lively village of Robin Hood's Bay, where Leland observed twenty fishing boats,[69] each of which may be reckoned the livelihood of one family at the very least.

With wealth distributed so as to give a highly distinctive social structure, the Craven District was quite unlike any other part of England. The semi-occlusion of categories between £2 and £39 sharply divided society into two classes. Upwards of £40 there were the landowners, or gentry, though a good many below this point might have been counted as gentlemen. The remaining 90 per cent or more included the majority of the peasants. In the absence of precise definition, 20s. might be taken as marking the dividing line between husbandmen and labourers, were it not that at Long Preston Edmund Clarke (nil) was stated to be servant to Thomas Squyer, who was worth only 6s. 8d. Contrary to the usual practice elsewhere, 'less than £1' means a few shillings leavened by a sporadic nil assessment, rather than the opposite, for only one man in nine was actually given as nil, the majority ranging from 3s. 4d. to 18s. In place of the even sums of pounds and marks of the bigger assessments, all those below £2 were precisely stated in shillings and pence, producing a finely graduated hierarchy of wealth (see Table 2.3).

Table 2.3   Wealth of Staincliffe wapentake, 1523

Assessments £	Persons	Group wealth	
		£	%
100 and above	2	300	12.6
40–99	7	180	7.6
20–39	24	510	21.4
10–19	1	13	0.5
5–9	33	183	7.7
3–4	26	85	3.6
2	38	76	3.2
30–39s.	182	–	–
20–29s.	377	670	28.5
10–19s.	394	362	15.2
Under 10s.	450	–	–
Nil	104	–	–
Total	1,638	2,379	100.3

With upwards of four-fifths of people here having less than 30s. in personal property, nobody at all was worth as much as 40s. in one township out of every three, especially upland ones like Arncliff, Hellifield and Kettlewell, though these were not the only ones.[70] So the man worth just under £2 might well have been a person of some consequence in the community.

In relation to the harsh physical environment holdings were small and (it was said) getting smaller, thanks to partible inheritance: few exceeded 20–25 acres. This, coupled with spacious commons, encouraged a relatively dense population. Although the soil of Craven was good loam, little corn was grown, even less up the dales; oats alone could withstand the damp climate and formed the staple food of the common people. Most tillage was temporary, and some quite large farms had no implements. The grazing of sheep and store cattle was the main occupation, although in the course of the sixteenth century dairying was to assume increasing importance.[71] At this time, however, the problem was almost certainly one of finding outlets, so far did the region lie from major markets, if indeed any great proportion of its products was marketed. Values obtaining south of the Humber – at least 5s. for a cow or 4s. for a steer[72] – can hardly have applied: even the smallest stock farm must have carried more than just one or two; sheep fetched 1s. apiece in other parts. All added up to subsistence farming in its most rudimentary form, with minimal trading and scarcely any money circulating, so that the assessors' valuation of livestock – and household effects – may well have been frankly notional. The alacrity with which northerners enlisted for military service whenever warfare flared up on the Border speaks for itself. The pay was welcome and there might well be plunder to boot, not to mention the excitement. While the Vale of York and the Wold country might have been reasonably fruitful, the province as a whole lived close to the margin of subsistence – so much so that periodic military activity on the Border was invariably handicapped by the need to import virtually all supplies, even of forage.[73]

Not only were nearly three-fifths of the people here unable to scrape together sufficient personal property to reach the tax threshold of £2, but none got the alternative of 20s. wages in the year, as did many in the Midland and southern counties who were in the same position. On the one hand, it is not easy to see who would have been in a position to pay them; on the other, the incidence of wage assessments fell away steadily as distance from the London region increased. In Leicestershire only 22 per cent of taxpayers overall were classed as wage earners, compared with 37 per cent in Rutland next door. In Staffordshire and Shropshire this was even more marked, and, unlike in Gloucestershire, the shortage is not readily explained. Nonetheless, there are no grounds for imputing laxity to local officials operating at a safe distance from central supervision. The qualifying 20s. was no arbitrary figure but the maximum (16s. + 4s. for livery) laid down for a common servant in husbandry by the wage-regulation act of 1515. These maxima were subject to the proviso that 'in such shires and countries that where it hath been and is now used to give less wages, that in those shires and countries they shall give and the taker of the wages be compelled according as they have been used to take'.[74] If the published rates were basically those applicable to the Home Counties and tended to decline proportionately to the distance from the metropolis, many labourers and servants in the provinces may not have earned enough to be assessed. At the same time there was no particular reason why rates in these two West Midland counties should have been materially lower than in the adjoining shires of Warwick and Worcester where wage assessments were not uncommon, while in Devon, which is actually farther from London than Staffordshire, they amounted to 36 per cent of the whole.[75]

The ninety-one resident freeholders in Craven – about one man in twenty – were, as everywhere else, measurably better off than other people, almost half owning goods worth at least £2, and only sixteen having less than £1's worth. Yet since, in contrast to that of personal property, the range of landed incomes bears comparison with what was recorded in other, wealthier counties, there were some curious exceptions. John Clarke of Swinden, for one, must have been a gentleman, with his income of £10 a year, yet his moveables were valued at no more than 30s., with which he only just scraped into the top 20 per cent. Lord Clifford, if not an eccentric peer, might almost have been the archetypal spendthrift one, for, despite a rental of £453 a year, his home in Skipton castle was appraised at a mere £60; similarly his son, Sir Henry Clifford, had £80 a year, but only £8 in personal estate.[76] Altogether, nearly half the gentry owned goods worth very much less than their net rentals. In particular, Anthony Talbot of Alton was worth only one mark, though his income was ten. A relative in the same village had goods valued at no more than 6s. 8d., though enjoying an income of £3. 6s. 8d. from land, which, in this poor region, may, rather than £5, have been the minimum for gentlemen, many of whom are only identifiable by their landed incomes. Such tiny personal estates owned by eminent persons underline the initial impression of a thoroughly spartan standard of living in the North Country.

THE CELTIC FRINGE

Beyond the Tamar lay a land where things were ordered differently (see Table 2.4). Although Cornwall was not the only county where nothing less than 40s. was reckoned as substance,[77] the making of an independent return by each hundred[78] resulted in five sets of officials taking different views of the native poor, the complement of which tapered off from the modest (15 per cent) in the eastern parts to the negligible (0.4 per cent) in the far west, balanced to some extent by aliens, who were classed as poor and accounted for one-eighth of this category, making Penwith the antithesis of East hundred, notwithstanding that many who were subsequently taxed in Kerrier hundred were passed over in 1522.

Here something of a special case, aliens were common in most maritime shires, chiefly in seaports, like Great Yarmouth and Rye, though here and there penetrating farther inland, to work, for example,

Table 2.4 Wealth of Cornwall, 1522

Assessments £	Persons	Group wealth £	%
100 and over	7	1,166	4.0
40–99	66	3,201	11.1
20–39	212	4,749	16.4
10–19	532	6,182	21.3
5–9	751	5,037	17.4
3–4	1,485	5,685	19.6
2	1,433	2,947	10.2
Nil	671	–	–
Total	5,157	28,967	100.0

at ironmaking in the Weald of Sussex, a county where they amounted to about 3 per cent of all taxpayers.[79] In Cornwall almost all were Bretons, who bore a close affinity to the indigenous population, speaking a related tongue, and as yet imperfectly assimilated into the kingdom of France: 'ther use many Britons with smaul shippes to resorte to Padestowe with commodities of their countery and to by fische,' Leland observed, adding that the port was also full of Irishmen,[80] Most, however, must have come to work, especially if native labour was in short supply in the parts where they were most numerous.

Since little corn was grown in the county a big labour force was not needed. Although in the end a good many men were taxed on wages, a number in Kerrier hundred initially had goods worth £2, making the true overall percentage of labouring people a fairly normal 36.6, almost the same as in Devonshire.[81] The wage earners of the central districts were largely concentrated in Bodmin borough, leaving about 14 per cent in the villages of Trigg and West hundreds where there were no other major towns.[82]

Not only were most holdings too small to provide much work for hired labour, but the big villages that would have housed such a workforce did not exist. Husbandry was so neglected the population could not feed itself from local resources. Their staple diet was 'whitsul', compounded of sour milk, cheese, curds, butter and suchlike – yogurt, traditional Cornish style! – washed down with water rather than ale. In addition the greatest single cause of a landless peasantry was missing: Carew contended that 'In times past, and that not long ago, holdings were so plentiful and holders scarce, as well was the landlord who could get one to be his tenant'.[83]

During the preceding century there had indeed been no pressure for subsistence, yet at the same time demand had been strong, especially in the east where the growth of a thriving cloth industry along the border, combined with the prosperity of the Devon stannaries, situated within a day's journey by cart, had created a market lively enough to make small-scale farming a practicable alternative to labouring for wages.[84]

Very commonly two or more men shared a single assessment, mostly members of the same family, though the occasional bracketing of different surnames suggests cousins or, rather, in-laws – the husbands of co-heiresses who were commonplace among landowners locally; and maybe business partnerships of the kind often formed by miners to save expenses.[85] Here, though, the family was a larger, more cohesive unit than in the Saxon shires, keeping its property undivided. Carew describes how when a bargain is so taken to these three [father, mother and son], it often falleth out that afterwards the son marrieth and delivereth his yerning-goods (as they term it) to his father, who in lieu thereof, by his wive's assent departeth to him and his daughter-in-law with the one half of his holding in hand [sic].

Now, though after the father's decease, the mother may, during her life turn them both out of doors, as not bound by her own word, and much less by her husband's, yet I have never known the same put in practice[86]

Irrespective of any causal link, the additional personnel in joint assessments presumably comprised men who elsewhere would have been returned as wage earners or young and poor, but except in Kerrier, where it led to 880 native assessments comprehending as many as 1,179 individuals, it did not add greatly to the numbers of poorer men; and if it tends to raise the true proportion to a clear quarter in a couple of hundreds, it hardly made any difference in West and Trigg.[87] Of course it need not follow that separate assessment must have cast the younger members of every family as wage earners, any more than it did in other shires where traces of an emergent discrete labouring class were already manifest. It is, for instance, improbable that, on a joint assessment of £133. 6s. 8d., any of the three Thomases of Lavale would have been mere labourers.[88] Nevertheless, as members of relatively poor peasant families, and so technically landless, most of these people can have owned little or no personal property in their own right.

If Cornwall was anything but a land of rich squires and yeomen, it may also have enjoyed some immunity from the scourge of absolute poverty. Many symptoms point to a rude equality, and the average level of wealth was not significantly lower than in other shires. In some respects Kerrier may have constituted an exception, yet although the mean of £4.4 per head may need scaling down to take account of the multitude of labourers discovered and roped in for the subsidy, upwards of seven-tenths of the assessments made in 1522 were at £2–£4. As the chief location of tin mining, conditions confirm that an abundance of cheap labour tended to stimulate industrial growth, although naturally mineral extraction has to be carried on where the workable reserves happen to be located, using imported labour if necessary, as, it would seem, was precisely what was done in Penwith. All round the coast fishing provided the chief by-employment, outranking both clothing and tinning in the south-eastern quarter of the county.[89]

THE URBAN DIMENSION

When John Leland was touring England, observing and recording, in the years 1534–43, he was not always certain how a town differed from a village, and so concluded a list of Staffordshire market towns with 'Tetenhaul a village and a college about a myle from Wuluerhampton',[90] although there is no confirmation it had ever been anything more.

Little or nothing beyond the holding of a market distinguished the smallest towns from mere villages, for no small number contained not more than two or three hundred inhabitants.[91] Uppingham in Rutland, which just reached 300, was almost exactly the same size as the big villages Langham and Lyddington. Consisting of 'but one meane streete, and but a very meane chirche,[92] it also resembled them in lying, like many another market town, amidst its own open fields. Many of its people were farmers too, though several were merchants as well – two drapers, a mercer, a haberdasher and a wax-chandler, and in 1584 Archdeacon Robert Johnson chose it as the location of one of the two grammar schools with which he endowed the county. Even at this size it completely outclassed most Rutland villages, quite two-thirds of which had populations of fewer than 150. Oakham, the only other town, and easily the biggest place there, scarcely reached the 500 mark (see Table 2.9 below)[93]. Although the range of its occupations was wider and more comprehensive, its mainstay was agriculture, with most of its tradesmen farming on the side – unless their crafts were the subsidiary pursuits. Yet it had a castle, was the county town, and in due course would become another beneficiary of Archdeacon Johnson's munificence.[94]

If Rutland was but a miniature county its towns were far from untypical. Half the market centres of Sussex had populations below 500; indeed, places such as West Tarring, Broadwater, Hailsham and Storrington are best described as villages where markets happened to be held. But there were also tiny towns that ranked as boroughs, like Steyning (population about 300) and East Grinstead, which, though much smaller, was privileged to assess its own taxes (see Table 2.5). New Shoreham, now sadly decayed, had barely 100 inhabitants, while Bramber, the site of a ruined castle, was minute and had already lost its market.

From 500 to upwards of 1,000 in population, towns became much more recognisable as such, even those which, like High Wycombe, Bucks., or Battle, Eastbourne and Petworth in Sussex, formed part of extensive rural parishes (Tables 2.8–2.9). At the same time, some remained in essence overgrown villages resulting from the establishment

Table 2.5   Wealth of East Grinstead, 1524

Assessments £	Persons	Group wealth £	%
100 and over	–	–	–
40–99	–	–	–
20–39	2	40	26.3
10–19	1	10	6.6
5–9	7	49	32.2
3–4	6	20	13.2
2	8	16	10.5
Under 2	17	17	11.2
Total	41	152	100.0

of rural industry. In the Stour Valley of West Suffolk these were thick on the ground in the heyday of the clothing trade, but they probably lacked a truly urban ethos,[95] and consequently fell easy prey to the winds of economic change. Lavenham, which must have had a population approaching 1,000 and ranked as one of the dozen or so richest towns in the kingdom,[96] went into decline following the death of the great clothier Thomas Spring in 1523. Dedicated solely to the pursuit of wealth, it evolved no institutions beyond the ubiquitous parish guilds, of which there were at least four. Places as diverse as Petworth, Birmingham and Manchester remained manors. Against the implacable opposition of its lord, Aylesbury failed utterly to hold on to the corporate status granted it in 1554. Markets and fairs remained perquisites of the manor even at Lewes, the capital of East Sussex, where otherwise a rudimentary form of self-government was well established.[97]

A fair number of towns of this rank were reputed to be boroughs, though incorporation was something of a rarity and might well depend on special circumstances: Rye, Winchelsea and Hastings, for example, were Cinque Ports. In Buckinghamshire, High Wycombe (Table 2.9) was still the sole chartered borough at this date. Sudbury in Suffolk (see Table 2.6), though comparable in size and much superior in wealth, did not achieve incorporation until 1553. Fortifications were another variable. There was not a single walled town in either Buckinghamshire or Rutland, while other counties might possess several; Sussex had at

Table 2.6 Wealth of Sudbury, 1522

Assessments £	Persons	Group wealth £	%
100 and over	9	1,240	46.7
40–99	11	509	19.2
20–39	12	270	10.2
10–19	26	306	11.5
5–9	21	139	5.2
3–4	23	79	3.0
2	37	78	2.9
Under 2	37	37	1.4
Nil	45	0	–
Total	221	2,658	100.1

least five, including the Cinque Ports and the two county towns.

In remote, less populous areas, urban development was inevitably minimal. In the heart of the Pennines, Skipton (Table 2.9), traditionally the centre of Craven, was the only place for many a mile recognisable as a town in any real sense; its population cannot have reached 500. The idiosyncrasies of the certificates make Cornish towns exceptionally difficult to characterise. In any case most were tiny. This was a region of hamlets and little towns which, in the Middle Ages at least, had been inhabited largely by aliens imported by borough patrons.[98] However, by early Tudor times this had changed, and strangers, though still a substantial element,[99] were generally less in evidence than in rural parts, while natives show few signs of having flocked in to replace them. With something like 1,000 people, Bodmin was the biggest town; Helston was barely half this size, and Launceston, its importance notwithstanding, was not much better.[100]

Whilst the smallest kind of town can only have served as a market point, those with populations exceeding 500 usually provided more extensive services to their localities, and some had developed specialised manufactures even if on a modest scale. Kerseys were made at Midhurst and Petworth and leather workers were prominent in Horsham, one of the most flourishing towns in the Weald of Sussex,[101] as well as a prime example of a town which, despite an outstanding rate of economic

Table 2.7 Wealth of Horsham, 1524

Assessments £	Persons	Group wealth £	%
100 and over	–	–	–
40–99	5	242	37.3
20–39	7	170	26.2
10–19	4	49	7.6
5–9	11	68	10.5
3–4	7	23	3.6
2	21	43	6.6
Under 2	52	54	8.3
Total	107	649	100.1

growth since the last general fiscal revaluation in 1334, remained unplaced in the national league table (see Table 2.7). The market might be held several days a week, and if, like the great Cotswold wood marts at Cirencester, Tetbury and so forth,[102] it was noted for some speciality, business might be attracted from well outside the five-mile radius considered reasonable for day-to-day requirements in the Middle Ages.[103] Seldom, however, was a market area a tidy territorial entity; rather it was the product of a complex of factors.

Not only might a town look much like any big village, but in some essentials its economy was inseparable from that of its rural hinterland. As the market-centre of a district the town owed its existence to, and gained its livelihood from, handling the produce of the local agricultural community which, in turn, depended on the town for industrial goods and professional services.[104] The trade of Leicester centred on handling local wool and leather – its craftsmen, headed by tailors and shoemakers, were mainly occupied in making cloth, clothing and footwear for local consumption. York served a wide area as the processing and distribution centre for foodstuffs.[105] It was no accident that a good many towns were sited on the borderline between arable farming and pastoral regions. While each could be self-sufficient for food, neither could manage well without the products of the other: stockmen needed cereals to balance their diet, not to mention barley and malt for brewing; corn growers needed butter, cheese and meat to alleviate the monotony of bread. In Sussex both Lewes and Steyning lay at the foot of the South Downs on the edge of the Weald. Norwich had grown up where the cornlands of Norfolk meet the wood-pasture country. Near the foot of the Chilterns, Aylesbury was the natural point of exchange for the two regions of Buckinghamshire. Also in every shire one town at least, like the two latter examples, served as the focus for community affairs and local administration. In one way or another towns exerted an influence over the farming population. The right of holding markets and fairs was a jealously guarded privilege and (needless to say) a source of profit to the lord, or the community of the freemen of an incorporated borough. Corn and seed factors could regulate the conditions of small farmers by setting prices and extending credit:

At Michaelmas time poor men must make money of their grain, that they may pay their rents. So long then as the poor man hath to sell, rich men will bring out none, but rather buy up that which the poor bring, under pretence of seed corn For this cauze therefore they must buy in the markets though they be twenty miles off, and where they be not known, promising there, if they happen to be espied (which God wot is very seldom) to send so much to the next market, to be performed I wot not when.[106]

A major development in rural industry often took the form of town based capitalists organising the labours of village artificers. Nayland in Suffolk was obviously a centre of the clothing trade; a couple of miles away, Stoke, though equal in size, was completely different, having only a handful of clothiers whose businesses, by local standards were not large. Cloth-finishing processes tended to be concentrated in towns and urbanised villages; Wiltshire fulling mills were nearly all controlled by the clothiers.[107]

Contrasts between town and country (Tables 2.8 and 2.9) were less apparent than is implied by contemporary insistence on an antithesis between towns and their agricultural environment. Townsmen in Cornwall, Carew supposed, 'conceive themselves an estranged society from the upland dwellers and carry an emulation against them, as if one member of a body could continue this well without a beholdingness to the rest'.[108] In 1549 the citizens of Exeter believed the rebellious peasants to be intent on pillage; Norwich merchants concealed their valuables and fled. In rich provincial capitals these apprehensions might have been well-founded, but the men of smaller towns made common cause with the country folk: Kett's rising actually began in Wymondham,

Table 2.8 Wealth of towns and environs, 1524–5

Assessments		Under £2	£2	£3–4	£5–9	£10–19	£20–39	£40–99	£100+	Total	£ per capita
PETWORTH	Number	67	47	13	22	12	6	3	–	170	
	Wealth, £s	67	94	46	104	157	165	147	–	780	4.6
Environs*	Number	318	185	114	131	53	41	12	2	856	
	Wealth, £s	328	370	381	800	623	841	540	400	4,283	5.0
MIDHURST	Number	43	34	10	2	8	6	–	–	103	
	Wealth, £s	43	68	36	13	90	160	–	–	410	4.0
Dumpford and Easebourne	Number	211	113	66	65	33	13	4	2	507	
	Wealth, £s	212	229	328	381	360	289	284	860	2,943	5.8
CHICHESTER	Number	114	105	46	22	25	11	6	1	330	
	Wealth, £s	122	211	174	144	312	287	363	200	1,813	5.5
C. Rape, excl. Weald	Number	642	287	194	174	106	51	24	9	1,487	
	Wealth, £s	659	581	646	1,059	1,307	1,292	1,250	1,276	8,070	5.4
BURY ST EDMUNDS	Number	298	125	79	51	48	26	16	8	651	
	Wealth, £s	298	255	282	310	575	664	738	1,093	4,215	6.5
Thedwastre and Thingoe hundreds	Number	521	190	91	87	46	25	10	6	976	
	Wealth, £s	538	397	323	344	525	606		505	3,238	3.3

* Rotherbridge, West Easewrithe and Bury hundreds.
NB Under £2 means down to £1; under £1 is peculiar to the musters.

the Prayer Book rebellion in Bodmin.[109] Recent work stresses rather the common attributes of village and town.[110]

If the sort of town represented by East Grinstead was too insignificant to accumulate much wealth, even a burgeoning one like Petworth, which was primarily a big village in an extensive parish, was hardly differentiated from the Wealden parts of Arundel rape at large; in fact, its per capita wealth was marginally lower. With a top assessment of only £30, Midhurst was distinctly poorer than the surrounding hundreds of Dumpford and Easebourne. But there was no necessary correlation between population and wealth; Midhurst compares unfavourably with its neighbourhood only because village wealth was boosted by a handful of big landowners whose personalty accounted for most of it. Skipton comprehended a broader spectrum of wealth than most villages in Craven, with only three-quarters of its inhabitants, instead of nine-tenths, valued at less than 40s. At this point we must look at what the loan and muster books have to say, although the examples cover a more limited range.

Appreciably bigger than Skipton, High Wycombe, as the leading town of Buckinghamshire, contained a solid merchant class which made per capita wealth there half as high again as in the villages of the Chilterns where really rich men were thin on the ground. Chichester, with a population approaching 2,000, also had its substantial merchants, yet its wealth was matched by that of the prosperous farming community of the coastal strip and the South Downs, despite £5,850 coming yearly into the city from all corners of Sussex as the income of the cathedral dignitaries; almost certainly the moveable wealth of the clerical establishment was proportionately every bit as high as in Exeter, where it equalled one-sixth of aggregate lay wealth.[111] Unless some merchants had withdrawn to the country, while continuing to manage their businesses there must have been significant investment in urban industry and commerce by the agricultural sector to maintain the balance between town and country in West Sussex. Industry and tourism helped to make Newbury and Little Walsingham people, respectively, worth twice as much as the country folk of the vicinity.

Misconceptions can penalise too rigid definition of hinterlands. Superficially the lack of any considerable contingent of men of undoubted substance in the Soke of Oakham and Alstoe hundred hints that the townsmen of Oakham's average of £5.8 apiece was achieved at the expense of the immediate market area. The rest of Rutland, of which it was the administrative as well as commercial hub, was measurably richer at £6.5 per capita, the slight tendency to a

Table 2.9 Wealth of towns and environs, 1522

Assessments		Under £1	Under £2	£2	£3–4	£5–9	£10–19	£20–39	£40–99	£100+	Total	£ per capita
SKIPTON	Number	44	27	7	6	4	–	1	1	–	90	
	Wealth, £s	17	34	15	21	24	–	30	60	–	201	2.2
Staincliffe	Number	945	562	38	26	33	1	24	4	2	1,635	
	Wealth, £s	362	670	76	85	183	13	510	180	300	2,379	1.5
HIGH WYCOMBE	Number	60	31	40	25	25	20	18	9	1	229	
	Wealth, £s	nil	33	83	90	163	235	441	393	240	1,678	7.3
Chilterns*	Number	160	192	160	112	107	63	37	9	1	841	
	Wealth, £s	2	223	320	390	619	750	857	430	100	3,691	4.4
OAKHAM	Number	49	19	8	9	24	6	5	2	1	123	
	Wealth, £s	nil	19	16	33	156	81	118	90	200	713	5.8

Alstoe and Oakham Soke	Number	100	70	54	79	81	79	19	3	–	485	
	Wealth, £s	nil	78	109	257	579	790	312	60	–	2,185	4.6
Rutland	Number	289	182	162	180	200	180	88	20	9	1,310	
	Wealth, £s	nil	200	321	602	1,273	2,102	1,906	1,045	1,053	8,502	6.5
NEWBURY	Number	62	61	39	24	24	10	14	10	4	248	
	Wealth, £s	15	65	82	81	154	121	315	587	1,013	2,433	9.8
Environs†	Number	620	371	247	226	207	129	71	39	6	1,916	
	Wealth, £s	97	389	516	778	1,308	1,549	1,709	1,996	884	9,226	4.8
L. WALSINGHAM Number		52	23	26	7	14	13	10	10	4	159	9.9
N. Greenhoe Number		106	111	92	71	52	36	13	7	2	490	
hundred Wealth, £s		nil	119	193	246	349	351	325	322	340	2,245	4.5

*Desborough and part of the Aylesbury hundreds.
†Compton, Faircross, Kintbury, Lambourn hundreds.
NB Under £1 includes many at nil.

concentration of wealth at the top of the town community being offset by an exceptionally high proportion (for this shire) of labourers and poor men. Even the smallest county town could become the Mecca of the surplus rural population.[112] Although yet greater extremes of poverty might be expected to exist in bigger towns, an outstanding feature of Chichester was the clearly higher level of wages effective there, with many artificers assessed at 40s. a year, though these were sure to have been balanced by an anonymous mass of recorded paupers.[113] Among the better-paid men were employees of the cathedral, some of whom were clerks in minor orders.[114] Not only were other Sussex towns strongly characterised by the number of £2 assessments, usually on goods, but Bury St Edmunds and Newbury, also county centres, had a smaller proportion of people at the bottom of the heap than their immediate neighbourhoods, though at the latter, the suburban hamlet of Speenhamland was crowded with poor. Wycombe too returned more nil assessments than the surrounding countryside, but the overall proportion below £2 was slightly lower.[115]

A strong bloc of townsmen worth £10 and upwards made the average wealth of Bodmin, Cornwall, a trifle higher than in the rest of Trigg hundred, even though the taxed wage earners, who formed a negligible element in the country parishes, exceeded 40 per cent in the borough itself, numbers which point to a concentration of men who had effectively severed kinship ties with the Celtic extended family that so influenced the social structure of many villages. Helston was measurably poorer, and, except for just one £40 man, had no inhabitant worth more than 20 marks (£13. 6s. 8d.). With half its population taxed on wages, this minute borough precisely reflected rural conditions in the far west. In fact per capita wealth was marginally below average, notwithstanding the existence of municipal institutions which included a guild of cobblers whose rules were promulgated (or reissued) in 1517. One of the members, who included seven householders, three servants (presumably journeymen) and a clerk,[116] was Janyn Perowe, assessed at 40s.; another was John Richard, a £10 man, and presumably not the labourer of the same name.

What, more than anything else, distinguished towns of all sizes was a narrow £3–£9 band which, with a relatively high proportion of assessments upwards of £10, left something of a gap between, on the one hand, the upper tradesmen, and, on the other, artificers and labourers at 40s. or less;[117] the big £3–£4 group at Bury suggests nonetheless either a strong contingent of master craftsmen or unusually well-to-do workmen. On the land the position tended to be reversed, with considerable numbers of £5–£9 men, representing the middling sort of peasant farmers, and far fewer of the more prosperous husbandmen and yeomen. Yet if urban communities divided into well-defined upper and lower classes, the sharp edge of inequality was not infrequently blunted by a numerous £2 group, the diffusion of wealth amongst a solid bloc of merchants and master craftsmen worth upwards of £10, and, in most small towns, the absence of very rich people.

As the centre of a miniature shire, Oakham was neither populous nor wealthy. Not only was Buckinghamshire small, its inadequate internal communications served to check the evolution of a true county town.[118] Also lacking through routes, as well as extending over seventy miles, Sussex has always been administered in two divisions with two county towns, of which the second, Lewes, was similar in size to Chichester, though less prosperous at this time in having far fewer affluent burgesses and no well-paid artificers. Its central location probably terminated its influence well short of the eastern extremity of Sussex, where Rye was almost certainly its peer in size and superior in wealth.[119] More compact shires usually focused on a single centre of the order of two or three thousand inhabitants with wealth to match: Leicester had a good 2,000 or more, including a leading burgess worth £600; in a smaller, poorer county, Nottingham was both smaller and less prosperous.[120] Worcester was closer to 3,000.[121] Bury St Edmunds, hub of the ancient Liberty of St Edmund, with well in excess of 3,000 inhabitants, had fewer labourers and a higher proportion of middling and richer men than its immediate environs; but this apart, there was little to chose between town and country, except at the top of the scale, despite a Hawstead knight's £500 in the latter. Only in per capita wealth did the town have a slight edge, and then perhaps less decisively than might be expected for so important a centre. Comparisons, however, are tenuous, with information about many villages incomplete.[122] Babergh hundred and, to a lesser extent, Cosford, comprised the clothing district where conditions were fundamentally different, and towns such as Sudbury and Hadleigh were important in their own right. Bury, in short, reflected the wealth of an ordinary country district and displayed no strong individual characteristics. Some effects of the historical struggle against the domination of the abbey might arguably have persisted – the town was not incorporated until 1553 – though its evident prosperity shows that this no longer constituted a serious handicap.

Foremost among provincial towns were a handful of regional capitals with populations upwards of five or six thousand. For these too the

Table 2.10   Wealth of Coventry, 1522[123]

Assessments £	Persons	Group wealth	
		£	%
100 and over	20	5,973	52.4
40–99	40	2,141	18.8
20–39	54	1,257	11.0
10–19	65	750	6.6
5–9	96	580	5.1
3–4	66	240	2.1
2	152	311	2.7
Under £2	128	130	1.1
Nil	714	(20)	(0.2)
Total	1,335	11,402	100.0

experience was a varied one. Rather more than half the wealth of Coventry belonged to men whose assessments reached three figures in 1522; in Exeter just under half. In both cities men of £40–£99 accounted for a further 16–19 per cent. The difference was that inequality was more pronounced in the Midland one, where the two top men had upwards of £1,000 apiece, in contrast to Exeter, where the highest was £300,[124] and altogether there were twenty-nine three-figure fortunes compared with just twenty in Coventry (see Table 2.10). At lower levels the proportion of wealth belonging to each group was smaller in Coventry. The lowest ranks of society showed the most striking and significant contrasts. The Coventry muster put 53½ per cent at nil, or a few shillings, with a further 9.6 per cent at 20s. or so. The situation was almost the same at Exeter, but 48 per cent of the subsidy assessments were at £1, mostly on wages, while in Coventry these were only a handful out of a total of some 700 taxpayers,[125] meaning that almost half the population literally 'possessed absolutely nothing but the rags they stood up in, a few sticks and boards for "furniture", and the tools of their trade, if any',[126] Exeter clearly enjoyed full employment – as full, that is, as was attainable in the conditions of the time – while Coventry languished in the grip of severe unemployment, and indeed in the early 1520s was undergoing a series of acute economic crises.[127] Nor was its misfortune unique, for Norwich, the capital of East Anglia, returned a moderate 40 per cent under £2, far less than the adjoining countryside, yet within a dozen years the worsted manufacture commenced a decline that was to contribute largely to the total of more than 500 unemployed males, and altogether upwards of 2,500 destitute persons by 1570. Except that it was nearly twice as large, its social structure closely resembled that of Coventry.[128]

The biggest provincial cities and towns had reached a stage of urbanisation at which the scale of wealth far exceeded that of the countryside. Conversely, the smallest market towns were scarcely distinguishable from populous villages. Between these extremes conditions varied endlessly, with so many towns sharing the social structure of their rural environments that cases of exceptional wealth can only have been the outcome of special circumstances. Great Yarmouth's lead over its hinterland may be attributed to maritime enterprise, its fisheries in particular.[129] Its considerable size – population about 2,500 – certainly cannot be the whole explanation, for a much smaller place could display a more distinctive social structure. With barely 800 inhabitants, Little Walsingham comprised almost a quarter of the population and a clear two-fifths of the value of North Greenhoe hundred, Norfolk (Table 2.9): four men in the £100 class shared 30 per cent of the town's wealth, and ten at £40–£99 owned a further 35 per cent. In the remainder of the hundred these two groups accounted for just under 30 per cent. For a town of this rank it seems almost incredible until we recall that Walsingham enjoyed a lucrative tourist trade as far and away the most popular resort of pilgrimage, the shrine alone deriving an income of £250 a year from the pious offerings of the faithful, compared with the meagre £36 to which that of St Thomas at Canterbury had by then shrunk.[130] The insignificant proportion of men in the £3–£9 range would appear on the face of things to betoken no handicraft beyond what would suffice to satisfy demand in a small hundred, while the many nils, amounting to very nearly one-third of the total, strongly suggests that many of the inhabitants of Walsingham were mendicants subsisting on the alms of the faithful.

For towns of medium size a big stake in the woollen textile industry was the surest foundation of prosperity. If Lavenham is the outstanding example, it is also of interest to look at Newbury, a borough of some 1,250 people, or about 1,600 including the surburban hamlet Speenhamland. Its per capita wealth was nearly double that of the four nearby rural hundreds,[131] with almost four-fifths of the aggregate concentrated in the hands of twenty-nine rich, or very rich, men; no less than 41.6 per cent belonged to the top five, compared with the 'normal'

9.6 in villages and small towns. A leading centre of kersey manufacture, Newbury had been the stamping ground of the celebrated John Winchcombe until his death as recently as 1519. As in a good many other towns, the £3–£9 category was smaller than in the local villages, but the most telling contrast is to be seen at the foot of the scale. Not only were there more 40s. men and fewer at £1 or less, but in the borough itself the poorest class was much smaller than on the land, implying that the more skilled, more remunerative trades were carried out there, while poorly paid weavers and the like lived and worked in Speenhamland. Neighbouring towns such as Hungerford, Lambourn and Wantage conformed to the usual run of little market centres, with populations of 500–600. Three-figure assessments were altogether lacking, though a certain amount of cloth working did support reasonable groups of the second rank in Hungerford and Wantage.[132] Lambourn was never anything greater than a country market.

LONDON

The capital was distinguished from provincial cities and towns on three counts: it was at least five times the size of any other, almost ten times as rich, and possessed a vastly more complex social and occupational structure. Its population at this time can hardly have been less than 50,000 and may easily have been well over 60,000. The mass of the people were not recorded because the evidence is limited to the loan book,[133] which of course excludes everyone with less than £5, a class which in Coventry amounted to as much as 80 per cent of the total,[134] though in other provincial towns the proportion was not as high, that of sub-£2 assessments being lower than in the countryside. At the same time much of London's growth resulted from the influx of the rural poor, so that it early acquired its reputation for slums and crowded tenements. A great deal of growth was, however, in suburbs outside the limits of the city, which, until much later, was the preferred domicile of the affluent, and so the population of the City itself may not have exceeded 50,000.[135]

The size of Norwich, the second city of the kingdom, is also problematical. The population of little more than 7,000, indicated by the total of only 1,414 taxpayers in 1525, seems on the low side, and since it has been estimated at 10,625 (exclusive of aliens) in 1569,[136] a figure closer to 10,000 would be more realistic for the 1520s. The index of the

Table 2.11   Wealth of London[137]

Assessments £	Persons		Group wealth	
	Number	%	£	%
0–4	8,588	80.0	18,209	7.2
5–9	728	6.8	4,016	16
10–19	328	3.1	2,655	1.1
20–39	242	2.3	5,666	2.3
40–99	314	2.9	17,008	6.8
100–499	448	4.2	98,147	39.2
500–999	42	0.4	26,347	10.5
1,000 and over	45	0.4	77,952	31.2
Total	10,735	100.1	250,000	99.9

city's wealth is its contribution of £1,704 to the subsidy, which, although far ahead of that of any other provincial town, was only slightly more than a tenth of London's £16,675.[138]

The most telling comment on the wealth of the metropolis is that it had more men worth upwards of £100 than most other towns had taxpayers of all grades; indeed, the number of four-figure assessments equalled the total taxpayers of some tiny market towns. In order adequately to represent these it is necessary to extend the classification (see Table 2.11).

In provincial towns we noticed the relatively small numbers of £3–£9 assessments, corresponding to the main body of husbandmen in villages; similarly in London there was a shortage of £10–£39 assessments, even of the £40–£99 ones, which in other, smaller towns would have belonged to local merchants and leading master craftsmen. The precise composition of the £0–£4 group can only be guessed at; nevertheless it is clear that the gulf between the merchant class and the artisan population was a very wide one indeed.

The contrast in wealth between merchants and the possessors of rare skills on the one hand and manual workers on the other is clearly demonstrated by their median assessments. The twelve richest occupations were:

Merchant Taylor	£300
Mercer	£167
Physician	£100
Vintner	£ 67
Embroiderer	£ 59
Stockfishmonger	£ 45
Goldsmith	£ 41
Fishmonger	£ 40
Poulterer	£ 40
Ironmonger	£ 40
Leatherseller	£ 38
Waxchandler	£ 36

As the two fish trades came under the same livery company, they may be considered as one; grocers, bakers and haberdashers came next with a median of £26.13s. 4d., closely followed by the dyers on £25. The median for upholsterers works out at £95, but the sample of four is too small to qualify for inclusion in the table. Of the manual occupations, hosiers, cappers, founders, and barbers, to mention but a few, all had the minimum assessment of £5 for median; so also had the various building trades, with the exception of the marblers who averaged £50 on a small sample. Only slightly better off at around £6 were tailors - probably the yeomanry of the Merchant Taylors – shoemakers and smiths, while everyone connected with transport, whether by land or water, showed a median of £5–£7. Rather more skilled crafts, such as fullers, shearmen, cutlers, painters and butchers, were around the £10 mark.

Figures of this kind cannot avoid concealing a great deal. Goldsmiths, for example, included manual workers who tended to depress the average; the richest member of the Company had £2,000. One painter was worth 2,500 marks, the richest grocer 4,000. These examples can be multiplied.

The City differed from other towns in two major respects: first the division of the membership of most companies into the 'livery', who controlled them, and the 'yeomanry', and secondly the distinction between the great companies and the lesser ones. The former, eleven in number – the Clothworkers being formed by amalgamation of the Fullers and Shearmen in 1536[139] – comprised most of the merchant class. The loan book must contain virtually all the liverymen of the various companies, though not necessarily all the yeomen, nor indeed any but a fraction of the membership of the poorest crafts: only a single weaver is listed, though there was a livery of thirty and a full membership of seventy in 1546.[140] By the turn of the century their numbers seem to have declined; they evidently tended to move out of the City, yielding place to wealthier residents.[141] At the top of the scale, business must have taken a number of leading men out of town at the time the assessment was made, including, for example, Robert Thorne, Merchant Taylor and a notable benefactor to the City; worth more than £20,000 at the time of his death in 1532, he must have been one of the very richest men in England.[142]

It is instructive to compare the members of the eleven great companies taxed in 1522–3 with the statistics compiled by Professor Thrupp (see Table 2.12).[143] Here the tailors and Merchant Taylors are counted together, though distinguished in the loan book. One man at least was wrongly classed as a tailor, namely Stephen Jenings, who had served as Mayor in 1508–9,[144] and was now the highest assessed citizen at £3,000; the same must hold good for other rich tailors, since the craft itself was poorly remunerated. As there was only the one company it is reasonable to infer that everyone roped in for the first loan was in fact a Merchant Taylor. Further, it is noticeable that the grand total is very close to Professor Thrupp's estimate of the Company membership, while the numbers valued at £40 or better and £20 or more closely match the livery lists of 1501 and 1537–8, respectively. This is the only company whose entire membership appears to have figured in the loan;

Table 2.12 Membership and wealth of the great companies

| Company | Membership | | | Assessments, 1522–3 | | |
| | Total | Livery | | Total | £40+ | £20+ |
		1501	1537/8			
Mercers	*c.* 273	55	66	113	87	90
Drapers	248	76	80	104	46	66
Grocers	177/191	59	84	119	58	71
Merchant Taylors	230	84	96	216	82	104
Fishmongers		76	109	98	55	70
Goldsmiths	168	51	52	69	44	49
Skinners	[151]	54	151	71	33	45
Haberdashers	[120]	41	120	87	41	47
Vintners		26	33	28	18	18
Salters		30	40(50)	31	14	17
Ironmongers	93	25	27(44)	30	15	15

in the case of such as the Goldsmiths and the Ironmongers it seems clear that only the livery was assessed. Seventy-nine fullers and shearmen, later to form the Clothworkers, were assessed, compared with a combined livery of eighty-five in 1501.[145]

Comparisons such as these must not be pressed too far. Although it is not certain that property qualifications were required for liverymen, several companies are known to have imposed minima for admission to their freedom. The Mercers fixed it at £100 in 1503; either it was not enforced or the assessments are thoroughly unsatisfactory. The Goldsmiths settled on £40 in 1480, but did not stick to it for long;[146] whatever their rules, it is clear that they were exceptionally wealthy, no fewer than fifty-seven having £200 or more, much the same as the number of liverymen. Although under-assessment was nowhere more flagrant than among rich Londoners,[147] it was always possible for a fortune to be wiped out by an unsuccessful business venture, as in the case of Alderman Aylmer, draper, who was assessed at £40 net, 'his debts paid', when others of this rank were normally worth a thousand or more.[148] Lesser companies had smaller qualifications, if any. Fullers and carpenters required 20 marks for admission to the livery in the late fifteenth century,[149] but in each case the total number of assessments was much less than the number in the contemporary lists, twenty-six and twenty-four respectively, compared with between thirty and forty. Of companies of this sort only the liverymen, if indeed all of them, were likely to find their way into the returns. Below the exemption line there must have been many small masters. The Founders had eighty-five members in 1522, with a livery ranging between twenty-two in 1501 and a possible sixty-five in 1537–8; yet only eight were assessed. If their complaint to the Star Chamber in 1507 be credited, they were a weak group at the mercy of any sharp speculator.[150] Even in the great companies not all the leading members were rich. In the Mercers an assessment of £100, or even £200, was appropriate for a liveryman; in the Merchant Taylors, Haberdashers and (perhaps) Grocers, £40; for Drapers, Fishmongers, Goldsmiths and Skinners, approximately £20; and as little as £5 in the remaining three.

Save for the obvious case of a handful of Staplers, the returns do not distinguish merchants. There can be little room for doubt as to the status of wealthy citizens, but the lower limit is more problematical. Thrupp estimated that the eleven great companies contained some 700 merchants towards the close of the Middle Ages.[151] The loan book identifies 926 members. Presumably men of modest means would scarcely have qualified, but only 502 were worth £20 and upwards, and

406 had £40 or more, a figure that might be regarded as a reasonable minimum for a substantial businessman. However, while these companies were by nature primarily mercantile, there was a varying proportion of merchants among the less eminent ones. The return shows in all 849 persons of £40 and above, which should yield a net figure of something like 700 possible merchants, since a good many of the assessmented belonged to gentry, clergy, members of non-mercantile companies, or men of unstated occupation. Unless the size of the class has been exaggerated, it is, nonetheless, clear that merchant status was not of necessity synonymous with large-scale activities and great fortunes. The aspiration was

> argosies with portly sail,
> Like signiors and rich burghers of the flood,
> Or, as it were, the pageants of the sea

but, as Antonio points out,

> Thou know'st that all my fortunes are at sea;
> Neither have I money nor commodity
> To raise a present sum[152]

Judging from the number of Londoners who ended by having to pay more than they were initially assessed for, this refrain could have been sung a bit too often to be convincing.

Whether or not there was substance in the belief that London's prosperity worked to the detriment of provincial cities, the contrast between them was little short of dramatic. At a time when London's population can hardly have exceeded 2 per cent of the entire nation, it contributed more than one-ninth of the total subsidy. It is no accident that Londoners were to be found financing enterprises in the shires – Henry Fyner, a goldsmith, had built the first English blast furnace at Hartfield, Sussex[153] – and helping to create the country's stock of 'social overhead capital' – roads and bridges, schools and colleges. Hugh Clopton, a mercer, erected the bridge at Stratford-upon-Avon that still bears his name; Sir William Horne, salter, left 500 marks for repairing the road to Cambridge; Sir Thomas White, Merchant Taylor, founded St John's College, Oxford, and others endowed grammar schools at Holt, Macclesfield, Wolverhampton and many other places. Much of the provision for the relief of the poor at this time was the benefactions of Londoners. The charitable bequests of Robert Thorne, Merchant Taylor, who died in 1532, amounted to no less than £4,400, a sum that was indeed higher than any assessment for the loan, levied when he was evidently abroad on business. Many endowed almshouses. One of the most evocative of early sixteenth–century legacies, was that of Henry Keble, grocer, which included 140 ploughshares and 140 iron coulters for poor husbandmen in Oxfordshire and Warwickshire.[154] Merchant princes did not forget their native towns and counties and the people there who might want for the means of providing themselves with even the most basic tools of their trade.

THE EFFECT OF INDUSTRY

Although craft activity in some form was carried on almost everywhere, whether it can properly be termed industry depends very much on the objective and scale of the undertaking. A great deal of it amounted to little more than an adjunct to farming, typically by smallholders plying a trade on the side.[155] Commonly geared to the demands of a constricted local market, not all these crafts could provide continuous employment. Many small town craftsmen worked on much the same plan. The sale of sheep and barley made up 35 per cent of the estate of Richard Jerard, a Chepping Wycombe pewterer and brazier, the residue including a few more animals, a little grain and hay, and an iron harrow, although another metal worker there owned nothing but the tools of his trade. On the other hand a Stony Stratford shoemaker's connexion with agriculture was limited to a cow and (possibly) a white horse; his sideline was petty capitalism, if not simply money-lending, for his assets, totalling more than £28, included £18. 1s. 8d. owed by seven different persons.[156] In sizeable towns the volume of trade offered wider scope for specialisation, but even there the connexion with agriculture remained intimate: in most the victualling and food-processing trades formed one of the principal groupings, as in Leicester or York;[157] only if there was a manufacturing speciality would they take second place. In some small towns, such as Sudbury or Oakham, just under one-fifth of the workforce was engaged in textiles and in victualling as well. In villages, where people did their own cooking, baking and brewing, food handling was restricted to milling, malting and butchering, leaving clothing and footwear the commonest occupations – indeed, tailoring was one of the largest single crafts anywhere.

Industry, strictly defined, can be regarded as having established itself only where production so exceeded local demand as to be aimed at a wider market, for a trade might flourish and yet remain no more than a subsidiary activity, like the leather trades of the Weald of Sussex. It was observed: 'In most villages of the realm there is some one dresser or worker of leather, and in most of the market towns iij or iiij or v, and many great towns and cities x or xx^{tie},' and indeed, with cattle and timber its chief products, the Weald was a natural location, and local bark, of which colliers and ironmasters had plenty to spare, was much in demand by tanners.[158] A modest, though steady, export of hides reached its peak, for the reign of Henry VIII, with just over twenty lasts (each of twenty dickers) in 1528–29, tapering to a minimum of sixteen dickers ten years later.[159] Yet less than 4 per cent of wills, 1525–60, were made by leather workers, two-thirds of whom were tanners, manufacturing crafts being relatively inconspicuous.[160] The one or two well-to-do tanners identified in the subsidy rolls were so scattered, and formed so small a part of the population, that the contribution of leather working to the local economy can have been no more than marginal at best.

The effect of a dense concentration of the woollen textile industry is emphatically expressed by the manner in which the seventeen manufacturing villages and towns of Babergh hundred, Suffolk, differed from the purely agricultural ones (see Table 2.13). The relatively small £3–£9 element gives these a pronounced urban flavour but, in contrast

Table 2.13 Industrial wealth of Babergh hundred[161]

Assessments £	Persons	Group wealth £	%
100 and over	42	10,605	53.7
40–99	60	3,200	16.2
20–39	97	2,248	11.4
10–19	136	1,610	8.2
5–9	132	839	4.3
3–4	122	435	2.2
2	244	492	2.5
Under 2	297	304	1.5
Under 1	273	nil	–
Total	1,403	19,733	100.0

to the majority of little country towns, it was men worth upwards of £40 that were specially numerous, while for size and wealth the topmost class had no parallel outside London. So, although the gap between rich and poor in Babergh may look wider than in most parts of the country, the distribution of wealth was complex. Great as they were, the numbers of the labouring poor did not approach the level of the arable-farming areas of West Suffolk. Even in the clothing district, wage earners reached almost 53 per cent in the villages of Cosford hundred, but since they fell short of a third in the rising manufacturing town of Hadleigh, it seems that vigorous industrial growth pushed up the level of earnings. At the same time this trade was notoriously unstable. Babergh starkly illustrates the brittleness of its prosperity at any given moment. In 1522 an affluent society was depicted in which inequalities, albeit wide, were offset by an above-average overall standard: the profits from textiles were widely diffused. Yet within two years the percentage of sub-£2 assessments jumped from a modest $39\frac{1}{2}$ to more than 56. In confirming the wealth of the district the subsidy exposed a scale of poverty that more closely approached what was to be found in the rest of Suffolk.[162]

Almost certainly textiles had fallen into some disarray by early 1524. Following the death, on 29 June 1523, of Thomas Spring of Lavenham, 'the rich clothier', his commercial empire had been dismantled, and his immense fortune, £3,200 net, dispersed among his heirs, most of it to his widow and daughter; his son had already chosen to live as a gentleman and was duly taxed on £20 from lands in 1524, and the firm ceased trading. Something like £1,500 shared among the family, not to mention generous bequests, including £200 towards the completion of Lavenham steeple and cash distributed among the parishes where Spring owned property,[163] virtually accounts for what was far and away the greatest personal estate owned by any commoner, or for that matter almost any peer: only the duke of Norfolk's £4,000 topped it.[164] Spring's actual goods, doubtless including his stock-in-trade, were appraised at precisely £1,800, a further £1,400 consisting of money owed to him, £800 having been written off as 'desperate' debts. This netting of his assets doubtless conceals the fact that, like any businessman, he in turn had extensive liabilities, making him the centre of a complex web of credit, the effects of which had to be reckoned with.

Spring's vast fortune comprised upwards of 40 per cent of the combined assets of the Babergh clothiers. The abrupt cessation of his trading cannot but have caused more or less severe dislocation until others were ready to take up the slack, just as Bath became 'somewhat decayed' after the deaths of three of its clothiers.[165] A phase of acute unemployment is likely to have supervened; it was certainly alleged to be rife by 1525 when it was put forward as the precipitant of the riots against the levying of the Amicable Grant – the tax of one-sixth on the valuations of 1522 by which Wolsey sought to make good the disappointing yield of the subsidy – albeit attributed to the dislocation of business caused by the severity of taxation.[166] By this point the wealth of the local clothiers had in fact been reduced by more than half, though taxation, while extracting huge sums from the community at large, had taken little more than £1,100, far less than had been withdrawn from the industry by the Springs.[167] Sharp rises in the national export statistics in both 1523–4 and 1524–5[168] rule out any general depression; any unemployment can only have been temporary and localised, as the disorders in the eastern counties were not repeated on the same scale anywhere.[169] Very likely there was a general cut in wages brought about by a combination of causes, not the least of which was the loss of an employer who may very well have paid premium rates in order to attract and retain labour; in any case the living standards of the cloth workers had fallen sharply by 1524, and with them those of the farm labourers of the other villages in the district.

With this episode commenced perhaps the decline of the Stour Valley woollen industry, the symptoms of which were all too obvious by the middle of the century. In the end it was overtaken by the advent of the 'New Draperies',[170] but the downward trend had set in well before the establishment of these in East Anglia; indeed, in the event they came to replace the contracting broadcloth manufacture which, even as early as 1523, had shown signs of instability: it was symptomatic of recession that no less than 35 per cent of Spring's liquid assets had to be written off as irrecoverable, and the winding up of his affairs cannot but have dealt its prosperity a mortal blow. Lavenham was never the same without him; by 1568 it paid only half as much tax as Long Melford, compared with two-and-a-half times as much in 1524, and its place had been usurped by Hadleigh, which had paid only three-fifths of Lavenham's quota in 1524, yet now ranked as the third town in Suffolk after Bury St Edmunds and Ipswich.[171] This, however, lay still in the future, and for the time being the seventeen industrialised towns and villages (out of thirty-two) in Babergh hundred contained almost three-quarters of its population and 87 per cent of its wealth.

Cloth was also made in north-east Essex, in and around Colchester, though on a much smaller scale. Outside this borough, however, only

Dedham counted for much. Coggeshall was neither large nor particularly affluent; John Paycocke, nephew of Thomas and inheritor of the imposing Paycocke house, was assessed at no more than £53, though the richest man in Coggeshall, his son having £10 as well; to all appearances Thomas's munificent bequests had depleted the family fortune.[172] In the Middle Ages clothing had also flourished in the small towns westwards as far as Saffron Walden. Halstead did have one man worth £300, but among the remaining 148 taxpayers there was only one worth £80 and one worth 40 marks.[173] Already, it seems, industry was coming to be concentrated on the north side of the Stour – Dedham lies opposite East Bergholt, a booming village – and that the gap was opening which forty-five years later was to be filled by the arrival of the Dutch bringing the techniques of the 'New Draperies'.

Except in the colourful person of the legendary John Winchcombe, the Berkshire woollen industry had little in the way of glamour. In addition to Newbury it centred on Reading and Abingdon, about which information is scanty, and had flourished at Wantage during the fifteenth century.[174] It was also carried on in some few villages: fulling mills operated at East Hendred, near Wantage, Brimpton and Colthorp, as well as one at Bagnor owned by no less than Jack of Newbury himself.[175] Generally, though, the manufacture was primarily an urban one, any slight activity in the villages of the Vale of the White Horse escaping Leland's notice; not only was it most unlikely to have spread to the Downs, but the social structure of the countryside north of Newbury was typical of corn-growing chalklands. Already the trade showed signs of becoming restricted to the immediate neighbourhood of Reading, whose clothiers seem to have controlled most of the output of Berkshire.[176] By any standard the industry was not extensive: Berkshire was bracketed with Herefordshire at the bottom of a list of clothiers fined at Blackwell Hall in 1561–2 for marketing substandard cloth, with just one offender, a Reading man;[177] unless Berkshire workmanship in general was above average, production was clearly small in volume. The fact that Kent headed this unworthy league by an ample margin suggests that the industry there hastened its eventual downfall by inferior work.

By the early 1560s the Berkshire trade was unquestionably in the doldrums when the Privy Council admonished Reading clothiers against putting men off work by ceasing to trade. Abingdon's trade had been waning for some time, with its fulling mills lying in ruins and unemployment rife by 1538. New enterprise was urgently needed, and in 1558 Abingdon started manufacturing sailcloth for the Admiralty.[178] Newbury had attained its zenith in the reign of Henry VIII, traditionally with Winchcombe. An elusive figure, there is nothing to show that his wealth approached Thomas Spring's in scale, his wider fame owing more to a flair for the flamboyant gesture. As a businessman the great William Stumpe of Malmesbury was no doubt Winchcombe's superior.[179] Together, nevertheless, these three men indicate that each district was apt to throw up one great entrepreneur at a time who stood head and shoulders above his contemporaries and competitors. Besides John Winchcombe, junior, who was assessed at the unusually high figure of £630, Newbury in 1522 had three residents worth £100 or so and ten more in the £40–£99 range, including William Dolman who had been the elder Winchcombe's works manager; now, at 100 marks, he might already have set up in business for himself. The subsequent history of the town is confused; by 1564 its trade was said to be in decline, and it sustained a further blow when William's son retired to the fine house he had built at Shaw on the outskirts of the borough, leaving his men to sing ruefully:

> Lord, have mercy on us miserable sinners,
> Thomas Dolman has built a new house and turned away all his spinners.

The formation of a company of clothworkers in 1601 suggests not only something of a revival but equally a closing of ranks in the face of

Table 2.14 Wealth of Bisley hundred, 1522

Assessments £	Persons	Group wealth	
		£	%
100 and over	6	1,006	36.9
40–99	4	190	7.0
20–39	26	596	21.9
10–19	45	532	19.5
5–9	41	241	8.8
3–4	24	85	3.1
2	39	78	2.9
Under 2	–	–	–
Nil	10	nil	–
Total	195	2,728	100.0

adversity. As things turned out, the seventeenth century saw a total collapse which left both Newbury and Reading only the remnants of their former trade. Nonetheless, in the 1520s Newbury's position in south-west Berkshire remained unchallenged. Wantage was a decent little town but had less than half the population of Newbury and no inhabitant worth more than £80, though four others had £40–£60; average wealth of well under £6 compares poorly with almost £10 in Newbury and was not much higher than in most villages.[180]

The Stroud district of Gloucestershire was well developed, 'Stroudwaters' having been a household name for nearly a century.[181] Bisley hundred returned the large number of six three-figure assessments out of a total of 195, though only four at £40–£99 (see Table 2.14); Lower Lipyatt parish, including Stroud town, had three worth £122–£240. Although places along the river Frome were as rich as, or richer than, any other part of the county, by Cotswold standards they were not outstandingly affluent. For per capita wealth Bisley (£14.0) was rivalled by Bradley hundred (£13.5) and outclassed by Brightwells Barrow (£15.4), which contained the market towns of Fairford and Lechlade; as representatives of the rural Cotswolds these make an interesting contrast (Table 2.15). Also outclassed on an average of only 59.4 by most other hundreds of the region was Langtree hundred, which included Horsley and Munchinhampton. The wealth of manufacturing Stroud looks modest beside that of trading Cirencester where, of eighty men listed, nine had upwards of £40 and four more than £100.[182] Nowhere was there a clothier of the stamp of Spring, or even Winchcombe, and comparatively few of major stature. Away from Stroudwater the industry seems rather to have remained in the hands of independent craftsmen: in eight places where cloth was made, the structure of wealth resembled what was commonly found in parts where it had not taken root, with perhaps three of the four £100 men belonging to the gentry.[183] Although Tortworth had 'some good clothiars', £30 was as much as anyone there was worth. Wotton-under-Edge also was 'welle occupied with clothiars having ane faire longe strete and welle buyldyd', but nonetheless £60 was the top assessment, though three other men, out of seventy-six, had £40–£50 each. Nobody in Wickwar, 'a hamlet', admitted to more than £4, while the lord of the manor owned more than half the wealth of Alderley, where a man of £50 was the only one who looks a potential clothier. 'A pretty' manufacturing town, Dursley had several residents who look as though they operated the water trucking mills; unusually for the area, more than half the fifty-two persons listed were rated at less than 40s., some of

Table 2.15 Wealth of Bradley and Brightwells Barrow

Assessments £	Persons	Group wealth £	%
100 and over	5	680	16.3
40–99	23	1,188	28.4
20–39	29	649	15.5
10–19	76	962	23.0
5–9	68	956	10.9
3–4	52	177	4.2
2	33	66	1.6
Under 2	–	–	–
Nil	1	nil	–
Total	287	4,178	99.9

them probably millhands, though others must have laboured in the stone quarry which caught Leland's eye.[184]

As yet, industry hereabouts may not fully have 'taken off', but at the same time the many £2 assessments downgraded for tax purposes in the Vale region indicate a degree of recession, the state of some towns hinting at an uneasy period of relocation. Around 1540 Berkeley was 'no great thinge'; quite small, it contained one potential big businessman worth 200 marks, and, other than Sir Thomas Berkeley, the local magnate, no one else of note. Thornbury had known 'good clothing' but was no more prosperous than any other little country town, and 'idelnes muche reynithe there'.[185] In the busiest centres clothing was a major source of employment, nearly half the Bisley hundred taxpayers being assessed on wages, as the working weavers, fullers, shearmen and so forth, a far higher proportion than in most villages.[186] If the record of those who organised and controlled production is anything like complete, they did not begin to compare with their peers in East Anglia. Nor for that matter could Wiltshire clothiers, for, although a dozen or more were rated for the Anticipation at upwards of £100, the highest was only £250: for some reason the great William Stumpe of Malmesbury was not assessed. Devizes, with one man worth £160, one £100, and six in the £40–£99 class, compared poorly even with Newbury.[187]

The wealth of Worcester, its size and eminence in the textile industry notwithstanding, showed similar characteristics. Although also a shire town and centre of a big diocese, the absence of truly rich citizens made it hardly more impressive a place than Chichester, which was much smaller (Table 2.8). Since work was not put out to rural artificers, clothmaking remained craft-based.[188] Kidderminster depended 'most' and Bromsgrove 'somewhat' on clothing.[189] Hardly more than a village, the latter possessed no more wealth than any sizeable one and no distinctive characteristics; most of the population of the huge parish was scattered among hamlets, locally called 'yelds', which showed few signs of industrial growth. Nearly twice the size of Bromsgrove, Kidderminster returned a handful of men of the second rank and many poor as well; the Forens, or out-parish, looks in part an artisan suburb. An Act passed in 1534 granted a monopoly of clothmaking in the county to Worcester and four other boroughs including Droitwich and Evesham. Designed to nip in the bud any incipient growth in villages, it was successful, so far as the city was concerned, probably because it did no more than sanction the existing situation, even though in the fifteenth century the trade had flourished at Hartlebury, which remained an important centre of the specialised craft of fulling.[190] Generally conditions in Worcestershire in 1522 add a sombre background to the apprehension that rural competition was injuring the towns; by the date of Leland's visit things were possibly looking up once more.

In Sussex the manufacture of cloth had never reached major proportions; what little there was of it was scattered, chiefly in the Weald. In 1562–3 clothiers from East Grinstead, Petworth and, unexpectedly, Alfriston, in the heart of the Downs, even Chichester, were fined at Blackwell Hall; as well there are signs of a minor centre of activity near Steyning; and at least five clothiers of Midhurst controlled weavers in Bepton, Lodsworth and other villages nearby. In the middle of a prime corn-growing district, Chichester is unlikely to have been a centre of putting out; high wages there probably showed the influence of a craft-based manufacture, though on too small a scale to have any marked effect on the level and distribution of wealth. Midhurst and Petworth were actually less affluent than their respective market areas. As £20 in goods was the most any of them owned, the business of the Gobles of Petworth, one of whom was fined in 1562, must have been quite modest; a namesake of Thomas Page, the Alfriston defaulter, had 20 marks, and a possible forebear of George Partrych of East Grinstead was a small landowner with £5 a year.[191]

Mineral extraction and quarrying were the only other enterprises

Table 2.16 State of Droitwich, 1522

Assessments £	Persons	Group wealth £	%
100 and over	–	–	–
40–99	–	–	–
20–39	2	50	27.0
10–19	7	77	41.6
5–9	5	34	18.4
3–4	4	17	9.2
2	3	6	3.2
Under 2	–	0	–
Nil	54	1	0.5
Total	75	185	99.9

producing for more than immediate local demand, though practical considerations must generally have limited the distances stone could be transported. Leland regularly noted quarries on his travels;[192] doubtless the one at Dursley, Gloucs., was the reason for the great number of poor labourers there.[193] Seldom did extractive industry bring prosperity. Salt burning, on the contrary, made Droitwich (Table 2.16) one of the poorest communities in Worcestershire, almost without parallel anywhere, the township itself being 'somewhat foule and dirty when any reyne faullythe, with moche carriage throwghe the stretes, being over ill pavyd or not pavyd'.

Leland added:

The great avancement of the towne is by makyng of salt; and yet thoughe the commoditie thereof be syngular great, yet the burgesses be poore for the moste parte; by cawse the gentlemen have for the moaste parte the great gayne of it, and the burgesses have all the labowre.[194]

Since nonetheless the gentry of the vicinity were anything but affluent, the profits may have been largely illusory.

Impoverishment is a recurrent theme in accounts of Cornish tin mining; very much later John Norden observed that

The poore hirelinges worke for 8 pence per diem or 6 poundes per annum, and in all theis to find themselues of all necessaries the parishes wherin their workes moste abounde are for the moste parte of meanest wealth. And they that stand vpon tillage are in best estate[195]

Carew added that 'as by abandoning this trade they amend, so by reviving the same they decay again'. Towards 1540, when earnings were certainly much lower, it was mostly fishing villages like Newlyn, Bodinick and St Germans that looked poverty-stricken to Leland,[196] though the jottings of a tourist, primarily on the look-out for antiquities, hardly stand comparison with systematic investigations of Carew, a professional surveyor and a life-long student of local matters. Leland's gloomy view of Droitwich must have been prompted by visual symptoms – the foul streets and the sickly faces he encountered in them: 'the people that be about the fornacis be very ille colorid'.[197]

Around 1540 mining was most active in the far west of Cornwall, in particular between St Just in Penwith and Newlyn, and 'from ther to Looe Pool' and Helston, and there were 'no greater tynne workes in Cornwall then be on Sir William Godalchan's ground' in and near Breage.[198] Penwith and Kerrier hundreds were obviously poorer than the eastern parts of the shire; a high proportion of men were taxed on wages who had not been thought worth mentioning in the earlier survey, many of them poor immigrants variously described as tinners or labourers. Even though the ranks of labourers were thinner and the level of wealth higher than in the west, tinning was not unknown in eastern parts, though parishes containing tinners differed little from ones that did not: not only were the former only slightly poorer in East hundred, but in West and Trigg they were actually rather better off.[199] To Cornish people as a whole tin brought little tangible benefit; whether it was a social disaster is less certain. Carew's bleak diagnosis can hardly have been uninfluenced by several decades of mounting concern at the impermanence of non-agricultural employment compared with the stability of farmers fully occupied tending their land, and men continuously employed as servants in husbandry engaged for a year at a time. Of the handful of men who made real money out of tin, Godolphin, besides being a leading figure in the industry,[200] was also the richest resident in the county, assessed at £200. (Sir Piers Edgcumbe was indeed rated at £400 for the subsidy,[201] but, equally a Devon man, was absent from Cornwall in 1522.) In the long term, moreover, the profits were creamed off by London capitalists who kept a tight grip on the marketing of tin.[202]

Iron was increasingly worked in the Forest of Dean and the high Weald in Sussex, which in wealth and social structure had much in common. Wealden ironmasters, and even more so their men, are elusive figures, but a Wadhurst miller, taxed at £4 on land, looks much like John Barham of Woodlands and Butts who in 1521 purchased Brooklands forge along with Bartley Mill. Eight Barhams taxed there included his brothers Richard (£15 on goods) and William (£8); Henry, a wage earner, was probably the son, though listed as servant, of Thomas (£10 in goods). At this time most of them were minor landowners, but they were of gentle descent, and although John of Faircross, son and heir of the ironmaster, styled himself yeoman all his life, his descendants eventually moved up into the gentry.[203]

No great number of people need have been directly engaged in iron-making, for the Wealden industry was still in the 1520s no more than poised on the threshold of greatness, with only three blast furnaces in operation, and indeed the original one at Newbridge standing idle without a tenant. Not until around 1540 did undertakings begin to proliferate, and even then the work was never a whole-time occupation, production being organised in 'campaigns' lasting from two to six months, mainly in winter when the rains swelled the streamlets and filled the ponds which powered the furnace bellows and the tilt-hammers of the forges. Only three of the twenty-six hands at the Sheffield works (commissioned *c.* 1540) were permanently employed: a manager 'hired by the year to attend upon the works and workmen at all tyme, and wey the iron from the workman to the merchaunte', and two waggoners for the slow, laborious process of collecting raw materials and delivering the forgings. At Worth the supervisor was the sole full-timer. Only one out of eight men employed to carry coals, mine and sows of iron at Robertsbridge worked all 140 days of the campaign in 1542–3, the remainder putting in anything from two to forty-eight.[204] Salt-burning at Droitwich was confined to the six months Midsummer–Christmas – to keep up the price, Leland was told, though he himself thought the real motive was to conserve wood, since the exhaustion of supplies nearby obliged the salters to buy it from as far away as Worcester, Bromsgrove, Alvechurch and Alcester.[205]

Doubtless many iron workers put in a few days at a time on different sites; until quite recently putting out much of the work to contract in small stints on a 'labour-only' basis was a regular practice in mineral extraction, so leading tax collectors to class earnings as profits rather than wages. Alongside the new-fangled blast furnace the traditional bloom process must have continued to occupy many people for short periods every year. Far-fetched as the notion of a forge in the yard of every sizeable farm[206] must seem, it would in principle have been perfectly consistent with fragmented and seasonal production.

Most families prominent in the iron trade came from the yeomanry and lesser gentry, though there were a few bigger men. Richard Sackville of Buckhurst, in the business of making shot, was a major landowner with 200 marks a year. William Wybarn of Ticehurst (goods £110) took on Bayham forge in 1525, and Thomas Oxenbrege of Northiam (£52) demised the Darfold Wood furnace in Mountfield and a forge at Etchingham in 1535 to a Thomas Walsh, who was perhaps the man taxed on £5 per annum in Danehill Sheffield hundred. John Levett, gentleman, of the same (goods £30) must have been the brother – also in iron – of William, the parson of Buxted, who in 1542 directed the casting of the first one-piece cannon. John Warner of Hartfield (land £20) was probably the supplier of gunstones as well as a relative of Richard Warner who owned the Parrock works in 1518.[207]

Men of this standing were mostly considerable landowners in the first place. The Barhams were more typical. John Bowley, or Bowyer, a shot maker who took on the Hartfield steel forge in 1525, might have been related to either Valentine or Nicholas Bowyer (land £2 and £3 respectively). John Collins (Collen), who already owned Sockernsh furnace in Burwash, had £28 in moveables. William Spycer of Dallington might have cherished visions of instant fortune when he leased the site of the projected Panningridge furnace, but they soon faded, and, having assigned his interest to the wealthy Sir Henry Sidney, he carted stone, and lime for the constructors;[208] if his personal property was limited to the £3 on which he was taxed, he was under capitalised.

The marginal impact on the local economy left few traces on the record. The condition of the people of Hartfield, Hawksborough and Shoyswell hundreds differed from that of the rest of the region only in so far as the usual string of £1 assessments was balanced in each of them by one of the very few three-figure ones (see Table 2.17). Jobs were certainly created, but generally as by-employments, and limited in number. Big undertakings like Sheffield and Worth only required twenty or thirty men each, and of course for just a few weeks at a time. Furnace construction naturally provided opportunities: a fair number of men, mainly of the smallholding and labouring type, fetched materials

Table 2.17 Wealth of Wealden iron districts, 1524[209]

Assessments £	Persons	Group wealth £	%
100 and over	3	433	20.2
40–99	1	49	2.9
20–39	13	219	10.2
10–19	43	527	24.5
5–9	45	281	13.1
3–4	53	189	8.8
2	89	181	8.4
Under 2	256	269	12.5
Total	503	2,148	100.6

and performed other services during the building of Panningridge in 1542–3.[210]

As with Cornish tin the profits were creamed by the London capitalists who financed a good many undertakings.[211] Nonetheless, the workmen were not necessarily the hapless victims of exploitation. Levels of earnings might well have been limited by their own work-psychology, as were those of lead miners in Derbyshire and the Mendip Hills, where the labour force consisted almost entirely of smallholders and cottagers. The interdependence of farming and mining, added to technological constraints, restricted the number of days annually available for mining; the farmer-miner's smallholding had first claim on his time, and he went to the mine with the limited aim of satisfying, with a minimum of effort, the desire for a particular level of cash-income expectation determined by the need to pay the rent of his holding and purchase a given packet of 'industrial' goods. The cottar, subsisting on an inadequate holding, had a greater need for cash earnings and more time to spare, but because he accepted the hierarchical consumption ethic of the village community his aspirations were lower, so that, although working longer, he did so at a lower intensity. The professional miner seeking to achieve a higher standard of living through maximisation of earnings scarcely existed in the early sixteenth century.[212]

Although on the whole wages in the iron industry were good,[213] real earnings would not have been high enough to produce a tangible effect on the structure of taxable wealth. High wages at some undefined earlier date had very possibly induced many Cornishmen to abandon husbandry for tinning.[214] Then during the period 1410–50 the falling price of tin had necessitated increases in the number of work days and productivity to maintain the level of earnings, and more and more men, finding tinning an unrewarding way of satisfying their expectations, had turned to occupations such as cloth making and fishing.[215] Enough of them might also have left the county to reduce the population to a point which, by the 1520s, created a need for Breton workmen.

At first the native community of the Weald may have been little affected by the expansion of the iron industry. Almost certainly the key positions, and perhaps many others, were filled by Frenchmen. The new era having dawned with the introduction of the blast furnace from France in 1496, French experts were naturally recruited to install them. By 1524, thirty-eight Frenchmen comprised almost a third of the taxpayers and well over half the labourers of Hartfield hundred. This, the biggest single enclave in Sussex, not only demonstrates the continued dependence of the prototype works at Newbridge on immigrant workmen, but also implies that there had been no great pool of indigenous labour to draw on in the first place. Although later works made more use of Englishmen, foreign technicians continued to be needed, and the several groups located in the Weald add up to a directory of the industry in 1524–5.[216] The traditional bloom process was still capable of meeting all needs, for a negligible outlay; the exotic indirect process had been introduced as an act of state policy simply in order to make cannons, the need for which had been proved by the effectiveness of French artillery – against the English themselves – in the wars of the fifteenth century; Newbridge, where the first successful gun had been cast in 1509, was Crown property.[217] Here for once a rural industry had been set up regardless of the availability of local labour or any need to create employment; at first people in the Weald lacked not merely skill but also, it would seem, sufficient incentive. The number of sub-£2 assessments was primarily a function of the natural poverty of the region, most being returned by smallholders – some of them owner-occupiers – rather than labourers. Viewed against the abnormally small numbers in High Suffolk, the many wage earners of the Stour Valley also give the impression that expanding industry sucked in labour from far and wide. If a common phenomenon, this goes some way towards accounting for the ingrained belief that such growth engendered serious economic and social problems, not least Carew's conviction that the opening of tin workings impoverished a parish, whilst their discontinuance restored prosperity.[218] In fact it might well have been that such developments generally attracted more labour than could be fully employed, which departed once the enterprise was terminated, leaving behind a sleepy farming community not unlike the fifteen undeveloped villages of Babergh hundred (Table 2.18). If anything these somewhat stereotyped complaints sound not unlike the protest of agrarian society at the higher wages and extravagant consumption patterns of the industrial sector, at the dissolute habits of miners and the St Monday custom observed by many artificers.[219]

Iron production in Sussex stimulated a variety of related activities, not least charcoal burning. The Sidney works and others on great estates did their own coaling, though Ralph Hogge of Buxted purchased fuel from independent colliers and it formed one of the biggest items in his accounts. Carriage of wood, coal and iron also created work for carters and watermen. William Boys of Battle, worth £30 in goods, had inherited from his father a lucrative business employing several waggoners and assistants, plus a leading position in the town hierarchy.[220]

In many ways the most valuable product of the Weald at this time was timber, much of which was exported as sawn wood and fuel. At Robertsbridge coaling was merely one branch of a complex operation which produced cordwood for fuel, as well as inch-board, ship board

Table 2.18 Pastoral wealth of Babergh hundred, 1522

Assessments £	Persons	Group wealth £	%
100 and over	1	133	4.5
40–99	6	281	9.5
20–39	36	834	28.2
10–19	62	742	25.1
5–9	67	409	13.8
3–4	85	295	10.0
2	80	166	5.6
Under 2	92	97	3.3
Nil	102	nil	–
Total	531	2,957	100.0

and planking, which of course kept numerous sawyers busy. Almost certainly most of it went to Rye, the chief centre of shipbuilding, where, as well as at Playden, ropemakers were working some years later. The whole Robertsbridge undertaking was indeed a highly diversified one incorporating a large farm that sold corn and beer to the workmen, and hides to tanners and glovers. Parrock furnace was similarly linked with a 40-acre farm.[221] These enterprises present an alternative aspect of the supposed conflict of interest between ironmasters and the rest of the community that ordinarily commanded attention.[222] The reality was less dramatic: far from exhausting stocks, the demands of the ironworks lay well within the capacity of the Sussex woods, and the landowners themselves led the development of the industry as the only way to exploit their timber resources profitably.[223] Therein also lay perhaps the supposed profits of the gentry in the neighbourhood of Droitwich, which also devoured timber, 'for the makyng of salt is a great and notable destruction of wood': 6,000 loads annually, mostly young growth, was the local estimate.[224]

In North Worcestershire also industrial growth made little or no visible impact on the structure of wealth, possibly because a man's position in the rural hierarchy determined his choice of trade. In Yardley tile making had evolved as a major activity early in the fifteenth century; along with tanning, which may still have been the principal industry in nearby Birmingham, it was practised by farmer-craftsmen, who mostly had well under £20 in goods, the £3–£9 range forming a good two-thirds of the list: Thomas Walton, whose £11 was the highest assessment, made tiles and practised cooperage in winter. Metal, which became more prominent later in the sixteenth century, mainly attracted cottagers: Thomas Jeffereys, a wire drawer, had only 30s. in goods. Already there were signs of the wide range of West Midlands trades: a weaver was recorded in Yardley in 1556, and there were several millers and brewers.[225] Birmingham of course was largely engaged in metal working.[226] It does not, however, say much for the Worcestershire industries that, apart from salt, cloth making was the only one noticed by Leland, although it was unimportant except in Worcester and towns like Kidderminster, where there were swarms of poor artificers, and Bromsgrove. Droitwich was supposed to be a textile centre, but evidently not even the Act of 1534 had saved clothing from total eclipse by salt burning; the town's poverty being symptomatic of chronic unemployment which the hazards of the salt trade did little to alleviate. So widely dispersed was industrial activity that there can have been few parts of the country that did not support it in one form or another.[227]

Yet, significant as many of these developments were, the majority seem chiefly remarkable for the wealth they did not generate. Too thinly spread to have much impact on the structure of wealth, so many were subsidiary to farming that, far from being divided into industrial and agrarian regions, England consisted of various farming regions of which certain pastoral ones had attained some degree of industrial development, in some few cases to the extent of substantially modifying their fundamental characteristics. At the same time it was doubtless the case that by-employments, which were probably the rule rather than the exception, were decisive in bringing the level of wealth in districts unfavourable to husbandry more or less into line with that of the more eligible farming regions. Certainly there is no corroboration of the contemporary belief that mining engendered poverty. What does emerge beyond dispute is the primacy of large-scale cloth making as the great national industry and by far the most important export, leaving the rest more or less nowhere, as attested by the massive wealth of many clothiers and the prosperity – albeit a brittle one – of the workers in the major textile districts: high earnings in Suffolk and Gloucestershire at least resulting in a disposable surplus of income which not infrequently enabled artificers to accumulate sufficient goods for assessment, in contrast to agricultural labourers, who seldom had anything but their wages to be taxed on.

THE CLERGY

Although incomes had to be given, assessment of the personal property of 'spiritual men' was not stipulated, and since the clergy were customarily taxed more heavily than the laity a good many of them may have been less than forthcoming. In certain areas no figures were given for a good many parishes, even the values of some livings being omitted. Some certificates tend to lapse into impersonal references to 'the rectory' or 'the chaplain'. Absenteeism will account for some gaps, and temporary vacancies[228] for inability to state a clerk's name. Individually, of course, monks and nuns were bound by their vow of poverty, but although their communities often possessed great wealth the moveables of some monasteries and other corporations were also ignored. Friaries such as those at Aylesbury and Coventry could hardly have owned much anyway, but at the opposite end of the scale, the omission of rich abbeys like Cirencester and Tewkesbury leaves a serious gap. Nor are all assessments entirely reliable: Brooke Priory in Rutland owned goods valued at £52 and had no serious debts when it was dissolved in 1536, yet fourteen years earlier it had been assessed at a mere £13. 6s. 8d.[229] Coventry Cathedral Priory declared possessions worth £500, but its debts left it £52 in the red; similarly its net income was less than a quarter of the gross. The Charterhouse, also deep in debt, was passed over in silence.[230] As the income of the much smaller Missenden Abbey was given as £160, compared with £262 net in 1535, its goods may have been worth much more than the £140 assessed.[231] £140 was perhaps a fair valuation of the chattels of Hickling Priory, Norfolk, yet the tally of the secular clergy of its locality is incomplete, and, conversely, the very areas where ecclesiastical wealth was consistently recorded were ones which contained no important monasteries. Apart from Brooke, an obscure little house, all that survived of the medieval foundations of Rutland was the hospital, or almshouse, at Oakham, which only had goods worth 40s.: clearly its income of 20 marks only just sufficed to maintain the twelve poor inmates: Warden Gunby was no Septimus Harding.[232]

Although chantries were not established everywhere, the recording of the priests who served them looks erratic, many being ignored, although the expression 'singing at' in some Norfolk parishes probably denotes one whose days were occupied saying masses and other prayers for the repose of the souls of the founders. Here and there the line dividing them from the parish clergy may have become blurred, for some chantry certificates claimed, in 1545, that the cantarist was the only minister available, and generally give the impression that they regularly shared the parish duties. Yet although in 1545 the chaplain at Barrowden received 40s. a year for the cure of souls, founders usually inhibited the holding of other benefices, and pluralism was rare save in cathedrals. Pleas for the retention of cantarists are suspect as ploys aimed at keeping the endowments in the parish.[233] Such pluralism as did occur was excused on grounds of the poverty of one or both livings. Barrowden had easily the poorest chantry in Rutland, valued at less than 50s. a year, while, although the curacy was assessed for taxation at £5. 6s. 8d., the parish priest's stipend in 1522 was a beggarly 26s. 8d.[234]

Typical of the late Middle Ages were secular funds created for religious purposes. In most parishes the churchwardens held a stock in the church box; in some a guild or fraternity of lay people maintained a stock of its own. Commonly not exceeding a couple of pounds, the church stock reached an exceptional £7. 6s. at Waddesdon, Bucks., though as often as not it was nil, or else no figure was given, some certificates consistently omitting it.[235] At least one was lumped in with the guild stock. The guild at Ketton had £10 and the Uppingham one ample funds, while both church boxes were empty.[236] It was easy to confuse the two. Guilds were formed to supplement the slender resources of benefices by financing additional services and so forth; any friendly-society function was likely to be subsidiary, only a minority providing financial assistance for needy members. In the normal way a fraternity held an annual social function, after its festival mass, to collect the stock which was forthwith paid over to the churchwardens, less any sum retained for guild purposes. Some stocks, however, were permanent and might be invested in animals (for example) which were hired out to produce an income.[237] Distribution of guilds was uneven, many rural

Table 2.19 Comparative wealth of the clergy

District	Laity £	Secular clergy £	Regular clergy £	Churches and guilds £	Total £
Bucks.: Newport	4,557	374	69	36	5,036
Cottesloe	5,148	209	274	64	5,695
Aylesbury	5,715	126	140	107	6,088
Chiltern	12,883	406	122	38	13,449
Cornwall	28,969	1,444	443	–	30,856
Norfolk	30,925	2,391	380	225	33,921
Rutland	9,223	348	15	54	9,640
Worcestershire	10,518	369	94	563	11,544
Coventry city	12,520	363	–	321	13,204
		Percentages			
Bucks.: Newport	90.5	7.4	1.4	0.7	100
Cottesloe	90.4	3.7	4.8	1.1	100
Aylesbury	93.8	2.1	2.3	1.8	100
Chiltern	95.6	3.0	0.9	0.3	100
Cornwall	93.9	4.7	1.4	–	100
Norfolk	91.2	7.1	1.1	0.7	100.1
Rutland	95.6	3.6	0.2	0.6	100
Worcestershire	91.1	3.2	0.8	4.9	100
Coventry	94.8	2.8	6.0	2.4	100

parishes having none at all, while a town might contain several. They were thickest on the ground in Norfolk and the clothing places of Suffolk.[238] Population, however, was not the determinant. Coventry possessed two big ones with assets totalling £321, while the little village of Burnham Sutton, Norfolk, had no fewer than four, though they could scrape together only £11.[239] The few mentioned in Buckinghamshire included the rich guild of Our Lady at Aylesbury with a stock of £50 and £17 a year from real estate. None at all were recorded in Worcestershire or Cornwall, although there had been forty or more in Bodmin alone which had been the most generous contributors to the rebuilding of the parish church. Almost everyone there was a member of a guild, and since the population can hardly have exceeded 1,000 some people must have belonged to several.[240]

These uncertainties need not inhibit a broad comparison of lay and clerical wealth (see Table 2.19).[241]

Generally reliable, the Rutland figures make a useful yardstick.

Table 2.20 Goods of secular priests

		Number	Minimum £	Maximum £	Median £
Rectors	Buckinghamshire	51	0	200	$6\frac{2}{3}$
	Cornwall	20	0	60	$8\frac{1}{3}$
	Norfolk	63	$1\frac{1}{3}$	200	$13\frac{1}{3}$
	Rutland	17	2	40	10
	Worcestershire	13	0	$26\frac{2}{3}$	6
Vicars	Buckinghamshire	45	0	30	5
	Cornwall	25	2	120	20
	Norfolk	45	$1\frac{1}{3}$	$33\frac{1}{3}$	5
	Rutland	10	2	$16\frac{1}{3}$	5
	Worcestershire	6	7	$26\frac{2}{3}$	$21\frac{1}{2}$
Chaplains	Buckinghamshire	101	0	20	2
	Cornwall	103	0	$13\frac{1}{3}$	34
	Norfolk	101	0	40	3
	Rutland	21	1	$13\frac{1}{3}$	2
	Worcestershire	16	$1\frac{1}{3}$	40	$3\frac{1}{2}$
	Coventry	40	0	18	$2\frac{1}{2}$

Besides being not untypical, 3½ per cent was a fair enough share of the community's wealth for the fifty-two secular priests, who formed almost exactly the same proportion of the 1484 adult male inhabitants. As a similar percentage of the population, Norfolk priests were very much more affluent.[242] In contrast, however, the omission of information for the Westwood nunnery leaves the Worcestershire aggregate defective, while data relating to secular clergy in the Aylesbury hundreds of Buckinghamshire are probably inadequate.

In regard to the wealth of individual secular priests we are on firmer ground. Most fell neatly into one of two primary categories, beneficed and unbeneficed: rectors and vicars on the one hand, and parish priests, chaplains or curates on the other (see Table 2.20). Materially the average incumbent approximated to the middling sort of tenant farmer; the unbeneficed, who lived on stipends, to smallholders, or even labourers.[243] In practice the range covered by the former was much narrower than the bare figures suggest, few of them having less than £2 or more than £25–£30. Being mostly confined to Buckinghamshire, the handful of parsons reported as having no personal property serve as much as anything to highlight doubts about the approach to clerical assessments there. In this certificate 'nil' normally indicates an indigent inhabitant, though not consistently. Wherever there was no chaplain the incumbent could very well have been truly poor, unable to afford the stipend. Alternatively, such an entry might mean a temporary absence, on Church business if not a foray in quest of preferment.[244] But it is difficult to make anything of the sort of entry which assesses the rector at nil and omits the chaplain's name, implying that he was not in his post.[245] At the top of the scale only seven Buckinghamshire parsons were worth £40 or more, compared with a good fifth of the total in Norfolk, where no fewer than four reached three figures. The top Buckinghamshire man, the prebendary of Buckingham, was an isolated figure, £71 being the second biggest assessment.[246] Predictably, vicars tended to conform to more modest standards; indeed, in Norfolk as many as twelve were rated at a mere £2. In Cornwall the situation was reversed, with half having at least £20 and only five less than £10; similarly only two of the small Worcestershire sample had less than £10. In principle parsons had the advantage, but in practice rectories with cure of souls tended to be the poorer ones, for many of the best were impropriate to their monastic patrons, which in almost every case had ordained a vicarage and endowed it adequately – rarely with less than £5 a year, more commonly £6 – while rectory incomes tended to vary widely. Nonetheless, income differences were not commensurate with some of these exceptional examples of personal wealth, and regional influences cannot be ignored. In Cornwall and Worcestershire even the unbeneficed clergy were better off than the average, the overall position being that of an affluent clerical establishment alongside a relatively poor laity. In addition, Cornwall was the only one that was without question adequately staffed, every parish having at least one priest, frequently several. Whatever factors might have operated behind the scenes, the existence of an inverse proportion between economic development and ecclesiastical wealth cannot be discounted. It appears implicit in the contrasts observable in a small county like Buckinghamshire. In the Newport hundreds, where the level of lay assessments was low and left substantially unchanged by the subsidy, the proportion of wealth owned by the Church was much higher than in the more advanced Chilterns, not only in 1522 but also after the initial assessments had been scaled down for the subsidy. The exception to this rule was Norfolk, but here clerical wealth must have reflected the yield of tithes in the leading cereal-producing region, momentarily augmented perhaps by the high grain prices of recent years.[247]

By no means all priests were dependent on income from the Church. Throughout the survey clerks occur as (generally) small landowners, and some were taxed in this capacity in the lay subsidy. Antony Carswalle, vicar of Whitchurch, who died in 1521, owned land in Garsington, Oxon. Much above the average in wealth for a Buckinghamshire incumbent, his estate totalling nearly £19 included £7. 1s. 4d. in ready money, a substantial amount for the times by any reckoning. Doubtless it included rent from Garsington as well as from the Whitchurch glebe, which must have been let to farm seeing that his own agricultural interests were limited to a couple of dozen sheep and some poultry. His lifestyle, in a word, was gentlemanly; his effects included a saddle and bridle, a riding hood of chamlet and another of sarcinet, although he no longer owned a mount. His wardrobe was also unusually large and varied. Although in no sense 'a povre Persoun of a Toun' this did not prevent him being 'also a lerned man, a clerk'. And not only was he a graduate, he had retained the habits of scholarship. His books – not itemised – totalled £2 in value, there was a lectern to stand them on, a desk, and 'a horn with ynk' priced at a penny. The income of the vicarage was an average £8 a year, and Carswalle's successor, who presumably did not enjoy private means, got the more or less average assessment of £6. 13s. 4d.[248]

Most parish priests or chaplains were hardly distinguishable from smallholders, or even labourers; the standard stipend of £5–£6 a year was equivalent to the agricultural wage of 4*d.* a day and there was no job security. The possessions of William Willesley of Leckhamstead, who died in 1521, amounted to 57*s.* 9*d.*, of which a third represented the value of three mares, while the rest consisted of clothes and bedding. The administration of his estate took 22*s.* 8*d.* of this, half of it going on fees, plus 2*s.* to the pardoner for letters of pardon and 5*d.* to the summoner.[249] Except in Cornwall, the fortunate few who enjoyed a measure of affluence were chiefly to be found in towns where lucrative guild appointments were available. In Buckinghamshire four of the five wealthiest lived in Aylesbury, Amersham and Buckingham, and elsewhere they were to be found at places like Bromsgrove and Kidderminster, Worcs., and Blakeney, Little Walsingham and Great Yarmouth, Norfolk.[250] But these were exceptional. Four-fifths of the chaplains in Buckinghamshire and Rutland owned personal estates of 5 marks or less, while if one out of three in Cornwall had £5 or more, a good 10 per cent were assessed at nil, and indeed at Gwinear and Towednack were described as 'pauper'.[251]. Almost certainly alternative sources of income played an important part. William Willesley very possibly had one, for although his personal circumstances were slightly better than average his stipend was a wretched one, £3. 13*s.* 4*d.* a year. One of the priests of Holy Trinity, Coventry, owned goods valued at no less than £100, nearly three times as much as his eleven colleagues put together; he was also vicar of Priors Hardwick. Again, in St Michael's there was a chantry priest worth £40 and two more with £20 each; their incomes were normal – round about £6 a year – but they (and others) must have had opportunities to officiate on behalf of the wealthy fraternities in the city, of which the Trinity Guild had £209 a year. Apart from infrequent exceptions such as these, chantry priests were indistinguishable from parish chaplains. Half the nine cantarists in Coventry had £2 or less in goods, which, although numbers generally are hardly sufficient to average, was typical of their condition.[252] Very occasionally a priest is mentioned who appears not to have any official connexion with the parish. Such a man was Sir John Sargent of Datchet, Bucks., who had no less than £50 a year and 100 marks in moveables;[253] quite possibly he was a fellow of Eton College or a canon of St George's Chapel, Windsor, both of which lay within walking distance.

If only because of the nature of the record, the wealth of the clergy is not readily assimilable to that of the laity. Religious of course were withdrawn from the world. Although secular clerks, especially at parish level, were fully integrated with the community, the structure of their personal property differed from that of the laity. The richest ones, the bishops, were remote from local communities, and, as lords spiritual, were as much 'them' (as opposed to 'us') to ordinary parish priests as to their congregations. At the opposite extreme of the scale, although the lists teem with wretchedly paid chaplains, assessments of less than 40s. were relatively few and far between, most lying in the middle ranges, between £3 and £20. A pair of spectacles and 40s. worth of books set the late (graduate) vicar of Whitchurch somewhat apart from his parishioners, who probably did not appreciate his erudition, yet his private collection was certain to be innocent of both profound and frivolous titles, limited to practical works such as collections of sermons, primers of divinity and apologetics, plus, naturally, his Breviary, perhaps too a copy of the Vulgate, or Latin scriptures.[254] Lords temporal were not mustered as members of the county community: it would never have done for 'my lord' to be paraded on the village green by some Dogberry and Verges, even a Justice Shallow, made to line up with Mouldy, Shadow, Wart and the rest, to be handed over to a red-nosed, pot-bellied mercenary captain, to be abused and maybe put on a charge by his blustering subordinates, and finally

> Be shot for sixpence in a battlefield
> And shovell'd up into a bloody trench[255]

If the greatest and richest in the land were exempted from the indignity of assessment, so many of the poorest were simply overlooked that every list ended up short of about one-third of the men it should have included, and since almost all of these were worth less than £2 the general level of wealth is made to look higher than it really was.

CHAPTER THREE

LANDOWNING

ALTHOUGH the outlines of the structure of landed wealth are clearly delineated, the piecemeal execution of the survey creates a number of problems. The unit of registration was the township, and the instructions called for certification of the owner of each piece of land there, not for a statement of the property of each inhabitant. Complication is introduced by the fact that while most constables followed their orders to the letter, others tried by means of a global sum to represent the value of anything an inhabitant might own in another place. This, added to the inevitable errors and omissions, results in a picture in which some of the details are blurred, even at times distorted. Further, the neat division of society into a minority of freeholders sharply contrasted with the mass of tenant farmers and landless men stops far short of the whole truth in its failure to acknowledge the interest of copyholders whose security of tenure made them freeholders in all but name, or to distinguish leaseholders with long terms from mere tenants at will. The assessment in some places of the incomes head tenants received from subletting, while a valuable addition in itself, serves also to confuse the issue, as also do sporadic attempts to assign a value to the unexpired term of a lease.

THE VILLAGE LANDOWNERS

In order to form an estimate of both the range and the limitations of the record of landholding we cannot do better than commence by examining the section devoted to a single parish, Empingham in Rutland.

95

EMPINGHAM LANDOWNERS

Name	Land £	s	d	Goods £	s	d
George Mackworth, esq. chief lord	40	0	0	36	0	0
Wm Overton, steward fee		3	4			
Chris Massingberd, clerk, parson	24	0	0			
Ric Fowler, priest, vicar	5	6	8			
Prior of St John of Jerusalem	2	0	8			
The Lord Souch		7	0			
Wm Dall, gent.	1	5	0			
John Eldred, yeoman	2	0	0			
John Parker, yeoman		6	8			
Elizabeth Edmonds, widow	3	0	0	50	0	0
John Collyn, husbandman, tenant to Mackworth	—			21	0	0
Wm Barnys „ „ „	—			23	0	0
John Laxon „ „ „	—			21	0	0
Ric Collyn „ „ Dale	12	0		10	0	0
John Spenethorn, husbandman & hath land their	10	0		10	0	0
Thos Exton, husbandman, tenant to Mackworth				8	0	0
Wm Sisson „ „ „				7	0	0
Raff Caterans, servant & „ „				3	0	0
John Faux „ „ „				1	10	0
Nich Fowler, husbandman, tenant to the parson				13	0	0
Rob Williamson, tailor, „ Mackworth				8	0	0
Ric Brown, husbandman „ „				4	0	0
John Leyff „ „ „				4	0	0
Gye Spenethorn „ „ „				5	0	0
Robert Careby „ „ „				2	0	0
Thos Langton „ „ „				8	0	0
Thos A Brown, miller „ „				3	0	0
Thos Turnor, husbandman „ „				6	0	0
Wm Gooll, laborer* „ „					nil	
Thos Prodfote, husbandman „ „				2	0	0
Rob Wright „ „ „				13	6	8
Thos Wright „ „ „				2	0	0
Ric Turnor „ „ „				2	0	0
Rob Whithed „ „ „				3	0	0
Wm Paper „ „ the vicar				12	0	0
Margaret Wetherby, widow „ Mackworth				3	0	0
Wm Fox, husbandman „ „				3	0	0
Ric Robynson, husbandman „ „				4	0	0
John Hyll, laborer „ „				1	0	0
John Wezelhed, laborer „ „				1	0	0
Ric Wetherley, husbandman „ „				2	0	0

Thos Collyn	,,	,,	,,	4	0	0
Rob Burney, laborer		,,	,,	1	0	0
John Brown	,,	,,	Prior of St John	1	0	0
Thos Symys	,,	,,	Mackworth	2	0	0
Ric Puts	,,	,,	Prior of St John	1	0	0
John Brown, husbandman		,,	Mackworth	2	0	0
John Careby, servant to Elizabeth Edmonds				11	0	0
Chris Banys, laborer,* tenant to Mackworth					nil	
3 labourers, tenants to Mackworth, John son of Eliz Edmonds, & Wm Toller, servant to the vicar, all*					nil	

* 'Pore men, & yong' (except Banys).

The first feature to note is that only a small minority of the listed inhabitants – five persons out of forty-seven – owned any land at all. As one of these was the lord of the manor and another the vicar, only one in fifteen of the 'ordinary' folk was returned as a freeholder: two husbandmen and a woman who looks like the widow of a yeoman or maybe a minor gentleman. In Rutland this was a normal proportion; elsewhere freeholders might form a clear majority, and in many a Norfolk village embrace virtually everyone above the condition of labourer. Only in the case of two men at Fleet Marston, Bucks., is any hint given of what else they owned, and its utility is minimal. Mr Colte, who 'hathe landes ther and in Quainton, Doddersell, Hartewell and Stonne', is not mentioned under any of these headings. Sir Robert Lee, who was also stated to have property in the selfsame places was a prominent local figure. He owned Little Marston and farmed the rest of Fleet Marston, a moiety of which belonged to Colte.[1]

It is a reasonable inference that a 7s. parcel formed but an insignificant fraction of the estates of a nobleman like Lord Zouche, whose goods alone totalled 500 marks. Inclusive of the manor of Clipsham his Rutland property alone exceeded £12 in value, and from Buckinghamshire he drew a further £43.[2] As a gentleman, the absentee William Dall (or Dale) could also be expected to have other property, and was in fact lord of the neighbouring manor of Tickencote, where he resided. Squire Mackworth was similarly likely to possess more than this one estate, and sure enough land worth £5 a year is found in Normanton. A subsidy assessment of £40 suggests that this completes the account of his lands; any there might have been in other counties cannot be deduced from the available evidence.[3] Inquisitions *post mortem* can sometimes fill such a gap, but because a separate one had to be taken in every county involved we can never be certain that the record has survived in its entirety. Only a feodary survey, made in the event of a minority, gives a complete account of a man's lands. None of the remaining small proprietors of Empingham had other holdings in Rutland, and on the whole it seems unlikely that their interests extended beyond its boundary. The vicar also held the chaplaincy of the deserted hamlet of Horn in plurality, but it yielded only a trifling 13*s.* 4*d.*, and he seems to have had no other benefice.[4]

If Empingham people were representative the outlines of a typology can be detected. A single township would contain no more than a fraction of the estates of a nobleman or other great landowner. The lands of the middling sort of squire were usually confined to a handful of parishes, often in the form of a main property, on which he probably resided, with smaller outlying holdings. Even an estate worth upwards of £100 a year might well consist of no more than a couple of manors plus an assortment of lesser parcels, all located in a single county.[5] Persons of inferior degree rarely owned more than a single parcel, irrespective of whether they lived on it themselves or let it to a tenant.

So far as resident proprietors went this rough yardstick makes a useful indicator as to the probability of their owning land in other places. For non-residents, other than the nobly born and well connected, it is less informative. Most are difficult to trace; their names are apt to be commonplace and we do not know where to commence looking for them. The return for North Marston in Buckinghamshire is unique in giving the 'addresses' of nearly half the absentee landowners; a few more are supplied in half a dozen other villages there, but in general examples are rare and isolated.[6] A piece of land at Yardley (Worcs.) was owned by a certain John Arden of Castle Bromwich; absentee proprietors at Windrush included citizens of Bristol and Gloucester. There is a scattering in Berkshire, especially in Wantage hundred; most resided within the county, in the towns of Abingdon and Newbury in particular, though a few lived as far away as, for instance, Salisbury. Two somewhat indefinite entries under Letcombe Basset specify only Hampshire. The broad conclusion must be that the majority of owners of small parcels lived within a radius of a very few miles.[7] Coming back to Empingham, yeomen called John Parker resided in Belton and Clipsham, both in Rutland, though there is no clue as to which, if either, was the man listed under Empingham; if he was the Belton man he could also have been the owner of a piece of land there – the MS is faded at this point.[8]

William Dall illustrates a further complication – inconsistent spelling. Here the style 'gentleman' identifies him as Dale of Tickencote: the name of Richard Collyn's landlord is spelt the same way. In the absence of these rare pointers guesswork may be the only recourse. The christian name of 'Shallowe of Hollendon', owner of a small property in Singleborough, Bucks., is illegible, and since this is the sole reference to him one is almost tempted to dismiss him as a fictional character! When, as not infrequently, an owner proves untraceable, yet another obstacle has to be negotiated – a wrong name. Now so far as we are in a position to judge, the information was reliable. When the owner was resident there was no problem; if he was not, the occupier would be able to tell the constable how much rent he paid and to whom. Inevitably, however, cases would occur when the information was out of date, if the owner had recently died or disposed of the property or, if a woman, had changed her name by marrying. Nor was it just the humble and obscure whose exits went unnoticed. At Caldecott, Liddington and Stoke Dry no less a personage than the bishop of Lincoln, lord of all three towns, was erroneously named as William Atwater, who had died and been succeeded by John Longland the previous year.[9] If a flagrant oversight like this could occur it says little for the prospects of men of lowly status being correctly recorded.

Land might also be vested in a feoffee to uses (i.e. trustee) or managed by an attorney. A parcel worth £2. 6s. 8d. at Stony Stratford was held by the executors of the late Sir Edward Belknap. In Grendon Underwood we read: 'The rente of Grendon to ye executors of Thos. Pigott to fulfill his will.' Whether these should be equated with his 'heirs', who held land worth £4. 6s. 8d. in Elesborough, his widow, who lived at Whaddon and was a prominent landowner, or someone quite different, is not clear. The formula 'the heir of' (e.g. John Cordwan of Shepley Yeld in Bromsgrove) is not uncommon. More often it takes the plural form, indicating partition of the property between co-heiresses, like Agnes Chaplayne and Beatrix Salesbury at Gayhurst, Bucks. Three Stourbridge men shared a rent of £2, while in Chadswith Yeld, Bromsgrove, Edmund Harwell divided 2 marks yearly with 'his co-parcenor'.[10] Generally, though, the heirs are not identified; in any case such entries are sporadic except in Cornwall, where the Celtic custom of partible inheritance caused them to be widespread, and incidentally obliterates the trail of the persons concerned in a great many cases.

With trifling exceptions the record is restricted to monetary values. When for once it is stated that Sir Raynold, the chaplain of Ridlington, Norfolk, owned a house and three acres, the reason must have been some difficulty over determining the value, which in this case is omitted. One Cawston man was credited with £1 per annum in respect of a mill, another with the same amount for 'a house and land'. Some properties can be identified with little difficulty: Dale's holding in Empingham was the manor of Hardwick, once a flourishing hamlet, which by 1522 had evidently shrunk to the single farm it has long been; there was just one tenant. Similarly, 'Vernand's Lands' are named at Adstock, Bucks.[11] In the Midlands and south of England values average out at roughly £20–£30 per thousand acres, but although this represents an average of about 6d. an acre – which was near enough the going rate for rent[12] – it cannot be employed as a general conversion factor, for while it may be applicable to a county or other major division, the ratios for individual parishes and hamlets are subject to extreme variations. Feasible explanations of this phenomenon can be grouped loosely in two main classes. On the one hand, assuming the assessments to have been broadly accurate, the level of exploitation might have varied widely: it was, for instance, regarded as axiomatic that enclosed ground was worth substantially more than common,[13] while manorial custom and estate policy could exercise a profound effect on rents. On the other hand there are problems inherent in the composition of the certificates. Lacunae, which must always be reckoned with, are both overt and latent. In certain cases the value is left out, perhaps pending further enquiry. A high proportion of these relate to lordships, the Crown's especially, doubtless in the belief that these particular details would not be required. Many deficiencies can be made good from alternative sources: time and again the *Valor Ecclesiasticus*, compiled barely a decade later, gives virtually the same values as the survey for Church properties. But even the most painstaking officials could overlook some estates. The probability is that casual omissions tended to be unimportant, but occasionally evidence of a more serious oversight can be detected. The feodary survey of the lands of the infant daughter of Thomas Ramsay in 1527 shows that the family had substantial holdings in Buckinghamshire including the manors of Hitcham, worth £20. 3s. 7d. a year, and Losemere in Little Marlow, which was valued, along with other parcels there, at £20. 12s. 6d. Of all this only 40s. was recorded, at Marlow, in 1522, in the name of Thomas, who was then a ward himself. His status may go some way towards clearing up the misunderstanding which must have arisen, for in Gloucestershire manors belonging to another royal ward were also left unassessed. Hitcham, furthermore, which contained only seven taxpayers, was so insignificant a place it was surveyed jointly with Dorney, and we can readily imagine the constable becoming confused and forgetting to insert the name of the juvenile lord of the smaller township; anyone subsequently checking the certificate could be forgiven for failing to realise that the first line referred to the lord of Dorney only.[14] Fortunately errors of this magnitude are rare.

Equally troublesome, if not more so, is the domiciliary assessment which turns out to express total income from all sources. As the manor of Whitwell was valued by a feodary survey at £3. 13s. 9d., it is virtually certain that the £80 assessment of Richard Flower, the resident owner, must be interpreted as meaning his whole income scaled down by 20 per cent. Further examples can be deduced in Rutland, notably the £46 credited to David Cecil at Tinwell, a small parish from which the abbot of Peterborough received £21 as lord; Cecil was his bailiff and lived in the manor house.[15] All big assessments that are not accompanied by an explanatory gloss have to be approached warily. The tiny hamlet of Dixton, near Winchcombe, contained not only William Hygford, who was worth £66. 13s. 4d. a year, but also a second man with £50. Fortunately (for us) the commissioners of depopulation in 1517 discovered that Hygford's father had enclosed 190 acres of arable land a few years earlier; estimated to be worth £6 a year, this was probably all, or most, of what he owned there.[16] Smaller assessments could also be global ones. The most explicit was that of John Goodwin of Over Winchendon, 'landes in this shere vij*li* viij*s* and in all other shires of England xij*li*'. Even assessments as tiny as the £4 of Robert Fonten of Burcott in Wing and the 20s. of William Taylor of Soulbury were both annotated 'in all England'.[17] What finally got recorded may have depended on how much the individual chose to reveal to the constable, though in Coventry – thanks no doubt to the existence of a highly organised local administration – the citizens' circumstances were thoroughly investigated. The prior of the cathedral produced his accounts and was duly assessed at £483. 7s. 6d. in 'clere yerlie Revenues and Possessions' after sundry deductions from a gross £1,004. 4s. 8d. 'as appereth by Rentalles and Bookes of Accompte'.[18] In every case, so far as can be judged, property located inside the city was carefully distinguished from what was owned elsewhere, and so here alone there is no ambiguity.

Many assessments do not represent ownership as such. Much of the income of rectories and vicarages consisted of tithes. Usually there was a glebe as well, but the proportion attributable to it was far from consistent. Overall it would appear to have accounted for less than a tenth of the income of spiritualities; in seven Norfolk parishes in 1658 the glebe varied from one-eighth to two-thirds of the living, though the average scarcely exceeded a quarter; acreages ranged from one to fifty-two with a median of twenty-four in these and three other parishes.[19]

Glebes could be anything from large farms to little or nothing. At Frocester, Gloucs., it was restricted to a single close of five acres; the priest of Saul chapel had 5¼ acres in the common fields of Fretherne, the mother parish. The rich vicarage of Churcham, valued at £20. 4s. 5½d., had no glebe at all, while not only was there none at Tirley, the vicar's income of £9. 6s. 8d. came wholly from the farm of the tithes. In Buckinghamshire nineteen parishes, or more than 9 per cent, had no glebe by the seventeenth century, several had also been depopulated, and in a further half-dozen the living was impropriate. Glebes here could be anything from twenty to 100 acres.[20]

The abbot of Halesowen received £1 a year from the tithes of Dudley, Worcs., and the vicar of Hailes 10s. The certificates provide numerous examples of these 'pensions to religious or spirituall men'. At Little Brickhill, Bucks., 'Robertus Crofton clericus habet pencionem extra dictam ecclesiam sursum et desuper predictam summam de vjli xiijs ivd', which formed the vicar's portion: the pensioner enjoyed the handsome share of £8.[21] Pensions originated in various ways. Some were imposed by monasteries on benefices of which they were the patrons, sometimes as a halfway stage to appropriation.[22] Evesham drew them from several Cotswold parishes; the abbot of Owston received 2 marks a year from Tickencote. There was an unusually complex situation at East Hendred, with three pensioners in addition to the parson all taking their cut: the abbot of Abingdon and the archdeacon of Berkshire each had 'a portion out of the rectory' of two marks and one, respectively, while a clerk named William Jones was entitled to 'a portion of tithes' to the value of 8s., leaving £16. 1s. 4d. for the incumbent. The fact that the prior of Shene was lord and two other monasteries as well as the bishop of Salisbury all had interests there may have exercised some influence. Pensions were also assigned to parish churches; Cirencester got 8s. from Througham rectory and Rodborough chapel 20s. from Upper Lyppiatt.[23]

Pensions were peculiar to clerks: £4 a year paid out of the parsonage of Wendover to layman Richard Byrch was described as an annuity. As the majority seem to have been charges on benefices, the two enjoyed by the rector of Marsh Gibbon were additional to his living and presumably from a different source. Annuities generally issued from lay land, and a technical distinction was evidently maintained at Water Stratford, Bucks., where the abbot had a pension of 6s. 8d. as well as an annuity of 4s.[24] At the same time allowance must be made for local preferences in the matter of terminology: annuities were not specified in Gloucestershire, nor were pensions in Worcestershire where, for example can be found payments of £5 from Kidderminster to John

Rooke, serjeant at law of Bristol, £4 from Droitwich to another layman, and £1. 6s. 8d. from Cradley to the vicar of Halesowen. Occasionally precise definition was evaded, as in the case of the 22s. which Lord Bergavenny received 'out of the chantry' at Kidderminster, or the pound which formed the 'portion' of Mr Gregson (presumably a clerk) at Inkberrow. Kidderminster also yields an isolated reference to an obit of 4s. per annum.[25]

Thomas Blunt, the bailiff of Chaddesley Corbett's annuity of 20 marks looks very much like a salary, similar to Thomas Solley of Hindlip's 'fee of one mark for the bailiwick of Abbotsey'.[26] All sorts of people got fees for services of many types, not all of which found their way into the survey. Not only was John Barnesley's remuneration as bailiff of Hartlebury omitted, he was credited with no landed income at all.[27] The most frequently stated office was the stewardship of a manor, as specified in the instructions; it too was frequently omitted. The fees covered a wide range. William Overton held the courts of Empingham for as little as 40d., compared with 40s. for the same duty at Burley. Ten shillings or less was the usual rate in Rutland, and the amount was seldom large anywhere. However, the bishop of Worcester normally paid £10, while at Feckenham the fee was given as no less than £14. 16s. 10½d., but this perhaps included services in connexion with the forest administration.[28]

As charges against the profits of manors these payments were naturally classed as income from land. Similarly the stipend of a parish priest or chaplain formed a charge on the living paid by an incumbent, who was, more often than not, an absentee. Fees in general were listed under land, in some cases perhaps for no better reason than that they were annual income. However, although there is no indication of the source of 10 marks payable to Roger Blomfeld of Buxton, Norfolk (where he also owned land worth 13s. 4d.), the £1. 9s. 8d. assigned to Thomas Parker, a servant of the king at Elmley Lovett, Worcs., could well have been a payment from the manor, which was a royal estate, and Parker himself did not live there.[29]

Finally there was a complex miscellany comprising the endowments of chantries, guilds, lights, obits and so forth, the recording of which was far from perfect. The Empingham return fails to mention the annual rent charged on a tenement of Mackworth's for the finding of a torch at the second mass of Christmas Day, together with 5s. in ready money, which by 1545, and with the consent of all interested parties, had been converted to a rent of 2s. The income of the chantry at Clipsham was assessed at £7, which further enquiry reveals to have included a pension of 7s. issuing from certain lands in Lincolnshire. Chantries and their possession in Worcestershire are also recorded fitfully.[30]

Even those entries – unquestionably the majority – which represent profits accruing from physical possession of land cannot be assumed to hold a uniform significance. If the freeholder was an absentee the natural inference is that the property was tenanted and that the value shown represents the net rent, as indeed is made clear in several entries at Langley Marish, and implied by the uniform addition of the phrase 'per annum' throughout the three hundreds of Newport. Rent is also specified in the case of John Swyft at Hene, Worcs., as well as the three co-owners of a property at Stourbridge; even more circumstantially the prior of Worcester was assigned £5. 13s. 4d. a year 'for rente of ye farm of ye manor' of Bredicote. Conversely, the Coventry volume enters the rent *paid by* nearly every householder.[31] Two entries at Aylesbury, nevertheless, warn against rigid categorisation, viz. Sir Thomas Boleyn as 'lord ther in land by ye yere x*li*', and 'My Ladye of Salisburye in Rente, xl *li*'. This latter was in fact the fee farm of the borough, which had come to be permanently assigned to the earls of Salisbury, whose titles and possessions had been conferred on Margaret Pole, daughter of the duke of Clarence.[32] If an owner dwelt in the township where his land was situated the logical inference is that he occupied it himself, although there was nothing to prevent him letting off part or all of it: the Langley Marish man Richard Collis features as 'tenaunt to ye Queene, in landes the yerely rente, vs'. A resident's assessment could also take the form of an attempt to quantify the pecuniary benefit of owner-occupation. This was the practice in Coventry, where Henry Pysford, for example, was described as 'dwellyng apon hys owne Frehold to the yerly value of iiij*li*'. Nowhere else, however, are the meanings of residents' assessments explained. In Rutland the tenant to a small proprietor is mentioned here and there, while larger landowners would in any case have been landlords. The incomes of the resident incumbents of Dorney and Taplow were expressed as rents, possibly to draw attention to something out of the ordinary: leases granted by previous absentee parsons had not yet expired. Rectories were often leased by absentee incumbents; several were so leased in Rutland, mostly by gentlemen like John Digby, who farmed Preston.[33]

In spite of a host of imponderables it is possible to speculate on the composition of some of the smaller properties. A few shillings might represent a messuage or cottage with, perhaps, a little land attached; alternatively it could be a small close or a croft. At an average of 6d. per acre the fairly common assessment of 20s. might well indicate a more or less standard yardland of some 30–40 (customary) acres, depending on what buildings were included, if any. In mid-Buckinghamshire the average of 6*d.* or 7*d.* looks to have been inclusive of house and outbuildings for, according to an Aylesbury rental dated 1532,[34] land without buildings commanded not more than 4*d.*, examples being 3 acres for 1*s.*, three roods for 3*d.*, and 55 acres for £1. 2*s.* 10*d.* Cottages – even one described as decayed – rented for 3*s.* 4*d.*, houses and tenements for 6*s.* 8*d.* and 11*s.* 8*d.* As prime business premises the Bull inn 'with a lyttyll pyttyll' was let for 13*s.* 4*d.*, and the garden attached to it for 1*s.* 2*d.* Land presented as having been imparked at Thornbury affords an interesting comparison: with buildings it was valued at 6*d.* per acre, without at 4*d.* At the same time it is not altogether clear how much weight to attach to figures quoted in the charged atmosphere of a hearing by the Royal Commission in 1517. Elsewhere in Gloucestershire they varied between 5*d.* and 1*s.* or more per acre. In the Vale of Evesham, around Broad Marston and Weston-on-Avon, high values come as no surprise, but the variations indicated at Meon in Quinton seem instructive. Seven farms had been enclosed in 1512 in a move that must effectively have crippled this tiny hamlet. Four of these, all of 30–40 acres, had been allowed to go out of cultivation and the houses left desolate; owned by four different people, they were valued at from 8*d.* to 1*s.* per acre. The remaining three farms, all owned by Sir Edward Greville, the local lord, amounted to 70 acres worth £7 a year, or 2*s.* per acre. The difference was that although the three ploughs were alleged to have been laid up, 'the houses are up to now standing and occupied'; precisely what Greville had done is obscure, but whatever it was it had undoubtedly achieved a dramatic increase in productivity without uprooting the tenants.[35]

Very seldom can an actual assessment be translated into spatial terms. William Baten of Long Crendon had an assessment of 3*s.*, and bequeathed his wife 5¼ acres of arable ground. A Cold Brayfield husbandman, William Bateman, who was assessed at 10*s.*, left his wife 'half my crop of 5 acres of corn this year [1526] growing on the ground'. This does not tell us a great deal. Assuming a three-course rotation, it implies 7–8 acres arable plus meadow and grazing (or common rights), making a farm of perhaps a dozen acres – bigger if 'corn' meant only the cereal crop. As, however, he directed his son-in-law to apply 2*s.* of the yearly rent to the keeping of an obit for six years, it sounds as though his tenement was larger and that part at least of the assessment represented income from letting. With John Ingram we are on firmer ground. His father had left him 20 acres called 'Margarettes Stacyes land' in North

Marston which, with common rights added, must have been equivalent to something like 30. Assessed at 26s. 6d., it must have been tenanted, since John did not reside there. His younger brother Thomas, who had stayed in Marston, was assessed on goods only in spite of having inherited 3 acres called 'Dauers'. As a small owner-occupied parcel it could have been missed; alternatively he might have preferred to sell it, possibly to John, whose own assessment could therefore have embraced this as well. We can only speculate.[36]

A manor, it now seems unnecessary to reiterate, might be worth much or little, depending on a combination of factors: the size of the demensne and the efficiency of its management, whether the customary fines were certain or arbitrary, and if the latter, the vigour with which they were exploited. Empingham netted its owner £40 a year, and up and down the kingdom could be found a good many manors worth at least as much. In contrast, while few were quite as poor as Whitwell at a mere 22s. – not to mention the virtually notional 4s. produced by Buscot in Berkshire – a considerable number yielded no more than about £5 a year. Certainly by the end of the sixteenth century some had been broken up; in wooded districts they might not only be small, but also bear scant resemblance to the 'classic' manor of arable farming areas. Rolfehedges in the Sussex Weald 'hath no demesnes but consisteth onely of a fewe copiholdes' – in fact four, containing 91 acres and paying a total of 15s. 8d. annually; tenure was hereditary and fines limited.[37] While some landowners such as the Staffords, Herberts and Seymours might have been conspicuously successful in exploiting their estates,[38] others, including the king and many monasteries, were far less so.[39] Where the demesnes had been alienated and the customary dues (if any) were negligible, the lordship might be no more than nominal, as at Great Linford, Bucks., where the profits totalled only 15s. divided between the king and the earl of Shrewsbury, with 1s. payable to the honour of Berkhamsted. In contrast the absentee landowners alone were worth £33, of which two-thirds belonged to a single leading proprietor, Lady St Leger; the inhabitants totalled nearly £8 more. To complicate matters, figures quoted on different occasions often disagreed. A valor of Crown lands put the rents of Great Woolstone at £6. 13s. 4d., or ten times what the survey states; at North Crawley rents were £11. 12s. 9d. compared with 2s. Another valor gives £22. 10s. 9d. net for Buckland, compared with £42, and Olney as £72. 14s. 2½d. (£53. 0s. 6½d.) as against £67 in 1522.[40] Revenues were diverse and variable. While demesne rents and, in some cases, customary fines were related to acreage and profit, copyhold rents had long ceased to reflect market conditions, and freehold ones were notional. Tending to follow market values, heriots might form realistic death duties, but other seigneurial perquisites, such as profits of the court, rarely added much to the total income.

COPYHOLDERS AND FARMERS

The exclusion from the survey of land held by customary tenures not only restricts attention to a minority, but seriously distorts the profile of effective ownership, for not infrequently the lord of the manor's control was more apparent than real:

> in all my life I looke not that the thirde parte of my lands shall come to by dispocition, that I maye enhaunce the rent of the same; but it shalbe in mens holdings, either by lease or by copie, graunted before my time, and still contynuinge, and yet like to continewe in the same estate, for the most parte duringe my life, and perchaunce my sons

And he was fain to acknowledge the tenant's insistence that the bargain was sacrosanct:'I cannot much saie against that; but yet I perceaue I shalbe a losser still by this bargaine, thowghe I cannot tell the reason why'[41] More prosaically, landownership was hedged about by varying degrees of limitation resulting from the security of customary tenures, accompanied as often as not by inelasticity of rents. As a result, many men who in law ranked as tenants were for most practical purposes the *de facto* owners.

The central problem of the agrarian history of Tudor England has been the nature of the security enjoyed by copyholders. As long ago as 1893, I.S. Leadam demonstrated that they did in fact enjoy the protection of the courts. Rejected by Tawney (1912), this has now been fully vindicated by Dr Kerridge, who has shown that the security conferred on the copyholder by the law was not inferior to that enjoyed by the freeholder, and that it was not a subject for dispute in the courts during the sixteenth century 'for the simple reason that the question had been settled long before'.[42] There was, of course, a diversity of tenures – so much so that it can never be assumed that the customs of any two manors were identical, or even similar, unless perhaps they formed part of the same feudal honour, for example the barony of Lewes in Sussex, which had evolved a set of common customs.[43] Nonetheless, a clear regional pattern divided eastern England, where copyhold by inheritance prevailed, from the west, where copyholds were usually granted for three lives, occasionally fewer; grants for term of years were rare. In most practical aspects heritable copyhold differed little from socage. With rents normally frozen at an obsolete level, entry fines were either certain, or, if technically arbitrary at the will of the lord, required by custom to be reasonable, which amounted to much the same thing.[44] There was little to prevent tenants disposing of their land as though it was freehold. In the barony of Lewes it was not unknown for heritable copyholds to be entailed, to such an extent indeed that even though the common law harboured reservations as to its legality, the judges 'haue bene sparinge to deliuer their opinions because it concerned very many of the kinges subjectes'.[45] Here is clear evidence that the judiciary could and did temper the law with common sense, and did not habitually turn a blind eye to social and economic realities.

The entry for Slapton in the Buckinghamshire muster book contains the almost unique line, 'Eliz. Turney her copye landes in all England, xl'. If this was anything more than a straightforward clerical error – the only parallel case being Robert Harold of Hungerford, who was stated to own a copyhold worth 8*s.* – it poses the question, was customary land ever assessed, whether by accident or design? At Slapton, as on not a few other manors, a degree of confusion is understandable, for tenures were complex, embracing not only freeholds and copyholds – mostly heritable, though including a few for lives – but also what were described in a survey made in 1548 as 'The Farme Landes', which were probably parcels of the demesne that were let by copy of court roll, the larger ones for fifteen years, the rest at will. In addition the manor and the mill were demised for twenty-one-year terms.[46] From the point of view of the lord of the manor there were five freeholders, all of whom had earlier featured in the musters, two as inhabitants of the village.[47] However, in addition to the lord (Barking Abbey), and the king, who received 12*s.* 'in Certentye', the muster lists a total of ten absentee and sixteen resident landholders, i.e. more than five times as many as in 1548. Now it is not beyond the bounds of possibility that during the intervening twenty-five years the lord had bought out most of the freeholds, which, with few exceptions, must have been very small, and might just be identified with the sixteen 'Farme Landes'. The five surviving freeholders included the dean of Windsor, Robert Dormer of Wing, who was one of the richest landowners in the county, and a lady who was principal proprietor of the hamlet of Horton in Ivinghoe, not the kind of tenants to yield to pressure to sell out, if pressure there was: most of the small landed families of 1522 were still there as customary

108

tenants at the later date. But were they really freeholders in the first place?

The Turney family provides a few clues. Elizabeth was much the wealthiest inhabitant of Slapton, her goods being appraised at £66. 13s. 4d. There was also a Thomas, mustered as an archer, and Malyn, who was described as a 'mayde'. Neither owned any property, but from the fact that Elizabeth's assessment was reduced to £30 for the second instalment of the subsidy in 1525, while Thomas and Malyn were now taxed on 20 marks apiece, it is logical to deduce that they were her children, lately come of age. A guardian would be assessed on the stock he was holding on behalf of his wards, as was Francis Brown of Little Casterton, Rutland, in respect of his four brothers and sisters. Land worth £2. 1s. 4d. per annum was owned by Bernard Turney, who lived at Hudnall in Edlesborough and had goods valued at 40 marks. Until recently he must have lived at Horton in Ivinghoe, where he had £2 a year in land, for the entry there concerning him was cancelled with the gloss 'quia in Edlesboro non computetor?' One called John lived at Cheddington, owning land worth £1 with goods of £20, another at Linslade, assessed at £2. 6s. 8d. and £6. 13s. 4d. respectively; either could have been the owner of £1. 6s. 8d. in land at Soulbury, where William Turney also had the same income from land, together with £5 in moveables. Taken as a whole the Turneys formed a not unimportant family of landed peasants and yeomen all living in the neighbourhood of Leighton Buzzard. In 1548 two held land at Slapton. William was a small farmer occupying a messuage and yardland as a copyholder in inheritance, together with half an acre of meadow and another piece of the 'Farme Landes' of unstated dimensions, as a tenant at will, for a total rent of 11s. Bernard had been farming the manor on a 21-year lease since at least 1536, and paying £9. 10s. a year for it. He was probably not the Bernard listed in 1522, for one of the copyholders, occupying half a virgate, was Joan Pace, who is described as the widow of Bernard Turney, while the lease of the manor was renewed without a break until the eighteenth century.[48] Thus the importance of the family's position at Slapton was growing. Bernard was at the least reckoning an ambitious yeoman, the kind we expect to find purchasing land, like the Chibnalls of Sherington,[49] not selling – unless, of course, he had done so in order to finance the purchase of his lease, or to stock the new and very much bigger farm; but this is pure speculation.

It would seem strange for the lord to have pursued a policy of buying up freeholds while leaving undisturbed copyholders who for the most part were virtually owners too. The alternative solution is that the structure of ownership had changed little since 1522, and that most land values recorded at that date represented the profits from subletting customary holdings – mostly in small parcels since the sums involved did not generally exceed ten or twelve shillings. Exclusive of absent freeholders there were twenty-six tenants at Slapton in 1548, who are matched by thirty resident laymen in 1522, four of whom owned no property of any description. The solitary subsidy list adds a dozen more, including two of some substance.

It is an established fact that copyholders regularly sublet their tenements either whole or in part; the manor of Rodley, Gloucs., evolved a complex framework of rules to govern it.[50] The extent of the practice is, however, obscured by the widespread custom that permitted tenants to make demises for up to a year – in some places as much as three – without licence from the lord of the manor.[51] At Wigston, as at Stoke Gifford, information derives largely from remarks made in the course of lawsuits.[52] Its economic importance is attested by the provision in the subsidy act for the assessment of income from customary land, conceivably in the light of knowledge gleaned from the preceding survey. Slapton was no isolated case. Haddenham returned forty-five landholders in 1522, of whom thirty-five were resident, yet the survey of 1555 lists only eleven freeholders. One or two holdings were probably outside the manor. 'Grenville's manor belonged to Edward Grenville of Wotton Underwood, and was worth £10 to him; in 1606 it may have comprised a house and 89 acres. Another holding could have been the obscure Bigstrupp Farm, or hamlet, of which there is no record between 1346 and 1797. Haddenham copyholders held in inheritance. The 1555 survey contains forty-six (exclusive of men who were also freeholders), and it is reasonable to assume that something like thirty held land that was sublet in 1522, an estimate that finds a measure of confirmation in the subsidy schedule which, perhaps in deference to the provision for the taxing of income from customary holdings, mentions the landed wealth of twenty-six men who were assessed on goods.[53] At Cuddington, an adjacent manor belonging to the same lord, there were thirteen land assessments in 1522 compared with only two freeholders a generation later. At Datchet and Stoke Hammond freeholders formed a majority of the tenants, but even so the number of men assessed on land was greater. At Steeple Claydon, on the other hand, where nine land assessments compare with only three actual freeholders, there were some fifty inhabitants all told, of whom only four drew income from land.[54] Either custom or convention hereabouts militated against subletting, or officials in the Buckingham hundreds ignored land that was not freehold, for far fewer owners were recorded there than in the remainder of the county. The paucity of property-owning residents in Rutland suggests that attention there was confined strictly to freeholders, yet the situation delineated by two surveys taken in 1537 appears much more complex. At Stretton, where there were two freeholders, most tenants held at will, and only six out eighteen can be identified in 1522. At Woodhead (Great Casterton) all held by lease or at will, and again only seven out of twenty-six can be traced in 1522; the two non-resident freeholders were disregarded.[55] Clearly a high turnover in the course of fifteen years cannot be ruled out, but nonetheless subletting looks probable unless tenurial conditions discouraged long occupancies: the lease of the manor farm was dated 1534.

The situation varied greatly from manor to manor and region to region. Most tenants at Ravenstone, Bucks. (which overlapped into Stoke Goldington and Weston Underwood), were freeholders, a numerous class in this district, the remainder lessees for term of years or at will. Copyhold was by inheritance in thirteen out of twenty-five Buckinghamshire manors surveyed in the reigns of Edward VI and Mary; on two there were lifeholds only, and at three either a term of years or tenure at will; six had a medley of all modes. Around Newbury from one to three lives was the rule, while at Faringdon tenure was hereditary, reflecting perhaps the mainly pastoral economy of the district.[56] How far these variations affected the ability of tenants to sublet is difficult to determine in the absence of objective criteria. That subletting was widely practised cannot be doubted, for not only in the cases examined was the number of proven freeholds relatively small, but, even in regions where they were most numerous they still formed a minority of all holdings.[57]

The evidence is undeniably circumstantial; the rare examples of actual letting usually come in the form of licences to demise. In West Sussex in 1547 Richard Stygant of Yapton got leave to sublet three crofts containing 9 acres for five years, as did John Standen of Nutbourne in respect of a messuage, garden and 3 acres. At Nutbourne also Thomas Croft, upon being admitted, applied for licence to demise a cottage and 3 acres because, as a minor, he was unable to manage them personally. Though too few to be presented as typical, examples such as these confirm that letting was apt to be of small parcels – commonly portions of tenements – for short terms. Five licences were granted at one session at Singleton; three related to tiny parcels, while a whole virgate was let by a recently admitted tenant to his brother, presumably the elder, the younger having inherited under the custom of borough English, and probably under age. The fifth case belonged to a different category: a gentleman named Thomas Arundell was given leave to demise a tenement and three yardlands which he presumably treated as an investment.[58] The fines for these licences were uniformly trifling, implying that they were obtainable without difficulty.

Frequently it is necessary to read between the lines. Fulco, son and heir of William Michell, surrendered by attorney his copyhold at Cradley, Worcs., to the use of Richard Smith; both were non-resident, as was William Bere, who surrendered in the same way at the next court.[59] Exactly half the families who took up or vacated tenements at Hagley in 1521–9 were absentees. Alice and John Underwood lived thirty miles away at Stratford-on-Avon; the former was one of three co-heiresses of John Dauncer, senior, sometime bailiff of Hagley, who had all espoused men from other villages. In 1528 Underwood, as life tenant in right of his wife, transferred the property to another non-resident, again by attorney. All but two of the jurors attending the courts in 1522 featured in the muster book, while seven of the ten essoins were absentee tenants. One man, John Wright, is a bit of a mystery. In October 1522 he conveyed two freehold houses and 1½ virgates to a certain Thomas Hyll, but subsequently seems to have taken up residence at Hagley, for in October 1526 he was presented for operating a brothel in which his own daughter was the star attraction: prostitution, it has been suggested, was a concomitant of deferred marriage, widespread among the peasantry of the West Midlands. This mis-demeanour did not debar Wright from election as ale-taster at the same court, and constable the following year.[60]

Not only had most manorial demesnes been let to farm well before the beginning of the Tudor epoch, small freeholds and customary tenements were also regularly managed in the same fashion – indeed, they must frequently have been treated as investments. The copyholder, often equated with the poor peasant farmer, might well have been every bit as much a rentier as the lord of the manor, especially if a gentleman or wealthy townsman, earning thereby the disapprobation of Robert Crowley:

> ther bee certayne tenauntes, not able to be lande lordes, and yet after a sorte, they conterfayte lande lordes, by obtaynynge leases in and vpon groundes and tenementes, and so reyse fynes, incomes and tentes; and by such pyllage pyke out a porcion to mayntayne a proude

112

porte, and all by pylynge and pollynge of the poore commons, that must of necessitie seke habitations at their handes.[61]

Conversely, the husbandmen who bulked so large in the assessments of the 1520s, and formed the majority in later subsidies when the experiment of taxing wage earners was abandoned, were far from being exclusively freeholders and copyholders on advantageous terms. Not only were customary tenants in the West Country, for instance, powerless to resist rising fines, it is quite feasible that everywhere the land was, to a great extent, actually cultivated by leaseholders or tenants from year to year paying an economic rent. In 1605 at least forty out of seventy-five holdings of less than 60 acres in Arden were sublet.[62] It was not uncommon for one man to hold land in several different tenures and to combine the roles of tenant and landlord. Some conception of the resultant complexity may be gained from a survey of the freeholders of Bedfont, Middx., in 1546, which records a wealth of detail that was more often than not disregarded. There were 140 parcels, of which only forty-seven were occupied by the head tenants, the remainder being in the hands of subtenants. In all there were thirty-eight occupiers, of whom twenty were owners as well. Three of these had let off part of their land, and five others had rented some themselves. One man occupied 14 acres of his own, sublet the same quantity, and rented 8½ acres from an absentee. Two more had let all their own property, while leasing other land; one of these styled himself gentleman and was perhaps an example of a counterfeit landlord.[63]

For Cannock, Staffs., the fortuitous provenance of the requisite documentation, notably a field book drawn up in 1554, has enabled C.J. Harrison to compute the scale of subletting. While the number of tenements held of the manor came to fifty-two, the number of separate farms totalled seventy-three, resulting of course in an increase in the number of smaller units, both absolutely and relatively; in particular the number below 10 acres amounted to forty-five (62 per cent) compared with twenty-eight (54 per cent) head tenancies. Sixteen head tenants were absentees who let all their land, while thirty-seven (or half) of the cultivators occupied their entire holdings as undertenants. Some leased part of their own tenements while renting additional land. All told two-thirds of the land was cultivated by subtenants.[64]

The identification of these petty landlords, though at times a tortuous process, is not impossible; their tenants are another matter. Manorial records in general concerned themselves solely with the head tenants;

the name of an undertenant might occur only incidentally, as at Long Crendon in 1535 when the vicar of Thame was presented for letting two tenements by indenture for ten years to William Byrte, from whom, in fact, he had purchased them a few years previously.[65] At Cannock, for once, they are on record, and here many of the smallest subtenants were entered as 'landless' in a survey of the manor.[66] The military survey of 1522, in theory at least, confined itself to ownership strictly defined. However, a characteristic of the Worcestershire record is the attempt in some cases to estimate the value of a lease to the tenant. Thus at Inkberrow Richard Russell's 'lease by year' is valued at £1. 3s. 8d., and Henry Woodwar's 'lease for years' at £1 – clearly distinguished from his own property, which was valued separately at £1. 10s. The precise significance of such entries is not explained. Totalling fewer than twenty and confined to a minority of townships, they can hardly have represented more than a fraction of the real number of demises, most of which were likely to have been annual tenancies anyway. At Warley the abbot of Halesowen's rent for the farm of the manor is entered as a separate item, but the identity of the farmer is not revealed; we may hazard the guess that he was William Hardeley, whose personal estate, amounting to £30, made him much the wealthiest man in the village. All the same not every lessee was enumerated as a resident of the parish where the land was situated: in Kidderminster Foreign only one out of the five named was. Could the others have been examples of the 'leasemongers' on whom so much opprobrium was heaped?[67] These entries are reminiscent of the leases mentioned in some probate inventories, the wording of which occasionally implies that they were valued on the basis of the number of years they still had to run, calculated perhaps as a proportion of the original fines. One couched in the form of an account of the sale of the deceased's effects says, 'Of Mr Marshall for the fine of the yeares to come of the lease of the house'[68]

Rigid adherence to the letter of their instructions by commissioners can only have served to obscure important aspects of the structure of landholding. The meticulously executed Rutland survey does not go beyond naming a handful of rectory farmers. In 1517 David Cecil took a 21-year lease of land in Essendine at a rent of £18. 3s. 3d.; not being the freeholder he was not mentioned in the muster, and there is no means of telling whether his global assessment of £46 at Tinwell embodied the profit of this farm which he very possibly sublet. On the same date the crown lordships of Preston and Uppingham were let for £49. 17s. 8d. a year to a certain Robert Symmys, who also had a lease for £10. 3s. 8½d. at Ridlington. By 1522 there is no trace of him; the only person of that name was a widow living at Ridlington, where she owned property assessed at 4 marks, with £10 in goods. She could have been his mother, for he was the son of John Symmys of that parish, or even his relict, for he himself must have been dead by 1525, when the Ridlington lease was granted to the duke of Richmond.[69] Although the Rutland book does give everyone's landlord, for information regarding terms of tenure we are dependent on the chance provenance of supplementary evidence. Only very occasionally is it possible to read between the lines, as in one instance at South Luffenham, where Henry Bonytt, as the sole tenant of freeholder Edward Sapcote, presumably held a lease; he also had 10s. a year in land and a subtenant called William Clark, who must *mutatis mutandis* have held from him by lease, if not from year to year.[70]

THE ELUSIVE ABSENTEE

The difficulties of identifying and evaluating absentee landowners have already been touched on. The return for North Marston, Bucks., is exceptional in giving the addresses of half the individual owners, and since several others are readily identifiable, approximately three-quarters can be placed in context (see Table 3.1).[71] Places marked with an asterisk (*) in Table 3.1 are stated in the return itself. Lady St Leger and the Prince speak for themselves; Pigott and Eversbye were major figures in the locality, Redmond was distinguished by a unique name and was a minor gentleman resident in an adjoining parish. As a Bedfordshire man William Taylor remains an unknown quantity.

Of the remainder, the Bornes illustrate the type of vexing question these lists so frequently raise. Several lived not far away in Worminghall, a middling sort of family which included a Richard who had seven marks in goods. A Richard *Barne*, who also held *in absentia* land worth 43s. 4d. in Long Crendon, may have been the same man. Peter Borne, presumably a clerk, was, by contrast, a person of substance with possible pretensions to gentility. There was a Bele family in Wendover which included a Richard with 20s. in land and £10 in goods, but he was not a priest; others dotted about the county were mainly of the labourer type. Not infrequently we can find the right name, yet no positive identification can be made. Baron is rare, one other example occurring at Olney. It could be a corrupt spelling of Barne or Borne, but Katherine, as a woman, might recently have changed her name by marrying. Mistress Fatchyll is equally obscure.

Table 3.1 Non-resident landowners in North Marston

Name	Residence	Marston			Elsewhere			Goods		
		£	s	d	£	s	d	£	s	d
Lady St Leger (lord)			8	6						
'My lord prince'				3						
Elizabeth Pigott	Whaddon	3	5	8	96	14	4	100	0	0
Mrs Eversbye	Quainton		10	0	41	12	0	100	0	0
Henry Cowper	Shipton Lee	3	0	0		19	0	53	6	8
John Deverall	Swanbourne*	1	6	8	2	13	4	30	0	0
Tho. Redmond, gent.	Oving		3	4	1	0	0	26	13	4
John Hardinge	Whitchurch*		8	0	1	6	8	15	0	0
John Boston	Winslow*		19	0	1	6	8	10	0	0
John Parott	Pitchcott*	1	6	8		2	0	10	0	0
John Polle (Pott)	Aylesbury*		5	4	2	0	0	10	0	0
William Reade	Fulbrook*	1	13	4				4	0	0
Richard Prentice	Soulbury*		5	0		1	8	3	0	0
Thomas Prentice	Bierton*	1	6	8	1	0	0	0	0	0
William Taylor	Leighton Buzzard*		14	0						
Mr Peter Borne		7	4	6						
Richard Borne			10	0						
Richard Bele, priest		1	1	0						
Katherine Baron			17	0						
Mrs Fatchyll		2	9	0						

Other than the two eminent personages – curiously, Lady St Leger was also lord of Hagley – the freeholders comprised three of the local gentry, three or four of the yeoman type, and six or seven husbandmen or tradesmen. Redmond's credentials look slender; 'gentleman farmer' seems to fit him better. All save two or three lived within a dozen miles or less of Marston, eight certainly within three. Of the unknowns, Bele and Richard Borne probably came of peasant stock. There were also institutional proprietors, Oseney Abbey and Magdalen College, Oxford, had £2 and £7 respectively, while the parsonage, valued at £18. 6s. 8d., belonged to St George's Chapel, Windsor; the small payments of 7s. and 6s. 8d. due respectively to the churchwardens of Aylesbury and Stony (or Fenny) Stratford could well have been rent charges. The village community comprised twenty-seven farmers and smallholders assessed at 40*s*. or more on personal property; seven of these had land of their own, leaving precisely twenty to match the same number of holdings belonging to absentees. Unquestionably this is too neat; the structure of occupancy was doubtless more complex. Nevertheless, it has some claim to consideration. The position with respect to copyholds is uncertain, though the lord's negligible income implies that they were unimportant or sublet to few restraints.

The situation as it appears in other counties is governed by the criteria on which their returns were based. The well-known fact that small freeholds were abundant in East Anglia[72] is amply attested by the great number of resident proprietors recorded there, though this is offset by the conspicuous failure of some of the Norfolk books to deal adequately with non-residents. In the severely limited number of resident landowners listed, Berkshire resembles Rutland; at the same time the many small parcels noted in some parishes are reminiscent of the copyhold estates of Buckinghamshire. In passing it is worth remarking that the addresses of a handful of absentee proprietors at Grove in Wantage were mostly confined within an eight-mile radius.

By rigidly segregating the landowners from the inhabitants, the Cornish commissioners made it unnecessarily difficult to distinguish resident proprietors. The structure of ownership was exceptionally complex. The lands of most parishes comprised a welter of tiny parcels, forty-three in St Kew, for example, and upwards of sixty in St Stephen's, Launceston, the biggest of which was worth no more than £6 a year. Only in one or two small places was property concentrated in a few hands, as at Botteslemming, where Sir Piers Edgcumbe had £20 a year as lord of the manor and a local farmer owned a holding worth 33*s*. 4*d*. Similarly in Ruan Minor the lord's income amounted to £5, in addition to which two smallholders had 3*s*. 4*d*. and 10*s*. respectively. Nevertheless, nearly everywhere owner occupiers could be comfortably numbered on the fingers of one hand. In five townships of Penwith there were none at all, in eleven more there were two at most, while of twenty-nine freeholders in Uny Lelant just one belonged to one of the forty-nine listed inhabitants.[73] In the west especially the unsettled state of surnames complicates matters: there was a marked discontinuity between the local population, who commonly answered to patronymics, and owners of land who were consistently identified by family names.[74] However, Trigg, West and East hundreds, where the use of family names was general, may afford some clue to the real numbers of peasant proprietors. Out of 3,373 listed inhabitants, 220 – some 6½ per cent –

can be identified as landowners, but since some ranked as gentlemen the proportion of husbandmen occupying holdings of their own can scarcely have reached 5 per cent.

A further complication is the fact that Cornwall was a Celtic society; the field system was Celtic and, at least in earlier times, partible inheritance was practised.[75] The resultant fragmentation of estates could easily have led to uncertainty as to the precise identity of the owner of any given parcel in the unprecedented circumstances of 1522.[76] The formula 'the heir(s) of' occurs too frequently to be limited (as the rare examples found in other counties probably were) to heirs general and co-heiresses. Land in several places in Penwith was owned either by John Vyvyan or the 'heir of Richard Vyvyan' of Trelowaren who had died in 1516 leaving three sons, the eldest of whom had died without issue in 1520.[77] The 'heir' could mean either John, the second, or Michael, the youngest, who in fact is not mentioned anywhere. In two instances in which heirs can be identified they turn out to have been women: in the one the three daughters of the important landowner John Glyn of Morval, who all married eminent local gentlemen; in the other Anne, wife of John Croker, the sister and sole heir of Sir Edmund Arundell, a member of the great family of Lanherne whose lands extended to all parts of Cornwall.[78] Time and again we find an inhabitant bearing the surname of an absentee owner of land in the same township. Many of these must have been related, but while the assumption is tenable in the case of Nicholas and John Talgarrick at Camborne, the commonplace patronymic Jamys makes any connexion between Richard, a resident of St Just in Penwith, and John, a landowner there, speculative.[79] Nothing short of investigation in depth can turn suspicion into certainty.

With the added drawback that the certificates for four of the nine hundreds are lost, it is well-nigh impossible to trace the majority of non-resident landowners. In St Levan near Land's End, a geographical factor that limits the possible whereabouts of its proprietors, there were thirty-three freeholds, not one of which apparently belonged to an inhabitant of the parish. Two may be traced to the adjoining parishes of Senan and St Buryan, seven to persons living within a radius of some twenty miles, and seven more to gentry families which owned widely dispersed estates. The remainder cannot be satisfactorily attributed; some belonged to 'heirs', while three were held by men with problem names. One of these was John Hicka, a name found in Gulvall and Towednack. Another was John Hoskyn, a very common name, who might have lived in Paul, less than three miles away, but could also have belonged to Cambourne, Gwithian or St. Hillary. The third was Pascoe John Thomas, and here the best that can be done is to note that men called Pascoe John resided in Gulvall and Gwithian.[80]

St Levan partially confirms the impression of a considerable class of peasant proprietors in west Cornwall, for while a full third of the freeholders can be identified more or less confidently as gentry, the rest were almost certainly of humbler status. Their main characteristic is that their property tended to lie dispersed and that they seldom (as far as can be seen) occupied it themselves. John Cuswyn of Phillack owned parcels totalling £4. 13s. 4d. in six parishes, though none in Phillack itself; William Clemowe of Marazion had tiny parcels in Maddron and Zennor.[81] Untraceable owners possibly tended to reside much further away from their property. Few foreigners, we are told, cared to acquire land in Cornwall,[82] and anyway the great majority of owners bore Cornish-sounding names, even in parishes nearer to Devon. As no doubt was the case in other shires, it was hardly worth while for small men to purchase or retain tiny holdings in remote places, and indeed, with few exceptions, the only Cornish landowners who can be found living at any great distance from their property were gentlemen. Finally, the humble status of many of these elusive people finds confirmation in the fact that few seem to have owned more than a single holding.[83] The values of most parcels were less than 20s., many less than 10s.

The prevalence of small scattered parcels of land forms a striking contrast to the more compact estates usual where primogeniture prevailed. James Erisy of St Grade, a squire of moderate standing, held lands totalling £38. 2s. 0d. in no fewer than eighteen places in west Cornwall, the biggest, in Redruth, being valued at £8, the smallest, in Mellion, at only 3s. 4d.[84] The estates of the various branches of the Arundell family hold great interest. John of Trerice had interests in twelve parishes, ranging from 1s. 4d. in the borough of Liskeard to £5 in Gyrogh; but this was a mere fraction, amounting to less than a fifth of his £80 subsidy assessment.[85] John of Tolverne's lands extended from Cape Cornwall to Launceston, fragmented into tiny parcels spread over seventeen parishes, as follows:

	£	s	d		£	s	d
Penwith				Kerrier			
Camborne		13	4	Gwennap	1	13	4
Crowan		12	0	Penryn		14	4
Gwithian		9	0				
Ludgvan		15	0				

	£	s	d			£	s	d
Maddron		15	0	West				
Phillack	2	10	0	St Neots		2	0	0
Sancreed		13	4					
St Buryan		19	0	East				
St Hillary	13	10	0	Launceston			13	4
St Leven	1	12	0	Menhenniot		3	0	0
St Just	1	1	0					
Zennor	1	14	0					

The total value topped £32 compared with his loan assessment of £50, which must have comprehended much property in Powder hundred where he lived, but of which there is no record.[86]

As we have seen, the phenomenon of untraceable freeholders is not exclusive to Cornwall, and it is tempting to speculate that behind some at least of these seemingly insignificant proprietors lurked rich men unobtrusively extending their estates with an eye to profit. Certainly there was a deep-rooted belief that big landowners pursued a policy of buying up freeholds, and the distaste with which this was viewed provided an incentive for being discreet. Kett's followers petitioned 'that it be not lawful to the lords of any manor to purchase lands freely and to let them out again by copy of court roll to their great advancement and to the undoing of [the king's] poor subjects'.[87] The knight in the *Discourse* implies that lords wanting to resume control of customary tenements had to buy out the tenants[88] – and why not? It made sound business sense, and we should not fall into the trap of assuming that behind every entry in a court roll recording the surrender of a holding into the hands of the lord lay a story of harassment and intimidation.

SOCIAL DISTRIBUTION

It will by now have become apparent that interpretation of these assessments is fraught with hazards. Questions of accuracy apart, allowance has to be made for a variety of distorting factors. Tending towards exaggeration are, firstly, the intrusion of global assessments, most of which are large, and, secondly, the tacit insertion in some returns of income from copyholds – suspected though not conclusively proved. Tending towards understatement are omissions, not merely the overt sort which merely leave the value blank, but also the more insidious ones which ignore a landowner and his property altogether.

120

Rectification is practicable only where alternative sources are available, leaving little option but to assume that these factors tend in the long run to cancel one another out.[89]

Potential major discrepancies are detectable by comparing ratios of value to area. The broad indications are that in the south-eastern half of England they approximated to £32 per thousand acres. In Babergh the total value came to £2,339, the area 71,000 acres, giving £32.9; the omission of the clergy of eight parishes indicates that the true figure should be slightly greater. For Surrey the equivalent figures are £16,819–£14,831 exclusive of the wealthy metropolitan borough of Southwark – and the acreage 485,000, producing of £34.7 overall, and £30.6 for the rural hundreds.[90] Buckinghamshire yields a ratio of £31.5, and Rutland £30.3., or £31.6 if it is assumed that the deserted villages of Horn and Pickworth were overlooked by the survey.[91] The aggregates for these two counties are bulked out by global assessments. Babergh seems to contain none, indeed it is clear that they were not applied to the two richest landowners there.[92] As the Surrey data is restricted to an abstract there can be no question of even guessing at the make-up of the original lists. Values could quite easily have been inflated by global sums, and although the high average does not suggest many serious omissions, it is nonetheless possible to visualise a combination of the two producing an eccentric result. It has also to be borne in mind that any similarities between these two counties could be fortuitous. Babergh was much the richest part of Suffolk, while overall values in Surrey must have been depressed by expanses of poor heathlands and woods.

Table 3.2 Average land values

County	Value £	Area 1,000 acres	£ per 1,000 acres
Norfolk	4,382	202	22
Buckinghamshire	14,970	476	32
Berkshire (part)	5,418	223	24
Gloucestershire: Cotswolds	7,136	343	21
Vale	6,529	256	26
Forest	1,933	100	19
Worcestershire (part)	4,169	168	25
Cornwall (part)	8,051	455	18

Elsewhere there are marked divergences from this norm (see Table 3.2). Here we have done no more than aggregate the raw figures, making no allowance for possible distorting factors except insofar as it has been practicable to make good unstated values of Crown lands from contemporary sources.

One county alone approaches the 'standard' value, appropriately enough Buckinghamshire, the southern tip of which touches Surrey. It is singular, therefore, that Berkshire, which borders on both, should appear measurably poorer than either. Were it not for the obvious omissions, the low value of the rich farmlands of Norfolk, with the important town of Great Yarmouth thrown in, would appear even more surprising. In South Erpingham, where the valuation looks more thorough than in other hundreds, the ratio works out at £30.66. The Cotswolds too appear grossly undervalued; in any case the survey is problematical. The figure for the Vale looks more promising, though depressed by several unvalued Crown estates. In fact roughly half the

Table 3.3 Ownership of land[93]

County		Crown £	Laity £	Church £	Total £
Rutland	(say)	725	1,212	972	2,909
Buckinghamshire		713	8,632	5,625	14,970
Berkshire (part)		292	2,431	2,695	5,418
Worcestershire (part)	(say)	200	2,433	1,650	4.283
Cornwall (part)		391	4,330	3,330	8,051
Gloucestershire: Cotswolds		274	2,791	4,071	7,136
Vale		383	2,823	3,323	6,529
Forest		25	1,422	742	2,189
Percentages					
Rutland		24.1	44.3	31.6	100
Buckinghamshire		4.7	57.7	37.6	100
Berkshire		5.3	44.9	49.8	100
Worcestershire		4.7	56.8	38.5	100
Cornwall		4.9	53.8	41.4	100.1
Gloucestershire: Cotswolds		3.8	39.1	57.1	100
Vale		5.9	43.2	50.9	100
Forest		1.1	65.0	33.9	100

region, containing 146,996 acres,[94] which seems to be better recorded than the rest, amounts to £4,347, averaging £29.6 per thousand acres, and so close to the norm. For a poorish area like north-east Worcestershire £25 may not be unrealistic; by comparison the figure for the Forest of Dean is less convincing.[95] Remote and containing broad tracts of moorland, Cornwall could be expected to produce a lower ratio, though whether the recorded values are in fact adequate cannot be precisely determined.

The *Valor Ecclesiasticus* confirms that the Church's possessions were correctly assessed, sometimes down to the last penny in Buckinghamshire and Rutland, and if a number of Gloucestershire livings tend to be undervalued, the difference is insufficient to account for the lower overall level of wealth there. So the question is, were other categories properly assessed? It is particularly appropriate to examine the broad division of land between Church and laity, more especially in view of the possibility that in the immediate pre-Reformation atmosphere the commissioners might have been inclined to accord their fellow laymen preferential treatment. The holdings of the basic groupings were as shown in Table 3.3. While the proportions vary a good deal, the Church's share in the two counties which conform to the £32 norm, as well as in Surrey, was not far off a third. Now in the speech he may or may not have delivered in the House of Commons, Thomas Cromwell claimed that the national annual revenue from land totalled £1 million,[96] while a near-contemporary computation, judged by Alexander Savine to be 'evidently derived from a trustworthy source',[97] placed the Church's income prior to the dissolution of the monasteries at £320,180. 10s. 0d., in other words the equivalent of 32 per cent. Although Cromwell did not indicate the source of his information, we do know that he would have had ready access to a comprehensive one – no less than the muster books themselves. Not only was he Wolsey's servant, he was pre-eminently a man of facts and figures, and it is not taxing credulity to ascribe to him the authorship of the general proscription. There can be no doubt that the certificates were eagerly processed to establish the basis for a subsidy of £800,000: someone certainly skimmed rapidly through the Rutland one totalling each page. The conclusion can only be that the popular conviction that the Church owned at least a third of the land[98] rested on a solid foundation of fact. Indeed, the question must arise, could pamphleteers of the ilk of Simon Fish have had access, however indirect, to the record? Speculation apart, we are presented with a working hypothesis that the Church's share lay generally in the range 30–40 per cent.

In several counties the unadjusted figures make the Church's holding appreciably larger. Can they be trusted? In the Gloucestershire Vale, where values look to be below standard, the proportion tops 50 per cent. However, we have seen that there are grounds for believing that the true ratio was about £30 per thousand acres, even a full £32. Now this last figure would give a theoretical aggregate of £8,192. If it can be assumed that as a general rule ecclesiastical property was assessed at its full value, and that laymen were better able to conceal their assets or secure preferential treatment – not to mention the certainty that the incomes of some Crown lordships were omitted – real wealth can be reconstructed as follows:

The Crown	£383	4.7%
The laity	£4,486	54.8%
The Church	£3,323	40.6%
Total	£8,192	100.1%

Though still on the high side, the Church's holding now works out not much greater than in Worcestershire, and the overall picture certainly gains in verisimilitude. (The fact that the Crown's share should be substantially larger is immaterial as this would simply reduce the amount theoretically allotted to the laity.) A similar calculation in respect of the Cotswolds produces a revised total of £10,976, of which the £4,071 attributed to the Church comes to 37.1 per cent, somewhat below the Worcestershire figure. Little is to be gained by attempting a rectification of the Forest of Dean values. Despite the superficial inadequacies of the record, the Church is represented as having almost exactly one third, which the £32 ratio would actually reduce to about 23 per cent. Indeed, this 'normal' apportionment between Church and laity implies that the raw figures are by no means misleading.

Before attempting any adjustment of the Berkshire figures it will be of some interest to observe the wide variations in the recorded land values of the eight hundreds covered by the survey (see Table 3.4). The small size of these divisions inevitably magnifies any exaggerations, but even so there is scant consistency. The low average of Faircross, which included the rich borough of Newbury, admits of no explanation other than defective assessment, nor does the contrast between Wantage and the neighbouring hundreds of Ganfield and Shrivenham. Lambourn is depressed by the omission of the king's important lordship there. The

Table 3.4 Berkshire land values

Hundred	Value £	Area (1,000 acres)	Average £
Faringdon	392	8	49
Wantage	1,167	28	42
Ganfield	518	17	31
Shrivenham	951	31	31
Compton	351	16	22
Faircross	948	46	21
Lambourn	356	19	19
Kintbury Eagle	736	41	18

valuation of Kintbury Eagle can only be regarded as thoroughly unsatisfactory. The overall impression is that much of the work was poorly executed.

The area of Berkshire covered by the survey is 223,000 acres, which multiplied by £32 produces a total of £7,136 which may be apportioned thus:

The Crown	£292	4.1%
The laity	£4,149	58.1%
The Church	£2,695	37.8%
Total	£7,136	100.0%

Here too 'correct' relativities are restored, and perhaps more convincingly than in Gloucestershire inasmuch as fewer royal lordships are left unassessed. At the same time a note of caution must be sounded, for the limitations of the model are exposed by the fact that in the four richest, and presumably most accurately assessed hundreds, the Church actually owned half or more of the land.

Emendation of the Cornwall and Worcestershire data is less obviously called for. In both, the Church's property lies within the hypothetical range, and in the former moreover it is by no means clear what to aim for. As a Midland shire Worcestershire is potentially suited to the £32 model, which would have the effect of increasing its value to £5,376, and reducing the Church's £1,684 to 31.3 per cent, almost exactly the same as in Rutland. But the solution is anything but straightforward. The grand total is distorted by the omission of several Crown lordships while simultaneously inflated by several global assessments, notably Sir Gilbert Talbot's £200 'in all places', of which not more than £21.10s. can be traced, and the rents of Bordesley Abbey amounting to £99. 15s. 4d. over and above demesnes rated at £26. 4s. 8d. a year. These are offset by royal manors that were not assessed: the queen's income from Droitwich was estimated on another occasion at upwards of £7.[99] Coupled with the relative poverty of the district, the fact that the proportion attributed to the Church falls just inside the theoretical range makes adjustment unnecessary in the absence of compelling reasons. Similar considerations apply to Cornwall, especially since reconstruction of the Crown's income is for once practicable.

If any significance attached to variations in the proportion owned by the Church in one district or another it is not immediately apparent. A tenuous correlation with the number and importance of monastic and similar establishments can be detected. In Rutland, where the proportion was minimal, there was only Brooke Priory, an obscure house with just one canon remaining in 1535. Its income was then given as £40–£47, though the survey had put it no higher than £20. The sole surviving medieval hospital at Oakham was impoverished, and the muster takers ignored it.[100] Great religious foundations were less in evidence in the north-east Midlands than in some other regions, and in Rutland account must also be taken of the close historical links with the monarchy; not only did the Crown lands bulk unusually large, the most important monastic proprietor was none other than Westminster Abbey. Nevertheless, in Cornwall, where the Church's wealth reached nearly 40 per cent, the local monasteries were also small and there were comparatively few major ones in Devonshire either. Buckinghamshire too lacked great establishments, although St Albans, Westminster, Woburn and several Oxford houses were all generously endowed there. Similarly the rich abbeys of the Severn Valley exercised a marked influence on the Gloucestershire Vale and north Worcestershire, even though none was located in the districts covered by the survey, except for Tewkesbury. Against this Cirencester, with a revenue exceeding £1,000 a year, and Winchcombe, would not appear to have exercised any very marked effect on the position of the Church in the Cotswolds.[101]

THE CROWN LANDS

Despite gaps in the survey the Crown emerges clearly as by far the greatest single landowner. In addition to the estates attached directly to the king there were also the independently administered duchies of Lancaster and Cornwall, the queen's jointure, and sundry receipts from a wide range of sources.[102] Owing, however, to the absence of any comprehensive record for the period 1509–36, the overall situation remains elusive. Narrowly defined, total revenue from land averaged some £40,000 yearly towards the close of the reign of Henry VII, slumping dramatically to about £25,000 in the early years of his son.[103] Nationally, therefore, the king may be taken as owning at least 2½ percent of the £1 million computed by Cromwell. Against this a contemporary official estimate represents 'rents and farms with other issues' as having declined in value from £55,000 in 1508–9 to less than £35,000 in 1511–12,[104] and having regard to the fact that royal lordships accounted for between 4 and 6 per cent in districts, for which figures, despite imperfections, are available in 1522, it is reasonable to conclude that the commissioners worked to this broader, more comprehensive definition. At the same time the possibility that the sample is weighted by counties where the monarch had a special interest cannot be ignored. The exceptionally high proportion in Rutland may perhaps be traceable to the origin of this minute shire as a royal estate in the eleventh century,[105] over and above which it had been greatly augmented by the manors of Oakham, Egleton and Langham following the recent attainder of the duke of Buckingham, an accession of £196 per year that increased its total share by something like 50 per cent.[106] Berkshire of course contained one of the principal royal residences and had acquired the title of 'royal county'. Cornwall had the Duchy; nevertheless, important as this estate was to the local economy, the Crown's overall share was not dissimilar from what it was in Buckinghamshire or Gloucestershire, and in consequence the county is not necessarily unrepresentative. The sample consisting of five of the nine hundreds gives an average of 5.7 per cent, though the distribution of the Duchy lands was uneven: in East, West and Trigg hundreds they formed nearly 10 per cent but very much less in the west. Moreover, the total over the whole county came to little more than £600,[107] which is well short of 4 per cent of the notional £15,600 obtained by applying the ratio of £18 per 1,000 acres to the whole area. Support for a true figure in the region of 4 per cent comes from Worcestershire, where the values of only three out of eight royal lordships are wanting. As contemporary valors put the revenues from Droitwich at £70. 17s. 10d. and Yardley £20. 7s. 9½d.,[108] and there were besides the immense parishes of Bromsgrove and King's Norton, the total could very well have reached, or exceeded, £200, upwards of 4½ per cent of a revised figure of £4,317. This, nonetheless, is hypothetical. The profitability of a manor bore no necessary relationship to the size or importance of the place where it was located. Although sixteen royal lordships in the Newport hundreds of Buckinghamshire yielded £174 in all, no less than £162 was produced by Hanslope and Olney alone, with the remainder being assigned nominal values of between 2s. and £2.

In other respects too the proportion of land owned by the Crown cannot be precisely determined. If, for obvious reasons, we eschew the counting of manors, we are left with only net monetary values to compare, the utility of which is impaired by the fact that Crown property was often farmed at a fraction of its real value, while inefficiency and malpractice deprived the sovereign of much of what was his due.[109] Further, revenues fluctuated so that any statement can only be true of the time to which it refers. As recently as 1521 they had been substantially augmented by the forfeiture of the duke of Buckingham, but although he had been by far the greatest peer of the realm, with an income of £6,045 – or £4,906 net according to another account – much of it was speedily alienated, with several East Anglian manors (for instance) being granted to the dukes of Norfolk and Suffolk. Dietz's assertion that this acquisition, among others, had gone some way towards restoring the decline in the Crown revenues has been shown not to be well founded.[110]

Finally it must be remembered that the area under the control of the Crown was proportionately greater than crude monetary values imply. In Cornwall, for example, the king owned as much as 8.8 per cent of the temporalities, that is, of land as such; in Buckinghamshire something like 6 per cent. In Rutland nearly 300 persons, say one-fifth of all householders, were his tenants. Similarly, if the net rate of yield was in fact less than that from privately owned estates, the acreage it represented must have been correspondingly greater.

THE CHURCH

Considering the controversy surrounding the subject in the run-up to the Reformation, it is strange that the Church's share of the wealth of the nation has remained something of a mystery and, moreover, one that has persistently frustrated attempts to solve it. Deterred by the conflicting results, the one systematic investigator, Alexander Savine, restricted himself in the main to criticising the estimates made by his predecessors.[111] The musters cannot be expected to settle the question once and for all, if only because the remnants now cover only a fraction of the kingdom. Nevertheless, the striking similarity to the *Valor Ecclesiasticus*, not only in the values placed on benefices, but also in the categories that were made the subject of scrutiny, has prompted Jeremy Goring to liken the proscription to a 'dress rehearsal' for the later project.[112] Insofar as the assessments of 1522 were substantially repeated in 1535, albeit with the round sums of pounds and marks refined down to halfpence and farthings, they contain few surprises. Their significance resides in the fact that they integrate the wealth of clergy and laity into a unified statement: *valor ecclesiasticus* becomes *valor rei publicae*, enabling the wealth of the Church to be analysed in context as a sector of the national economy.

Although assessments are cast exclusively in terms of income produced by land, there need be little doubt that this was what propagandists had in mind; as the reticence of many manorial records, backed by the authority on the art of surveying,[113] attests, spatial dimensions were not the prime consideration at that time. In fact spiritualities made much the largest contribution to ecclesiastical revenues. In Rutland they accounted for a full three-quarters, while temporalities, totalling £270, represented little more than a tenth of all profits arising directly from tenure of land. Church estates in Buckinghamshire, although much more extensive, still amounted to little more than a sixth of all temporalities: £1,996 out of £12,220. By contrast the holdings of a bishop and several great abbeys combined to boost the percentage to 26.3 (£854 out of £3,235) in Worcestershire, although in Cornwall the situation was reversed with temporalities totalling no more than £454 out of £5,282. Of course spiritualities comprehended glebe, but since some livings contained very little it contributed but a fraction of the gross revenues of benefices.

A clear half of the Church's resources was appropriated to the support of the secular establishment, primarily the parish clergy whose share in Rutland came to no less than two-thirds. Superficially it fell somewhat short of one-half in Buckinghamshire, mainly because in many parishes of which the incumbents were non-resident no record was made of any stipend paid to a parish priest. That cures really were neglected cannot be doubted in the case of Rutland, where all clergy seem to have been meticulously enumerated. Such thoroughness is less evident elsewhere; all too frequently information is confined to an impersonal reference to 'the parsonage' or 'the vicarage', and while this may indicate that the living is vacant or the incumbent non-resident, it says nothing as to the presence or absence of a chaplain.

The structure of ecclesiastical wealth was complex. To the distinction between temporalities and spiritualities was added the division of the clergy into regulars and seculars. As a classification this is not wholly satisfactory. Secular clerks comprised several subgroupings, according to the levels and the sources of their incomes from which they were drawn. In strictly economic terms, moreover, some were barely distinguishable from the regular clergy, for cathedral chapters, communities of secular canons, and university colleges, to say nothing of a miscellany of hospitals and similar small establishments, were all corporate owners of property on exactly the same terms as houses of the recognised orders of monks and nuns. The fact that, with the exception of seats of learning, all were swept away indiscriminately in the dissolution of the monasteries leaves us in no doubt that much more weight was attached to functional similarities than to constitutional differences. As it happens the division of the clergy into individual and corporate landowners corresponds very closely with that between the pastoral function of the Church and its manifold other interests. Anomalies cannot be avoided; one at least resulted from the inability of the constable of Manton to explain an unconventional arrangement. On the surface the sole rather unusual feature (for a small Midland parish) was that it had both a parson and a parish priest in residence. But a chantry certificate of 1548 describes a college there, consisting of a master and two stipendiary priests, which had in fact been founded two centuries earlier to staff the parish church. As its endowment included the rectory, making the master (or warden) in effect the parson, the misunderstanding is not entirely surprising. To add to the confusion, it is not entirely clear whether the rector was resident or not. His successor in 1548 was certainly an absentee, the holder of another living in Oxfordshire. Presumably, too, Mr Newton's Christian name would not have been unknown had he dwelt in the parish. At the same time an assessment of £30 in goods gives him the appearance of a resident. The solution – assuming that it is more than a coincidence – may lie in the chantry certificate, which appraised the ornaments of the church, which would have been assessed in the name of the master, at £27. 3s. 4d.[114] Cases of this type do not slot neatly into a formal taxonomy.

Among the secular clergy the bishops were sharply differentiated from the rank and file by their great wealth. What made them individually affluent was their 'fat' manors – an epithet,[115] incidentally, that is thoroughly misleading. The bishop of Worcester's six manors in the county of the same name formed a mixed bag, with Alvechurch and Claines worth upwards of £60 apiece, Hanbury, Hartlebury and Stoke Prior £26–£35, and Stock and Bradley a mere 8 marks. On his home ground, as it were, he enjoyed almost 13½ per cent of all clerical revenues, a total of £223. 10s. However, these figures emanate from one corner only of a shire that was dominated by his possessions, and represent fewer than half his manors there. From Gloucestershire he received little more than £165, approximately 2 per cent of the Church's wealth; the bishop of Hereford also had £102 a year there.[116] In all essentials episcopal estates were identical in composition to those of lords temporal. Spiritualities contributed little to their revenues – in Gloucestershire nothing except trifling pensions from a couple of Cotswold parishes. In Buckinghamshire the receipts of the bishops of Lincoln and Winchester, which together totalled almost £160, included only a single rectory, that of Wooburn, valued at £13. 13s. 4d., which belonged to the former. From roughly half of Cornwall the bishop of Exeter got £102 a year, consisting entirely of temporalities. Like the lay nobility members of the episcopacy were excepted from the proscription of provincial communities; their lands were scattered far and wide, and their interests tended to be national rather than local. An income of £3,500 raised the archbishop of Canterbury above the greatest lay magnates. Other prelates also enjoyed £1,000 a year or more, though like the baronage others were not nearly as rich; Rochester had to manage on £411 a year.[117]

A complete contrast, the parish clergy, with few exceptions, were men of modest means; the income of incumbents averaged around £10 a year. Their personal estates, as we have seen, placed the great majority on much the same footing as the peasant farmers among whom they lived and worked, and from whom for the most part they were sprung. Yet in the aggregate their wealth formed the largest single constituent of the possessions of the Church as a whole, in particular spiritualities with which they were characterisically endowed, whether as beneficed clerks, that is to say rectors and vicars, or parish priests and chaplains whose stipends were charged against livings.

These figures in Table 3.5 underline what has already been established respecting the state of the clergy. Three-quarters of all parish livings at the end of the Middle Ages yielded less than £15 a year, half less than £10; and with not a few worth under £7 many incumbents

Table 3.5 Values of secular benefices

		Number	Minimum £	Maximum £	Median £
Non-resident rectories	Buckinghamshire	121	$3\frac{1}{3}$	$46\frac{1}{3}$	$13\frac{1}{3}$
	Cornwall	74	4	80	16
	Norfolk	18	$4\frac{2}{3}$	$26\frac{2}{3}$	$11\frac{2}{3}$
	Rutland	26	$\frac{2}{3}$	49	12
	Worcestershire	29	$\frac{2}{3}$	32	9
Resident rectories	Buckinghamshire	52	$5\frac{1}{3}$	40	10
	Cornwall	20	2	55	10
	Norfolk	63	$4\frac{2}{3}$	$33\frac{1}{3}$	10
	Rutland	17	$3\frac{1}{3}$	22	10
	Worcestershire	12	$4\frac{1}{3}$	21	7
Vicarages	Buckinghamshire	68	$5\frac{1}{3}$	$40\frac{1}{3}$	8
	Cornwall	42	6	30	11
	Norfolk	47	$4\frac{1}{3}$	20	8
	Rutland	12	$5\frac{1}{3}$	$13\frac{1}{3}$	$7\frac{1}{3}$
	Worcestershire	15	$6\frac{2}{3}$	20	9

Notes

1 In Norfolk the values of many non-resident livings are not stated.

2 The value of Bradwell rectory (Bucks.) (which is counted as non-resident) is given as 6s. 8d.; the rector was the prior of Bradwell, who was also lord of the manor.

3 Pilton rectory (Rutland) is stated as 13s. 4d., but in 1535 it was £4. 17s. 2d.; (*VE*, iv, 343). The next higher is Stretton at 26s.; in 1535 it was £7. 17s. (*VE*, iv, 344).

4 A vicarage of Owlswick, Bucks., is assessed at £3. 6s. 8d., but this was a chapelry of Monks Risborough (Bod., MS Eng. Hist. e. 187, f. 44v).

endured a life of 'hardship and strain'.[118] The clergy of Buckinghamshire and Rutland were typical of Lincoln diocese, where the gross income of most parsons lay in the range £5–£15 (average £9. 8s. 6¾d.), and of vicars £5–£10.[119] As with personal wealth the extremes can be misleading. In Worcestershire the effective minimum for rectories held *in absentia* was £5; in Cornwall very few working parsons had less than £5. For Buckinghamshire vicarages, £20 a year was the effective maximum, and the median £8 was also the most frequent valuation. Some assessments were clearly eccentric. Stretton was valued at 26s., though taxed at £5 in 1526, while the wretched 13s. 4d. assigned to Pilton was one-eighth of its taxable value; in 1535 they were assessed at £4. 17s. 2d. and £7. 17s., respectively.[120] As previously remarked, higher levels of personal wealth in Cornwall and Worcestershire were related to more lucrative benefices, vicarages especially. Everywhere it is noticeable that the choicer livings tended to belong to absentee incumbents, irrespective of whether they were religious houses or secular clerks. This was only to be expected, since a poor rectory could not support a chaplain and leave a reasonable profit for the incumbent. The stipends of parish priests and chaplains covered a much narrower range. The rates, standardised as long ago as 1414, provided for a maximum of £5. 6s. 8d. if the cure of souls was involved, £4. 13s. 4d. if it was not; £6 might be paid by special episcopal licence. Stipends were halved if board was provided.[121] According to the musters the scale was rarely exceeded: nearly all chaplains in Rutland got between £5 and £6. In Norfolk, however, the discretionary higher rate was not uncommon, and was occasionally stretched to 10 marks or more, especially when there were several curates. Six men were classed as parish priests at Aylsham, of whom two got as much as £8, one £6, two £5. 6s. 8d., and one, possibly a probationer, nothing. The £8 men were unusually affluent, one having goods amounting to £10, the other £30, in addition to a house of his own and lands worth 20s. a year. It is conceivable that they augmented their incomes by acting as chaplains to guilds, of which there were more than 900 in Norfolk alone, many possessed of great wealth. As it happens only one was listed at Aylsham, dedicated to St Nicholas, and its stock of £3 was hardly exceptional.[122] Clerks who may have ranked as the senior curates of St Michael's and Holy Trinity, Coventry, were each paid £8 a year, the second man at the former getting 10 marks; but the great majority of the city's priests, including all at Bablake church, received the standard 8 marks.[123]

Here and there a clerk was assessed on temporalities, a few even paid the lay subsidy. The vicar of Felsted, Essex, was rated at £2 for land 'purchasyd', presumably as an investment; other parcels, most of which were relatively small, could have been inherited. As private property they rendered their owners liable to assessment on the same terms as lay proprietors. Their presence makes the temporalities of secular clergy an ill-assorted medley. A rare exception, which bridges the gap between these small properties and the great estates of prelates, was the lordship of the manor of Walton in Aylesbury, worth £21 a year, which belonged to an obscure clergyman named William Frankleyne.[124]

A residue of temporalities is collected for convenience under the heading 'chantries and guilds'. Essentially the class defined by the 1547 act suppressing these institutions,[125] they comprise a miscellany dedicated to purposes which can be described as fulfilling the needs and aspirations of the laity. Here too anomalies creep in. The college at Manton was, as we have seen, indistinguishable from the rectory, and for this reason we have followed the survey and classed its endowments as spiritualities. An entry dealing with land – presumably temporal – held by the rector is indeed left blank. Chantry property included land, rent charges and annuities; objects such as obits and lights were funded almost entirely from the two latter sources. Although the assets of parish guilds consisted for the most part of common stocks, a few included landed endowments as well. The fraternity of St Rumwold at Buckingham owned property in seven separate places, producing upwards of £44 a year. In contrast the income of the village fraternity of St Katherine, North Crawley, was limited to 40s. (Because they were exempted from the confiscation of guild property, the holdings of the London Mercers there, totalling £30, are classed as lay-owned.) Among a few miscellaneous entries the commonest are those attributing a parcel to 'the (parish) church', as at Rushock, Worcs., where Elmley Lovett church owned one valued at 4s. 4d. Alternatively the tenants might be defined as the churchwardens or, as at Bisley, Gloucs., 'the keepers' of Rodborough chapel.[126] Few in number, such small endowments, which rarely exceeded a pound or so, were probably dedicated to maintenance and running costs. Only in Buckinghamshire does anything resembling a comprehensive survey of chantry property seem to have been attempted. In Cornwall the subject was virtually ignored, unless we are to infer that some of the apparently supernumerary chaplains listed in a good many parishes were in reality cantarists. Any uncertainty as to their status comes as less of a surprise when it is recalled how many chantry certificates state categorically that the chaplain is the only priest in a parish; doubtless there were absentee parsons who grasped the opportunity to avoid the cost of a substitute. In the two Midland shires chantries owned at most between 1 and 3 per cent of ecclesiastical property, and hence a negligible proportion of all land. The priest, as at Clipsham or Kidderminster, generally received a stipend of the order of £5 a year, though at Salwarpe, Worcs., it was as little as 38s. 6d.; the endowment of the chantry at Ford in the parish of Dinton, Bucks., was 5 marks.[127]

A by-product of the military survey is the light it sheds on the state of the ministry. An acute problem, which is difficult to measure precisely, was the practice of non-residence, especially on the part of parsons who sought advancement in the service of the king and other exalted personages,[128] delegating the cure of souls to stipendiary priests, and even neglecting their parishes altogether. The full impact can safely be estimated only in Rutland, where no fewer than eleven out of fifty-one churches and chapels were deprived of ministers. Although Margaret Bowker has reckoned that the incumbents of fully 25 per cent of the parishes of Lincoln diocese were absentees, she claims that the great care taken to ensure that deputies were provided made cases of outright neglect rare.[129] The case rests on the clerical subsidy of 1526, according to which almost every church in Rutland deanery had a minister of some sort. Apparent instances of deprivation are attributed speculatively to temporary vacancies; this, however, is demonstrable only in the case of Tickencote, where a new parson had been instituted by 1526. She argues further that Braunston and Tixover were only chapelries, but overlooks Barrow and Essendine where, significantly, the pay offered was only 7 marks, the rate set for a chaplaincy without cure of souls. The curacy of the parish church of Greetham, which was worth only £4 per annum, was also vacant. The incidence of unserved daughter churches points to the conclusion that they were prime targets for economies. Barrow, a hamlet of Cottesmore, was small and poor; not only did it have no priest in either 1522 or 1526, the chapel itself could already have been falling into disuse: it was destroyed by 1660.[130] On each of these occasions the rector of Cottesmore was in fact in residence, and could conceivably have claimed to serve the hamlet from the parish church. The exposure in detail of the abuse could have led to pressure being brought to bear on incumbents either to resume residence or to appoint substitutes; hence it is arguable that the 1526 subsidy reflects the results. Nonetheless, to hire a curate was one thing, to see that he performed his duties conscientiously another. It is of some interest that in the four parishes of Ashwell, North and South Luffenham and Preston the taxman denied the parsons any relief in respect of the stipends they claimed to be paying, very possibly to penalise them for the absence of their subordinates, who were themselves certainly taxed. Parson Alcock of Pilton, who was absent from his post at the taking of the musters, looks to have been prevailed upon to resume his duties by 1526. What day-to-day arrangements were made for these neglected congregations it is impossible to surmise. Edith Weston, Wing and Whitwell – the last a tiny village – each enjoyed the ministrations of a resident rector and curate; in Oakham there was a parish priest, two assistants and the chaplain of James Waren, a gentleman and Merchant of the Staple, who was the principal inhabitant of the town.[131] Some of these might have held services in unstaffed churches.

Closely allied to non-residence was the problem of pluralism. Although normally signifying the tenure of two or more benefices, there is no compelling reason why it should not on occasion indicate an unsupervised chaplain contriving to occupy more than one post. Certainly it is not surprising to find William Elys, an assistant priest at Buckingham, serving as chaplain of Bourton, a hamlet in the same parish. The curate of Essendine in 1526, a man named Thomas Sommer, could also have been the parish priest of Barkby, Leics., which lay not many miles away. As vicar of Duston near Sleaford and master of St Leonard's Hospital in Northampton, William Borowe, the incumbent, couldn't have had much time to check on his subordinate's comings and goings. The inference that we are dealing with the same two men in every case rests on the fact that their names occur with below average frequency. Commonplace ones makes cases of pluralism extremely difficult to detect: the chantry priest of Barrowden, the rectors of Husbands Bosworth and Glooston, Leics., and the curates of St Peter's, Northampton, and Yelling in Huntingdonshire, were all called Thomas Clarke. Of the eighty-seven taxed in Rutland in 1526 at least eleven can be identified with some assurance as pluralists through being the possessors of fairly distinctive names or (in four cases) a master's degree, including Richard Parker, prebendary of Stow in Lincoln Cathedral, who had lately been preferred to the mastership of the college at Manton. Though the number of MAs presented to livings was on the increase – from 3½ per cent in 1495 to 11½ per cent by 1520 – they remained a minority.[132] With Robert Hodgkynson, rector of both Wardley in Rutland and Stonton Wyville, Leics., the problem is largely resolved by the fact that the same man was lord of both villages.[133] Inclusive of marginal cases the incidence of pluralism might have been as high as between 17 and 19½ per cent: Mrs Bowker has noted that most cases of non-residence were due to this cause.[134] Among the forty-three incumbents in Rutland the percentage lies somewhere between 20 and 40; greater precision eludes us.

In Rutland no churches were held in plurality with others in the same deanery. Barrow was annexed to Cottesmore. The 'Custos' of the chapel of the deserted hamlet of Horn was the vicar of Empingham, and the depopulated parish of Martinsthorpe was evidently a sinecure. Few clergy held more than one benefice within Buckinghamshire. William Hands was vicar of both Langley Marish and Wraysbury, two parishes a short distance apart, but the only flagrant pluralist was Thomas Jakeman, rector of Aston Clinton and vicar of Buckland, Bierton and Stoke Mandeville, an arc of parishes round Aylesbury, worth in all £43. 6s. 9d. This should perhaps be regarded as a gross figure since neither of the two curates he employed was assessed for a stipend. Buckland had no priest in 1522 and was ignored in 1526; located a bare mile from Aston, it could have been served by the vicar in person. If appearances demanded that pluralities should not as a rule be held in the same deanery, Jakeman must have been an insensitive fellow, for, these few examples apart, some such convention does seem to have been observed.

The economics of pluralism form a complex subject. Buckland and Stoke Mandeville were poor livings worth £5 and 10 marks, respectively, Bierton being rated at £8. According to the *Valor* Aston was worth as much as £23. 6s. 9d., but for the subsidy it was assessed at £18 gross, and as little as £9. 5s. 5d. net. With Bierton similarly reduced to 45s., Jakeman's true income might not have exceeded £20. Langley (omitted from the subsidy) and Wraysbury combined yielded £30, the united livings of Cottesmore and Barrow £22. Need cannot have been the sole motive for pluralism, for a considerable number of poor livings were held in singularity. Nor is Mrs Bowker's theory that it resulted from the number of ordinands falling well short of the number of vacancies[135] wholly convincing; indeed, it is numerically unsound, since it fails to take into account the large number of unbeneficed clerks who must have been on the lookout for preferment but evidently were unable to get it. Deeper causes must have been at work, as when the absentee parson of North Luffenham, Richard Stokesley, appoints his brother John executor of his will shortly before his death in 1526, and a few short months later it is none other than one John Stokesley, MA, who pays the clerical tax there.[136] The sober truth is that more often than not the choicer livings were held by absentees, leaving the poorer ones to working parsons. In Rutland the median income of non-resident priests was some 40 per cent greater than that of residents - £14 compared with £10. Elsewhere the two types tended to be somewhat less sharply differentiated, though in Cornwall the corresponding figures were £20 and £10, respectively. In Buckinghamshire, where there are grounds for suspecting that the shortcomings of the record tend to exaggerate the degree of absenteeism to the point where it affected more than half the beneficed clergy, the differential appears less pronounced – £12 as against £10 – while rectories impropriated to monasteries averaged £13. Observing no distinction between residents and absentees, the subsidy roll provides no corrective. Finally, it cannot have been entirely a coincidence that the Reformation took root soonest and flowered most vigorously in the eastern counties where so many parishes were deprived of pastoral care, dependent at best on the services of an itinerant priest[137] or the accident of having a cantarist. In Cornwall, on the contrary, there was at least one priest resident in every parish, and it can be no mere coincidence that it was here that the people, led (it was alleged) by their pastors,[138] were to take up arms in 1549 in defence of the ancient faith.

Ecclesiastical foundations drew their revenues from a combination of spiritualities, including both rectories and pensions charged on benefices, and temporalities ranging from whole manors – 'fat' and otherwise – down to small tenements, annuities and rent charges. Incomes of £2,000 a year and more placed the richest abbots on an equal footing with the higher nobility. At the bottom of the scale some 9 per cent of monasteries got by on less than £20; eight nuns at Fosse, Lincs., existed on £7. 3s. 6d. net, while the only income that can be traced for St Katherine's Hospital in the impoverished town of New Shoreham is £1. 6s. 8d. The median of 654 monasteries, exclusive of friaries, hospitals and houses suppressed by Wolsey, was less than £160.[139] Monastic wealth has formed the subject of intense scrutiny with results that in the final analysis remain inconclusive. In the present context attention focuses rather on the ranking of religious houses in the hierarchy of landowners. Taken as a whole they would appear to have owned between two- and three-fifths of the revenues of the Church, according to locality. A preliminary note of caution must be struck. The districts which show the highest levels, namely Berkshire and the Gloucestershire Cotswolds, are two where the record of land values is not entirely satisfactory. Apart from these possibly overweighted examples, the range lies rather between 40 and 50 per cent, slightly more in Buckinghamshire where the possessions of Oxford Colleges, aggregating upwards of £240, helped to inflate the total, but disproportionately low in the restricted area of Rutland where it failed to reach as much as one-third. Savine computed the net value of monastic income, narrowly defined, as £136,362, a sum which colleges, friaries and so forth might have raised to a round £150,000; Knowles plumped for £165,000 to take account of establishments of every type as well as houses omitted from the *Valor*.[140] These estimates form, respectively, 46.9 and 51.7 per cent of the possible grand total of £320,180.

Their share of gross landed wealth was distinctly more uniform, generally of the order of 15–20 percent, though slightly greater in the problem areas, yet even there not far outside this range. Of greater significance is the position of ecclesiastical corporations as landlords, and hence the amount of land that was to change hands in the course of the next few years. Allowing for cases of special difficulty this was remarkably constant, irrespective of district. In Rutland their total share was well below average in any case, but in Cornwall, although owning just over 15 per cent of all property, two-thirds of their revenues (totalling £1,221) took the form of spiritualities; moreover, since the sample covers those parts of the county where the chief houses – Bodmin, Glasney, Launceston and St Germans – were situated, the figures could well prove to have been biassed in their favour. In Buckinghamshire temporalities formed a clear two-thirds, a proportion that was very nearly matched in Rutland too. And if it was only in Worcestershire that they attained the four-fifths estimated by Savine – actually 86.3 per cent – this is not unexpected in view of the fact that the most recent authority puts it no higher than three-quarters.[141] Once again the somewhat less convincing Berkshire and Gloucestershire figures point towards a higher ratio, but here allowance has to be made for ambiguous entries such as that relating to the dean of Windsor's liberty at Wantage which reads, 'The Dean Lord and Parson'. A similar confusion occurs at Hawkesbury, where the abbot of Pershore was assessed as lord at £124, a sum that must have comprehended the rectory since the other clerical entries were those relating only to the vicar and several curates. The prior of Tickford, Bucks., was assessed at £16 as parson of Chicheley 'et pro aliis terris ibidem' when the value of the rectory alone was £8. Nor are lacunae wanting: the Greyfriars of Aylesbury, for instance, had a net income of £3. 12s. 5d., which is wholly ignored. Fortunately the estates of small establishments of this class were neither extensive nor of great value. The hospital of St John at High Wycombe had a revenue of just £10, in lay terms equivalent to the income of a minor gentleman.[142]

There is little in the make-up of monastic estates that calls for comment. The possessions of some great houses lay dispersed around several counties. Westminster Abbey owned the rectory and a manor in Oakham, and four manors plus several small parcels in Buckinghamshire; Rochester cathedral priory held a large and profitable block in the country between Aylesbury and Thame. Yet as often as not, the nucleus was concentrated within easy reach: all but two Winchcombe manors were situated in Gloucestershire, and, like the abbey itself, in the Cotswold district.[143] The logic of estate geography points to the conclusion that, in their formative phases at least, monasteries had in a very real sense served as foci and expressions of local aspirations. The most pronounced manifestation of this occurs in relation to the smallest houses. The lands of Medmenham Abbey and Little Marlow and Snelshall priories, each of which was worth only about £20 a year, were situated wholly in Buckinghamshire. Lavendon, with £80 per annum, had 80 per cent of its property there. So too did Tickford Priory; a good four-fifths of its endowments of £115 per annum formed a compact block in the adjoining parishes of Newport Pagnell and Chicheley, other than which there were only trifling pensions payable from half a dozen nearby parishes. All it owned outside Buckinghamshire was the parsonage of Aston near Birmingham. Of the two biggest houses in

Buckinghamshire, nearly four-fifths of Missenden Abbey's £261 accrued inside the shire, all but a negligible sum from places in and around the Chiltern Hills. Much of the remainder came from Hertfordshire and Middlesex and may be counted as part of the nucleus. Woburn Abbey, just inside Bedfordshire, drew £165 a year from Buckinghamshire, all its properties, with the exception of Chesham rectory, lying not more than ten miles from the house itself. Notley Abbey was something of an exception. At £437 per annum the richest of the local monasteries, nearly half its possessions lay dispersed across eight other counties, from Lincolnshire to Wiltshire. It was further atypical in that more than half took the form of spiritualities, although in Buckinghamshire the temporalities were almost equal in value. Spiritualities contributed about a third of the incomes of most other foundations. Notley, nevertheless, retained its essential character as a local institution, with half its Buckinghamshire holdings, including the only two manors, located in a handful of parishes just west of Aylesbury.[144]

THE LAITY

Discussion of the landed wealth of the laity hinges primarily on the question of its social distribution. Lay landowners comprised all sorts and conditions of men, from the nobility and gentry, who owned most of the soil, through yeoman freeholders (including a variable sprinkling of husbandmen) down to cottagers and even the occasional labourer. In addition there were a good many town dwellers, although it is not certain that the majority of these owned more than the houses they lived in. In two counties the different groupings can be isolated with tolerable assurance: Rutland, where status is defined with reasonable consistency, and Buckinghamshire as the result of a detailed analysis. Subject to the limitations mentioned above, the structure of ownership in Berkshire and Gloucestershire can also be reviewed, although some of the data relating to the latter are less than clear cut. Everywhere, however, the line of demarcation between the gentry and others remains tentative. An assessment of £5 will serve as a rough yardstick, but there must have been more than a few instances in which the absentee owners of tiny parcels were in fact gentlemen, though not so described. The status of the Buckinghamshire man Thomas Redmond, a resident of Oving and owner of a 20s. holding in North Marston, is shown only in the subsidy

Table 3.6 Lay landownership

	Buckingham £	Rutland £	Berkshire £	Gloucester £
Total value	15,359	2,980	5,418	15,534
Total lay-owned land*	9,744	1,937	2,723	7,557
Peers	599	35	381	589
Gentry	5,402	1,050	1,600	5,153
Others	3,029	127	450	1,113
	Percentages			
Peers of all land	3.9	1.2	7.0	3.8
of lay-owned land	6.2	1.8	14.0	7.8
Gentry of all land	34.8	35.2	29.5	32.3
of lay-owned land	54.4	54.2	58.8	68.2
Others of all land	19.5	4.3	8.3	7.2
of lay-owned land	31.1	6.6	16.5	14.7

* Including Crown lands.

roll, which here, fortunately, is available for cross-checking. Examples of men of rank owning very small properties abound, such as one worth £1 at Frilsham, Berks., belonging to a gentleman named Basset, or another of only 2s. 6d. owned by Lord Audley at Loveston.[145] No satisfactory apportionment between gentlemen and others is feasible as regards Cornwall, while the scope of the Worcestershire muster is limited by its fragmentary nature. In Cornwall peers held 4.7 per cent of all land and 7.8 per cent of lay property; in Worcestershire little more than 2 per cent.

The figures assembled in Table 3.6 emphasise the fundamental division of society into the small class which owned much the greater part of the land and the mass of small proprietors who shared what was left. In some respects the picture tends to be contradictory. In the aggregate the sheer quantity held by farmers, smallholders and townsfolk in, for example, Buckinghamshire must be regarded as impressive, amply justifying the contemporary stereotype of a nation of small owner occupiers; but since there were twenty of them for every gentleman, individual shares were correspondingly modest.

There is not a great deal to add to recent work on the temporal nobility. Peers were not returned in the muster certificates as members of the county community, and consequently feature only in the role of absentee landlords; in the subsidy they were assessed separately. Prior to the evolution of a Parliamentary peerage in the fifteenth century the distinction between the baronage and the untitled gentry was tenuous,[146] and it remained a subtle one as late as the 1520s. Both lived 'for the most part on the yearly revennewes of the landes and fees given them by the kinge', as the *Discourse* put it.[147] Nor is it necessary to look far for commentators who regarded them as subdivisions of a single class. In Edmund Dudley's eyes they were equally members of the 'chivalry'; to Sir Thomas Smith they formed the 'greater' and 'lesser' gentry.[148] Had the peerage formed a closed caste the position would have been straightforward, but it did not. The writ of summons to the House of Lords had not yet acquired the character of a hereditary right; noblemen who were unable, through poverty, to maintain their status, were quietly dropped from the list, though eligible for reinstatement once their fortunes revived. In this way the Lords Clinton were excluded from parliament between 1460 and 1514, and the earls of Kent between 1523 and 1572.[149] The personnel of the upper house was never static; as fast as peerages were extinguished by natural processes or the hazards of politics they were replaced,[150] in most cases by recruits from the ranks of the non-titled gentry. Some earned promotion by meritorious service to the Crown: Thomas Cromwell furnishes the outstanding example, as well as being one of the few whose origins were genuinely lowly. A few men like Charles Brandon, duke of Suffolk, Henry VIII's friend and brother-in-law, simply happened to enjoy royal favour.

If the combined wealth of the peerage appears unimpressive there are conditioning factors to be borne in mind. In the first place their numbers were not large, remaining, with fluctuations, fairly constant around fifty. Secondly, before the Reformation the lords spiritual not only equalled the lay aristocracy in terms of numbers, but differed little from them in the economic role. Like the baronage the bishops and the mitred abbots were all great landed magnates. The backlog in recruitment that was to become a marked feature of the last years of Elizabeth I was intensified by the growth of population and wealth in the interim, while the dissolution of the monasteries had removed the twenty-eight mitred abbots from the stage. The effect of these changes on the possessions of the peerage as a whole lies outside the scope of the present work; in a single county and in the short term it would of course depend on how much property any of the persons in question happened to own there. The attainder of the duke of Buckingham in 1521 had reduced the peerage's stake in Rutland from a handsome 15.1 per cent (at least) to a negligible 2½ per cent or thereabouts.[151] Conversely the elevation of Sir Henry Marney and Sir Nicholas Vaux in 1523 added £165 to the total in Buckinghamshire, augmenting it by more than a quarter; yet so substantial was the wealth of the untitled gentry, the proportion owned by them slipped only marginally from 35.7 per cent to 34.6. Lord Zouche, one of the lesser barons, assessed at 500 marks, had relatively small estates in each county, about £43 in Buckinghamshire and £12 in Rutland. In western Berkshire, noblemen, with £381, accounted for 15.7 per cent of the land of the laity. Nearly half of this (£178) belonged to the Duke of Suffolk, who had been ennobled as recently as 1513; the earl of Devon, executed for treason in 1538, had £21. Technically too the situation was affected by wardship. The fourteen-year-old earl of Derby owned the rich manor of Ardington, the profits of which, £70 a year, accrued to the royal treasury for the time being.[152]

These reservations must not be allowed to obscure the fact that individually most of the nobility were men of great wealth. First among the thirty-four who were assessed on their landed incomes in 1524[153] stood the earl of Northumberland with £2,920 a year, and although at the lower end of the scale seven of them had less than £300 apiece, a full half were worth £800 or more. Several of the poor ones were northerners, including the earl of Westmorland and Lord Greystoke, assessed at a mere £40 each. The list omits several of the wealthiest. The duke of Norfolk was taxed on personal estate of £4,000; his income was at least £2,800,[154] and in 1534 the Howard estates were assessed at 5,000 marks. The earl of Derby left his infant son £2,903 per annum in 1522, which of course was held in wardship by the Crown for the time being. Only four peers were rated at more than £2,000 a year, with the earl of Worcester making a possible fifth since his goods were taxed at £2,000. No one else exceeded £1,400, the point at which the earl of Shrewsbury was assessed. At the bottom of the list Lord Montague was exempted on grounds of poverty. Some, perhaps all, of these fortunes were underassessed, though not outrageously so. The earl of Arundel's true income was computed at £2,207 in 1524 compared with £1,820. 13s. 4d. on which it was taxed ten years later. In his day the greatest of the magnates, Buckingham, had enjoyed a total income of £6,045; the net £4,906 to which sundry reprises had reduced it may afford some clue as to how it might have been assessed had he survived. And of course there must always have been families going through difficult patches – even the Percys, whose revenues had fallen substantially during the preceding century and did not show much change until the later 1530s.[155]

The straitened circumstances of a few peers meant that they were overlapped by the richer gentry; indeed, two courtiers were assessed at no less than £1,100 apiece. But although this may be regarded as symptomatic of a closing of the gap between the two orders, it can all too easily be exaggerated; nothing can be gained by seeking to reopen the debate on the rise of the gentry at the expense of the titular aristocracy here. Certainly the incomes of the nobility still covered much the same range as in 1436, at best no more than marginally higher. With the gentry, in contrast, anything in excess of £200 a year had been quite exceptional in the fifteenth century; for practical purposes it had marked the boundary between the two orders.[156] By the 1520s there were already knights and squires who could vie with the baronage, having to all intents and purposes become magnates themselves, inferior only in the power and influence they were able to wield – or maybe in the will to do so.[157] A Northamptonshire knight, Sir Nicholas Vaux, had an income of £719 to which enclosure and depopulation perpetrated in north Buckinghamshire had contributed.[158] In Suffolk alone might be found three with £400 a year, with as many more who must have owned broad acres that lay concealed behind assessments made on goods.

This trend was nevertheless contained within relatively narrow limits. Very rich commoners were not really numerous; they were predominantly courtiers, and in several cases already on the threshold of the peerage. Of the two £1,100 courtiers, Sir Thomas Boleyn was shortly to be elevated; Sir William Compton was passed over for some reason, though well able to support a title on an income that was actually £1,655 – advancement was to elude the family for a further fifty years. A long record of service to the monarch carried much weight. Even among the ranks of the remaining members of the royal household only the treasurer and the comptroller had more than £500, and were in fact, in common with several others, assessed on personal estate. In practical terms there was a well defined cut-off point in the region of £300–£400, a figure that was less than the income of all but a minority of more or less impoverished noblemen.[159] And even this level was comparatively rarely attained. Outside court circles anything in excess of £200 remained exceptional; in some small counties it might not be reached by anyone at all. Moreover, of the two Sussex knights who declared incomes upwards of £400, only Sir Roger Lewkenor could be called truly provincial; Sir David Owen, the other, was primarily a courtier.[160]

Whether styled knights, esquires or plain gentlemen, the gentry already by a wide margin possessed the greatest share of the land, including well over half of what did not belong to the Church. In contrast to the nobility, sheer weight of numbers ensured their pre-eminence. In Sussex, where, unusually, three or four peers were assessed, there were 130 or more, and in tiny Rutland alone 35. Individually their estates were usually moderate in size, although covering a very wide range; many were quite small. Estimates of their incomes have for the most part to be drawn from the subsidy rolls, since the muster books do not, as a general rule, state totals; consequently the recorded figures have to be regarded as minima. However, contemporary feodary surveys, executed when estates were taken in wardship, afford an alternative and presumably more realistic statement (see Table 3.7).

Since in nearly every case the feodary surveys and the assessments related to completely different men, they are perhaps not entirely comparable. Nonetheless three separate cases provide strong evidence

Table 3.7 Incomes of the gentry

	County	Number	Minimum £	Maximum £	Median £
Knights	Sussex	8	50	460	120
	Suffolk	12	20	400	130
	Buckinghamshire	3	48	200	160
	Feodary surveys	18	54	1,655	204
Esquires	Sussex	17	5	180	50
	Suffolk	27	20	200	50
	Buckinghamshire	13	9	120	67
	Rutland	6	31	120	64
	Cornwall	13	20	133	60
	Feodary surveys	124	10	618	80
Gentlemen	Sussex	39	2	67	15
	Suffolk	41	2	80	13
	Buckinghamshire	28	2	160	18
	Rutland	8	5	42	12
	Cornwall	13	6	30	11
	Feodary surveys	42	5	29	17

that assessments could be too small by a third or more. Sir William Compton was taxed on £1,100 against an income of £1,655; Roger Flower, a Rutland squire, and Thomas Tyringham of Tyringham, Bucks., who were both assessed at £85, had incomes of £103 and £146, respectively. There could of course have been valid explanations of these discrepancies. With Sir Roger Lewkenor the situation was reversed: the feodary could only account for £344 of the £460 at which he was assessed, though this was many years later in 1545.[161]

In contrast with the peerage, rank and wealth interacted to a greater degree than a summary statement is capable of demonstrating. According to the feodary surveys the largest estate owned by a mere gentleman was well below the median value for esquires, while three-quarters got along on £20 a year or less. This serves as a corrective to the fiscal record which displays a marked ambivalence with regard to status, frequently writing off as a gentleman a man who was really of higher rank. Such was the treatment accorded to Robert Dormer of Wing, who was one of the richest Buckinghamshire landowners with £160, to say nothing of goods appraised at 700 marks. Although not yet a justice of the peace, he served as sheriff in 1522 and a subsidy commissioner in 1524, and was well on the way to an eventual knighthood and a leading place in the county hierarchy. A relative newcomer with a mercantile background, he evidently encountered a certain reluctance among the local community to accord him the deference to which wealth entitled him. Extremely fine distinctions might be drawn. Not only did the esquire differ from the mere gentleman in quartering his arms, the nucleus of his estate was likely to be a manorial lordship, probably held in chief of the king. The limited number of gentlemen subjected to wardship shows that these lesser proprietors were not typically tenants-in-chief, but rather a comparatively recently formed class of men who assembled small estates out of mesne tenancies.[162] And in the crudest material terms the average esquire had five times the income of the average gentleman.

In essence the comparatively small number of provincial knights were esquires writ large, owning estates that were similar in composition and between two and three times as large on average. A clear majority of esquires possessed the official qualification for knighthood of £40 a year, though it is clear that few were prepared to undertake it on less than £100, while the feodary surveys place the average at double that figure. In fact the median assessment of all knights featured in the table was £180, and the account for the anticipation in Norfolk yields the same average.[163] The similarities between knights and esquires are emphasised when allowance is made for the fact that the average for the latter is depressed by the inclusion of a number of men whose incomes were very low. These for the most part were cadets of wealthy and important families, such as John Waldegrave, Esq., of Bures, who had only £8 a year while his father, Sir William, was assessed at 400 marks, or in Sussex John Ashburnham with £10 compared with his father's £100.[164] By concentrating on full-sized estates the feodary surveys present a much more realistic picture.

All told the gentry, though forming at most 1 or 2 per cent of the population, possessed more than a third of the land; with the holdings of the aristocracy thrown in, it was probably as much as 40 per cent, and if spiritualities are discounted they must already have controlled at least a half, and possibly two-thirds of the soil.

By common consent the measure of a yeoman was the ability to 'dispend of his owne free lande in yearly reuenue to the summe of xl.s. sterling':[165] a 40s. freeholder in short. This contained a solid kernel of truth, yet although primacy among humbler proprietors belonged clearly to the yeomanry, the situation was far more complex. Half the yeomen of Rutland owned no land at all. Nevertheless, the median for those who did was precisely £2, and even though the minimum was as low as 12s. and holdings as large as £5 exceptional, the maximum reached no less than £8. Half a dozen husbandmen, though their lands were valued at less than 40s., might also be deemed yeomen on the basis of goods worth upwards of £20. Several more particularly affluent husbandmen owned personal property – up to £50 – sufficient to put them well inside the yeomanry range, but they were not freeholders and for this reason may not have laid claim to higher status. In Babergh, where small landowners were much more numerous, a full four-fifths of the yeomanry were freeholders with assessments from 6s. 8d. to £6; the median, though, was appreciably lower at 28s.

That even as few as half the yeomanry ranked as freeholders sufficed to lend them a distinctive character, for in marked contrast to them few of the thousands of husbandmen, who formed the nucleus of rural society, indeed of the nation, did so. In Rutland they added up to a meagre 7½ per cent, worth for the greater part between 2s. 4d. and 40s., with one placed as high as £4. Put another way, the yeoman's average was the husbandman's maximum, except in certain rare, ambiguous cases. Similarly the husbandman's median of 12s. was identical with the yeoman's minimum. In Suffolk, although a good 40 per cent of the husbandmen had land of their own, the situation was not dissimilar; the median works out at 13s. 4d., and there were a couple of men owning £3 and £4, respectively, who again could be classed as yeomen on the basis of their goods. Compared with Rutland classification was less thorough, and there were a good many other men, landowners included, who must have ranked as husbandmen; judged by their goods it looks improbable that any yeomen were missed. Some could even have been labourers, for nearly 7 per cent of those so designated held land, a phenomenon that was almost unknown in Rutland. The grounds on which they were classed as labourers are obscure, for not only were their holdings comparable with those of husbandmen, ranging from 4s. through a median of 12s. 8d. up to 20s., their goods were valued at anything up to £5. Nor are other anomalies wanting, such as the Morcot husbandman who, though possessed of a £6 estate, could not raise more than £5 in moveables, or four so-called yeomen of Belton assessed at £2–£8 who can hardly have owned anything more than a cottage apiece since their holdings were worth less than 10s. a year.[166]

The diffusion of property among the mercantile and industrial population would seem on the whole to have been governed principally by regional conditions. In rural Suffolk there was a marked preponderance of farmers and clothiers among landowners; the overwhelming majority of artificers occupied rented accommodation. In towns incidence varied greatly. More than a third of the listed inhabitants of Sudbury were assessed on hereditaments, and well over half in Great Yarmouth including nearly everybody of any substance. Over a quarter of the people of High Wycombe (including the rural parish) may have been proprietors, though the schedule is ambiguous in places, and some of the sixty-two persons in question look like non-residents. Elsewhere the proportion tended to be very much smaller, less than one in eight at Newbury, well under 10 per cent in Tewkesbury and Wotton-under-Edge, Gloucestershire, and only five out of ninety at Skipton in Yorkshire, exclusive of Lord Clifford, who was of course a big landowner. To all appearances there were very few at Bodmin and other Cornish towns, though here we are confronted with the problem of long lists of landowners who cannot be linked with any of the inhabitants. Oakham, despite being the county town of Rutland, remained a manor without burghal institutions. Only three men, less than 3 per cent of the inhabitants, owned any property of their own, two being the principal residents there, a gentleman and a yeoman-cum-pewterer. This was closely paralleled at Coventry, capital of the Midlands, where only 63 out of 1,335 persons were registered as 'dwellyng in his owne'. Judged by the values assigned to them, no more than a couple of pounds except in rare instances, the majority of these properties cannot have amounted to more than a house or cottage, normally, perhaps, the one in which the owner resided. This certificate alone gives any idea of the intricacies of urban housing. Of the two richest citizens, Richard Marler was in the property business to the extent of letting out forty-six tenements, and was assessed at £40 for lands; the other, Julian Nethermill (who had no land assessment), owned just one property let for £2 a year. Interestingly, both rented the houses they lived in, the former from the wardens of the city for £4. 13*d*. 4*d*., the latter from the Trinity Guild for £4. 6*s*. 8*d*. Thomas Towley, another considerable landlord, owned fifteen houses, which brought in £13. 10*s*. 8*d*. per annum, and must have had other parcels elsewhere to raise his land assessment to £20. In marked contrast to the others, with their four-figure assessments, his goods were valued at £60. Few residents figured as major property owners; much belonged to outsiders, including several Londoners, while three tenements were owned by William Pulteney, an inhabitant of the foreign hamlet of Radford. But corporate owners formed by far the most important group, headed by the cathedral priory and the wealthy Trinity and Corpus Christi guilds, landlords to more than half the city. On paper they also took half the rents, although in 1522 these were in nearly every case remitted in consideration of the poverty of most of the population.[167]

The compactness of Rutland allied with the intrinsic quality of the data allows a detailed analysis of its landholders. Out of 1,433 lay inhabitants, which the subsidy augments to some 2,000, 154 owned land there to the value of £700, with a median holding of 20*s*.; non-residents, who totalled fifty-six, held an estimated £512, with a median of 46*s*. Inclusive of the possessions of king and Church far less than half the land belonged to the people who lived on it and worked it: only about one Raddleman in twenty owned so much as a cottage. Of the resident freeholders thirty-four ranked as gentry, including one lady, Isabel Conyers 'Gentilwoman' and widow, and one other whose status is confirmed by lands worth £10. 13*s*. 4*d*. This handful shared revenues of upwards of £494, leaving a mere £206 to go round 118 yeomen and husbandmen.[168] In most townships there were not more than one or two freeholders to be found, and in some like Stretton and Teigh not even that. Almost half lived in Wrandike hundred, where twenty-eight out of seventy-one were concentrated in the two villages of Liddington and North Luffenham. This might conceivably be ascribed to local custom of the Welland valley, especially since Ketton, also on the riverside, contained nine of the twenty-three freeholders of East hundred. In these three parishes they amounted to a quarter of all persons listed in the survey, indeed to well over a third at North Luffenham. Disregarding the labourers and the poor naturally makes the proportions much higher: at Ketton eight out of twenty-two farmers owned land worth anything from 2*s.* to £5. Whether their holdings were accurately represented is less certain. Most can be regarded as owner-occupiers, though two create problems. On the face of it John Oxon, yeoman, occupied no other land since he was not described as anybody's tenant; his assessment of 40*s.* presumably incorporated the rent paid by his own tenant, Thomas Porter, labourer, yet he must have farmed a considerable acreage to be able to declare goods worth £20. Henry Bretten, worth £12 in personal estate, owned land valued at 46*s.*, which must almost certainly have comprised the rents paid by his two tenants, one of whom was another husbandman with £10 in goods. Unless, as tenant to one of the absentee proprietors, he himself farmed rented land, he might not have been a freeholder but the occupier of a large holding part of which was sublet.[169] Some men, of course, held land in parishes other than where they were domiciled, although this cannot always be established with certainty unless the person in question had the status of gentleman or a name distinctive enough to leave little room for doubt as to his identity, like, for example, Christopher Webster, of Ridlington, where he had no property, who was clearly the owner of a 4*s.* parcel in Belton.[170] Important though it is to be able to determine precisely how many of the inhabitants of the county had land within its borders, the problem is not a major one. The weight of evidence indicates that the smallest proprietors rarely held land in more than one parish, and thus the risk of underestimating the wealth of any of them is minimal. A county resident who did not live where his land was situated was still an absentee proprietor in the context of the parish. Conversely two distinct individuals can be mistaken for one if they bear the same commonplace name. Fortunately only eighteen definitely had land in two or more townships, and most of them were gentry.

Bigger counties than Rutland, containing proportionately more proprietors, respond less readily to the same treatment, for it is difficult to

Table 3.8 Gloucestershire landholdings

| Region | Residents | | | | | | Non-residents | | | | | |
	No.	Minimum s d	Maximum £	Median £ s d			No.	Minimum s d	Maximum £	Median £ s d		
Cotswolds	166	2 0	200	1 6 8			344	1 0	109	1 0 0		
Vale	254	1 6	93	1 6 8			187	2 0	168	2 6 0		
Forest	381	1 8	78	1 0 0			58	2 4	66	1 6 8		

establish definite links between putative owners and properties located in parishes other than where they resided. Nevertheless, in view of the sharply contrasted character of its three regions, the attempt is worth making in the case of Gloucestershire, even at the risk of exaggerating the number of small estates, and in the absence of data for the county town and one large hundred (see Table 3.8). Not every multiple holding, of course, was confined to a single region,[171] but since most were sited preponderantly in one or other the underlying pattern is sufficiently clear. Peasant proprietorship was deeply rooted in all parts, and, with the exception of absentee owners in the Vale, three-quarters of all holdings were worth £3 or less. Maxima too are misleading. Apart from a dozen or so very big estates the effective top value was closer to £40–£50, and not much more than £30 in Dean. A few assessments must have been global ones; Richard Sapcote of Minetty had £22 'in all places', which in fact included at least £30 in Rutland.[172]

The difference between the Cotswolds and the Forest of Dean – and in lesser degree the Vale – was profound. Small parcels were numerous enough in the hills, but only a minority of the owners lived there – in fact over two-thirds of the proprietors of the district were absentees. Distribution, furthermore, appears very irregular. No less than 30 per cent were returned in the two little hundreds of Cheltenham and Cleeve,[173] beyond which there were sizeable clusters in towns like Stow-on-the-Wold and Tetbury, though not, curiously, in Cirencester. Conversely, in many villages the lord, very frequently a prelate, might be the sole proprietor; in others freeholders were limited to one or two persons. Nor is the position clarified by suspicions that the valuation of lay-owned land hereabouts was incomplete. With husbandry favouring big farms the small freeholder might well have seen more profit in letting off his land rather than working it himself. It is attractive to speculate that he migrated to one of the industrialised villages of the valleys, or that successful tradesmen made a habit of investing in Cotswold land. However, the only feasible example is John Carpynter of Leonard Stanley, owner of small parcels in Hampnett and Winstone;[174] all other traceable men lived in Cotswold settlements, and in any case the overwhelming majority of residents had only the holding on which they (presumably) dwelt.

A sizeable population of petty freeholders was much as would be expected in the generally pastoral Vale district. But the most distinctive region was Dean, where the balance between residents and absentees was the reverse of that of the Cotswolds, influenced no doubt by the rights and privileges enjoyed by the commoners, so that, admittedly at a much later date, there was complaint of 'the great number of unnecessary cabins and cottages built in the forest by strangers, who are people of very lewd lives and conversation, leaving their own and other countries and taking this place for shelter'.[175] Unnecessary or not, mining and ironworking superimposed on the basic pastoral economy provided plenty of incentive to settlers. Once there they formed a curiously enclosed society in which absentees, apart from great landowners, played a minor part. Whatever the reasons, freeholders made up nearly a fifth of the inhabitants, who were far more comprehensively listed than in the rest of Gloucestershire, with a density approaching eight times what it was in the Cotswolds, which covered more than three times the area of the Forest.

The multitude of holdings recorded in Buckinghamshire (Table 3.9) form an unwieldy whole inhibiting any firm distinction between non-resident landowners domiciled within and outside its boundaries. Attention consequently focuses rather on the parcels themselves than on the persons to whom they belonged. Wide though the range of values was in every case, the medians show remarkably little variation. Again the contrasts between the maxima for the various hundreds are more apparent than real, for the highest assessments were all global. With only a couple of exceptions the holdings of absentees were approximately double the value of those in the hands of residents. In Burnham and Stoke there was a relatively large number of substantial resident proprietors, while in Buckingham it is almost certain that copyholders were not assessed, as they seem to have been elsewhere. In general, though, the difference may be attributed to the fact that absentee holdings included most of the manors and other major properties, while

Table 3.9 Buckinghamshire landholdings

Hundred	Residents No.	Minimum s	Minimum d	Maximum £	Maximum s	Maximum d	Median £	Median s	Median d	Non-residents No.	Minimum s	Minimum d	Maximum £	Median £	Median s	Median d
Newport	386	0	6	50	0	0		8	0	340	0	4	160	1	0	0
Cottesloe	412		3	160	0	0		6	8	218		4	160		13	4
Buckingham	64		8	69	0	0		10	0	137	1	4	52		12	0
Ashendon	105		6	66	13	4		6	8	197		3	50	1	0	0
Aylesbury	327	1	0	81	0	0		10	0	243	1	0	63	1	6	8
Desborough	171		3	26	13	4		10	0	145	2	0	62	1	6	8
Burnham	230		6	26	13	4		13	4	199		2	200		16	0
Stoke	158	1	4	60	0	0		13	4	124		8	45	1	0	0

those of residents were much more likely to be limited to single farms, if not little more than a cottage or a patch of land. Nor is it unlikely that under both headings some of the smallest values were really rent charges. What is beyond question is that, as in Rutland and Gloucestershire, more than half the individual holdings were extremely small.

CHAPTER FOUR

THE COMMON WEAL

ENGLISHMEN in the sixteenth century possessed a deep sense of economic justice and held strong views about how wealth ought to be shared among the community. Anything but egalitarian, the consensus concept of the common weal was an imprecise mixture of 'to each according to his needs' and 'according to his works'. Needs were determined by men's roles in society. The true gentleman required a rental of at least £40 a year, not only to enable him to live in proper style, which meant employing a lot of servants who otherwise would have had no means of livelihood, but also to fulfil his duties as magistrate, local administrator and agent of central government. The husbandman or family farmer required some 20 acres of arable land – the equivalent, inclusive of common rights, of about 25–30 acres – to pay his rent and support his dependants. Yet with human nature, stimulated by market forces, asserting itself, most men and groups easily persuaded themselves that whatever was advantageous to them as individuals was beneficial to the commonwealth, and so, rather than a harmonious equilibrium, the *Discourse of the Common Weal* depicted at the middle of the century a scenario of conflicting interests. Relations between landlords and tenants were soured in more ways than one. For the former, the Knight complained of his inability to raise to more realistic levels the rents of tenants who were assured of possession for long terms at a time when everyone else was free to raise the prices of their wares. The Husbandman protested at the gentry taking over and converting to sheepwalks land that by rights belonged to the farming community, and, regardless of the higher prices his own produce now commanded, stoutly refused even to consider paying more rent. Cheap foreign products imported by the Merchant, complained the Capper, competed unfairly with the wares of native craftsmen. Rising prices afflicted everybody, wage earners above all; farmers and master craftsmen could not afford their men's wages, the cost of running their country seats forced gentlemen to dismiss their servants and withdraw to lodgings in London. General insistence on a decided worsening in conditions since around 1530 makes the first question to be addressed that of how these matters stood immediately prior to this date, taking fresh stock of the central issue, the situation of the peasantry, in the light of the special features of the sources, while holding over for independent consideration the contingent problems of wage-labour and poverty, and concluding what is really an interim report with a re-examination of the all-important land question.

At first sight the summary statistics of personal property make a simple statement of stark inequalities between rich and poor, as a result of which almost everywhere something like half the community had to make do with a negligible share, while at the same time in many parts of the country – the affluent south-east in particular – the top people, who formed at most half of 1 per cent of the population, owned no less than 14 per cent of moveable wealth, while extension of the definition to include those worth £40 and upwards locates some 25–30 per cent in the hands of a bare 2 per cent of the nation. And this is only a part of the complete picture. On the one hand, the true numbers of the poor are generally understated, matched by a scaling down of the fortunes of some of the rich, added to which there was nationally a disproportionate and growing concentration of mercantile wealth in London, coupled with a propensity on the part of many of the richer gentry to congregate at court and so be lost to the view of provincial taxmen. On the other hand, a close look at the details modifies the elementary observation that a few people owned a great deal and the multitude very little, showing that in most counties even men of unquestioned eminence were not all that wealthy and, save in a few well-defined districts, their aggregate share was less than overwhelming.

The essential inequality lay in the distribution of land as the prime source of wealth; in this too the outward appearance is not definitive. Superficially the lower orders owned no more than 18 per cent of landed wealth in Buckinghamshire and as little as 10 in Rutland where possibly only freeholders were counted. Of land itself, exclusive of spiritualities, they accounted for 23 and 13 per cent of temporalities. Not only did proportions vary greatly from shire to shire, they also did inside each county: in Buckinghamshire resident small proprietors amounted overall to some 22 per cent of the inhabitants, but this embraced a wide range from 25–35 per cent on the eastern side to as little as 6–10 – much as in Rutland – in the western hundreds of Ashendon and Buckingham, where it looks as though the view was also limited to freeholders.

Conditions in other shires were every bit as varied, and almost everywhere much of the land was fragmented into little parcels. Doubtless some of the holders were owner-occupiers, but obviously even the smaller kind of small absentee owners could not have been, and if the majority were what outwardly they look to have been, that is peasant farmers and craftsmen, the stereotype of the condition of this class needs to be modified to take account of the fact that significant numbers of them must have been rentiers. Since so many defy identification, it looks as though, as often as not, it was *reputed* owners who got recorded, just as at Lyddington, Rutland, it was forgotten that the bishop of Lincoln, the lord himself, had recently changed. Over the names of lesser men, who were not held in any special esteem, little care may have been taken. It may be no coincidence that the Chibnalls, whose holdings in five north Buckinghamshire parishes were precisely listed, were a yeoman stock who had pulled themselves up by their bootstraps into the ranks of the minor gentry and were now worth nearly £20 a year.[1]

Dissimilarities in social distribution as between personal and real wealth are not so difficult to accept if it is assumed that a major part of the value of chattels represented not a consumable surplus but the means of production, and the further down the scale the greater this was bound to be. When some six-sevenths of a Midland peasant's estate consisted of the stock and tackle of his holding,[2] the great majority were left with very little that could be described as accumulated profit. In contrast, much of a gentleman's wealth might comprise personal effects and domestic comforts together with capital assets and status symbols combined in the form of gold and silver plate and ornaments; a full half was not uncommon, and it could run to as much as the entire inventory of £55 of a Norfolk knight in the 1550s. Drawing much of his substance from rents, the greater landowner was free to choose whether or not to sink his capital in productive enterprise, but since his status was directly linked with his scale of consumption, his personal estate was frequently smaller than that of a prosperous yeoman.[3] The profits from land, moreover, cannot be fully evaluated within the context of a single county. As many of the greatest proprietors were the king's servants and courtiers, wealth was constantly being siphoned from the shires to the metropolis, though naturally much would eventually find its way back in the course of internal trade. Even when, rarely, magnates were assessed locally, the resultant impression can be misleading. Though in 1524 the duke of Norfolk was in residence at Framlingham castle, his goods, rated at £4,000, represented the issues of far-flung estates and not merely those situated in Suffolk, or even East Anglia. Similarly had an assessment been made in the summer of 1542, when his successor was keeping house at Chesworth, it would not have borne much relationship to the wealth of Sussex.[4] Important as this distinction is as a corrective to the raw data, it is in some sense academic, a question of who skimmed the cream off the economy.

LANDLORDS AND TENANTS

The crux of the problem was the ability of landowners to control and exploit their property; alternatively how large or small a share of the profits were retained by their tenants. In the owner-occupier situation no difficulty arose except insofar as an occupier's activity might disrupt the finely adjusted mechanism of common-field management.

The landlord–tenant relationship hinged on two contentious issues – security of tenure and rent. Manorial custom backed by the common law conferred effective security on those tenants who held 'according to the custom of the manor', especially if they could produce written evidence of title in the form of a copy of the court roll of the manor; but those who held simply 'at the will of the lord' enjoyed no such protection,[5] and the volume and intensity of condemnation of large-scale evictions of husbandmen raises the feasibility of a gap between judicial pronouncements and the harsh realities of conflict between lords and tenants.

Faced by rising prices, landlords found that custom imposed a rigid ceiling on rents. The only certain way of increasing their income was to turn land over to more lucrative uses, which happened to be sheep farming and wool production, and this meant getting rid of existing tenants who stood in the way of change. Faced by the problem of bridging the gap between a stable income and rising costs, even the best landlords might find the temptation to resort to extra-legal and even illegal methods of ridding themselves of 'protected' tenants irresistible.

The indictment of agrarian abuse did not stop short at polemics. Graphic accounts of actual incidents are preserved in the record of cases in which groups of peasants prosecuted oppressive lords in the courts. However, the total number of cases of forcible eviction to facilitate change is not great; some were collusive actions brought in order to get a judicial ruling,[6] and the testimony of others is less than conclusive. As the decrees of the Star Chamber, which dealt with most of them, were later destroyed, the outcome is usually unknown. In some cases the surviving record is limited to the plaintiff's initiating bill of complaint, which, in giving only one side, does not mean that the charge was well founded. Some suits no doubt failed, or were withdrawn, for want of proof. In the well-known Angmering case a parallel suit was alleged against the same 'wicked' lord in the Court of Requests and he successfully showed that he had exchanged the land in dispute with the plaintiff, another tenant, who had not only refused to vacate it but had persistently disturbed his peace and quiet with her livestock. However, in confirming the landlord's title, the court obliged him to make good any discrepancy in the acreage allotted to the plaintiff and repair her house if necessary. Finally the old lady was excused rent for the remainder of her life, a clear hint that the owner was deemed to have overstepped the mark and deserved to be penalised. Here is an excellent example of a prerogative court showing willingness to temper law with equity in a spirit of compromise and conciliation, and it surely affords the best possible clue to the verdict in the Star Chamber suit, in which it appears that the defendant had resorted to force only when other tenants had reneged on an exchange.[7]

The background puts this case in a very different light. The 'victims' of landlordism at Ecclesden came through unscathed and were still carrying on 'business as usual' some years later. The depopulation of Dunsby, Lincs., was in fact alleged by a member of a prominent family. True he claimed to represent 'all the pore inhabitantes and parishioners', but since none was identified they could have been dragged in to camouflage the pursuit of his personal interests. At first glance it looks a classic case, for only five households, say a couple of dozen persons, remained there in 1563, ten years or so after the supposed débâcle; however, the five taxpayers listed in 1524 represent much the same level of population, and the village had never amounted to much anyway.[8]

If some landlords dealt harshly with their tenants they were not alone in flouting the rules. In another Lincolnshire case it was an enclosing landowner who prosecuted other tenants – he was not the lord – for invading his land over which they claimed, rightly or wrongly, to exercise right of common; it was the kind of dispute in which erroneous assumptions might have grown up over a period of time.[9] The row between some Somerset villagers and Sir John Rodney in 1516 involved *inter alia* the general allegation that the latter had defaced copyhold deeds, to which he riposted, let specific instances be cited so that each can be dealt with on its merits; the free use of generalisations detracts from the evidential value of statements made in legal proceedings. This dispute was rounded off by a cross-petition alleging riotous assembly, attempted assault, and malicious damage.[10] In another episode of seemingly flagrant landlordism Robert Delavale, having bought up the freeholds at Hartley, Northumberland, evicted all fifteen tenants at will and threw the land into one great farm; after 1578 cottagers were the only tenants recorded on the court roll. Yet it was not a clean sweep, for six farmers were resettled in newly created husbandry tenements at Seaton Delaval, five more received cottages, and only three appear to have gone away, making an actual reduction in the number of tenants of from twelve to five. It should be added that the customary rights of 'husbandry tenants' were minimal.[11] What Delavale in fact did was to purchase various small properties and give the sitting tenants, who were probably on short lets, notice to quit, exercising his option not to replace them. At Slaidburn it was the copyholders who petitioned for regulated enclosure, opposition coming from the poorer commoners who could not afford the attendant expense – and were in the event forced out – as well as from under-tenants fearful that their landlords might not sublet any of the allotments to them. In practice the copyholders leased their allotments to their tenants on the same terms as before, while at West Bradford special arrangements safeguarded the interests of the poorer occupiers. In this part of the West Riding improvement followed enclosure, with the years 1560–1630 witnessing a real rise in the prosperity of the copyhold farmer as a result of a strengthening of his tenurial position arising in the first instance out of a dispute about customs.[12] Consideration of the wider impact of enclosure and depopulation may be deferred at this point.

TRENDS IN RENT

The share of the produce of the land that returned to the lord in the shape of rent was determined by many factors. It is generally taken for granted that, freeholders apart, the majority of farmers held by the custom of the manor, whether as copyholders with written evidence of title or by some less precisely defined tenure. The outgoings of the customary tenant consisted chiefly of the fine paid on admission, annual rent, and heriot on death or alienation. Rent was almost always fixed by custom at a level which inflation made increasingly unrealistic in the course of the sixteenth century. Heriot, commonly defined as the tenant's best beast and more often than not compounded for in cash, amounted to a substantial, though not necessarily oppressive, exit duty. Here and there labour services were still rendered, generally in the form of boonworks at harvest and other busy seasons, but they were usually paid for on the nail with food and drink and other allowances.[13] Some copyholders, notably in the Wiltshire chalk country, also rendered annual quotas of corn which had the effect, more or less, of rack rent.[14] Generally, however, it was through the entry fine that the landlord increasingly endeavoured to secure a due share of the output of customary land.

Fines require careful definition. In broad terms fines were arbitrary towards the west where tenure was for lives, but usually limited in the east where copyholds were heritable. On some manors fines were certain, equal to one or two years' rent, and virtually indistinguishable from the socage tenant's relief. If technically arbitrary they were very often required by custom to be 'reasonable', again usually meaning a year or two's rental, and this, or something not dissimilar, was the courts' interpretation. Alternatively there was the common-sense practice of certainty or reasonableness on succession, and arbitrariness on alienation.[15] A Chancery decree of 1605 confirmed that fines on descent at Ryhall, where most copyholds were heritable, were certain, and on purchase arbitrary, which meant reasonable, i.e. two years' rent.[16] The boundary between the two systems has not been traced in detail and was probably much blurred. In Sussex the river Arun may have formed the effective line of demarcation, and indeed the arable coastal plain may be regarded as an eastward extension of Wessex. Throughout most of the county copyhold of inheritance with limited fines was the rule; only three out of ten manors using lifeholds and two out of eleven having both forms of tenure were situated east of the river Ouse.[17] The few which had arbitrary fines were all in the neighbourhood of Chichester.[18]

Although a sustained rise in the level of rents, chiefly through the adjustment of fines, in the sixteenth century has been demonstrated,[19] the process was subject to variations at different periods, from region to region, and even on different types of estate. One difficulty is that much the best evidence emanates from two big estates in Wiltshire. The very full and systematic records of the Herbert estates, in particular, testify to efficient, possibly exceptional, management which would have included making every effort to maximise returns; put another way, persistently rising rents and the successful preservation of the archives, which provide the evidence for them, were equally the outcome of sound administration. The Seymour estates in the same area were run with comparable efficiency, but as for others, not only did standards of management vary a great deal, but also more often than not no records have survived; for this the hazards of time are partly to blame, but how often did it happen that administration, of small estates especially, was unsystematic and record keeping haphazard simply because owners did not attempt to run their properties as efficient businesses?

The time scale of developments becomes clearer when the century is divided into two periods at approximately the halfway point – at, indeed, the time of the rebellions of 1549 which specifically protested, *inter alia*, against rising rents; no doubt with good reason. Although most of the evidence earlier than 1550 is circumstantial, typified by Bishop Latimer's claim that the rent of his father's former farm in Thurcaston, Leics., had quadrupled since his own boyhood,[20] fines on the Herbert estates, the property of Wilton Abbey until its dissolution, were running in the 1540s at double the rate in 1510–19, accelerating later to treble by the end of the century. At first, growth on the Seymour estates was rather slower, just topping 50 per cent by the 1540s, though later sharp acceleration brought a further fivefold rise by the 1590s. By and large, the upward trend showed little sign of biting until the 1540s.

It is not entirely certain that Wiltshire, where copyhold fines were mostly arbitrary, was a true microcosm of the national trend, if only because the only parallel would appear to be a couple of isolated examples drawn from a single Northamptonshire estate which show a 50 per cent jump in 1545–6,[21] the point more or less at which significant rises began to take effect anyway. Conditions in Wiltshire favoured the landlord in a way they did not wherever copyholds were heritable and control over their outgoings restricted. In Essex between 1560 and 1640 copyholders generally were in a strong position and took advantage of every opportunity to improve their standing. Although many copyholds seem to have been granted for term of years only, and fines were arbitrary in half of a sample of twenty manors, lords were not on the whole unjust. Arbitrary fines were not necessarily at the unfettered will of the lord but a matter for bargaining, and at Dedham Hall were referred to arbitrators when no agreement could be reached. In 1584 the lord of Great Bromley agreed with his tenants to make the fines certain, and each holding was separately assessed at from 16s. 8d. to £12.[22] Here the trend was clearly to the advantage of the tenants. In Sussex in the same period there were only isolated cases of fines being raised.[23] Although fines were nominally uncertain on more than half of a sample of eighty manors in Norfolk and Suffolk, custom protected the tenants from any increase in the first half of the seventeenth century.[24] During the 1530s the level tended to be 2s. per acre, though in the following decade they averaged no more than 1s. on the Mettingham College estate; 5s. was accepted at Colkirk and Gatley, Norfolk, in the 1580s.[25] The *Chorography* (c. 1602) singles out some forty manors in upwards of 200 Suffolk townships as having arbitrable fines, possibly because they were atypical. Nevertheless, certain fines are specified only on two Long Melford manors, and at Lavenham for such copyholders as dwelt outside the 'borough'. They may perhaps be inferred on six or seven other manors from the fact that on others in the same townships – Baddingham, Preston and Stanton for example – fines were specifically stated to be arbitrary. A further exception was the gavelkind tenure noted at Deback.[26]

Prior to 1550 the situation is far less clear, though when it comes to cases evidence of general, systematic increases is seldom to be found, even in Norfolk where complaints of undue exactions featured prominently among the grievances of the insurgents in 1549. In rural Warwickshire the ancient custom of Knowle, a forest township, prescribed a fine of 1d. for an heir, and one years' rent for a purchaser; by 1635 these had risen to 1½d. and two years' rent, respectively. As late as 1601 the actual rental at Solihull remained less than one-eighth of the estimated 'improved' value of both copyhold and leasehold land, and rents lagged generally in the Arden district.[27] In the fifteenth century peasants had acted to force rents down. Tenants of the bishop of Worcester had refused payment in full on grounds of poverty, threatening to leave *en masse* unless their demands were conceded. This was no anarchic denial of the principle of rent; the tenants wanted a fair one, and like their predecessors in 1381, who had proposed 4d. an acre, had a clear idea of what it ought to be. On the principle that some income was better than none at all the bishops gave way. By the turn of the century conditions were changing. With increasing demand for land the peasants' bargaining position deteriorated, and henceforth withholding of rent was confined mainly to the upper classes. Another rent strike occurred at Henbury, near Bristol, in 1533, but it was provoked by the steward's unreasonable policy. Only here and at Whitstones, near Worcester, did fines on episcopal manors manifest a strong upward tendency as early as the 1530s and Dr Dyer attributes difficulties in both places to their situation close to major towns.[28]

'Fair rent' movements were not confined to the West Midlands, nor did they cease with the ending of the fifteenth century. The last duke of Buckingham always had large arrears outstanding and, though striving unremittingly to reduce them, never succeeded in solving the problem. Resistance was stiffest and most violent in Wales, but in 1513–14 a Northamptonshire tenant surrendered his holding and quit rather than pay an enhanced rent. Increased fines – equivalent to two, three or more years' rent – were resisted at Navisby, and the receiver had to seize tenements to enforce payment. Low rents were clearly valued more highly than security by the peasantry. In 1517–18 an attempt to combine a rise in rents with the conversion of customary tenure into copyhold at Navisby provoked the response, 'they wyll not consent thereto; they had lever to departe the lordshipp, for they say they wyll pay the rent from yere to yere according to their old custom and other wayes they will not.' Tenants of another lordship declared they would sooner die than go through with the deal.[29] Something of the kind seems to have occurred at Bramfield, Suffolk, later in the century, where the obduracy of the tenants proved self-defeating: 'The fine arbitrable nowe & many tymes & xijs an acre. Was certayne heretofore & but xijd an acre. The townesmen might have had it enroled in the chauncery by the L. Keeper for the certayntye of ijs an acre & would not'[30] This Lord Keeper was in fact Sir Nicholas Bacon, who built up a great estate, and it was his manor. The inference is that here at least the lord possessed some reserve power to vary the fines and that the unreasonableness of the tenants cost them their former privilege. Conservative in his approach to management, Sir Nicholas did not greatly exploit fines. The upward pressure came only after his death in 1578, even though in 1584 his tenants at Walsham alleged that he had tried to raise their fines above 1s. an acre; some had capitulated through fear, while others accepted the promise that the rate would never go beyond 2s. Subsequent inflation of fines was in fact made possible, as at Bramfield, by the tenants' own violations of custom. Even rents for leases advanced barely 50 per cent on his Mettingham estates, though in the 1580s they trebled, and they soared in the first half of the next century. Nevertheless, he himself effectively doubled the rents of Rickinghall Inferior before 1570.[31]

From Simpson's investigations the trend in East Anglia emerges as much less consistent than in the West Country. In the years 1540–5 Sir John Cornwallis's income remained virtually static around £100 except for changes due to purchases and sales; from 1544 to 1556/8 the real increment was modest because, although the total more than doubled, from £208 to £448, no less than £180 was added by new acquisitions.

Even after that, performance was patchy. The yield of the ten Suffolk manors increased more than two and a half times, from £199 to £513, between 1558 and 1595, but almost all of this came from two of them, and on the remainder the rise was negligible. Similarly, while income from one Norfolk manor rose 300 per cent, and that from two others was doubled, the increment at Thorpe Cornwallis was limited to 12 per cent. The doubling of the value of Basildon, Essex, and Wilton, Yorks., was balanced by the halving of that of Beauchamps in Suffolk. Demesne leases contributed much the most important element of growth, and here, as elsewhere, some manors consisted of little but heritable copyholds, and fines which were nominally arbitrary were often frozen in practice. The record of the Bures estate shows that in the middle decades of the century, 1530–60, improvements were not expected on the expiry of every lease. Acton, which was demised for £54 in 1525, was still producing the same rent in 1547, and remained at that level as late as 1559; it was over the next thirty years that the rental nearly trebled.[32] And not only was acceleration modest before the accession of Elizabeth I, some individual manors were undervalued prior to 1550,[33] around which time the *Discourse* remarked, 'yet the one halfe is [not] enhaunced . . . thoughe the owners wold'. And it continues:

> And noble men and gentlemen therbe, that whan there landes be set at disposition, yet they will enhaunce nothinge aboue the old rent; so as the most part of the landes of this Realme stand yet at the old Rent.[34]

Change was much less abrupt and dramatic than some authorities would have us believe.

Evidence relating to fines in other areas during this half-century is too scanty to be conclusive. At Cradley, Hagley and Warley in the pastoral north of Worcestershire they were uniformly very low and probably unalterable. Farther west, at Myddle and on other Shropshire estates, trends in the sixteenth century look sluggish, the explosion being delayed until the beginning of the seventeenth. In Buckinghamshire the fines on the Mercers' manor in Sherington remained nominal until at least 1550, even though tenure was not hereditary. At Long Crendon the sums taken were perhaps thought not worth recording; had fines been variable a note of precedents would presumably have been useful. In the 1550s fines were small or moderate on several other manors. Intermittent recording shows no rising trend at Apuldram in West Sussex in the reign of Henry VIII, and although the earlier practice at Bosham is obscure the fine there was fixed at two years' rent in 1619. At about this time too, Petworth copyholders, whose fines were arbitrary even though they held in inheritance, sued the ninth earl of Northumberland in Chancery over these and related matters; they offered to settle for two years' rent, which the court called 'very liberal', the earl accepted, and although fines continued to be negotiated individually, they never seem to have become oppressive.[35]. Here and there (see Table 4.2) the general condition of the farming community gives a clue to the nature of their liabilities. Fines were limited to two years' rent at Rodmell, in the valley of the Sussex Ouse, and, with a similar correlation between the sizes of their holdings and their tax assessments, the tenants of Boxgrove near Chichester no doubt enjoyed comparable protection. In contrast, at Prinsted on the Hampshire border, where assessments appear to match with considerably bigger holdings, farmers probably retained a smaller proportion of their earnings. Their position was relatively vulnerable; most copyholds were for lives and several tenants were villeins as late as 1586, while at the same time fines were certainly arbitrary on the manor of Woodmancote in the same parish.[36]

Compared with Wiltshire, where the upward tendency was strong and continuous, conditions in most other counties varied widely, but everywhere the maximum pressure on rents was delayed until at least 1540–50. Smaller landlords probably followed the example set by the greater ones, if only in passing on to subtenants their own higher costs; newcomers building up estates from the profits of commerce were not necessarily the first to apply the methods of the market to estate management: the smaller the estate the closer the personal contact with the tenantry.

'THE VERY AND TRUE COMMON WEALTH'

With law and usage operating to restrict the landlord's profit and safeguard the tenant's interest, it was no accident that the chief concentration of wealth was located below the topmost strata among men of intermediate standing. Who were these middling people? A rearrangement of the data offers a choice between three main candidates (see Table 4.1). Each of these groupings incorporates a large number of people possessed of a significant slice of the aggregate wealth of the community. The sole exception, and that a partial one, is Babergh where intense concentration in the highest brackets reduced the

Table 4.1 Wealth of middling men (percentages)

County	A £3–£19 Persons	Wealth	B £5–£19 Persons	Wealth	C £5–£39 Persons	Wealth
Norfolk	33.2	38.5	19.8	32.3	23.2	47.7
Suffolk: Babergh	31.2	19.1	20.5	15.9	27.4	29.5
Rutland	41.8	45.5	28.6	38.7	35.1	61.5
Buckinghamshire	34.4	45.0	19.5	36.2	23.0	50.0
Berkshire	30.9	35.5	18.3	27.6	22.0	44.2
Gloucestershire	49.0	47.8	33.1	39.8	38.8	57.2
Worcestershire	40.0	58.9	24.8	46.8	28.6	65.6
Cornwall	56.8	58.3	26.3	38.7	30.6	55.1

proportion available to the middling people, though without depressing their absolute wealth, as a glance at the figures themselves makes clear. Big cities, though not York,[37] also diverged from this pattern, as did some county towns of medium size; others broadly conformed to it. All three groups consisted predominantly of husbandmen and craftsmen. Group B interprets the concept of the peasantry more or less rigorously, excluding the yeoman and the merchant class above, and smallholders and petty tradesmen below. Upward extension of the range (C) to embrace yeomen, small merchants and a sprinkling of gentlemen does not add many more persons, but greatly augments the wealth held by the group. Conversely, extension downwards (A) pulls in a lot more people without a commensurate increase in wealth. Forty-shilling men, many of whom were indistinguishable from labourers, are probably best avoided at this point.

In the final analysis men worth £5–£19 were precisely those who were officially classed as intermediate. Unlike their inferiors they were burdened with the loan, though not approached until the contribution of the rich had proved inadequate, while at the same time deemed capable of being taxed at only half the rate prescribed for men of £20 and over. It makes a revealing gloss on Polydore Vergil's remark that 'When the assessment [of 1522] had been made the king could readily see that his people were by no means poor'.[38] More precisely it transpired that the top people were not as affluent as was commonly supposed, while those placed immediately beneath them disposed of worthwhile resources. In place of the initial crude categorisation of the rich and the poor, the outlines of a threefold division crystallise thanks to the identification of a numerically strong middle element comprising people who, if not wealthy, were certainly not poor in the sense of forming a proletariat. In approximate terms society was composed of a top layer of gentry and other men of considerable individual wealth, secondly peasant farmers, master craftsmen and others of comparable standing and some little substance, and last of all smallholders, labourers and servants. Granted this taxonomy errs on the side of simplicity, for nothing could be further removed from reality than a concept of society consisting of three homogeneous classes, much less anything as straightforward as an upper, a middle, and a working class, especially since the vast majority of members of the middle group were nothing if not manual workers themselves. Each of these primary categories was formed by an agglomeration of subgroups, and was flanked by marginal categories among which perhaps the most conspicuous were the £2 men and, less obviously, those worth £20–£39. (Indeed, there is much to be said in favour of plumping for Smith's fourfold classification modified to make cottagers and the like an autonomous group.) For all its shortcomings this scheme will, nonetheless, serve as a convenient starting point for the more precise charting of the ramifications of the social structure.

Set squarely at the centre of the spectrum, the £5–£19 class comprised roughly a quarter of all assessed persons and possessed personal property which exceeded by a handsome margin the wealth of the top 2 per cent of indisputably rich people in most counties. No individual member of it could be called affluent; few or none were likely to have farmed as much as 100 acres, more especially since the number of assessments in excess of £15 was negligible. Conversely, unless visited by disaster, they enjoyed a measure of immunity from the threat of indigence, since there can have been few among them who did not occupy a holding large enough to support a family, if not opulently at least securely. Subject to regional peculiarities, the £3–£19 range embraced some 40 per cent of the people owning a similar fraction of the community's wealth. The more affluent group covering £5–£39 amounted to nearly a third of the population and possessed a clear half of its wealth. But these additional recruits are liable to blur the pattern by introducing, at the lower end of the scale, people whose livelihood might at times have been precarious, and at the upper end, men whose aspirations outstripped those of the majority, marking them off as a separate species. When due weight has been assigned to all factors, the most acceptable solution is to treat the £5–£19 group as a nucleus to which in practice, and depending on individual circumstances, could have been added a proportion of each of the others – even some of the 40s. men, seeing that the distinction between these and £3 assessments can be tenuous – leading to a situation that can neatly, and not unrealistically, be summed up by saying that a third of the people owned nearly half the wealth.

The strength of this class is difficult to reconcile with the mounting alarm experienced by serious and intelligent observers at what they saw as a yawning chasm opening up between rich and poor – the genesis, one is tempted to murmur, of the 'two nations'. Yet with the advantage of hindsight it may legitimately be asked whether the true gap lay between empirical fact and a set of erroneous assumptions which gained currency and credibility in proportion to the vehemence with which they were asserted. The cold, impersonal statistics derived from contemporary fiscal records seem to expose as groundless, as irresponsible scaremongering, the dire forewarnings of mortal schism in society which culminated in the propaganda of the Commonwealth Men in the 1540s. It is true that the crisis did not break until 1549, but even so it is open to question whether the pace of change during the intervening years was sufficient to produce a radical transformation of society. Writers such as Sir Thomas More, in *Utopia* (1516), had already expressed concern;[39] by the early 1530s Parliament was having to grapple with a growing problem of indigence,[40] and might well have done so sooner had not the only session held between 1515 and 1529 been largely taken up with wrangling over taxation; it also insisted on a general pardon for offences uncovered by the inquisitions of depopulation in 1517, the product of Wolsey's deep concern with social problems.[41] In the absence of statistics – the subsidy rolls for 1543–5 are both less comprehensive and poorly preserved – the assumption must be that the broad outlines of the social structure underwent little change, other than perhaps some accentuation of inequalities; as late as the end of the seventeenth century small cultivators still made up a good fifth of all households.[42]

Having regard to the somewhat modest standing of many persons in the upper strata of taxpayers, it may be suggested, as an alternative, that in reality the crisis reflected the alienation of landless peasants from those fortunate enough to enjoy a secure living, a hypothesis that will be considered in due course. Most commentators were well enough aware of their existence but displayed little genuine knowledge of them. The *Discourse of the Common Weal* stands alone not merely in attempting a definition but in advancing the thesis that they formed a definable interest.[43] For the most part observers like More and Starkey confined themselves to deploring the growing numbers of vagabonds and beggars.[44] Servants as such did come in for rather more notice – their supposed idle and profligate ways were regularly (and ritually) castigated[45] – but their status as subordinate members of their masters' households disqualified them from consideration as an autonomous group.

The concept of pauperism only evolved during the course of the sixteenth century. In the early decades commentators referred not so much as to the 'the poor' as to 'the poor commons', or the 'commonalty', a term acknowledged by the people themselves. The Norfolk rebels in 1549 petitioned the king to redress 'the complaint of your poor commons', who have been shown to have consisted chiefly of solid, respectable husbandmen and yeomen, far removed from the riff-raff of sturdy beggars and discontented servants pictured by hostile propagandists. The king's 'power and faithful Subiectis Inhabitantes within the Townes and villages of Draycot and Stoke Gifford', who prosecuted their landlord in the Star Chamber, enjoyed 'astate in their holdes and tenures'. Again, 'At Michaelmas time poore men must make monie of their graine, that they may paye theire rents'.[46] Almost without exception 'the poor' turns out to mean small tenant farmers – the peasantry.

Hardly one social theorist betrayed the least hesitation at casting the rich in the role of villains, whether they were presented in the guise of big farmers or graziers, lawyers, merchants or gentlemen.[47] And it was on the last of these, the landlords, that the assault was ever and anon renewed: men who had it in their power to undermine the very foundations of an agrarian society by exacting extortionate rents and fines, expropriating tenants, engrossing farms, dividing and enclosing commons, and converting ploughlands into sheepwalks.[48] It was never for one moment suggested that there was no place for the great and powerful. It was taken for granted that, in order that they might diligently administer justice, rulers should be

> maintained in pomp and pleasure and in quiet life, without all travail and bodily labour by the labour and travail of the poor commonalty to the intent that they, a the other side may diligently with common quietness apply themselves to their labour and pains for the sustaining of the whole body, the which also is the chief point of their office and

duty, giving also reverently to their princes and lords all humble service and meek obedience required to their status and degree.[49]

No serious reformer proposed expropriating landlords, but simply admonished them to give their tenants a fair deal. A place would also be found for merchants whose trade contributed to the wealth of the nation.[50] But it was in the nature of things for the numbers of such men to be limited; the Norfolk insurgents sought to restrict the privileges of gentility to knights and esquires, which in almost every shire meant the merest handful. Outside their ranks society *was* the commonalty.

Who or what were the common people? The conventional ideal postulated a nation of small producers.[51] Although most clearly adumbrated in the writings of the Commonwealth Men,[52] it is heard also in the voice of the people themselves,[53] and plainly expressed in a good deal of legislation. The Weavers' Act of 1555 forbade any weaver to have more than one loom – two if he dwelt in a market town – on the grounds that cloth factories manned by 'Journeymen and personnes unskilful [tended] to the decaye of a greate nomber of Artificers which were brought up in the said Seyence of Weaving their Families and Households'. A gloss on the Statute of Artificers remarks:

For one man to be both an husbandman and an Artificer is a gatheringe of divers mens livinges into one mans hand, And therefore the lawe dothe not allowe such a one to keep or instruct Apprentices in any occupation [i.e. trade] to withdrawe from Artificers the occasion of their livinges, which have no other trade to live by but only their occupations.

The act itself provided for the fixing of maximum wage rates, not, as Thorold Rogers supposed, to cheat the workman of his due reward, but to protect one class of workers, the small craftsmen, from excessive demands made by another. Similarly the acts against depopulation sought to prevent, or reverse, the decaying of homesteads and ploughs: the Commissions of 1517 and 1548 investigated cases in which land had been let independently of a farmhouse, and as late as 1589 another statute tried to combat the problem of the landless labourer by prohibiting the erection of any cottage unless 4 acres of land were attached to it. At the very end of the century yet another was directed towards 'the maintainaunce of husbandrie and tillage' because it was by this means that 'the greater parte of the Subjectes are preserved from extreame povertie in a competente Estate of maintenance and meanes to live'. And in opining, 'But I think that whosoever does not maintain the plough destroys this kingdom', Robert Cecil did no more than voice conventional wisdom.[54]

Behind this lay an ingrained conservatism, a longing to 'call back yesterday' when, it was believed, life had been so much better. None expressed this feeling more eloquently than the Commonwealth Men who contrived to combine religious radicalism with an almost reactionary view of society,[55] never ceasing to contrast the miserable realities of the 1540s with the idyllic past. But impassioned rhetoric is not the best guide to actual conditions, and what they hoped to recover is not immediately clear.

REALITIES OF PEASANT LIFE

The reality behind the generalisations, the empirical facts on which supposedly they were founded, were never stated. At the same time the (unrecorded) details of the 'stocks and stocks of cattle', that were totalled to produce assessments, must have been much the same as the inventories of goods and chattels of people who died in the next few years, since in Buckinghamshire at least the values of the personal estates of most of them were more or less the same as their assessments. Although thirty-nine estates, in 1521–40,[56] totalled from 27s. 9d. to £71, only two topped £54, exactly two-thirds being less than £20, nearly half £5–£19, and rather more below £10. Including a couple of priests, a shoemaker and a whitesmith, they were of course people of all types, though most were probably farmers, similar to Leicestershire husbandmen at this time, two-thirds of whom left goods worth less than £20.[57] An average sort of man, Richard Perse, or Persenger, of Haddenham, assessed at £8, died in 1536 owning goods worth £7. 3s. 8d. He farmed a freehold virgate, later owned by his son William, and a copyhold which he left to his wife for life; on this he kept three mares, a couple of oxen, four cows and some hogs; as it was November the acreages of his crops were not recorded. A couple of Leicestershire farmers of 20 or 30 acres left similar personal estates about this time.[58]

Probably because smallholders and cottagers did not normally make wills, it was not thought worth going to the trouble of inventorising their scanty possessions, so few inventories total much less than £5, although half of all assessments did not exceed £2, which, as the minimum on which the standard rate of 6d. in the pound was payable, may sometimes have been employed to cushion the smallholder, like Richard Warwyke of Maid's Moreton who in fact was worth upwards of £6 and farmed on much the same scale as Persenger.[59] The estate of an actual smallholder, William Yonge of Burnham, totalled just £5. 3s. 2d. in which domestic and personal effects accounted for the relatively large sum of £1. 7s. 6d., though the chief item was 13 acres of growing wheat and barley – valued by the rent, 3s. 4d. an acre – implying a total arable acreage approaching 20 and a farm of 25–30 acres; livestock consisted only of two horses, three hogs and one or two sheep. Not listed in 1522, Yonge was taxed on wages as a labourer in 1524 when, perhaps a newcomer to Burnham, he was still trying to establish himself and pay off debts which for the moment depressed the net value of his property below the tax threshold, at the same time making ends meet by labouring work and being taxed on the proceeds.[60] Equally, he could have begun as a labourer who married a smallholder's widow, since the comparatively high value of the household effects points to an established holding that had got run down as a result of his predecessor's failing health and was having to be rehabilitated. Left with the holding on her hands, the widow had no doubt to hire a man to work it, and of course board him; marriage would follow almost inevitably.

On an entirely different plane, the yeoman farmer John Hill of Amersham, assessed at £30, left goods to the value of £36. 13s. 6d. to which the contents of his house contributed no more than £2. 9s. 10d. His livestock included two horses, twenty-three head of cattle and fourteen swine, with no fewer than nine score sheep and lambs. The contents of the barn amounted to 10 marks and winter corn in the ground was appraised at £3. 6s. 8d. which, reckoned on the same basis as Yonge's would have been 20 acres; with a similar area for spring corn and the same for fallow, he must have been cultivating some 60 acres, making, with meadow and grazing land, a farm of at least 100 acres, corresponding by and large with conditions in the Midlands.[61]

Occasional discrepancies between a man's assessment and inventory are inevitable if only because of the time interval during which prices fluctuated, those of cereals being especially volatile, and much of a farmer's assets usually consisted of stores of grain, bulking much larger just after harvest; as the years rolled by, moreover, values were increasingly distorted by inflation. Less readily accountable are the drastic changes – almost all reductions – in certain individuals' assessments, like that of William Bryghtmer of Morcot, Rutland, which plummeted from £14 to £3. In the whole of Sussex the sub-collectors of

Horsham town alone saw fit to offer a word of explanation in respect of the two richest inhabitants,[62] Avery Barwyke, who ended up paying tax on £54. 6s. 8d. from land and fees, was

> decayed sins the lone by the reason that he hath graunted the offyce of the controllership of the porte of Chichester to Thomas Awcokk and also ys decayed further of iiij[or] marks in londes that he hath gevyn to Eleynore hussay hys doughter in law.

The affairs of his neighbour Elizabeth Foys were stated more precisely, her net assessment of £53. 6s. 8d. was the result of being

> decayed ix[li] sins the lone by the deth of Richard Grover of Godylming whych ys decessed & left nothing to pay his dettes and also ys ferther decayed v[li] by the deth of one Rafe Furber of Shoreham whych ys deceased & left nothyng.

Annotations on one or two other returns show the wide variety of grounds for abatement, substantiated, as was Richard Furnes's of Cold Higham, Northants, 'by hys othe and the othe of his neybors' that he had suffered loss by the death of some of his cattle. In the three hundreds of Aylesbury, Bucks.,[63] a fifth of the taxpayers lodged successful claims, the great majority for the loss of corn and livestock – thirty-four for corn alone, sixty-seven for both. A serious fire in Aylesbury town could have been the cause of John Colyngborn the leading inhabitant's 'losse of corn schepe & byldyng' and destroyed more than half the buildings and household stuff belonging to the guild of Our Lady. Most relief was of the order of 20–40 per cent, rising to 50 or more in a few instances, among others William Barnard of Haddenham, reduced from £64 to £13. Similar reductions were allowed in parts of east Devon, where disease killed off 3,744 sheep, but although 1524 was a year of heavy rains there is no indication that losses on this scale were other than highly localised, even in Buckinghamshire, where the low-lying Vale of Aylesbury was prone to flooding; complaints came also from the Witham valley in Lincolnshire.[64] Rather less than 3 per cent of the taxpayers got abatements on other grounds, the proportion being similar in Towcester hundred, Northants,[65] where there were no crop failures and only one loss of cattle. Such were the normal hazards of life (see Table 4.2).

A man's circumstances could be drastically altered by a single event. Sickness was the obvious hazard: John Rokyngham of Towcester was laid up for a whole year before he died leaving his widow only £6 out of an original £10 after paying for the funeral and discharging sundry

Table 4.2 Reductions in assessments in Buckinghamshire and
Northamptonshire

Reason	Cases	%reduction
Loss of farm	1	46
Entry fine paid	1	50
Ordination of son	1	45
Marriage of son/brother*†	6	14–50
Sickness*‡	7	20–40
Evil servants and loss of wares	1	25
Bad debts*	3	20–40
[Law] suit and loss of cattle	1	50
Building and contents	1	60
Building, corn and cattle	1	28

* One includes loss of corn.
† One includes illness.
‡ One includes funeral expenses and bequests.

bequests. The English way of death was not cheap in the sixteenth
century. In 1521 the administrator of the modest estate of William
Willesley, chaplain of Leckhampstead, Bucks., consisting wholly of
clothing and bedding, and amounting to 57s. 9d., had to make payments
totalling 21s. 8d., plus 1s. for his own expenses. Six shillings were owed
to brother priests, but most went in fees of one sort or another,
including 2s. to the pardoner for letters of pardon and 5d. to the
summoner; the man who nursed him got only 4d., a penny less than was
laid out on ale for the officiating clergy.[66] If this was the everyday
experience, the case of Richard Hunne in 1514 gained notoriety not
merely on account of its tragic outcome but because his stand against
clerical avarice expressed universal resentment; significantly, excessive
probate costs and mortuary fees were among the first problems to which
the Reformation Parliament was to address itself in 1529.[67] It was
customary to set a young man up as a householder when he married,
though not girls, who, as the terms of many wills show, usually had to
wait for their portions until the deaths of their fathers; not dissimilar in
principle was the £9 (out of an estate of £20) it cost Edmund Dorman of
Great Missenden for 'makyn hys son a preeste'. This amply accounts for
many revised assessments, not only by way of reductions, but also new

and augmented ones.[68] Alternatively a man would be left as guardian of his younger brother, like Richard Ward of Cold Higham, who was 'Decayed be partyng of his goodes deliuered to hys brother Thomas Warde nowe of Laurens Marston ageynst hys maryage wherewith he stode charged and answered the Kynges grace at the fyrste Subsidie as parcell of his goodes', and was duly reduced by 7 marks to £7. For the first few years after coming into his patrimony a man would be committed by his father's will to finding the portions appointed for his siblings; later he would have to defer retirement as long as possible so as to be able to provide for each of his children and ensure an income for himself and his wife.[69]

Most circumstances are self-explanatory, though here and there more subtle influences may be suspected. Thomas Venner of Stone got his assessment halved in respect of the fine he had just paid for his farm. It sounds steep, but as a considerable yeoman, in receipt of £4 a year in rents, he could well afford it; besides he was the sub-collector and the only man in the parish to get any relief at all! Fines must have given grounds for a good many abatements, and, even though often paid by instalments, attempts would doubtless be made to claim the whole amount. Allowing that taxpayers tried to make the most of any liabilities or hardships, details such as these underline the care taken over assessments. Then as later, farm tenants came and went, and it is not at all certain whether the Weston Turville man who 'lost' his farm was evicted or simply failed to secure a renewal of his tenancy.

However severe the immediate impact of incidents like these, people's assessments were really determined by the source and size of their livelihood, which for most of them meant how much land they farmed. Manorial surveys should furnish this information, but even if the two units were identical in area, tenants of the manor, some of whom might have lived in another district, can rarely be identified as assessed inhabitants of an eponymous township, many of whom would have been sub-tenants and so no concern of the manor authorities. Making the most of a handful of near-contemporary surveys, supplemented by others of later date from manors where the long-term structure of tenancies was stable, we can look for any significant correlation between the tenements of a manor – though acreages were frequently omitted and details of freeholds are seldom adequate – and the assessments of the corresponding township arranged in order of magnitude (see Table 4.3).

Although no general average can be expected from an assortment like this, indications of a standard approximating to 15 acres confirm that most holdings were small, with few exceeding 40 acres in more favourable

Table 4.3 Assessments and manorial holdings compared

Boxgrove £ 1524	Ac. 1537	Great Casterton £ 1522	Ac. 1537	Stoke Hammond £ 1522	Ac. 1554	Foscott £ 1522	Ac. 1555	Rodmell £ 1524	Ac. 1575	Prinstead £ 1524	Ac. 1586
10	31	80	275	$13\frac{1}{3}$	140	50	75*	20	65	13	57
10	31	50	111	12	100	8	50	10	52	10	48
8	28	15	68	10	(100)	6	50	10	39	10	46
5	23	12	67	10	72	6	50	8	28	9	42
5	17	8	44	10	51	6	50	6	26	7	36
3	16	7	42	10	45	6	(50)	5	21	6	36
3	16	6	42	6	30+	4	(50)	5	21	6	30
2	12	6	30	$2\frac{2}{3}$	30	3	15	5	19	6	22
2	10	5	25	$2\frac{2}{3}$	20	$1\frac{1}{3}$		2	16	6	20
2	9	4	21	$2\frac{1}{3}$	19	1		2	16	6	18
2	8	3	21	2	13	1		2	14	5	17
2	5	3	20	2	(10)			2	11	4	16
2	4	2	$16\frac{1}{3}$	2	$9\frac{1}{3}$+			2	10	4	15

No.	yd	No.	yd	No.	yd	No.	yd	No.	yd
2	4	5	2	2	16	3	15	1	9
2	4	5	1⅓	2	16	2	14	1	2
2	3	2	1⅓	2	15½	2	14	1	cottage
2	3	2	1	2	13	2	12	1	"
1	3	1	cottage	2	12	2	8	1	"
1	3	1	"	2	3	2	7	1	"
1	3	1	"	1	cottage	1	6		
1	2			1	"	1	cottage		
1	1			1	"	1	"		
1	1			1	"	1	"		
1	cottage			1	"				
1	"			1 × 8	"				
1 × 7	"								
0 × 2	"								

177

* Holdings are stated as yardlands, which are assumed to average 25 acres, which was typical of many north Buckinghamshire villages: A.C. Chibnall, *Beyond Sherington* (Chichester, 1979), p. 165.

For Great Casterton and Stoke Hammond the combined 1522 and 1524 lists are used.

Sources Boxgrove, PRO, SC11/647, SRS, lvi, 26; Woodhead, Great Casterton, PRO, E315/254, RRS, i, 40, 96–7; Stoke Hammond, PRO, LR2/188, ff. 29–34, BRS, viii, 85, xvii, 333–4; Foscott, PRO, LR2/188, ff. 284–5, BRS, xvii, 60; Prinsted, PRO, SC12/15/76, SRS, lvi, 16; Rodmell, Lewes: Sussex Archaeological Trust, Aber. 129, SRS, lvi, 101–2.

Table 4.3   contd

Haddenham £ 1522	Ac. 1555	£ 1522	Ac. 1555
100	(demesne)	2⅔	30
63	180	2⅔	22
22	110	2	17
21	105	2	17
20	105	2	15
20	90	2	15
20	90	2	15
17	82	2	14
16	75	2	14
15	75	2	8½
15	60	2	7
15	60	2	7
15	60	2	7
14	60	2	7
12	60	2	7
10	60	2	7
10	60	1⅓	7
9	60	1	(5)
9	60	1	(5)
8	45	1	(5)
8	45	1	(1)
8	45	1	cottage
8	45	1	,,
8	45	1	,,
7	45	1	,,
6⅔	37	1	,,
6	37	1	,,
6	30+	1	,,
6	30+	1	,,
4	30	1	,,
4	30	1	,,
4	30	1	,,
3⅓	30	1	
3	30	0 × 5	
3	30	wages only × 27	
3	30		

Holdings are stated as yardlands, which are assumed to average 30 acres, and cotmanlands, which are taken as quarter-yardlands, There is also a 'worthy', or cottage holding, which is taken as a notional 1 acre. The 1522 and 1524 lists are combined. *Sources* PRO, LR2/188, ff. 13–21, BRS, viii, 4–5, xvii, 110–12.

conditions, like the sheep-corn region of Sussex, rising to about 60 on the heavy clays of the relatively inaccessible Midland vales. These acreages, mainly of common-field arable land, were of course complemented by a variable proportion of common pasture, which effectively made Prinstead holdings some 24 per cent bigger, and Rodmell ones more than double the recorded acreages.

Promising as surveys made as early as 1537 may look, it is more helpful to commence with Rodmell, where the rather late date of the earliest survey is offset by the fact that the structure of tenements scarcely changed throughout the century. Men assessed at 20s. (on goods in this case) were most probably cottagers and unlikely to have occupied as much as a whole yardland, which here meant about 10 acres plus ample common grazing. One yardland, or 1½, put a man in the 40s. class, perhaps a little higher, those worth £5–£10 having about 20–40 acres. Richard Aede, sen., the top man, with £20 in goods, occupied 52 acres, if not the 65 acre farm; one of these must have been tenanted by an outsider who employed one of the poorer villagers as bailiff; around 1620 the demesne was in fact leased to a wealthy gentleman farmer.[70] Copyhold fines were certain, and probably were at Boxgrove too, where the condition of the people was very similar and, compared with Great Casterton (Rutland) folk, they enjoyed the advantage of a superior location on the rich coastal plain of Sussex near Chichester. Prinstead, on the Hampshire border, was comparably situated, but the disabilities of serfdom, which still persisted there, coupled probably with arbitrary fines,[71] no doubt caused assessments to correspond with much bigger holdings; the omission of three freeholds from the survey leaves the picture incomplete. The big manor of Haddenham, in the Vale of Aylesbury, was measured in conventional units – virgates and cotmanlands – but conditions there nonetheless compare with those at Great Casterton, the best of the Midland examples; Foscott was not much of a place.

Although internal differentiation was well developed in rural communities by the 1520s, many retained a measure of rough equality with a relatively high proportion of the people having a substantial stake in the soil. Only here and there, as at Great Casterton, did a successful yeoman or two show signs of standing a little apart from the general run of peasants, who at Haddenham were outdistanced by a rich farmer-cum-merchant whom a landed income of £6 almost qualified for gentry status. Symptoms of incipient deeper inequalities also show themselves in the indications that the ratio of wealth to acreage increased towards the top of the scale, at precisely the point where we expect to find the more active and enterprising men. Significant too is the proportion of holdings of about 15 acres – the traditional peasant half–yardland – that match with £2 assessments. Since these were capable of producing substantially more wealth, while a much smaller plot could yield every bit as much, any doubts about the marginal position of many £2 men are removed: if evidence of smallholders being actively squeezed is scanty, their vulnerability is scarcely open to question.

The yesterday the Commonwealth Men ached to call back in the dreary 1540s is not difficult to pinpoint – 1485, the first year of the reign of Henry VII. Officially it was the *terminus a quo* in the definition of illicit enclosure and depopulation, and it was the land values of that period that the Norfolk rebels wanted restored. At government level, naturally, it expressed the official line that the Tudors had rescued the nation from the dark ages of tyranny. In the popular consciousness its mystique is to be sought not so much in some sly hint that everything had gone wrong since that event, as in the fact that it was simply a way of expressing 'upwards of sixty years ago', or beyond the limits of human memory in an age when few people lived that long. Most of the Commonwealth Men had not even been born in 1485. Hugh Latimer might remember helping his father buckle on his harness to go and fight at Blackheath Field,[72] but it was probably the only thing he did recall for certain, seeing that small boys normally take their parents' affairs for granted. 'Old men forget. . .' the rainy days; they have a knack of remembering the sun-drenched ones.

In this lost age of innocence the English (they never wearied of telling themselves) had been a contented race, busily cultivating little farms or making and selling artifacts in their shops. There had been an assured living for all. Rents had been low, frozen from time immemorial, fines reasonable, and all necessities of life could be purchased 'good cheap'. Enclosures and the pulling down of towns had apparently only begun some time after 1485; no one could possibly have read John Rous's MS list of fifty-eight Warwickshire villages depopulated much earlier.[73] Few of Latimer's congregation could have paused to reflect that his affectionate memories of life in the rural Midlands must have been coloured by the circumstances of his childhood: not many Leicestershire farmers in reality employed six men or owned thirty cows, a hundred sheep and a complete foot soldier's equipment, let alone were able to put sons through school and university.[74] This amounts almost to dismissing the reformers as a bunch of ranters who retreated from the material world into a fantasy conjured up by their fevered imaginations.

Yet although this is something of an occupational hazard for a good many clergymen (which indeed they were) and some sociologists (which they would nowadays be), the imputation does less than justice to their intelligence. Neither profound nor original thinkers, they reasoned from generalised impressions, of which the most obvious and cogent was the existence around them of a great mass of people – say a couple of hundred thousand households[75] – small farmers and independent craftsmen who controlled an important sector of the economy and added up to an interest of formidable proportions that embraced the destinies of hundreds of thousands of souls. There is no concrete evidence that this class declined measurably in size between the early 1520s and the late 1540s.

A broad correlation has already been established between taxpayers falling within the bracket £3–£20 and husbandmen, few of whom worked holdings big enough to do more than support a single family; their aim was subsistence as opposed to profit. Given the rude techniques available and the associated low level of productivity, this limitation was inevitable. But the testimony of the peasants themselves leaves us in no doubt that family farms was what the majority wanted. Their aspirations simply did not rise above feeding and housing themselves and their dependants, paying a reasonable rent for the right to do so. If only

> every man myght have. . . but one lythyll howsse or cotage to inhabyt and but a lytyl garden grownde wythe all thay wolde so order yt wythe thayr labor that thay wolde erne thayr lyvynge. . .a suffytyent and compleyte lyvynge. . .[76]

Equally material was lack of capital. Seldom could there be any question of putting something by for a rainy day; rather, so soon as the harvest was gathered the husbandman had to sell his grain in order to satisfy the landlord and the creditor.[77] With the stock of his farm comprising the bulk of his assets, the husbandman's meagre domestic effects were innocent of the gold and silver utensils and ornaments which then did duty as the savings accounts of the well-to-do. Even so, many farms may have been understocked: it is unlikely that animals, despite growing numbers, had as yet reached anything approaching the levels judged necessary to support arable husbandry in the nineteenth century.[78] In the most favourable circumstances the small farmer's income could rise only marginally above subsistence level, and a run of bad harvests might ruin him.[79]

In practice the mixed farming dictated by the need for self-sufficiency tended, as many inventories show, to mean a little bit of this and a little of that. Latimer, a farmer's son, tells the young King Edward:

A ploughland must have sheep; yea they must have sheep to dung their ground for bearing of corn; for if they have no sheep to help to fat the ground, they shall have but bare corn and thin. They must have swine for their food, to make their veneries or bacon off; theis is their venison: for they shall now have *hangum tuum*, if they get any other venison; so that bacon is their necessary meat to feed on, which they may not lack. They must have other cattle: as horses to draw their plough, and for carriage of things to the markets; and kine for their milk and cheese, which they must live upon and pay their rents. These cattle must have pasture, which pasture, if they lack, the rest must needs fail them: and pasture they cannot have; if the land be taken in, and enclosed from them.[80]

As on the clays of Latimer's native Leicestershire, dairy and suchlike animal products were the chief marketable commodities in both the cheese country of Wiltshire, and High Suffolk which produced 'butter and cheese in exceeding great quantitie of wonderful goodness comparable to any in the Realme. The commoditie thereof is unspeakable unto the inhabitants of the same...'[81] Yet everywhere, regardless almost of terrain and climature, the peasant engaged primarily in producing food for his own consumption.

Doubtless popular philosophy elevated necessity to a high principle. By its nature a peasant economy is self-perpetuating, a system from which it is difficult to break free. Ownership of land may never, as in some lands, have been legally vested in the peasant family,[82] but peasant aspirations were a potent force, and in fact the early principle that land belonged to the whole family retained its hold as late as 1700 at Kibworth Harcourt, Leics. In the long term, nevertheless, partible inheritance led to a tendency for kindred to narrow and unigeniture to develop as holdings got partitioned to an irreducible minimum size. Once a holding contracted to the size that could support only a single family it became reserved for one child, though equal provision of chattels was made for all,[83] and the extent to which some Buckinghamshire peasants' wills divided their livestock[84] seems calculated to keep the family together, unless the heir was expected to buy out the others. It has indeed been contended that there could be no inheritance in a true peasant society because property was vested in the family and a member could not leave it without renouncing his share; hence there was no social mobility.[85] However, not only was this never the case in England, it may also be observed that the smallness of holdings kept the majority of husbandmen firmly locked within the system, and indeed it is easy to exaggerate the degree of social mobility in Tudor times and misapprehend its nature: except for a few the only route was downwards, if only because the spread of unigeniture in an age of population growth was bound to create a surplus of landless men, dependent on working for wages.

Accepting his lot as inevitable, the husbandman believed the institution right, resented attempts by individuals to modify it, and defended it unquestioningly. At times a streak of complacency showed itself: an Italian visitor observed that the English made no attempt to grow more than sufficed for their daily needs, neglecting a potentially rich export trade in foodstuffs.[86] Starkey flatly declared:

> There is also likewise in the feet and hands which sustain the body and procure by labour things necessary for the same, as it were, a common disease. For both the feet and the hands (to whom I resembled a ploughman and labourers of the ground, with craftsmen and artificers in procuring of things necessary) are negligent and slow to the exercise thereof which pertaineth to their office and duty. Ploughmen do not diligently labour and till the ground for the bringing forth of fruits necessary for the food and sustenance of man; craftsmen also and all artificers show no less negligence in the use of their crafts, by the reason whereof there is in our country much dearth thereof and penury.[87]

Legally almost all peasants were now free men, villeinage having fallen into desuetude. Here and there, especially in Norfolk, isolated pockets persisted, but many serfs had left their manors (paying chevage) to conceal their status and better their position: the record is largely the outcome of a drive by Elizabethan government to trace them and persuade them to purchase their freedom.[88] As a class, bondmen tended to be of little account, even though the Buckingham valor, 1521–2, notes in respect of Thornbury, 'Boundemen of good substaunce be ther a good nombre', and in Norfolk, 'many of reasonable good substaunce and many of them be See men and maryners'. Nonetheless, if these have encouraged some scholars to point a meaningful finger at sporadic examples of prosperity, in reality John Norden's verdict on three bondmen he discovered at Falmer, Sussex, in 1617 seems nearer the mark: 'We think [manumission] is now out of season, yet were they men of abilitie they might vpon consideration be in franchised.'[89] Finally, although those belonging to the bishop of Exeter's manor of St Germans, Cornwall, included a Saltash merchant and his family, the only ones traceable there, or at Menheniot, in 1522 were comparatively poor.[90]

Convention reinforced the position of the countryfolk. During the preceding century, when the population stood at a low level, tenants had been scarce and holdings correspondingly easy to come by. Progressive abandonment of demesne farming had increased the stock of land available for leasing to the peasantry, besides phasing out the burden of labour services. The landlord's interest diminished as rent became the only return he could get from his property, and since tenants insisted on paying no more than they themselves considered fair, he was obliged to reconcile himself to the proposition that any was better than none at all. Although it was never suggested that rent should be abolished, tenants could be seen refusing to serve as jurors in manor courts until their demands had been met, while the proclamations of the insurgent commons of Yorkshire in 1536 urged men to 'Claim ye old customs and tenant right, to take your farms by God's penny, all gressums [fines] and heightenings to be laid down.'[91] Thus had evolved the proposition that every man enjoyed a prescriptive right to a farm adequate to support himself and his family at a reasonable (i.e. low) rental, which it was mandatory on landowners to provide. Thomas Lever argued as much when preaching at St Paul's cross in December, consciously or not echoing what Crowley had lately written:

For without a law to beare you, yea contrarie to the law which forbiddeth al maner oppressions & extortion & that more is contrarie to conscience, the ground of al good lawes, ye enclosed frome the pore their due commons, leauied greater fines then heretofore haue bene leauied, put them from their liberties (and in a maner enheritaunce) that they held by custome, & reised theire rentes. Yea, when ther was a law ratified to the contrary, you ceased not to finde meanes either to compel your tenantes to consent to your desire in enclosing, or else ye found such maistership that no man durste gaine saye your doinges for fear of displeasure.[92]

John Bayker besought the king to compel landlords to let smallholdings to men who wanted to earn 'a suffytyent and compleyte lyvynge by thayr labor' and prevent them amalgamating family farms into larger units to be run commercially. Latimer expounded the doctrine that 'The poorest ploughman is in Christ equal withe greatest that is. Let them, therefore, have sufficient to maintain them, and to find them their necessaries'.[93] In 1547 legislation to compel the breaking up of engrossed farms was actually planned even though not carried through. If an isolated gesture it was of a piece with the long series of acts against enclosure and depopulation, and an earnest of official approbation of the little man whom the state regarded as the true representative of the nation, and, in theory, cherished as vital to the preservation to the fabric of society.[94]

When Starkey could liken the tillers of the soil to the feet which 'by their labours sustain and support the rest of the body',[95] it is not difficult to appreciate that the wellbeing of this member should have been a matter of paramount concern. Blanchard argues that the peasantry formed an important consumer market, and Fisher depicts 1500–25 as a period of commercial prosperity. Declining purchasing power, which must largely have meant peasant consumption, was blamed for the collapse of the exchange in 1551 and, needless to say, was traced back to the ubiquity of sheep and sheepmen.[96] Of course this view did not go unchallenged. As Crowley was keenly aware, landowners were disposed to claim that

> The paisant knaues be to welthy, prouender pricketh them! They knowe not them selues, they knowe no obedience, they regard no lawes, thei would haue no gentlemen, thei wold haue al men like themselues, they would haue al thinges commune! Thei would not haue vs maisters of that which is our owne! They wil appoint vs what rent we shal take for our groundes! We must not make the beste of oure owne! They are ioly felowes! Thei wil caste doune our parckes & laie our pastures open! Thei wil haue the law in their own handes.[97]

It is indeed true that land was widely regarded as a form of community property, to the extent that the titular owners were expected to act as trustees for the Common Weal. One result of the conflict of views concerning the rights and duties contingent upon ownership was a sharp disagreement about the requirements of the law which led each party to ignore those aspects which did not serve its own purpose.

The peasant interest was defended with spirit. Founded on the assumption of an unchanging economic order, every person, every innovation that challenged it stood *ipso facto* condemned: the ultimate crime was to disturb the equilibrium. Antagonism towards, among others, the makers of larger, more efficient farming units rested on the thesis that engrossment of smallholdings necessarily deprived families of their rightful livelihoods. 'And one man shall have two or three such things, or more, in his hands, that a poor man shall scarcely have a hole to put his head. . .'[98] The tacit rule of fair shares could be extended to support the proposition that the law should prohibit any one man occupying two holdings unless their aggregate value was below a stipulated figure; three should not be permissible under any circumstances, so that, in the words of one statute, 'The wealthe of the Realme is kepte dispersed and distributed in manie handes, where yt is more ready to answere all necessary chardges for the service of the Realme. . .'[99] Not the least of these was national defence, the consideration that chiefly moved Protector Somerset to take up the question of depopulation. It was an indisputable fact that 'the mighty force of our enymies cannot be resisted with Shippe, be ther woll never so fyne', even if the related argument that enclosure 'is a great decay to artyllary: for that we do reckon that shepherdes be but yll artchers' sounds a trifle strained.[100]

The roll call of wrongdoers and anti-social acts seems at times endless. Enclosure, depopulation and conversion of arable land to pasture drove the peasant from the land; enclosure or overstocking of commons and the excessive raising of rents and fines rendered his position intolerable. The landlord who imposed it and the tenant who connived at it were equally culpable. So too was the lawyer who plumbed the darkest recesses of the Common Law in search of precedents and pretexts to circumvent the customs which protected the poor commons.[101] The attack broadened to include the middlemen whose intervention in the market forced up prices, and the merchant who, to his own profit, imported inessential foreign wares which both threatened the native artificer with unemployment and drained the kingdom of specie.[102] Crowley branded them impartially as 'greedy cormorants'; other polemicists echoed him. Of course 'greedy covetousness' meant profit. The offence was a dual one in that, on the one hand, the pursuit of profit necessarily disrupted the regular, leisurely rhythm of life and labour, and, on the other, success manifested itself in the unwholesome spectacle of go-ahead men outstripping their more conservative (or underachieving) peers. The *mores* of the age were such that their methods might at times be crude, even brutal, with the result that the process of economic change and development literally caused casualties. But it by no means follows that this was the principal cause of resentment; our present experience suggests something more general. In the hostility of organised labour to the modernisation of industry – lip-service notwithstanding – as well as membership of the European Economic Community, may be seen a vested interest defending its privileges as a matter of rigid principle. For all that effective measures may nowadays be taken to cushion the impact on the individual, the reaction is almost identical with that of sixteenth-century farmers. Reared in the shadow of the first industrial revolution, the pioneers of economic history could accept with little or no reservation the thesis that the poor were invariably the defenceless victims of the exploiting rich. Yet if any true parallel may be drawn between the embattled peasants of the Tudor Age, the handicraft workers of the early nineteenth century, and the miners, dockers and printers of recent decades, the conclusion must be that groups which have grown accustomed to occupying a position of unchallenged importance in the economy will stubbornly resist any developments which tend to erode it, and claim moral justification for so doing.[103]

THE LAND QUESTION

What was the whole truth as opposed to those facts, undoubtedly true in themselves, that were deployed selectively, possibly distorted, to bolster *ex parte* argument?

Population trends, unperceived at the time, go some way towards elucidating the problem. From less than 2 million around 1450 the nation had grown to at least 2.3 million by the early 1520s and, continuing to increase rapidly, topped 3 million by 1550.[104] There is good reason to postulate that a declining population had lain at the root of the movement from arable farming to sheep grazing. In the wake of the Black Death the acreage under the plough had steadily contracted, so that much of the enclosure movement became a matter of untenanted land reverting to grass, a retreat from marginal land. While clear records of the calculated destruction of thriving communities to make room for sheep do exist, the majority of deserted villages were tiny settlements which had already reached an advanced stage of decay before receiving the *coup de grâce*.[105] Instances when scores of people were turned adrift at a stroke to become vagabonds and beggars must have occurred, but, widely dispersed in time and space, can hardly have created the vagrant army of popular apprehension.

Rather than dismiss the land hunger of the first half of the sixteenth century as some groundless myth we should aim to define it and probe its complexities. Since the land on which so much of the population lived was a finite resource, demographic growth could not avoid adding to the total of landless peasants, and it is fair to assume that the type of person represented by the lowest assessments was becoming more numerous than formerly, moving towards the point, at the end of the seventeenth century, when wage labourers and servants would constitute a good two-thirds of the nation.[106] So long as there had been comparatively few mouths to feed, pastoral farming made good sense, but under changing conditions the omelet needed to be unscrambled. The difficulty was how to achieve it. Any extension of the arable acreage entailed an unavoidable time-lag while grasslands were returned to the plough. In the event this began to show tangible results in the years after 1551 when the slump in the textile market reduced the incentive to grow wool, while soaring food prices once again made cereal production profitable.[107] In any case calls for reconversion tended to be uncertain – naturally enough, seeing that where the previous population had been cleared there could be no demand for arable holdings.

The real demand was for new holdings to be created, for estates to be opened up to new tenants. If the *Supplication of the Poor Commons* (1546) is taken at face value, popular expectations were aroused by the dissolution of the monasteries, only to be dashed when their lands were sold off to the nobility and gentry.[108] But landowners were not the sole culprits. A good many were eager to take advantage of the rising value of arable land to let as many farms as possible; where hitherto manorial authorities and remedial legislation had concentrated on the problem of re-edifying dilapidated farm buildings, attention now switched to the need for some redistribution of the land,[109] an aim to which the entrenched rights of existing tenants constituted an insuperable obstacle.

It was at this point that engrossment of holdings surfaced as a major complication. Complaints about it began to be heard from the 1520s onwards, with the common people, once mute, adding their own voice to the chorus. But rather than large-scale abuse, the inquisitions of depopulation in 1517, and again in 1548, emphasised the insidious spread of piecemeal enclosures and the throwing together of relatively small parcels of land – accompanied by the decay of buildings – much of it the work of small farmers themselves, albeit with the connivance of their lords.[110] Much of this had clearly happened at an early date when a sparse population had required little land to support it. The sequence is easy enough to reconstruct. Far back in the previous century some husbandman had aspired to expand his activities. A holding stood vacant because no would-be tenant had come forward. He put in his bid, which the lord was glad enough to accept, even at rather a low rent. The farmer now had two houses and ranges of outbuildings and, having no use for both, left one of them to decay, perhaps taking some of the materials to repair the one he still occupied. From time to time he would be cited in the manor court for this neglect, but since he was merely mulcted of a few pence and the lord did not try very hard to make him amend, he paid up and did nothing; eventually the fine might become a regular small item in the revenues of the manor. Worked as one unit the holdings became inseparable in practice, and, although invariably identified separately in the court roll, usually passed together from hand to hand. The village grows; now there are men without land. They apply to the lord, offer a good fine which he would like to accept, but his hands are tied. The bigger tenants sit tight, assured of their land for life and passing it intact to a single heir at death, leaving their younger children empty-handed. Not only does the custom of the manor uphold their right to what they hold, it tends in practice to follow the Common Law rule of primogeniture. Formerly a shrinking population had led to fewer but larger farms: 'the ground of the parish is gotten up into a few men's hands . . . the rest are compelled either to be hired servants . . . or else to beg their bread', as Harrison observed in 1572, shortly after William Box had contrasted the growth of poverty with the broad tracts of derelict land to be seen everywhere, 'thes wastes that nowe be came first by decaye or lacke of people . . . But nowe the tyme is alterid . . . For the people are increasid and grounde for plowes dothe wante.'[111] As one of the few who managed anything approaching a realistic diagnosis he urged a programme of reclamation and resettlement.

Again it is imperative to distinguish sixteenth-century trends from earlier ones. Evidence for the continuation unabated of engrossment is, as Tawney conceded, inconclusive, and it is not satisfactory to assume, as he did, that engrossment must have continued because contemporary writers said so.[112] Instances certainly exist, but examples of the opposite tendency in later manorial surveys corroborate Dr Blanchard's contention that landlords now saw it as in their interest to create new tenancies.[113] The central question is whether the national stock of agricultural units was undergoing diminution, a singularly obscure subject which, as opposed to ownership, has been almost completely ignored.

As with many other enquiries the starting point has to be Gregory King's tables relating to 1688. The 330,000 freeholders and farmers make an obvious nucleus, though others are sure to have had agricultural interests as well; the clergy – 'eminent' ones at least – had their glebes and most peers and gentry presumably occupied home farms, some of the latter being really gentlemen farmers. All these might add a further 26,000 or so; superior officials, lawyers and other professional men probably overlapped the landed classes proper, and since rural tradesmen still retained farming interests,[114] a maximum of 360,000 units seems warranted, and it may be safe to settle for a round 350,000 holdings.[115]

To get round the lack of comparable figures for the sixteenth century let us adapt King's procedure to attempt an apportionment of the best available aggregate. The estimated population as of 1522–5 embodies the assumption that 30 per cent of the 2,300,000, i.e. 690,000, consisted of males aged sixteen and over.[116] These divided nearly equally into ones assessed at less than £2, who were mostly labourers and servants, and those at £2 and over who can be assumed to have enjoyed regular means of support, being in general householders.[117] For most people a regular livelihood meant an agricultural holding, giving a basis of 345,000 units of all sizes. This of course must be a maximum, since the inhabitants of the larger towns would hardly have engaged in farming; even so, in contrast with the more sophisticated society of King's day, the number of people who did not retain some more or less direct connexion with the land is certain to have been very limited.

Not only was there no significant reduction in the national total of farming units, there was even a slight increase, slight enough to be overshadowed by the short-term fluctuations which are bound to have occurred in more than 160 years when any imbalance can only have been accentuated by sustained population growth.[118] Any earlier tendency towards fewer, larger holdings would have been offset by some reversal of the movement in the second quarter of the sixteenth century, and subsequent consolidation balanced by gains due to reclamation, as, for example, in the Fens in the seventeenth. Piecemeal inning of the Lincolnshire marshes proceeded more or less continuously, and, although the initiative of landowners, the newly won land was usually let or sublet. Subject to some fluctuation, the median size of peasant farms seems to have fallen slightly, and, though mainly as a result of reclamation, bigger farms did appear in the Fenland, the arable acreage of peasant holdings did not change at all.[119] In Leicestershire too farm sizes remained pretty much the same in the seventeenth century as in the sixteenth.[120] At village level trends were conditioned by location. In Cambridgeshire, Chippenham, on the arable-farming chalklands, experienced a steady evolution towards fewer and bigger units between 1544 and 1636, including an abrupt drop of one-third by 1560. Fenland Willingham saw a 50 per cent increase in the number of smallholdings during the seventeenth century, while at Orwell, on the clay, growth overall was the result of medium-size units giving way to increased numbers of both big and tiny ones.[121] Little overall change occurred at

Myddle, Salop, in the sixteenth century or at Sherington, Bucks., in the seventeenth, while at Petworth, Sussex, the demesne, leased as a whole prior to 1500, was parcelled into as many as six farms in the early sixteenth century.[122] In mainly pastoral districts the small farmer not only held his own but even gained ground.

Polarisation in the village community followed divergent paths defined by Victor Skipp. In five parishes of the pastoral Arden district in Warwickshire the process was 'indirect' or 'contingent' on population growth, with additional poor households being created; inequity, in other words, was build into the system. In places like Chippenham, Cambs., the course was 'direct' – the 'removal of the middle', by the ousting of the small farmers, tending towards the stereotyped arable structure of big farmers and landless labourers.[123] As in most respects, each region had a distinctive pattern modified by localised variants which for the time being cancelled one another out.

If landlords as a class merited a good deal less than all the opprobrium that has been heaped upon them, the sheer volume of agrarian protest still demands attention. Of all grievances rent provoked the deepest, most sustained resentment, furnishing several of the articles of the Norfolk rebels in 1549, to the exclusion of most of the objects of official investigation the previous year. Indeed, in most of the stirs the throwing open of enclosures took on more of the character of spontaneous mob violence than of organised action. Kett's rebellion speedily developed into a movement of husbandmen and yeomen who, as occupiers of land and (in Norfolk) enclosers themselves,[124] were aggrieved chiefly by pecuniary burdens and the invasion of their fields by rich men's flocks, not by the plight of the landless. Time and again when we observe the farming community taking measures of self-defence – as opposed to reading pamphleteers' views about their tribulations – the crux of the matter turns out to be escalating rents and fines, and it can be no accident that this is the easiest one to demonstrate.

If custom restrained a lord from ruthlessly exploiting his estates, why the unending stream of complaints? Who if not the lord was getting the excessive rent by which the farmer claimed to be crushed? The Commonwealth Men inveighed bitterly against the 'leasemonger', typically a sharp operator who duped tenants into assigning him their leases, which he thereupon offered to renew at four (or more) times the old rent.[125] A shadowy class, whose existence (outside tracts and sermons) is suspected rather than demonstrated, these counterfeit landlords were represented as speculators, though in practice, no doubt, the term was prone to be stretched to embrace anyone who profited from renting out land untramelled by the sanctions of custom. Having taken the first step towards identifying them, can we now take the next and catch them, so to speak, in the act by showing that men registered as landowners were measurably better off than those who were not? On average (Table 4.4) they did in fact own three times as much personal wealth. At Slapton two-thirds of the former owned goods worth £3 or more, but none of the latter had more than £2 – indeed, at Haddenham and in Rutland generally most landed men had at least £5.[126] For working farmers, as most probably were, having their own land allowed them to pocket the bulk of their earnings.

In Rutland only were the tenants of a few of these men recorded, indicating that about one in ten was a petty landlord,[127] though the true proportion may have been slightly higher since a man holding of two lords was listed as the tenant of only one of them, and, pursuant to the overt purpose of the survey, priority would be given to naming the lord of the manor or (if appropriate) some other gentleman.

Although the holdings of these men in parishes other than where they resided are not readily ascertainable, the subsidy schedule for the Aylesbury Hundreds, Bucks., adds a note of income from land to many assessments on goods, doubtless as proof that it was too small to be taxed, most amounts being only a few shillings, a pound or two at most. Now assessments for the subsidy were specifically limited to income actually arising from land, and did not, as in the muster, signify the hypothetical benefit of occupying one's own property; thus for John Browne of Stoke Mandeville £2 may well stand for the rent element in the £5 assessed in 1522. The location of his property is not stated, but any not in Stoke must almost certainly have been let. Some considerable number of those who (according to the muster) did not have land in their home parishes must have been receivers of rent, and, as a result, averaging £13 in personalty, were more than three times as well off as those not in a position to draw income from their land who averaged £4. It can hardly be doubted that the latter were predominantly owner-occupiers, of whom fourteen in Monks Risborough can have been little better than smallholders, while many others were merely cottagers or labourers: Henry Kinge and William Syrett of Askett hamlet owned parcels rated at 6s. and 5s., respectively, but no goods, though one was subsequently taxed on goods of £1, the other on wages. All told, the goods of these – exactly half of which belonged to one of them – came to £32, while seven rentiers shared £96.[128] Throughout this district the contrast was decidedly more pronounced than in most others; not only was the mean personal property of men listed in the muster as landowners £13.6 compared with a mere £2.4 for everyone else, but also as a group landed men owned three-fifths of all the personalty there. As nine out of ten non-owners had moveables worth less than £5, it looks very much as if the threshold for the (second) loan was fixed at this point in order to exempt them; even small landowners were well able to afford their contribution since upwards of 60 per cent of them were assessed at £10 or more on goods, and indeed a good half belonged to the genuinely affluent strata of society worth £20 and upwards.

The unevenness that prevents us basing a realistic cross-section of society on its distribution cannot completely obscure the central importance of land as the ultimate source of all wealth. The richest people were mostly great landowners, even though, since their property consisted largely of manors, custom reinforced by the Common Law curtailed its benefit to them. At the opposite end of the scale, no one worth less than £3 in moveables was likely to own any land at all, and, since to be tenant farmers was the height of their aspirations, their personal wealth was mainly determined by the rent they had to pay. To own even a small parcel was to enjoy tangible benefits. The man who worked his own land, subject only to minimal outgoings, stood to profit from all he produced, and so was far better placed to accumulate chattel wealth than a neighbour who might have no choice but to pay a competitive rent. Most favourably situated of all the lesser proprietors, and in many ways answering to the description village capitalist, was the man in a position to play the part of landlord, if on the smallest scale, even to the point of investing his savings in the purchase of additional acres to expand his business.

In practice very often the only real distinction between owner and tenant was the legal definition. Even freeholders were tenants, usually to the lord of the manor, though for nominal rents and services. A manor too was normally held of a superior, and, if this was the king, was subject to the burden of wardship when inherited by a minor, being administered by the Crown until the owner came of age, the effect being a heavy and unpredictable form of succession duty. Copyholders by inheritance differed from freeholders only in that the tenure was socially inferior, and were actually better off because the legal costs of acquisition were negligible. Copyholders for lives and tenants with long leases, once the entry fine was paid, were also assured of undisturbed possession.

Very different was the situation of the occupiers of farms by agricultural tenancies from year to year, including a host of sub-tenants

Table 4.4 Personal wealth of landowners and non-landowners

| Value of goods £ | RUTLAND | | | | BUCKINGHAMSHIRE (AYLESBURY) | | | |
| | Landowners | | Non-landowners | | Landowners | | Non-landowners | |
	Number	Wealth £	Number	Wealth £	Number	Wealth £	Number	Wealth £
Under 1	1	–	332	6	1	1	205	205
1	5	5	194	208	–	–	181	363
2	17	34	152	306	1	4	64	213
3–4	18	68	168	565	43	282	29	160
5–9	14	86	208	1,328	42	531	14	152
10–19	19	226	158	1,940	34	729	3	77
20–39	25	530	60	1,730	3	143	1	40
40–99	9	500	8	358	–	–	–	–
100+	1	200	1	120	–	–	–	–
Total	109	1,649	1,281	6,561	124	1,690	497	1,210

Percentages

Under 1	0.9	–	25.9	0.1	–	–	–	–
1	4.6	0.3	15.1	3.2	0.8	0.1	41.2	16.9
2	15.6	2.1	11.9	4.7	–	–	36.4	30.0
3–4	16.5	4.1	13.1	8.6	0.8	0.2	12.9	17.6
5–9	12.8	5.2	16.2	20.2	34.7	16.7	5.8	13.2
10–19	17.4	13.7	12.3	29.6	33.9	31.4	2.8	12.6
20–39	22.9	32.1	4.7	26.4	27.4	43.1	0.6	6.4
40–99	8.3	30.3	0.6	5.5	2.4	8.5	0.2	3.3
100+	0.9	12.1	0.1	1.8	–	–	–	–
Total	99.9	99.9	99.9	100.1	100.0	100.0	99.9	100.0

195

on customary land whose lot was little less precarious than that of tenants at will on the demesnes of aggressively managed manors. And they probably formed a majority of the rural community. Even on manors where many of the head tenants were absentees, very few licences to demise were recorded; on some, indeed, tenements could be freely demised without licence, some lords merely reserving the right to veto individual under-tenants. It may be assumed that as a rule the head tenant preferred to retain the option to vary the rent from year to year, which the sub-tenant found easier than paying a big fine for an extended term. The licence itself was no problem; 4d. a year was the standard fee in East Sussex, and indeed the steward of the barony of Lewes, who attempted, c. 1585, to increase it, was obliged to admit to an error; a limit of seven years on licences, which were readily available, at Petworth was not considered unduly restrictive.[129]

If, as seems likely, most of the actual tillers of the soil were tenants from year to year, it is hardly surprising that rent should have been the greatest single grievance. Although the most consistent evidence of an upward trend is restricted to certain parts of the country, nationwide discontent makes it improbable that others remained unaffected. Even where custom imposed restrictions on lords of manors there was nothing to prevent lesser owners enhancing rents; in fact it is significant that quasi-landlords were the chief targets of protest, and so have been depicted as the pace-setters, as newcomers to the land business, not only investing the profits of commerce but also introducing the ethics of the market place to estate administration. In reality it is clear that the trend was set by certain great estates, which are generally believed to have been managed conservatively, but all the same, counterfeit landlords cannot have been slow to follow their example.

In some circumstances the real rent was paid in advance as a lump sum, i.e. a fine which, unless specifically limited by custom, was fixed by the lord at will. Nevertheless, it is unrealistic to picture a hapless peasant faced with a take-it-or-leave-it demand for a preposterous sum. In practice 'arbitrary' meant negotiable; payment was sometimes by instalments, and some tenants raised it by mortgage. The experimental legalisation of usury in 1571 perhaps recognised the husbandman's need for access to loan capital, with a limit of 10 per cent to save him getting into deep waters,[130] for of course any serious fall in prices could leave him unable to meet his liabilities. Nor was it necessarily a case of paying up or going away empty-handed; the applicant might just as likely be mentally balancing the immediate down payment against the income anticipated from subletting the tenement at rack rent. The method appealed also to the gambling instinct of both parties: the lord hoping for the lease to expire before the twenty-one years the normal three lives were expected to average, advancing the day when he would get another (and bigger) fine, the tenant reckoning on profiting from rising values and one of the nominated persons outliving this period. Due perhaps to its uncertainties, rack rent has acquired sinister overtones, but although enabling the landlord to take a share of any increased profitability, the possibility of a reduction could help the tenant, who had not sunk a large slice of his resources in the purchase of a lease, to weather a depression.

The tensions of the common weal did not resolve neatly into a plain tale of unequal conflict between a powerful landed aristocracy and underprivileged tenant farmers. If anything, both tended to lose ground to men of intermediate status, those worth £5–£19 in personal wealth. The progressive division of village society into two classes meant, in the first place, that holdings of comparable size could be owned or tenanted by men of widely differing personal wealth; secondly, that many more farmers occupied land on competitive terms than manorial records indicate; thirdly, that the emergence of petty landlords seems to lie at the root of many of the stresses of rural society, nourishing the fundamental internal contradiction which could, and in the fullness of time did, precipitate the decline and fall of the peasant economy. Like the gentry, these minor proprietors, yeomen, are widely pictured as 'rising' from the 1540s onwards;[131] as with the gentry there is every reason to believe that their origins went back very much further. Finally, the institutions which guaranteed their property rights tended also to create a rural proletariat by excluding younger sons from the landholding hierarchy.

CHAPTER FIVE

THE LABOURING CLASS
AND THE POOR

IN ADDITION to any external threat from above and its own internal contradictions, the ideal society of small producers was coming under increasing pressure from the emergent labouring class and the related problem of rural poverty. Barely perceived in its initial phases, the evolution of this element, its genesis especially, has still to be investigated in depth.[1] The well-established fact that agricultural labourers were a prominent feature of seventeenth-century society is apt to be coupled with the implication that they 'just happened'. As regards the sixteenth century, unwonted emphasis on the lower social strata means that the assessment lists of the 1520s cannot be bettered for testing the validity of the sort of generalisation that would have it that 'wage-earners were a minority scattered in the interstices of village and borough, and . . . normally the sons of peasants'.[2] Because this requires a more systematic survey of the labouring sort of people than has hitherto been practicable, the first step must be definition, inclusive of wealth parameters, followed by an estimate of the relative size of the wage-earning element, leading to the question, did labourers remain cadets of the landed peasantry or form a separate class? Then comes the social problems arising from the growth of this class, concluding with some attempt to quantify the vexed question of vagrancy and mendicancy.

LABOURERS, SERVANTS AND OTHERS

The terms 'labourer', 'servant' and 'artificer' were all regularly employed during this period by official scribes and literary men. Any tendency in practice to blur these distinctions was due perhaps to mental inertia or, more importantly, to variability of role, and does not alter the fact that each expression had a precise meaning which should be adhered to as consistently as possible.

A servant was a regular employee, engaged normally for a year at a time, residing under his master's roof, and remunerated primarily with board and lodging, to which were added a small money wage and an allowance for clothing, termed 'livery'. In general they were young men and unmarried, although the Statute of Artificers purported at one point to impose in-service on married men below the age of thirty. By convention twenty-four was regarded as the minimum age for marriage,[3] and was certainly defined as the age of discretion: 'Untill a man growe unto the aige of xxiiij[tie] yeares, he (for the moste parte, thoughe not allwayes) is withoute judgment & not of sufficyent experience to governe himselfe . . . And therefore had more neede still to remayne under government as a servant . . .' In 1561 Buckinghamshire justices of the peace ruled that single men were to be hired for a whole year at a time. The official designation of a person as 'singleman' may reflect this practice and be intended to account for elderly bachelor servants.[4] 'Servant' could be stretched to cover a wide range. Certain types fell into a special category, chiefly officers in a nobleman's or other great household, who as such could be correctly described as servants. But in these cases the emphasis is on 'office', which fundamentally differentiates them from men employed at manual tasks and, as a result, subject to labour regulations.[5]

In marked contrast with the seventeenth century, contemporary writings and even official records display a curious reticence about agricultural labourers which makes precise definition difficult. The Statute of Artificers described them negatively as 'every person beynge an housholder and xxiiij yeres Olde at the least, and not occupienge husbondry nor beynge a laborer Dwellinge . . . in any Towne not beynge incorporat . . . and exercysinge any arte mysterye or Manuell Occupacion' – in a word the residue of family men who were neither farmers nor craftsmen: cottagers and, in some cases, smallholders as well, as has been convincingly demonstrated. Unlike servants they were hired by the day or the task, as most wage schedules make clear. Bound to no master, they were prone to wander from place to place in search of work, and consequently are marked out as the people to whom the embryonic concept of 'settlement' was particularly applicable long before the finalisation of the principle in and after 1662. Frequently linked with husbandmen and contrasted with artificers, they were regarded as typically farm workers.[6]

Since 'artificers' were quite simply workers in the mechanic arts, it is no great problem to distinguish them from agricultural labourers. However, as all members of a craft were usually labelled, irrespective of status, with the same description – weaver, tanner, or whatever – master craftsmen can only be distinguished tentatively from hired hands by their relative wealth, and rarely is there any means of separating servants from out-workers and day-wage men; many of the former must of course have been apprentices, among whom any juveniles would have gone unrecorded since cash wages were not payable below the age of sixteen. Older apprentices, whose terms might be extended to twenty-four would – skill apart – have occupied the same contractual position as farm servants. In certain circumstances artificers worked more or less full-time on their masters' premises and so have been classed as servants.[7]

Women, of course, formed a large part of the workforce, but information about their numbers is scanty. The majority of married ones were ancillary to their husbands, while low wages excluded all but a very few females from fiscal records.[8]

We have seen (Table 1.2) that about 38 per cent of the population could be classed as labouring people. Servants as such were not distinguished in Rutland in 1524, but 270 (or 37 per cent) out of 730 taxpayers in three hundreds there were designated as labourers, more than 85 per cent of them being assessed at 20s. on wages, though thirty-eight were credited with goods to the value of 40s. and one with as much as £3. At the same time thirty other £1 assessments, mostly on goods, were ascribed variously to husbandmen, tradesmen and women, or else no occupation was specified. Although in the military survey the richest labourer was worth as much as £6 and one servant had £4, the majority of each type were assessed at less than £2, and in fact more than half were rated at nil. Scarcely more than one in ten owned to £2 or more. As the percentage of sub-£2 assessments and designated labourers and servants were almost identical, there need be little doubt about the status of persons at this level in returns which omit occupational descriptions.

As an agricultural shire Rutland was straightforward. In highly industrialised Babergh hundred, Suffolk, where the woollen trade employed a large part of the wage-earning population, the situation was much more complex. Almost two-fifths of assessments in 1522 were below £2, and in 1524 nearly half were based on wages. In addition to this, 530 out of 1,934 listed inhabitants (of which some 400 were not classified) were labourers, though well over a third of them were rated at

Table 5.1 Assessments of labourers, Suffolk, 1522

Assessment* £	Persons	%	% of all assessments
Nil	168	31.7	46.8
1	171	32.3	46.8
2	105	19.8	33.7
3–4	63	11.9	32.3
5–9*	17	3.2	12.5
10–19†	3	0.6	–
20	1	0.2	–
Not stated	2	0.4	–
Total	530	100.1	–

* Highest in class, £6 13s. 4d; † highest in class, £13 6s. 8d.

£2 or better. The details are shown in Table 5.1. The background of the four top-rated men in the table is anyone's guess. Clearly, however, a personal estate of £5–£6 was not beyond the reach of the labourer hereabouts, while £3–£4 looks almost commonplace. This state of affairs no doubt reflects the unique concentration of industry in the district which opened up opportunities not found elsewhere outside London. Nor can the clothing trade have been the sole cause, since labour was at a premium in the wood-pasture region generally. Although only three-quarters the size of Rutland, Babergh contained a good 30 per cent more people and was more than three times as affluent. Not all these labourers could have been farm hands, but significantly the well-heeled ones were shared evenly between the industrial and non-industrial villages. Some may well have been servants, a description applied to a mere twenty-seven men, twenty-four of whom were in the household of Sir William Waldegrave at Smallbridge Hall. In the complex local economy the wealthier ones were employed in some kind of managerial or supervisory capacities which, even if the remuneration itself was not necessarily generous, provided opportunities for profit.

Deferring, for the present, consideration of the minority (naturally speaking) of workers outside the agricultural sector, let us now apply these preliminary observations to other counties (see Table 5.2). These lowest assessments lie generally within the range 37–47 per cent, inclusive of Rutland, to which the single Northamptonshire hundred of Towcester was similar at 35¼ per cent. In Lincolnshire at large the proportion was something above one-third, though approaching 41 per cent in the two wapentakes analysed; in Devon it averaged 36 per cent and in Leicestershire 22.[9] This in broad terms was the situation in the eastern counties, the Midlands and the south. It was probably not dissimilar in Gloucestershire where, making full allowance for regional variations and discrepancies between the sources, the average can safely be estimated in the order of one-third, and possibly rather higher.[10]

The low Leicestershire average results from the very small numbers of wage assessments recorded in some parishes – none at all in a few instances. Going northwards, the proportion of £1 assessments falls steadily away; indeed, in counties such as Staffordshire and Shropshire, even after allowing for a sparser population, the total number of assessments seems to become unrealistically small.[11] In these progressively poorer regions the market for labour is very likely to have been limited, but in addition, low wage rates could have been the means of exempting many labourers from taxation, for counties which already operated such rates were directed by the regulating act of 1515 to continue them and not raise them to the legal minimum.[12] In the northern shires the subsidy affected only the merest fraction of the population, literally no more than two or three individuals in many a township. In Cornwall the proportion of taxpaying wage earners varied from 15 per cent or less in the eastern hundreds of Stratton, Lesnewth and West to 26 per cent in Penwith and almost 45 per cent in Kerrier in the west.[13] The muster books here are distinguished, on the one hand, by the paucity of assessments of less than £2, and on the other, by the device of grouping several men together with a single assessment, usually members of the same family. The overall impression is that the labouring element was both smaller and less obviously differentiated than in most other counties. A good many wage earners, and men with nil assessments, in the muster were aliens, and it is only reasonable to conclude that the occasion of their presence in substantial numbers was a shortage of native labour.

According to the muster book there were almost precisely four labourers for every servant recorded in Rutland. The ratio was about three to one in mid-Sussex, where the collectors for Bramber rape thoughtfully differentiated wages derived from annual engagements from those earned by day-work, describing many recipients of the former as servants, and for the parish of Wiston grouping the latter under the subheading 'labourers by the day'. The resulting tally is 140 servants and 398 labourers,[14] exclusive of any who might have qualified for taxation as owners of personal property. These two cases represent the most consistent attempts at classification, and it is of interest to note that a similar ratio is implicit in Gregory King's tables of 1688.[15] Elsewhere many descriptions are unhelpful. The collectors of Avisford and Poling hundreds in Sussex uniformly called wage earners servants in 1524 and labourers in 1525, while in several other districts 'servant' was used exclusively; the only labourer mentioned in Petworth, Ralph Tanner, was stated to be 'seruant to John Tanner', who was probably his father. A number of servants were singled out in Wantage hundred, Berks., but only a handful of labourers: most other men were classed as householders, those with the lowest assessments presumably being wage-earning cottagers, but as a whole the return is uninformative. In townships for which the entries are subdivided into 'householders' and 'labourers and servants' the latter amount to 38.7 per cent, but almost a fifth of assessments of less than 40s. were placed in the householder section, and some must have also been labourers.[16]

In most areas servants appear to have formed more or less a quarter of workers who were mainly dependent on wages. If, as often as not, no clear distinction was observed, this was not necessarily because it was not understood, but rather the result of a habit of using related terms interchangeably, letting one meaning embrace both. This unintentional confusion was still cropping up in the middle of the seventeenth century.[17] The significance of 'servant' was well understood, but in the earlier part of the Tudor period at least, 'labourers' may have been a concept which caused both semantic and psychological difficulties. The description of

Table 5.2 Distribution of nil and £1 assessments

County	Total	Nil/£1	%
Berkshire	3,620	1,726	47.7
Buckinghamshire	7,842	3,359	42.8
Norfolk	6,862	3,103	45.2
Suffolk*	14,933	6,003	40.2
Worcestershire	2,302	897	39.0
Sussex*	10,517	4,466	42.5
Essex*	15,081	6,384	42.1

* Figures from subsidy rolls.

most men who had no goods as 'young and poor' evidently came easily to the Rutland commissioners, but the disproportionately small number of 'old' men suggests that they found the idea of ageing, indigent labourers (possibly with families) both unusual and disturbing.

In a wholly agricultural shire like Rutland the number of craftsmen or tradesmen was minimal and the majority were men of very slender means. More than half were taxed on wages, or would have been had they been assessed for the subsidy; several were described in the muster book as poor men. Two pewterers in Oakham were almost certainly employees of a third who was a wealthy manufacturer, but as for other craftsmen the source of their assessed wages is problematical and may well have been general labouring. Every man who was assigned to a trade by one return was described as a farmer or labourer by the other, an indication that this kind of community was incapable of generating full-time employment for even the most essential artisans. Some therefore gained part of their livelihood from small farms - perhaps the big ones too in one or two cases – while others took what work they could find, but whether as cottagers who took in craft work, or tradesmen who hired themselves to farmers in slack periods, cannot be precisely determined. A similar situation would have obtained in other farming districts. Where industry was more or less developed it must have employed a correspondingly larger number of men from the lowest ranks, but it was only in the clothing district of Suffolk that they were identified.

Most Suffolk tradesmen were either masters in a very small way or else wage earners – journeymen or cottage out-workers – but there is no clue as to their precise status save what can be inferred from their

Table 5.3 Textile workers in Suffolk

Occupation	Minimum £	Maximum £	Median £	Number @ £4 +	Total number
Clothmaker	2	3,200	27	113	118
Weaver	0	20	1	24	106
Fuller	0	13	2	9	40
Shearman	0	20	1	2	26
Dyer	0	30	1	3	13
Tailor	0	20	2	13	51

wealth. Three-fifths worked in the textile trades, their condition being as shown in Table 5.3. Purely distributive trades such as mercer and draper clearly find no place in this collection. Taking the labourer structure (Table 5.1) as the matrix, we may tentatively suggest that up to £4 most men were operatives, probably wage earners; some doubtless were working masters though enjoying a limited and declining degree of independence within the capitalist putting-out system.[18] Fairly obviously the clothmakers (or clothiers) were the sort of men who were unlikely to be found in the lower strata, although it is noteworthy that half or more must have been in a very small way of business: the handful who appear poor were probably men whose liabilities exceeded their assets. In contrast, some three-quarters of the manual workers were no different economically from men who were described as labourers, and a great many reappeared in the subsidy rolls taxed on wages. If we read the assessments correctly, shearing and dyeing were two trades in which, apart from a handful of potential employers of labour, nearly every member was more or less dependent on wages. Clothing occupied exactly three out of five persons not engaged in agriculture, 371 out of 612. Other trades were numerous and diverse, forming the extensive support echelon a rich and complex economy could be expected to attract. These divided into two categories, manual and distributive, and in the former, such as wood and metal crafts, the poor working element is similarly conspicuous.

In most returns the artisan element has to be inferred. The many tradesmen's servants noted at Coventry must, in the absence of evidence to the contrary, be assumed to have followed the same callings. Some must have been apprentices, of whom a good many were recorded in Exeter, one entry being particularly revealing: 'Richard Webber and John Townesen, servants and apprentices to Richard Coke', whose trade, unfortunately, is not stated; naturally neither owned any property.[19] Finally it has to be remembered that away from the larger towns and areas of major industrial development, the industrial workforce consisted mainly of farmers and smallholders during the slack season, the professional element being very small at this time.

A LABOURING CLASS

It was Tawney's contention, although conceding the impossibility of statistical demonstration, that the household which was wholly dependent on wages was atypical of sixteenth-century rural society.[20] By 1600 this may well be questionable,[21] but although the earlier years are shrouded in obscurity, a handful of pregnant statements exercise a potentially important bearing on the problem. Around 1550 a well-known passage in the *Discourse of the Common Weal* asserted that 'there be manie a M. cottagers in england, which, hauinge no landes to liue of theire oune but theire handie labours, and some refreshinge vppon the said commons, yf they weare sodenly thrust out from that commoditie might make a tumult and discorde in the common wealth'.[22] If it was literally true that, subject to some (variable) common rights, there existed a class of landless, wage-dependent labourers, the only question to be resolved is how many thousands had the writer in mind? Ten is feasible, so too is 100; the difference in a tiny population is immense. In 1525 there was distress in Suffolk. Alleging 'our goodes be taken from us' by Wolsey's Amicable Grant, clothiers laid off their workmen, and husbandmen their servants. A wave of riots swept the district in the course of which John Grene, the people's spokesman, is reported to have told the duke of Norfolk, 'We . . . lyve not of our selfes, but all we lyve by the substanciall occupiers of this Countrey, and yet they geve us so little wages for our workmanship, that scarcely we be able to liue . . .' and if they can't pay us we must perish.[23] Even this early there were a few areas at least where dependence on wages was the lot of many people.

Clearly not all the men taxed on wages can have been householders, far from it, but outnumbering servants nearly three to one, day labourers amounted to some 28–29 per cent of all taxpayers in Rutland and Bramber rape, Sussex, to which the corollary is that a similar proportion of households were dependent on wages. By the turn of the century it had certainly become large enough to cause deep concern; the act of 1589 which decreed the assignment of four acres of land to every newly built cottage,[24] acknowledged that far too many families had no resources to fall back on in times of recession.

With the notable exception of the *Discourse*, allusions to wage dependence seem more often than not to refer to artificers, who were vulnerable to the full force of economic fluctuations, unlike agricultural labourers who could hope for a measure of immunity. Yet the former not infrequently occupied smallholdings; indeed, manufacture tended to develop in regions of small family-holdings and pastoral farming precisely because these made fewer demands on the workers' time than cultivation. Conversely, the century witnessed a decline in the employment of full-time farm servants and a corresponding growth in the use of casual labour.[25] Either these factors cancel one another out, or else the artificer's lot was not as bad as sometimes represented, while the farm worker's progressively deteriorated. In fact the revolt of the Suffolk cloth workers is perfectly consistent with a relatively high standard of living which they sought to defend. In 1539 they were petitioning the government against clothiers who were combining to depress wages, 'By meanes whereoff many of your saide Supplyaunttes, that hath kepte good howsholdes, hathe exspendyd and wasted their substaunce, And are glade to become other mens servauntts, And many mo of them ys lyke so to doo . . .'[26] Equally, industry might well have been draining surplus labour from arable farming districts and thereby creating a new proletariat. Attempts to curb the growth of industry, to restrict entry to crafts, and to conscript labour for the fields[27] point alike to anxiety over an unhealthy situation – real or imaginary – in the major centres of manufacture, while certainly the reputedly gold-paved streets of the cities have always beckoned irresistibly to the rural poor. And for all workers a variety of factors operated to determine the ultimate degree of proletarianisation, not least the local conditions which governed the availability of small tenements and access to commons.[28]

Can a differentiated labouring class be identified in Tudor England? At first glance the concept of the village as a one-class community[29] seems amply supported by the deep overlap in the tax assessments of labourers and husbandmen and others: in Rutland some forty labourers – about 5½ per cent of the inhabitants – taxed at £2 or £3 were balanced by thirteen husbandmen at only £1, besides several men whose status was alternately one or the other, and their assessments 20s. or 40s. in different lists, while the significant number without status tags points to indeterminacy. A couple of yeomen, who were worth nothing, and were more realistically called servants in another list, might have been journeymen, by analogy with the yeomanry of certain London livery companies, unless use of the term represents a survival of the earlier connotation 'servant'. In wooded country, distinctions might be further blurred, as in the rape of Hastings in Sussex, where nearly 30 per cent of £1 assessments were based on goods as if the collectors limited taxation of wages to the irreducible minimum of persons mainly or wholly dependent on them and amounting to a good third of all taxpayers.[30] The high proportion of 20s. men in the Forest of Dean, in contrast to the rest of Gloucestershire, prompts the reflexion that the possessor of a personal estate of this size did not necessarily have a standard of living inferior to that of many men on considerably higher assessments. Much of the substance of a free miner – endowed with numerous privileges not enjoyed by (for example) a Wealden iron worker – would have consisted of domestic comforts with, maybe, a cow worth eight or ten shillings; the rudimentary equipment needed for his job was unlikely to be worth more than a shilling or two.[31] Compare the Midland farmer whose stock and tackle normally accounted for six-sevenths of his personal estate: an assessment as high as £5 could thus indicate as little as 14s. (£0.7) worth of household effects, leaving little to chose between the lifestyles of the smaller cultivators and the labourers. The true difference, of course, was that while the one had only his 'handie labours' to support himself, the other, so long as the weather was kind, might expect to enjoy a secure livelihood. If the line of demarcation defies precise definition, the effective difference was real enough, between, on the one hand, the smallholder who needed to eke out his subsistence with occasional labouring, and, on the other, the wage earner who might or might not have a patch of ground and/or some rights of common to fall back on. The former naturally merged at the upper level with the self-sufficient husbandman. Everitt has reckoned that 'cottage farmers' formed one-quarter of the agricultural working population, suggesting that they corresponded to labourers who possessed 2 or 3 acres.[32] The indications are that wood, marsh and moorland all favoured the semi-independent cottager, whilst champaign corn-growing districts, where in any case demand for labour was lively, were less likely to have land to spare for very small tenements and, as the population grew, spawned an ever-increasing multitude of landless families.

The existence, or at least evolution, of a landless peasantry before the later decades of the century is an elusive phenomenon. A good many Leicestershire wage earners were in fact farmers' sons with concrete expectations.[33] The custom of Borough English, by which a copyhold descended to the youngest son, was practised by 'a considerable minority' of manors,[34] and makes wage assessments particularly misleading, not least in Sussex, where it was especially widespread. At Graffham and Woolavington men classed as servants can be identified as tenants of the manor, whilst others of the same name and undeniable substance were technically landless. In practice of course the elder brother must have been the effective occupier: William Polinge of Tillington was only two years old when he was admitted to a 12-acre holding with his brother Thomas as guardian. In these circumstances the tenement was effectively a family concern, yet the custom does not seem to have promoted equality in Sussex; indeed, the evidence from these two manors, albeit not exhaustive, hardly suggests that most families had two surviving sons.[35]

The theory of the one-class village community would make labourers a branch of the peasantry because they sprang from its ranks.[36] At the same time it overlooks the implications of a self-perpetuating landless group of significant dimensions as opposed to the supernumerary individual members of landed families. Can such a group be identified? Family names should furnish a clue to putative relationships within a single village and thus sift out any residual discrete group of labourers and servants. This naturally can be only the first step; some, possibly many of them, would have had kin elsewhere, and the second stage must be to eliminate, as far as possible, those who could have belonged to the wider connexion of peasant landholders.

Centrally situated in Rutland and represented by three full returns, Hambleton provides a promising test case. A good deal has to be taken for granted for want of any ready means of determining how far any discrepancies between the lists are the result of population turnover, or, alternatively, mistakes and omissions, making it necessary, to avoid an arbitrary estimate, to assume that effectively the population comprised all fifty recorded persons.[37] Exactly half of these are described as labourer or servant, failing which[38] their status can reasonably be inferred from their assessments. This total can be progressively trimmed as follows:

	Number	% of 50
Designated labourer or servant	25	50
Deduct persons alternatively termed husbandmen	7	
	18	36
Deduct listed sons of husbandmen	3	
	15	30
Deduct men with same names as husbandmen	4	
	11	22
Deduct men with names of husbandmen resident in contiguous parishes	–	–
Deduct men with names of husbandmen resident in parishes bordering the inner ring	2	
	9	18

The residual nine persons cannot be connected with any family in the vicinity of Hambleton, except other labourers; these may perhaps be reduced to eight (16 per cent) if John Coole belonged to the same family as Robert Cole, husbandman (assessed at £30), of North Luffenham, a parish in the outer ring, but a labourer of the same name in Empingham makes it equally feasible that the Cooles were a separate labouring family.

Since as many as half the migrants whose progress can be monitored in detail tended to get no farther than the next-door parish,[39] the absence of any nominal connexion between Hambleton labourers and families domiciled in the inner-ring parishes makes a necessary relationship between two or three men there and families in the outer ring[40] dubious. All the same there is no rule that makes connexions in the inner ring a precondition of more distant ones, and due allowance must be made for links with more remote parishes and other counties.[41]

At most the proportion of labourers and servants not related to anyone of higher rank in the immediate vicinity was of the order of 22 per cent of the population of Hambleton, in fact within the range 19–23 if attention is confined to the forty-seven male inhabitants, the only women returned being householders. Of course, it is far from certain that every labourer would have been closely related to a husbandman of the same name. Among the ramifications of the Fowleres, a clan that must have comprehended several nuclear families, Henry, a labourer, may well, as a tenant of the manor, have been a householder in his own right; at best he was a poor relation of some of the leading people in the village, worth up to £30, including John (£24), who evidently died in 1523 leaving what must be his widow, Joan; Thomas (£3), who turns up in 1525 for the first time, was very possibly their son. Exclusive of designated servants and the supposed successors of householders who appear to have died, a maximum of forty family units may be tentatively estimated; with 'sons' and 'servants' similarly disregarded, the number of possible independent 'labourers' is refined to not more than ten, making one man in four – perhaps only one in five – at Hambleton safe to classify as landless and largely dependent on wages for livelihood, one whose line had grown right away from any landholding family.

Juggling with names alone is, however, inconclusive, if only because on their own they cannot prove kinship; nor, for example, is it feasible to tell how many (if any) labourers or servants were the sons-in-law of farmers who had no boys of their own. The most that can be suggested is that by the third decade of the sixteenth century some 20–25 per cent of the rural population showed signs of hiving off to form a discrete category of virtually landless men.[42] And yet so long as life remained short and uncertain there was always a chance for the survivors, and William Yonge of Burnham, Bucks.,[43] can hardly have been the only man who might have married a widow left with a smallholding on her hands and no male relative to work it. In any case names resolve no questions, for the working of the land law and the progressive discontinuance of partible inheritance among the peasantry led inexorably to the growth of a landless class, many of whom were doubtless closely related to farmers and small landowners, and in order to set up households of their own were obliged to take to labouring for day-wages.

THE LABOURER IN SOCIETY

Outside the fiscal records of the 1520s the subject of hired labour is shrouded in obscurity. Servants indeed were well understood. References abound, usually critical in tone, exhorting them to forsake the paths of idleness and vice for those of sobriety and diligence.[44] More precisely it was gentlemen's establishments that were reputed to be overmanned and underworked: well-bred commentators were presumably conversant with their subject. Farmers' men who toiled to 'get both their own and part of their masters' living'[45] almost certainly formed the great majority in practice. So far as can be ascertained from slender evidence, it was not at all rare for husbandmen in quite a modest way of business to keep a servant or two, many of them probably 'apprentices in husbandry', as envisaged by the Statute of Artificers, which probably did no more than reinforce existing practice in authorising the cultivators of half plowlands to employ them. In certain cases the roll for Arundel rape in Sussex links servants to their masters; figures relating to lesser men are as shown in Table 5.4. Apart from these the arrangement of returns is such that it is possible to infer the relationship in a good many more cases.

Towards labourers as such opinion maintained a curious ambivalence for much of the century. Officialdom employed the term with such freedom and assurance that there can be no question but that its meaning was perfectly understood. In complete contrast, literary circles studiously avoided the word itself, even in connexion with social

Table 5.4 Employers of servants in Sussex

Assessment of master £	Masters having	
	1 servant	2 servants
10	16	3
8	2	
7	8	2
6	2	1
5	3	
4	2	
3	3	
2	3	

problems, and (with the noteworthy exception of the *Discourse*) ignored the very existence of labouring folk.[46] The concept itself can hardly have been novel. As early as 1381 labourers were widely (if unevenly) distributed in the Midlands and East Anglia,[47] while by 1450 one in five of the Sussex participants in Jack Cade's rebellion who got pardons were so designated, and many more must have been subsumed in the portmanteau expression 'and all and singular of the same town'.[48]

This reluctance to face facts cannot have come about accidentally, but what can have been the motive? What did society have against labourers? The immediate focus of interest is the man without land who had to sell his labour to earn his bread. In principle this conflicted with the orthodox ideal of a nation of small producers, a theory which, as we have seen, was plainly embodied in much of the legislation of the period.

Now the regular term for a small producer was of course 'husbandman'; self-employed tradesmen were certainly a minority. But 'husbandman' did not connote any sort of norm, much less minimum or maximum acreages: at the foot of the scale it certainly embraced occupiers of a bare acre or two, and furthermore there is the suspicion – though no actual proof – that it could be stretched to mean simply householder, or association with agriculture in the broad sense. Philip Stubbes asserted in 1583 that

> othersome husbandmen haue houses with no lande belonging to them at all, and yet notwithstanding shall pay a good round some for the same also. And no maruelle, for landlords and gentlemen take all the lands and lyuelode, wherevpon there pore tenants should liue, into their owne hands, and suffer not the poore husbandmen to haue so much ground as willfinde them corn for the maintenance of their poore families . . .[49]

In a word there were two kinds of husbandman – landed and landless – and the latter was an all too familiar sight. Nevertheless, the polemicists of the first half of the century, from More to the Commonwealth Men, insisted on stigmatising him as a vagabond or beggar, and harped unceasingly on his idleness.

A significant feature of anti-enclosure propaganda was its timing, for it began around 1520, long after the wave of large-scale destruction of villages had died down. At its height this had excited little comment – the lone voice of John Rous excepted – so why the belated protest? Also we know now that most depopulated townships had been small in the first place, and had wasted away before their abandoned fields had been laid down to permanent pasture.[50] We have also to remember that a stagnant or declining population formed the background to these developments. The date when growth resumed is uncertain,[51] but by the middle of Henry VIII's reign, if not earlier, it was beginning to cause problems. Conceivably the change, the effect of which was naturally cumulative, had manifested itself with dramatic swiftness. If the *Italian Relation* can be trusted there had still been a surplus of land as late as the first decade of the century,[52] yet within twenty years the population was pressing hard on this limited resource which was already fully occupied not only by people but also by sheep. None was immediately available to accommodate the increased numbers; hence there arose demands for a redistribution of land and a reduction in the numbers of sheep to provide for the landless.[53]

The question is, was population growth creating a landless proletariat? It has already been established that in the early 1520s the population included some 690,000 males aged sixteen and over, very approximately divided equally into men assessed at £2 or more on goods, and ones worth less who can be counted as the labouring poor. The richer group necessarily represented more than half the total population, for not only may they all be reckoned householders, but the average size of their households must have exceeded the average for the nuclear family, the unit to which a labourer's would have been limited. Nationally the aggregate of households depends on the theoretical average, which has not been precisely determined, but probably lay between 4.5 and 4.75 persons. Despite the persuasive case in favour of a higher mean,[54] our preference must be for the conservative 4½ at a point of time when the great majority of householders were poor peasants and no inconsiderable proportion of the rest practised celibacy.[55] Dividing 2.3 million by 4.5 produces 511,000 households, and deducting 345,000 for men worth £2 and over leaves a possible 166,000 for labourers, that is almost exactly one family in three.

The next step is to devise an acceptable multiplier for each group. Gregory King is virtually the only guide: in his table the mean size of families 'increasing the wealth of the Kingdom' is 5¼, and of those 'decreasing' it – the labouring poor – 3¾. Thus –

$$345{,}000 \text{ households} \times 5\tfrac{1}{4} = 1{,}811{,}250 \text{ persons}$$
$$166{,}000 \text{ households} \times 3\tfrac{3}{4} = 539{,}500 \text{ persons}$$

Total	2,350,750

The slightly enhanced aggregate is not a serious defect.[56] It cannot be wholly coincidental that the 23.9 per cent formed by the labouring element is not far from the proportion already estimated. Of course, there should also be nearly 200,000 servants subsumed in the wealth-increasing households, but it is with labourers as such that we are primarily concerned.

Viewed as an isolated phenomenon the dimensions of the cottager class cannot have occasioned much disquiet; the point at issue is its impact on society. One fact is beyond dispute: it was on the increase and would, by 1688, comprise nearly two-thirds of all the households in the land. A simple graph (Fig. 5.1) illustrates the problem: if the 764,000 poor families of 1688 and the 166,000 equivalents of 1522 are plotted and the curve B–B' extrapolated, theoretical zero might be reached *c.* 1400, enabling us to postulate that the labouring class had remained below the 100,000 mark in the middle decades of the fifteenth century, passing it around 1485, and perhaps reaching 125,000 at the turn of the century, from which point the situation had deteriorated with dramatic swiftness, the landless class growing by as much as one-third in little more than two decades. Such a development is not inconsistent with the known facts: the upward trend in prices and decline in real wages had set in from about 1500.[57] Adjusting the curve to take account of (*a*) 85,000 families of soldiers and sailors and (*b*) the probability that growth slowed down after 1650,[58] makes it steeper, passing 100,000 just prior to 1500. Whatever the initial value – and any attempt to determine it would be unrewarding - the drop in real wages, unmistakable by the 1520s, shows that too many hands were chasing too few jobs. In the meantime the number of farmers' households remained constant at 345,000, A–A' which, plotted against the curve for labouring families, shows the gap between the two groups closing fast and reaching parity by approximately 1590. If in fact the population was growing at a faster rate, labourers could have overtaken the landholding class numerically in the 1570s. Very possibly the imminence of this event, which must have occurred earlier but for the epidemics of 1556–8, precipitated the tensions of the 1540s.[59]

There was scant recognition of the fact that the population was getting bigger. Alderman Box's diagnosis – is the date 1576 significant? – was an isolated one.[60] For the most part public opinion grabbed at the explanation nearest to hand and proceeded to flog a dead horse with gusto. Depopulation, with its concomitant abuses, suddenly became the eighth deadly sin. Faced with the growth of the landless element, the 'establishment' feared the imminent collapse of the social order. The

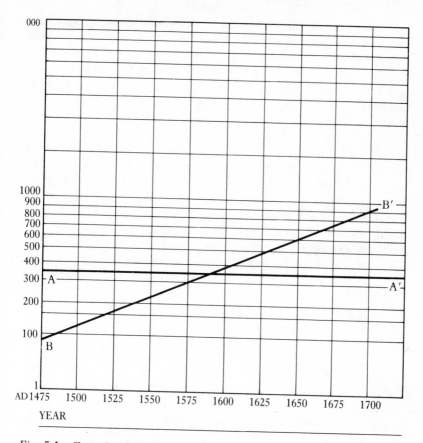

Fig. 5.1 Growth of the labouring class (semi-logarithmic scale)

peasantry, in whose midst the crisis was maturing, descried an ominous portent of their own fate and readily believed the worst. Whether or not John Palmer really did tell his tenants at Angmering, 'nowe is the tyme come that we gentilmen will pull downe the howses of suche poore knaves as ye be', that is how they chose to interpret his actions, and as such the affair bears witness to the tensions prevailing at the time.[61] The upshot was that the labourer could not be allowed a place in the commonwealth. Society rejected him, branded him (sometimes physically) a vagabond, and tried to ignore his very existence. There was no want of compassion for the victims of enclosure at the moment of dispossession, but once they had merged with the anonymous army of the disinherited no one really knew what to do with them, apart from hoping they would go away or that government would contrive some solution.

Any rational approach to the question was inhibited by the stubborn belief in some sort of Garden of Eden from which the nation had been expelled – recently, but far enough back in time to be just prior to the experience of most people, especially in the late 1540s when the Commonwealth Men fulminated against the sinfulness of the age. Perhaps the notion was not entirely fanciful, for the later fifteenth century had been a period of relative stability. Formerly, it is to be inferred, society had incorporated a limited, rather small complement of labourers. Utterly landless men were almost certainly a small minority. More typical perhaps was the 'cottage farmer', but even so, prevailing wage levels enabled those dependent on them to exist in reasonable security and so pose no problem: they were integrated. Equilibrium was destroyed when population growth swelled their numbers, partly from among their own ranks, partly from the younger sons of landed families, whilst all the time a minority of tougher peasants were acquiring the land of the weaker.[62] With insufficient land available to create new holdings, it was the landless element that was seen to be increasing fastest. Logically it was the husbandman class that demanded protection for its own sons, supported by informed opinion and official policy which regarded them as the backbone of society and the economy.[63] Since industry was embryonic and family farms could generate little employment, 'idleness' became endemic,[64] and with the depreciation of real wages the position of the labourer continued to worsen. Because there was no ready means of assimilating him he was branded a 'masterless man' and condemned to exist on the fringe of ordered society, whether as casual labourer, squatter, beggar, or even criminal. This too bred resentment in the second quarter of the sixteenth century, and since it is unlikely that the majority of such people were outcasts from choice, it looks remarkably like the commonwealth unloading its insoluble problems on to a convenient scapegoat.

UNEMPLOYMENT AND VAGRANCY

What little evidence there is goes to show that the initial impact of destitution on the national consciousness was both sudden and alarming. Overnight, as it were, around 1530, it blossomed forth as a burning issue of controversy and urgent concern, the target of increasingly stringent countermeasures which evolved rapidly from the first attempt to clamp down in 1531 to the climax of repressiveness in 1547.

Indigence and vagrancy were far from novel phenomena. Already in 1516 Sir Thomas More had deplored their prevalence, while the author of the popular ballad 'Nowe a Dayes' lamented 'much idelnes'. Harrison was to date their origins to a point less than sixty years before he wrote in 1577.[65] Disquiet prompted investigation of depopulation as a prime cause, though for all its harrowing descriptions of whole communities uprooted the evidence was, and remains, controversial.[66] Although the difficulty of persuading the parliament of 1515 to strengthen the earlier depopulation act[67] may have formed the overt motive of this fact-finding exercise, the meagre results invite the speculation that Wolsey's real purpose was to hold some sort of post mortem on the recent disappointing subsidy.[68] Certainly the 'Domesday of Inclosures' affords no better measure of vagrancy than it does of common arable land enclosed for pasture. The chronology is not in doubt. If the beginnings of demographic pressure, as opposed to the mere taking up of any slack, can be assigned to the turn of the century,[69] the first generation of disinherited peasants would have reached maturity in approximately 1515–25. Nonetheless, protest continued unabated. If no move was made to reinforce the relatively innocuous legislation already on the statute book,[70] public debate for a decade and more centred on war and taxation. Complacency too could have played its part in permitting the evil to fester unperceived beneath the surface until it erupted in an advanced stage of development. Equally a sudden upsurge of alarmism could have inflated the subject out of all proportion, but even though the image doubtless got distorted, the timing cannot have been wholly fortuitous. Formulation of an objective analysis took all of half a century. Although the familiar threefold classification – the impotent poor, the able-bodied willing to work but unable to find any, and sturdy rogues who could work but refused to do so – had crystallised by 1536, it was not until 1576 that the need to create employment was frankly accepted.[71] Initially the division was twofold, recognising only the impotent, and the able who were uniformly stigmatised as layabouts.[72] Although an abortive bill in 1536, which proposed setting up a national system of administration, went some way towards conceding the principle of unemployment,[73] it was clearly premature. The root of the malaise was defined as idleness, a concept which embraced both unemployed and lazy; the latent sense, however, tended towards worthlessness, and until unemployment was legally defined, idleness of every kind was deemed culpable. Chester city regulations pictured a 'multitude of valiant, idle persons and beggars which be strong and able to serve and labour for their livings, and yet daily go on begging'. Worse, though honest citizens might be inconvenienced, the real sufferers were 'the poor impotent and indigent people dwelling and inhabiting within the same city and having no other means to get their living but only be the charitable alms of good Christian people [who] daily want and be destitute of the same' through physical inability to compete.[74] Indeed, most beggars were feared as violent criminals. Besides furnishing the most comprehensive definition, the statute of 1531 expressed the terror inspired in ordinary folk:

> Where in all places throughe out this Realme of England Vacabundes & Beggers have of longe tyme increased & dayly do increase in great & excessive nombres by the occasyon of ydelnes, mother & rote of all vyces, wherby hathe insurged & sprunge & dayly insurgeth & spryngeth, contynuall theftes murders & other haynous offences & great enormyties to the high displeasure of God the inquetacion & damage of the Kynges People & to the marvaylous disturbance of the Common Weale of this Realme . . .

Nor did these miscreants operate in ones and twos; they roamed the countryside in 'great routs and companies' and were all the more menacing for it.

Whether sturdy beggars posed any serious threat to a society which tolerated a certain level of violence is debatable; as masterless men they were unquestionably a nuisance. Implying in the broader, pejorative sense a socially disruptive element, 'masterless man' strictly speaking indicated nothing more alarming than someone who was not answerable to a superior in a contractual relationship, most commonly tenant to lord, servant to master; it fitted the day-wage man who was bound to nobody and for whom no one accepted responsibility once the job for which he had been hired was done and the price paid. The intent of the Statute of Artificers to turn him into a regularly contracted servant was a response to the challenge of a growing social problem, the root of which was essentially economic.

The worst of it was that nobody really knew what to do about the problem; at first there was no machinery to cope with vast numbers of poor. In its heyday the manor, as the institutional framework of rural society, had taken care of that, but the time had long gone when it was a great farming enterprise based on the compulsory labour of the tenantry, which in practice must have meant using the spare members of their families, but who were no longer required, and the lord recognised no obligation towards peasants who were no longer tied to the soil.

Once the numbers of the permanently indigent reached major proportions masterless men became a burden which the community had perforce to resign itself to supporting. Justice Hext no doubt voiced Somerset opinion towards the end of the century when he blamed the increase of rogues for 'the vtter impoverysshinge of the poore husbandman that beareth the greatest burthen of all services' and confessed himself at a loss to 'see howe yt ys possible for the poore Cuntryman to beare the burthens dewly layde vppon hym, and the rapynes of the Infynytt numbers of the wicked wandrynge Idell people of the Land'.[75] The sentiment was mutual, for by his time the countryside contained two separate communities: on the one hand the cultivators of the soil in the old-established, mainly arable-farming villages, and on the other the burgeoning forest and heathland hamlets, the refuge of 'many Idell persons for lacke of worke, lyuinge in summer by the milke off his cowe, and in winter lyke to starue for meate, or dye for cold, hauinge many children that lyue by beginge', the outcasts from the farming community, which regarded them as alien because they represented a radical deviation from the norm. These settlements often originated as encroachments on the common wastes; they were frequented by such fringe elements as drovers and badgers of corn, vagabonds and layabouts, whose hovels would eventually become the meeting places of millenarian sects and the lunatic fringe in general.[76] With the passage of time the settled, self-sufficing peasant community must have found itself increasingly on the defensive, ground between the upper and nether millstones of oppressive landlords and landless paupers. If the copyholder did not necessarily live in daily fear of expropriation, husbandmen as a class were declining relatively in a century that saw the population grow by at least 50 per cent.[77] Small wonder that a deeply conservative society vented its frustrations on a new, burdensome and essentially defenceless type of person.

At first the solution looked simple: the idle could be coerced into working for their living. Arguing that earlier legislation had proved ineffectual, the act of 1531 abruptly stiffened the penalties for valiant beggars. Progressively intensified, these reached a climax in the drastic measure of 1547.[78] Yet 'the thinking which underlay an hysterical and really vicious statute'[79] is less impenetrable than has been supposed. At the time it excited little or no comment, partly because the severest sanction, i.e. the death penalty for incorrigible vagrancy, had already been decreed by the 1536 act, partly because it embodied universal prejudice. True, the most vindictive clauses were soon repealed, but simply because they proved unworkable.[80] Early Elizabethan legislation, including the Statute of Artificers and yet another act for the punishment of vagabonds, in 1572, clung to the belief that the obligation to labour could be enforced by law. However, in 1576 an act 'for the setting of the poore on worke and for the avoyding of ydlenes' frankly acknowledged responsibility for 'poore and needye persons being willing to worcke' and charged the parish with the duty of finding them employment,

> to the Intente Yowthe maybe accustomed and brought up in Laboure and Worke, and then not lyke to growe to bee ydle Roges, and to the Entente also that suche as bee alredye growen up in Ydelness and so Roges at this present, may not have any juste Excuse in sayeng that they cannot get any Service or Worke . . .[81]

So belatedly was conceded what everybody had known as a fact for the best part of half a century – unemployment was endemic, indeed you could easily be born to it.[82] Recognition of the phenomenon of institutionalised unemployment is thus dated to the third quarter of the sixteenth century, though its symptoms, even if misconstrued, had been evident much earlier.

In the middle decades answers to the two elementary questions, who were the vagrants and how many were there, are tantalisingly elusive. Their restlessness, of course, made them hard to round up and count; attempts to do so in Staffordshire in 1527 led, apart from the apprehension of a lot of suspected criminals, to the conclusion that any vagabonds as such had 'avoided and gone forth of the shire'.[83] Their mirage-like character casts doubt on their very existence. The stubborn conviction that the kingdom was infested with vagabonds looks much like a cliché, yet like most clichés it concealed a kernel of sober fact beneath the accretion of opinion and prejudice which imputed incipient vagrancy to anyone lacking the socially approved means of support, leading the authorities of some towns to drive the unemployed into vagrancy.[84] Very many of those dealt with by Elizabethan magistrates turned out to be weavers, labourers and servants travelling in search of work, usually within a restricted radius and not more than two or three days' journey from their places of origin. Two-thirds, moreover, proved to be under thirty-five years of age – young adults and adolescents, even children thrust prematurely out of home to mitigate family poverty. Significantly only a quarter of them were females, and one consequence of this predominantly male composition was that collections of beggars and other wayfarers could not fail to look far more aggressive than they really were, while conversely, counts of static paupers generally showed a preponderance of women. True to instinct, the young male was a wanderer, a rebel perhaps against a social order whose rejection of the migrant may be likened to the twentieth-century 'generation gap'. At all events his unreliability is attested by the militia officers who explained that their trained bands were depleted 'for that most are servants and artificers which change and remove . . . their dwellings daily.'[85] Also, although vagrant families were not numerous, they were by no means unknown,[86] and there were perhaps enough to give substance to rumours of whole communities being turned adrift by enclosures.

Concrete evidence is sparse and does not bear out the popular conception of vagabondage. Wild estimates of numbers stand in striking contrast to the handfuls actually picked up in the periodic drives undertaken by the authorities; the discovery of no fewer than seventy-two transients in one house at Westminster in 1568[87] is an isolated instance. English vagrants, as opposed to Irish, mostly travelled in small groups.[88] Obsessive, irrational fear of valiant beggars could easily have led to wild exaggeration, but, nevertheless, the depth of conviction has to be accepted as prima facie evidence of an acute social problem.

The issue is clouded by inability or unwillingness to distinguish between unemployment and vagrancy. Though debate might be triggered by protest at the former, it almost invariably resolved itself into condemnation of the latter. By the seventeenth century the situation had so far crystallised as to make it possible to estimate that something like a third of the workforce was either underemployed or wholly unemployed.[89] Starkey had claimed as much as early as 1530, though without stating his grounds. Less precisely, Clement Armstrong deplored the great numbers of 'idle' persons who, thanks to the engrossment of farms and other abuses, had neither 'workes' nor 'artificialitie' to support them. Typically he was somewhat vague about the composition of the workforce. Artificers were definitely comprehended, farm labourers perhaps by inference since he stopped short of asserting that all workers on the land were husbandmen, even while attributing rural unemployment to the expropriation of the peasantry. Starkey's mention – exceptional for the period – of labourers in association with ploughmen acts as a hint that their existence was to be understood. Unlike Starkey, whose estimate looks like an alarmist guess, Armstrong confined himself to samples. The trade of just one wool exporter could wreak the destruction of four or five villages inhabited by fourteen or fifteen hundred souls, and altogether deprive four or five thousand of their livelihood.[90] (Should this be taken as an invitation to multiply them by the number of Merchants of the Staple?) The difficulty is that figures like this are not altogether implausible. Although depopulation had become a rare phenomenon – assuming that it had ever been commonplace – a large Midland village might well contain 300 inhabitants, while the assertion that the laying up of a dozen ploughs might well impoverish forty persons is actually a conservative estimate since twelve households could be expected to contain upwards of fifty.[91]

Few people troubled to assemble systematic figures. Thomas Wilson, who had the opportunity, candidly admitted:

> The number of the poor is uncertain because there is no books or records kept of them ... but I can give a reasonable guess by reason of an office which for 7 years together I exercised, wherein I had occasion to take the names of all the inhabitants of 5 shires.[92]

At this point he abandoned the subject. Among the few surviving statistics, a survey made at Norwich in 1570 established that 21.8 per cent of the inhabitants were living in poverty. Although the number of men wholly unemployed, most of whom were heads of families, was small, few were able to support their dependants, and almost all households relied on the earnings of the wife and children. Few could have reached the tax threshold in 1524–5.[93] In fact the subsidy schedules for most big towns bear witness to massive unemployment. Urban poverty is well authenticated, yet, taken as a whole, town dwellers formed only a small percentage of the population, and in view of the propensity of the rural poor to drift to the towns, it is hardly a reliable guide to conditions in the countryside, except insofar as it might be a product of the interlocking economies of a town and its hinterland.[94]

Equalling fear of the valiant beggar was anxiety lest honest folk become burdens on the community through loss of livelihood. Already there were signs of the spirit that in coming centuries was to animate administration of the poor law, specifically in the removal of potential paupers to parishes where they had legal settlement and which were responsible for supporting them, when parish officers anticipated destitution by promptly expelling any new arrivals who happened to answer to the description of day labourers. The settlement principle certainly existed in Tudor times, at least for the impotent poor, who in 1504 were bidden reside where they had been born or else where they had dwelt for the space of three years.[95] Coleman has commented that the regularity of work and employment enjoined by the Statute of Artificers was a tribute to their very irregularity;[96] similarly the drive to impose settlement on the labouring poor may be construed as proof of a general restlessness which a series of statutes had to be designed specifically to counteract.

THE DIMENSIONS OF VAGRANCY

Contemporary apprehensions that vagrancy had reached a critical stage make it all too easy to imagine a veritable army of people who may never have existed at all; taken literally, the statements of polemicists and lawmakers imply tens or even hundreds of thousands of whom there is no record whatsoever. If, however, labourers and vagabonds were identical in all essentials, the rural workforce was migratory by nature. After the middle of the seventeenth century there is ample evidence of large-scale labour mobility,[97] and it is taken for granted that the persons involved were subsumed in the population estimates made by Gregory King and others; nor is it improbable that our own estimate of early sixteenth-century population fails to do the same. Since arguably the outstanding quality of both the military survey and the subsidy is the unique prominence they give to the lowest levels of society, they provide the materials for a model of the problem of poverty in general in addition to giving guidance to the special question of migrancy and vagrancy.

Now it has been seen that many persons assessed at less than £2 never appear in more than one list and that to make a complete nominal roll for a township requires a conflation of all three returns of a full set. The first step is to examine all available complete sets, paying particular attention to the frequency with which men worth less than 40s. were listed (see Table 5.5). Everyone falls naturally into one of three basic categories. Those whose assessments never reached 40s. are tabulated exactly as recorded.[98] Everyone at or above £3 in at least one list is assigned to that group on the assumption that he was a man of substance and that the highest figure given would have been the most realistic. Two-pound men occupy an intermediate position; the rate of turnover makes it a less stable group, a significant number being described as labourers and taxed on wages; also a good many alternate between this and some lower figure, and so, although settled, many must have been relatively insecure economically. Any not valued at £2 more than once are classed as £1/£2, reckoning a single entry at £1 or nil as a temporary phase.

The picture is completed by noting that the great majority of men worth £3 and above occur in every list, with drop-outs totalling no more

Table 5.5 Distribution of assessments in set of three returns

County	In one		In two			In three				
	nil	£1	£1 + 0 +	£1 + £1 + 0	£1 + 1 +	£1 + 1 + 1	£1/£2	£2	£3 and over	Total
Rutland: East hundred	42	68	12	18	7	4	21	36	138	346
8 other parishes	25	55	12	22	4	7	9	28	124	286
Bucks.: Ashendon hundred	51	216	23	101	43	59	34	150	294	1,014
Cottesloe hundred	50	179	5	40	10	36	36	129	294	779
			Percentages							
Rutland: East hundred	12.1	19.7	3.5	5.2	2.0	1.2	5.1	10.4	39.9	100.1
8 other parishes	8.7	19.2	4.2	7.7	1.4	2.4	3.2	9.8	43.4	100.0
Bucks.: Ashendon hundred	5.0	21.3	2.3	10.0	4.2	5.8	3.4	14.8	33.2	100.0
Cottesloe hundred	6.4	23.0	0.6	5.1	1.3	4.6	4.6	16.6	37.7	99.9

than are consistent with realistic rates of mortality and mobility. In contrast something like two-thirds of all persons with assessments below 40s. throughout are found in one return only.[99] East hundred in Rutland and Cottesloe, Bucks., share many features, except that in the latter, as throughout this shire, the poorer class gives an impression of greater stability. In this respect Ashendon diverges not merely from Rutland but also from Cottesloe, together with which it forms the central belt of Buckinghamshire. The broad picture here is one of a lower overall level of wealth appropriate to a mainly pastoral district – part of it belonged to the royal forest of Bernwood – containing few big farmers but numerous cottagers and commoners of whom only a minimal number were returned as worth nothing or, as was the local practice, just a few shillings. The number listed twice, or even three times, points to a relatively low propensity to migrate. In contrast with other areas, little more than half the Ashendon men worth less than £2 were confined to a single list.

The obvious explanation of the high turnover among the poor is that they were mostly transients, roaming the countryside in search of work and subsistence, and while it can readily be appreciated that some of them sought the latter without the former, there can be little question that the majority were genuinely looking for employment. Some (we are told) endlessly chopped and changed masters, others can have had little option but to move on once the demand for their services was exhausted. Should chance take them to a village where a muster was being held or a tax collected they would be roped in – some of them, for it is doubtful whether officials could ever hope to catch all of them, and the more worldly-wise decamped the moment performance of their duties to the state became imminent. Of course, different returns did not apply to exactly the same classes of people. Only the survey was intended to list all the inhabitants of a township; the subsidy specifically excluded anyone without taxable property or wages, and so in principle should be shorter.[100] Although men without goods in 1522 should have been the ones most likely to escape taxation, not seldom it was those assessed initially on goods who did so, while others not previously deemed worth mentioning under any head were called on to pay the subsidy, and many small taxpayers were replaced by an entirely new set of people for the second instalment of the subsidy. It could well be that the sub-collectors aimed to do no more than return whatever number of people would prove acceptable to their superiors, but this does not account for omissions from the muster, unless perhaps they were past militia service and did not own even a minimal amount of assessable property, like those who were classed as poor old men in Rutland.

The persistent omission of a full third of the men who should by rights have been recorded looks rather like normal practice, for a similar proportion would appear to have escaped the Gloucestershire muster of 1608; some naturally must have been unfit for service, and if, as is not improbable, persons of this type were peculiarly susceptible to disease and malnutrition, it still may not be fanciful to think in terms of 6,000–8,000 men living in nomadic or quasi-nomadic conditions.[101] This exceeds the total of labourers recorded on that occasion and is almost certainly similar in size to the wage-earning class as a whole, which must have included a majority of the craft workers, especially those employed in the local textile trades.

The turnover of Oxford wage earners was three times that of persons assessed on goods.[102] The propensity of this class of person to wander is further confirmed by the informative 1525 schedule for Towcester hundred, Northants, which explains all deletions from the one compiled the previous year. A good 15 per cent were stated to have gone away (*remotus*), more than three times the annual rate at Cogenhoe, in the same shire, a century later.[103] Against this the proportion given as deceased (*mortuus*) is much what would be expected.[104] A dead man caused no problem: he stayed in or underneath the parish – permanently. Only the merest handful of the alleged migrants can be traced, with no great certainty, to the nearby parishes which should in theory have been their first destination, nor can any be found in Buckinghamshire villages up the highway to London, the Mecca of the footloose,[105] though significantly in Towcester town, situated on Watling Street, the rate of removal was double what it was in the villages. Other cases throw doubt on the exact meaning of *remotus*, since it was applied to certain people who nonetheless turned up again very shortly afterwards.[106] So this evidence stops well short of corroborating popular tales of 'greate routes and companyes' of vagabonds; if anything it points to an indeterminate number of people of no settled abode who, if not habitual nomads, did not exactly belong anywhere, but drifted round a narrow circuit of villages picking up odd jobs and seasonal work interspersed with begging and poaching, until such time as a cottage fell vacant or some easy-going community decided to tolerate them as squatters.

Shortness makes the annals of the poor not simpler but harder to grasp, and the meagre details sometimes added to the bare record of names and assessments illustrate as much as anything the interplay of variable conditions and administrative inexperience. The Rutland survey described some as tenants (to a named landlord) which almost certainly implies householder too. Almost every owner of a nil assessment was called 'poor', meaning that the value of their goods was less than 20s., though a few – including perhaps husbandmen whose affairs were in the red – were also classed as tenants, indicating also the lack of any livelihood such as a farm or cottage holding. Of five poor men at Tickencote, one classed as a tenant was also the only one to be taxed in 1524, two can be found resettled elsewhere, and both the new arrivals can be traced back, one having occupied a tenement at nearby Tinwell, where three (out of six) poor men were tenants, of whom two do not occur in a later list, though two of the remaining three do. At Ketton the only man with a nil assessment to be listed more than once does so for the excellent reason that he progressed to £2 and eventually £5. Five out of seven described as 'old' as well were tenants; as elderly men were those more likely to have been settled cottagers, some could be expected to show up a second or third time, in contrast to younger men, who, having had less opportunity to put down roots, should have been more mobile. But it was only in eight places that 'old men & pore' were distinguished, while almost every village had its quota of 'yong & pore'. If 'old' meant past soldiering and they owned no substance either, it may as a rule have been considered pointless to mention them. Moreover, not only did comparatively few people pass sixty, but expectation of life was probably not unrelated to material condition. Finally, without a more reliable means of distinguishing the migrant poor from the settled, the result for small communities is less than conclusive.[107]

Similar inconsistencies crop up in other counties. In Berkshire many men with nil assessments were classed as householders, yet were not noticeably more settled than labourers; indeed, men of substance might not occur in more than one return.[108]

If the army of actual and potential vagabonds now begins to look more than a little insubstantial, the weighty authority of Sir Thomas More imposes the duty of giving it serious consideration. Too much importance can be attached to terms like 'tenant' and 'householder'. For the poorest class household need not have implied accommodation of a permanent character. In York and Salisbury the destitute from the countryside squatted in empty decayed houses and barns, or put up in ale- and lodging-houses, and if common soldiers on campaign were expected to bed down under hedges,[109] might it not have been precisely because they were unaccustomed to anything better than rude shelters and bivouacs? Having conducted a thorough survey of poverty in the city, Norwich corporation declared that beggars 'respected no worke to prepare them lodginge, but used churche porshes, mens sellers, doores, barnes and hay chambers, and other back corners to bestowe themselves, and such as had howses did not worke for lodginge other then that they layde upon the colde grownde'.[110] One hole is as good as another, and not a home to become attached to.

If the people who flit wraithlike in and out of the lists were in reality the masterless men of popular stereotype, ever drifting from place to place, pausing here and there for a few weeks or months, inexperienced officials would have had their work cut out to cope with them. It need not be doubted that they did their best, systematically registering all their staid, substantial neighbours, but floundering helplessly in a strange world of squatters, casual labourers and tramps, whose very identity was barely known to respectable folk, and whom no one had ever before tried to sort out. If constables reasoned that the most that could be expected of them was a rough tally, they could only too easily have missed some permanent residents while contriving to include others who happened merely to be passing through; the final roll might have amounted to little more than a guess. When yet another listing was required the obvious course was to check off the names in the original return, only to discover that while the more substantial inhabitants could be accounted for, a lot of other men failed to answer; when these proved mostly to be of no standing, a similar number of the same type were roped in to make good the total the new collectors had been advised to expect: their names were immaterial.

The abilities of the men to whom this work was entrusted should not be underrated; they may perfectly well have tracked down everybody and assessed them to the last penny.[111] A glance at Table 5.5 shows that far from being an undifferentiated agglomeration, the poor divide naturally into distinct subgroups. At the top came those who owned something tangible in the way of personal property, which might on occasion be reckoned as much as 40s., at other times a nominal 20s. or some figure in between: some assessors made a point of noting sums such as 26s. 8d. and 33s. 4d. Next came those assessed three times at £1 who, even if eventually taxed on wages, would initially have been assessed on goods. The third group might have owned little material property, but were nonetheless permanently settled, and like the second were judged capable of paying two lots of tax, 8d. in all. Men who were listed twice form the next two groups. One was straightforward: what goods they owned amounted to less than 20s. in value, and they were taxed once only, usually on wages. The other is rather more complex, consisting chiefly of men omitted from the musters though included in both parts of the subsidy, but secondarily of men represented by the survey as owning a worthwhile quantity of goods, yet apparently unable to pay more than a single groat in tax. Finally come those who were recorded once only. Some owned a little property but were exempted from taxation, others had nothing but the wages on which they were duly assessed; a few paid tax on goods which had apparently been overlooked in 1522. At the very bottom of the heap we find those unfortunates who did not even earn sufficient in wages to become liable for tax; in Coventry at least it has been seen that such people, unless apprentices, were very likely to have been unemployed.

Although in reality the gap between men who were more or less securely placed and those who had absolutely nothing was probably bridged by a series of steps, it is questionable whether the high constables and bailiffs of hundreds, let alone parish constables, were capable of the elaborate planning necessary for dividing servants and labourers into more or less equal groups to be taxed in rotation. It is easier to imagine a pragmatic approach which involved numerous errors and omissions resulting from the unstable condition of the labouring class. All the same the two need not have been mutually exclusive. Almost certainly the poor comprehended two primary groupings. On the one hand there were those who were permanently settled and probably enjoyed relative security from regular employment, cottages, patches of land and common rights, adding up to a standard of living not measurably inferior to that of small farmers; these were the archetypal cottage-dwelling labourers to whom nobody objected. Altogether different was the much larger class of ill-defined position embracing a wide range of conditions, including not only valiant beggars and the impotent poor, but also low-income people in general. It is these last that pose the greatest problem, rather than true migrants whose significance can easily be overstressed. Much more typical may have been the more or less static family enmeshed in the poverty trap of dependent children, low income, irregular work and poor health – the very people who were investigated at Norwich in 1570.

The evidence is insufficient to prove that upwards of a quarter of the population – well over half the labouring class – was inherently migratory. Nevertheless, it remains necessary to attempt a reconciliation between ingrained contemporary beliefs and such tenuous statistics as were actually produced. Part of the problem is definition. Elizabethan estimates ranging from 13,000 to the equivalent of 20,000 – 80,000 according to an ex-highwayman – can be considered as referring to the hard core of incurable vagrants.[112] Over and above these it is safe to visualise a number who were either unemployed or underemployed and who of necessity were obliged to move about in search of work. Not vagrants in any real sense, they probably gave little or no trouble, but being no doubt at times reduced to begging, they constituted an affront to society and a social problem. A great many were probably just destitute paupers who had no proper homes.

The imbalance of some returns is suggestive. In the Newport hundreds, Bucks., very few nil assessments were recorded in 1522, but the deficit appears more than made good by a disproportionate number at £1 in 1524–5; a sudden influx, though not impossible, takes some explaining. In 1522 only thirteen persons were registered at Clipsham, Rutland; by 1524 sixteen more had turned up, all of them labourers except for two who look to have replaced more substantial men who had either died or vacated farms; the four original labourers were still there and can be regarded as permanent residents. This long string of workmen must have been employed at the celebrated quarries there, which may or may not have been in continuous operation. So, although it is impossible not to be aware of a high rate of mobility among the labour force, there can be little doubt that some men were either omitted inadvertently from one return or another or exempted on grounds of poverty. Of course, some, like ten out of twenty-five wage earners at Wigston Magna, were the sons of farmers, and in Cornwall many of them were assessed jointly with their fathers. Treatment of a young man living at home presumably depended on whether or not he got regular wages, though it is not inconceivable that the father's assessment might sometimes be adjusted to cover the son's notional earnings. So the absence of a young man from any one return might mean that he worked for his father technically unpaid. John, son and servant to Robert Freman of Hambleton, appears only in the survey as a poor young man. Ralph Not, on the other hand, was the son of a husbandman of whom no more is heard after 1522; he may have died, but more probably had given up his farm and gone away, for Ralph, who owned no goods, remained to be taxed as a labourer in 1524, subsequently removing to Ketton, where he was working in 1525.[113]

There can be no doubting the existence of a class which lacked sufficient substance to bear repeated taxation; equally it must be recognised that many labouring people drifted around the countryside from job to job, like one 'idle fellow, who was a taylor, and went from place to place to worke' in Myddle, Salop, 'but had noe habitation'. Having gone off to fight for King Charles in 1642, he was written off as missing, presumed dead;[114] maybe he just drifted out of the army! All that is certain is that the representation of the poor was at best tentative, at worst chaotic.

CHAPTER SIX

NEW PERSPECTIVES

VAGABONDS AND beggars were already a distressing reality, in considerable numbers, even if the predatory gangs of popular apprehension often proved to be nothing worse than bona fide workmen travelling in ones and twos looking for employment, when not haunting the fringes of settled communities. If the nature and dimensions of the problem are thus subject to qualification, it is worth asking if the causes are too. On the broader plane it is at this point opportune to take stock generally and consider how far the essential truth of the evils that beset the commonwealth is confirmed and whether our perception of them stands in need of qualification.

Making the acquaintance individually of Henry VIII's subjects in their thousands opens up a novel vista in which formal categories become blurred as the familiar tensions and problems of the age recede into the background. Of course, looking for evidence of major changes brought about by long-term trends, such as inflation, as early as 1522 may, to say the least, be premature, and the military survey was certainly not designed to clarify current social and economic questions; indeed, rural depopulation had been investigated as recently as 1517–18. Nevertheless, the conditions actually existing at the time form the background to that exercise, and the peak of the late medieval urban crisis has been firmly dated to the second quarter of the sixteenth century.[1]

THE AGRARIAN PROBLEM

At the time the spread of vagabondage and poverty was unhesitatingly attributed to the twin evils of enclosure and depopulation, the most

231

obvious and disturbing features of the agrarian problem, the crux of which, according to the generally accepted version, was the progressive expropriation of the independent peasantry between the end of the Middle Ages and the outbreak of the Civil War, i.e. 1485–1642,[2] effected by pressure on tenants to vacate their holdings, forcible eviction and dispersal of whole communities, enclosure and conversion to pasture of open arable fields, division and enclosure of common grazing land, substitution of tenancies at will for copyhold, and raising customary fines to unreasonable levels.

Now by 1522 expropriation could hardly have made a deep mark; on the contrary, all the signs point to land being widely distributed throughout society, with much held in very small lots. As, however, owners are not clearly distinguished from tenants, generalisations based on aggregates are necessarily imprecise, and the true situation has to be sought in the condition of individual communities. The village prior to enclosure has been depicted as a tight-knit, well-balanced community of small cultivators.[3] Smallness of scale was the most constant characteristic. Had Constable Thomas Hyll decided, after completing the muster of Warndon, Worcs., that he had earned a pint of Richard Walle's ale at Cradley (and also looked up his kinsfolk there), it would never have occurred to the innkeeper to exclaim something like, 'It's a small world!' Indeed, Hyll would have thought this fatuous, having just listed 56 men at Warndon, which contained little more than 200 souls all told; Cradley was even smaller, and the population of the little county of Worcester was some 31,000 only. In a nation of only 2.3 million the typical Midlander belonged to a tiny community of less than 200 people, say, 30–40 households.[4] In wooded and moorland districts people were even more dispersed among hamlets and scattered farmsteads; 300 formed a big village, if not a small country town.

On the consciousness of minute communities the impact of even the most trifling change to a way of life hallowed by generations of observance could easily be devastating. Rumours of the obliteration of entire villages may be difficult to substantiate; some can readily be scotched. Space permits only one illustration: the median in size of the fifty-one Rutland townships was a typical East Midland community:

PRESTON[5]

The King, chief lord	land *blank*	
Edward Digby, Esq,		
steward	fees 6s. 8d.	non-resident

Christopher Goodworth, parson	living 10 marks	goods nil – absent
John Digby, gent. farmer to the parson	land 5	goods £4
Thomas Irelond, husband-man & tenant to chief lord	land nil	goods £25
Gilbert Thompson, ditto	nil	£15
John Sheld, ditto	nil	£10
William Rudkyn, ditto	nil	£10
Thomas Whetley, ditto	nil	£14
Thomas Coper, ditto	nil	£15
John Falconer, ditto	nil	£15
Robert Sheryngton, ditto	nil	£4
William Langton, ditto	nil	£3
Thomas Andres	nil	£8
Robert Ward, ditto	nil	£5
John Wynter, ditto	nil	4 marks
Robert Thompson, ditto	nil	£6
Richard Faconer, ditto	nil	£3
William Allen, ditto	nil	40s.
Clement Tiller, laborer & tenant to chief lord	nil	20s.
John Irelond, ditto	nil	40s.
John Jerman, ditto	nil	20s.
William Wynter, ditto	nil	nil
Robert Cooper, ditto	nil	nil
1 labourer, 6 servants, each	nil	nil yong men & pore

The nucleus in Preston comprised husbandmen worth £3–£15 each, who owned three-quarters of all moveable wealth, which one yeoman's £25 raised to more than nine-tenths for the farmers as a whole. At the root of their prosperity most of the parish belonged to the king, who was reputed to be an easygoing lord. The sole resident landowner also leased the rectory from the absentee parson, but with his own property situated somewhere else and at only £4 in goods, he probably ranked as nothing more than a gentleman farmer. The handful of 40s. men look like cottagers; the rest, including a few from the subsidy roll, were labourers and servants. The position of the peasantry was highlighted almost everywhere, not merely by the fewness of really rich landowners, but also by the embryonic state of the yeomanry, very many townships having no inhabitants in the higher range of taxpayers, £20 and more. Almost everywhere in southern England farmers and craftsmen of middling wealth formed the backbone of society; not just in agricultural communities, but even in the industrialised parts of Suffolk, London and the greater provincial towns, they were by no means eclipsed by rich manufacturers and merchants. Yet exceptions were plentiful: not five miles from Preston, middling men were conspicuously absent from Little Casterton, nearly the whole of which belonged to the Browns of Tolethorpe, whose father had enclosed it, and who between them owned well over half the personalty of the community. Significantly Francis, head of the family, was a Merchant of the Staple, or wool exporter; a £10 husbandman was his tenant and perhaps produced wool for him. The rest of the villagers were either labourers or servants, except for a yeoman worth £60 who farmed land owned by the priory of Newstead by Stamford which made him independent of Brown; it had taken the enclosure of 3 per cent of the area of the parish to reduce the community to this state.[6]

At worst a community might be reduced to a solitary shepherd and his dog,[7] the inhabitants having been expelled and dispersed, if they had not gradually drifted away to look for better conditions; in time the houses and cottages would fall down for want of maintenance, and finally the sturdier buildings, like the church, following perhaps a period of use as a barn. Some had been so long abandoned they were all but forgotten: Horn and Pickworth in Rutland seem to have been lumped in with other parishes and the onetime manor of Hardwick had shrunk to a single farm in Empingham; at Gunthorpe and Martinsthorpe only the land could be assessed.

Between these extremes, Longborough, Gloucs., which narrowly escaped depopulation, affords an example of a village ripe for enclosure. Already, as lord, the abbot of Hailes owned most of it. Anything but prosperous, it had no nucleus of middling men; besides a handful of yeomen, there were only ten of the better sort of husbandmen, worth from £5 to £13. 6s. 8d. (10 marks), and a similar number of smallholders and cottagers; more than a quarter of the villagers had less than 40s. in goods, and nearly a fifth had nothing. Yet while the net yield of £38 a year was small enough to make getting rid of unprofitable tenants to make way for more efficient management worthwhile, it was also high enough for the open scandal of enclosing abbots[8] to give pause for reflection.[9]

Not many Midland villages had got so completely into the hands of a single owner as Little Casterton, even in an area so hard hit by enclosure as the northern tip of Buckinghamshire, where Stantonbury was the only true parallel, although a handful of other little places[10] contained so few men of substance their condition was hardly better, indeed most of their inhabitants could easily be dispossessed if the small absentee proprietors, from which they probably held short tenancies, were bought out by speculators.

If contemporary jeremiads can be believed,[11] the landscape was thickly carpeted with the desolate remains of wasted townships inhabited, if not by a lone shepherd minding an immense flock of sheep, by a single 'capitalist' farmer and a handful of impoverished labourers, returning perhaps one assessment at £20 or more and a few of 40s. or less. In fact in most counties at this particular time not more than 2 per cent of all places did so, some being the tiniest of parishes, if not mere hamlets, and they were more characteristic of major cereal-producing areas than pastoral ones; nor were all rural, one of only three in Sussex being the Chichester suburb of Southgate.[12]

It is, however, superfluous to comb the records for evidence of enclosure and depopulation which cannot be anything but inconclusive, since the consequences of cases reported in north Buckinghamshire in 1517–18[13] can be precisely determined in the light of returns of actual inhabitants made exactly five years later.

THE DEPOPULATED VILLAGE

Although modern research has firmly pushed back the peak of the abandonment of settlements to well before 1500 the supposed threat of depopulation remained a lively issue far into the sixteenth century when 'depopulated' was not, as often nowadays, equated with 'deserted'. Abandoned at a remote, unspecified date and in circumstances that are now obscure, the deserted medieval site, or DMV, which is a familiar feature of certain landscapes, belongs to the province of the archaeologist; what really concerned Tudor society was the plight of communities crippled by enclosure. Scepticism about the intensity of this problem stems not only from the paucity of well-attested cases of serious depopulation but also from the testimony of the inquisitions of 1517, which are not statements of fact but allegations, frequently involving only tiny acreages and handfuls of people, many of which were rebutted in subsequent legal proceedings. At the same time, Kerridge's bold gambit, 'The returns of inquisitions . . . cannot be used as evidence of depopulating enclosure',[14] challenges reassessment. His strictures are of course directed principally at earlier attempts at statistical analysis. The solution to the problem should be sought in the state of actual village communities shortly after depopulation was reported.

At first glance the presentments, as specifications of alleged breaches of the law, look suspiciously like artificial formulae. Closer scrutiny, however, shows that only the descriptions of what was done with land and buildings are couched in conventional phraseology; what became of the people affected was variously described in what amounted to 'plain language', indicating a conscious attempt to define exactly what had happened. These repay re-examination in the light of the condition of the communities in question as recorded five years later.

Long defunct settlements where nothing remained to warrant a separate return in 1522 need not be lingered over; well before the last presentation to the church in 1554, Creslow, one of the few casualties directly attributable to plague, must have been reduced to the 'one manor house, seven closes of pasture, being 600 acres', and no tenants at all, described in a rental of 1607;[15] it was not even occupied by a single 'capitalist' farmer, like Tattenhoe where the church still stands and Thomas Worley was assessed at 40 marks.[16] Appearances, nonetheless, could be deceptive. Eythorpe came suddenly to life in 1524 on the arrival of the big household of its lord, Sir Edward Greville, a landowner of £200 a year with extensive interests in the Midlands.[17] Revival took longer at Burston in Aston Abbots; enclosed and turned over to grazing as far back as 1489, it did not even return a poor shepherd or two in 1522, when John Lamburne, the tenant, who had 20 marks a year from land besides £200 in goods, was dwelling on another leased property, Westcott Manor in Waddesdon, some miles away. When Leland visited it some years later, the lease of Burston had reverted to Sir Robert Lee, who had moved there from Quarrendon and was keeping 'a goodly house with goodly orchards and a park'. Although he too was a sheep farmer, the hamlet gained a new lease of life and by 1563 would have three households.[18]

A good many statements of the social effects of enclosure merely describe a situation, the most usual form being, '*mansionibus et suis occupacionibus* [or *laboribus] carent*', alternating with the slightly stronger verb '*deprivantur*', connoting 'to be actually deprived of', where *careo* means 'to be without' and approximates to the present-day cant usage of 'deprived'; irrespective of the precise word, the sense is that a shortage of both houses and jobs has come about. '*Otiose existunt*' applied to five persons at Liscombe and Bragenham suggests redundancy. Altogether these cover nearly half the cases alleged in Buckinghamshire, including Kingsey where, even after the demolition of one house and 'decaying of one plow', with the consolidation and enclosing of more than 200 acres in 1490 and 1496, as many as twenty-three men were returned in 1522–5 and twenty households in 1563. Nor had putting nine men out of work meant permanent loss of employment; indeed, as two-thirds of the people were still of the labouring type, the land must have been laid down to grass as temporary leys which had since been restored to tillage. Nonetheless, the peasant farmer nucleus had been eliminated, leaving, other than a couple of smallholders, only Thomas Boller, the encloser, who had £40 in goods as well as 6s. 8d. from land, and a lot of poor cottagers and labourers.[19]

Of course, for people summarily deprived of their livelihood, the obvious recourse was to look elsewhere, and at ten places they were said to have gone away: '*abinde recesserunt [abierunt]*', continuing in some cases, '*et otiosi facti sunt* [or *vagarunt*]', '*dolorose*' being added at Fleet Marston, but only here and at Bletchley combined with the assertion that they had actually been put out of work. More emphatically the exact number that went away, piteously bewailing loss of homes and livelihood, is sometimes added – in places a handful only, though eighty-eight people left Castlethorpe to wander weeping in search of relief and employment.

Straight eviction was alleged in just eleven instances. A total of fourteen persons '*abinde et in otiose perducti sunt*' from Grendon Underwood and other places, fifteen '*evadere coacti sunt*' or '*contra voluntatem suam depriuantur*' at Dinton and Waddesdon, and twenty '*compellebantur*' to quit Ashendon. In the end a mere four cases are sifted out in which the 'full treatment' was used, the pathetic exit into homeless destitution by no fewer than 150 people: '*lacrimose . . . recesserunt et in otiam perducti sunt . . . in extrema paupertate redierunt et eorum vitam sic finierunt*' at Doddershall, or '*lacrimose abinde otiose exire cohortebantur et misere vitam suam exinde duxerunt*' at Burston, where, it was added, the whole hamlet was turned over to sheep.

Summed up, the results of all cases were as follows:

Jobs destroyed	for	262 persons
Departed		98 „
Departed sadly/in tears		66 „
Expelled		199 „

At the risk of blundering into a variant of the numbers game, it is worth remarking that the qualitative approach reveals that up to half the redundancies were stated to be just that and nothing more; indeed, the formula most frequently used asserts only that potential accommodation and employment for a hypothetical number of persons, reckoned as a standard ratio to the acreage affected, had ceased to exist. Barely a third of the people involved were specifically stated to have been thrown out. As for those who simply went away (dry-eyed), there is nothing to show that a good many did not leave until some time later, as it became clear that they no longer had any prospects.

In the natural course of things some must have been absorbed by other communities, though at the time nobody so much as considered this as a possible solution. If there is no reason to accept that enclosure was the unique, or even the prime cause of vagabondage, its contribution was not necessarily unimportant, for the effect was cumulative: although the numbers made homeless and unemployed in any one incident and the numbers directly affected by enclosure might not be large, succeeding generations would inevitably grow up in a world short of work and housing.

Strung out over nearly three decades, the incidents recorded in 1517-18 each involved small numbers of people and comparatively few altogether, of whom only a minority were physically turned out in the process of enclosure, not nearly enough to make up the indubitably great numbers of vagabonds and beggars, but increasingly the surplus of the growing population was left with little alternative but to roam the land in search of work.

Of course, not all enclosed villages struggled on like Kingsey to revive in years to come. Of Hogshaw and Fulbrook, and Quarrendon, not a trace now remains, while only the church standing alone in the middle of a field shows where Fleet Marston once stood. Nevertheless, Latimer's gloomy image of a community reduced to a solitary shepherd and his dog is not borne out by the condition of these places on the morrow of enclosure.

Each parish was dominated by a single rich man; indeed, besides owning most of Quarrendon, Sir Robert Lee also farmed the manor of Fleet Marston where most of the inhabitants look like employees of his, managed by Richard Miller who, after removing to Quarrendon, was perhaps replaced by Harris. The name Sheppard, to which four wage earners answered, is suggestive. The overall impression for Fleet Marston is one of hired hands coming and going; any vestiges of a peasant economy must have been obliterated by Lee and his co-owners,

	Assessments											
	1522				1524				1525			
		£	s	d		£	s	d		£	s	d
Fleet Marston												
Roger Lee	goods	200	0	0	goods	100	0	0	goods	100	0	0
Richard Miller, servant	,,	10	0	0								
John Acars	,,	2	0	0	wages	1	6	8				
Hugh Cybbyns	,,	2	0	0	,,	1	10	0				
John Bytensall	,,	2	0	0								
William Cockes	,,	3	0	0	goods	2	0	0	,,	2	0	0
Thomas Vicars	,,	4	13	4	,,	2	0	0	,,	2	0	0
Robert Baston	,,	6	13	4	wages	1	0	0	wages	1	0	0
Raff Harris					goods	3	0	0	goods	3	0	0
John Vicary					wages	1	6	8				
John Coke					,,	1	0	0	wages	1	6	8
3 men, each					,,	1	0	0				
2 men, each									,,	1	6	8
3 men, each									,,	1	0	0
Quarrendon		£	s	d		£	s	d				
Sir Robert Lee	lands	30	0	0	goods	300	0	0	(no schedule)			
Richard Fawkener	goods	8	0	0	,,	8	0	0				
Richard Ball	,,	3	6	8	,,	3	0	0				
Richard Tredwell	,,	6	13	4	,,	6	13	4				
Raffe Rows	,,	2	0	0								
Richard Miller					,,	10	0	0				
William Grene					,,	3	0	0				
John Olney					,,	2	13	4				
10 men, each					wages	2	0	0				
Robert Cokes					,,	1	13	4				
Ralf Wayneman					,,	1	6	8				
Richard Haukyns					,,	1	0	0				
Sir Richard Muston, curate	goods	6	0	0								
Hogshaw and Fulbrook		£	s	d		£	s	d				
William Lane, gent.	goods	300	0	0	goods	300	0	0	(no schedule)			
William Brampton, chaplain	,,	—										
Chris. Caponhurst, chaplain	,,	2	0	0								
John Lincolne, shepperde	,,	6	6	8								
William Reade (Fullbrook)	,,	4	0	0	,,	10	0	0				
William Loblay, servant	,,	1	0	0	wages	1	6	8				

| | | Assessments | | | | | |
| | | 1522 | | | 1524 | | |
		£	s	d	£	s	d
John Wotton	,,	2	13	4	goods 2	0	0
William Hibbart	,,	2	0	0			
William Bristowe	,,	4	0	0			
William Herinsbye	,,	1	0	0			
Edward Warde	,,	1	0	0			
James Fynton	,,	1	0	0	wages 1	6	8
Edmund Bacon	,,	1	0	0	,, 1	0	0
Richard Archer	,,	1	0	0			
John Michell					lands 2	0	0
2 men, each					wages 1	6	8
5 men, each					,, 1	0	0
Geoffrey Haryson, Breton					—		
Hugh Farthynge (Fullbrook)					,, 1	0	0

Sir Ralph Verney and the shadowy Mr Colte, between 1507 and 1511 when they withdrew 324 acres from tillage in a parish of only 934 acres. Robert Baston, if not a superior servant, might have been a late survivor who had clung on till around 1523. The fate of other villagers is obscure. Although fifty were alleged to have 'departed sorrowfully into idleness', the population might not have dropped much by the 1520s, for if ten ploughs had been decayed only four houses were. Evidently there had once been ten farms, now reduced to the manor house, and five others downgraded to cottages: six dwellings but only one farm. Continuing wastage was to leave a mere three families by 1563 and eleven communicants at the turn of the century. Today the church of Fleet Marston stands alone in the middle of a field surrounded by the grass-covered sites of former habitations. No one remembered exactly what had happened at the neighbouring village of Quarrendon, but the remnants of a peasant community survived, and there was still a curate at the church there. Three men at least look like small farmers; their tenements could easily have been subsumed in the four households counted in 1563. An average parish of 1,922 acres, it had room for both them and the more ambitious enterprise of Lee, who was doing well enough to be able to pay the Crown £50 a year for his lease of the manor. Whatever the full story, Quarrendon faded away quietly and without fuss. Not unprosperous in the previous century, it had gained no tax relief in 1436 and only a negligible one in 1445. Clearly the Lees had been able to gain control without publicity, the decisive changes having come about before 1485, and it occasioned no comment until 1636, when it was described as 'a hamlet anciently enclosed and depopulated'.[20]

The more accessible history of Hogshaw and Fulbrook suggests how comparable conditions could have evolved at Quarrendon. The twenty-three taxpayers compare with about the same number two centuries earlier. As late as 1498 there had been eleven households, but in that year Roger Gifford and Ralph Lane, the lessees of the manor, had defaced seven houses and degraded the rest to shepherds' cottages, displacing (it was claimed) six persons; for this they were eventually pardoned in 1550. The composition of the remaining population is instructive. As a Merchant of the Staple, William Lane, Ralph's son, was temporarily absent in Calais in 1522. Two-thirds of those who were actually there were labourers, John Lincolne being presumably the chief shepherd; one or two might have been smallholders. William Reade either leased Fulbrook or managed it for Gifford, another very rich man living at Middle Claydon, who had acquired it by this time. Although unquestionably most of Hogshaw was a great sheep farm, the fact that only 380 acres out of 1,322 were said to have been converted to pasture, coupled with the number of labourers, implies that arable farming was continued on some scale, and indeed at Quarrendon too.[21]

The outstanding feature of all three villages, each an excellent example of a community fallen into the hands of one or two 'capitalist' landlords or farmers, is not merely the number of the inhabitants, but also the relative affluence of a good many of them who, even in the absence of a nucleus of prosperous husbandmen, were no worse off than the generality of peasant farmers. Even a small proprietor like John Michell evidently found it worth his while to work for the Lanes at Hogshaw: his 'land' of course could have been 'fees' charged to the revenues of the manor. At Quarrendon Lee paid premium wages, and rates at Fleet Marston were above average. Lane, Lee and Gifford may justifiably be termed capitalists, but they were in business to make money and were clearly prepared to pay the rate for the job.

Some flourishing villages had perhaps survived an earlier phase of adversity. Cublington had been partially abandoned between 1332, when it returned eighteen taxpayers, and 1340, when it was reported that 'there are two carucates of land in the said parish which lie fallow and uncultivated and thirteen houses stand empty and their tenants gone

241

away'. Complete decay might have followed, for the first incumbent of the new church was not instituted until 1410. Not classed as a village of fewer than ten inhabitants in 1428, Cublington by the sixteenth century was once again a thriving community with twenty-eight persons listed, including one worth £20.[22]

Recuperation could of course obscure even a phase of recent degradation. Although not hitherto reckoned a deserted village, Castlethorpe may have been more or less desolate for a time. In 1502 Lewis Aprice decayed a principal messuage and six others, enclosed 280 acres and evicted eighty-eight persons who went away in '*vagune querentes panem et occupacionem lacrimose*', leaving those who stayed in much the same plight through being denied right of common over the now engrossed holdings; in 1518 an amended specification alleged ten cottages and twenty ploughs decayed, 100 people evicted and no less than 500 acres enclosed. Whichever figures are correct, a large slice was taken out of a total area of 1,872 acres. In 1524–5 taxpayers numbered approximately fourteen, of whom two-thirds were poor labourers. Altogether the population then cannot have much exceeded fifty, though the census of 1563 shows a community approaching double this figure, with twenty-one families. Castlethorpe looks as if it had regained much of its former vigour, perhaps in conjunction with a revival of tillage, just as the change to pastoral farming had reduced the population. Lumping it in with Hanslope in 1522 might reflect the nadir of its fortunes, with the threat of prosecution stimulating the first steps towards the re-establishment of cultivation by 1524.[23]

The distinguishing characteristics of decayed townships are not readily pinned down. Even to say that they had few inhabitants must be hedged with qualifications, since none had ever been large and some still returned upwards of twenty taxpayers, though for the most part these formed the households and dependants of rich men, and consequently most assessments were low. Almost without exception a single big man owned virtually the whole place. Four of the six in Ashendon hundred, who had £100 or more in land or goods, lived in a depopulated village, while Roger Gifford, who dwelt at Middle Claydon, was a noted encloser. In some cases, notably at Littlecote and Stantonbury, only the great man himself was recorded, although he must have had servants who for some reason were not assessed, possibly because he paid them badly. It did not follow *ipso facto* that the former inhabitants were uniformly expropriated, and reduced to poverty, only that the upper stratum of peasants were no longer there. Tenacious freeholders might well hang on. Sir Robert Lee was not alone in paying good wages; top shepherds were often as well off as the average husbandman. Inevitably the management of great sheep flocks engaged sizeable staffs, even the *Discourse of the Common Weal* conceding that the minimum might be 'thre or four sheppards and the maister only'. Labour was required for driving sheep, greasing hogs, gelding lambs, hunting foxes, and, above all, shearing; large concerns needed a sheep reeve and in some cases a supervisor of the flocks as well.[24] Finally, depopulation was not the inevitable concomitant to agricultural change, even of enclosure itself.

THE URBAN CRISIS

If the nature and course of agrarian change have given rise to fundamental misconceptions, recent renewed interest in the phenomenon of late medieval urban decline now shows signs of losing its way in unproductive controversy.[25] There is, nonetheless, wide agreement that many towns were in serious trouble during the first half of the sixteenth century, and that the years around 1525 in particular were a time of acute crisis, making it a suitable point at which to take stock of the position.

Even in leaving on one side as misconceived the reservations expressed in some quarters as to the applicability of fiscal records to the urban problem, it should be stipulated that extreme care must be exercised in attempting to compare the tenths and fifteenths of 1334 with the subsidy of 1524–5, if only because of the gap of nearly 200 years that separates them. Recognition of the principles governing each should remove any difficulty in distinguishing urban wealth from rural. The tenths and fifteenths were straight percentage levies on moveables alone, and since they were assessed separately in the vills where they were located there can be no confusion; the abandonment of individual assessment in 1334 does not seem to have involved any change in the previous practice of taxing property *in situ*, and rare examples from earlier subsidies of persons taxed on assets in two or more places relate to members of the landed gentry, and the wealth in question can only be regarded as the contents of their respective demesnes.[26] Both real and personal property were taxed in 1524–5, though a man could only be assessed on one form of wealth, and the whole of what was due was payable at his habitual place of residence; only the muster books can give a breakdown of a man's assets;[27] but although this restricts the field to the inhabitants of a few smaller towns, it is clear not only that very few urban assessments were made on real property, but also that comparatively few townsmen invested in rural property, preferring to confine their interests to the town itself.[28] Even in really small ones, like Aylesbury, High Wycombe and Oakham, each of which had one man in the £200–£300 bracket, only John Collingbourne of Aylesbury cut much of a figure as a landed proprietor, yet though the subsidy credited him with an income of £40 a year, more than half of it accrued from the town; the property interests of the other two men did not extend beyond the parish boundary.[29] So much for one red herring.[30] Wages have only a marginal effect on the overall picture; not only did they turn out to be a transitory addition to the taxable sector, but the value of such goods as lay behind them was all but negligible. Prima facie therefore reservations as to the comparability of the wealth on which urban taxes were levied at different dates are superfluous and only create needless difficulties.

The simplest approach is to take a town's quota as the practical limit of its taxable capacity at a given date, treating the results of comparisons as indications of broad trends. The £73,973 raised nationally in 1524 was almost exactly twice the £37,430 agreed in 1334;[31] hence a doubling of the amount paid by any township represents standard progress over this period and affords a context in which to evaluate the Acts of Parliament which, in the 1530s and 1540s, prescribed a general rebuilding of dilapidated town properties, in particular the one passed in 1540 which scheduled three dozen towns believed to stand in urgent need of rehabilitation.[32] Nearly all of these had recently paid far more tax than in 1334 – three- and fourfold increases were commonplace – and thirteen ranked among the twenty-five leading provincial towns.[33] Since most towns grew in wealth faster than the nation as a whole, a mere doubling was really an unsatisfactory performance. Only six towns – York, Lincoln, Winchester, Great Yarmouth (all four in the top twenty-five), Oxford and Stafford – paid less than twice their previous quota. Strangely the list omits Boston, a leading town which also underachieved, and Shrewsbury which had been scheduled in 1535–6, implying that the requisite 'homework' had not been done or that some sudden crisis had hit many towns in the decade or so commencing in 1524.

Winchester had been pleading poverty for a century; its tax yield virtually unchanged, it had slipped behind the rest of Hampshire.[34] Lincoln was unquestionably in poor shape, population having contracted from well over 5,000 in 1377 to scarcely more than 2,000 by 1563; in 1500 there were not more than 3,000 inhabited houses, and decay continued throughout the century despite attempts by the corporation to prohibit demolitions. Prosperity founded on the wool trade had departed with the merchants, leaving a sleepy city living by its markets and fairs. Proposals made during the 1550s to establish a cloth manufacture led to nothing,[35] probably because this was now a rural industry; generally the city reflected the stagnation of the whole shire. In Boston too population had also been halved. Of old the greatest outlet of the export trade in wool, its commerce, especially with the Baltic, had collapsed: 'yet syns hath it beene manyfold richer then it is now'. wrote Leland, continuing:

> The Esterlinges kept a great house and course of marchaundice at Boston ontylle such tyme that on Humfrey Litilbyri, a marchaunt at Boston, did kille one of the Esterlinges there about Edward the 4. dayes; wherapon rose much controversie: so that at the laste the Esterlinges left their course of marchaundise to Boston, and syns the town is sore decayed.

The incident might of course have been made the pretext for withdrawal from a trade that no longer showed a decent profit; at all events by the 1530s the Steelyard there was 'little or not at alle occupied', and probably the Staplers' house was not much busier.[36] Alike in population and wealth Great Yarmouth resembled Norfolk as a whole, though Norwich, the county town, which had almost doubled in size and paid eight times as much tax as formerly, was perhaps more representative of the real wealth of East Anglia. Stafford's tax quota actually fell slightly, even though its population roughly doubled between 1377 and 1563.[37] It too was the centre of a poor county. As Shropshire as a whole declined absolutely in wealth it is not surprising that Shrewsbury lay becalmed in the doldrums, left in a backwater with the passing of the Welsh Marches. Ludlow had been chosen as the seat of the Council of Wales and the Marches; Leland noted the endowing of a chantry (subsequently transformed into a school) by 'a very rich merchant', but remarked only the size of Shrewsbury and almost nothing else about it.[38]

Among the lesser scheduled towns Buckingham had never been anything but very small, though this had been no obstacle to increasing prosperity, its tax quota nearly trebling to more than £11, while the surrounding district stagnated like the rest of north Buckinghamshire. In the south High Wycombe grew and flourished, paying five times as much tax as formerly. Chichester had grown rather less vigorously than some towns; its tax had somewhat less than trebled, but the 1,300 or so inhabitants of 1377 had become upwards of 1,600. Far more spectacular was the recent rise of Lewes, later to be described by Camden as 'for largeness and populousness one of the chief towns of the county

[Sussex]'. In 1496 it had been appointed the depository for standard weights and measures in Sussex, and from 1510 the sheriff held his tourn there in alternation with Chichester. This progress was not inconsistent with the decline of some of the town's medieval parishes. The absorption of St Mary in Foro (1538) and St Andrew (1545) into St Michael implies that it was redundant churches rather than abandoned houses that were falling down; in fact St Peter's was united with St Mary Westout in 1538 precisely because the parson's resources did not suffice to keep it in repair. In Winchester also Bishop Fox 'suppressid dyverse of the[m inv]iting the people of them to ma[intain the oth]er yet standing; and to make [some honest] lyving unto the incumbent'. Similarly the corportation of York got statutory power to suppress fifteen out of forty parish churches.[39] The tenfold growth of the wealth of Lewes over two centuries makes it hard to see how the Statute Book could lament:

Many beautiful houses . . . now are fallen down, decayed, and at this day remain unre-edified, and do lie as desolate and vacant grounds, many of them nigh adjoining to the high streets, replenished with much uncleanness and filth, with pits, cellars and vaults lying open and uncovered to the great peril and danger of the inhabitants . . . passing by the same, and some houses be feeble and very like to fall down, dangerous to pass by.

Similarly it would seem unlikely that urban landlords neglected their properties as a consequence of accepting uneconomic rents, an attitude that was to change after the middle of the century. Nonetheless, they had little option in towns where shrinking populations left houses vacant or having to be demolished, especially when, as at York, restrictions were placed on immigration, while the muster book shows that many rents in Coventry were uncollectable because of widespread poverty.[40]

Changes in the circumstances of urban life and work did of course take place. Leicester and York, like Lincoln, suffered from the contraction of the export trade in wool.[41] The port of Chester was throttled by the silting up of the river Dee, as was Winchelsea due to vessels jettisoning ballast in the fairway.[42] Other towns waxed and waned keeping pace with the regions they served; Wakefield, for example, ceded to Leeds the commercial leadership of the West Riding as the dales developed and the centre of gravity of the woollen industry shifted away from the Vale of York.[43] The function of towns was changing too: no longer was it axiomatic that they were 'chiefly inhabited with Marchauntes *Artificers and Handye craftesmen*';[44] instead industry

246

frequently abdicated to commerce, with imposition of excessive guild membership fees possibly hastening the transformation in some cases. Adversity made some inward-looking; High Wycombe excluded strangers from the trade of the borough.[45] However, generalising from analogy and stray examples serves little purpose; indeed, charges that crafts were driven away by excessive tolls do not stand up to investigation in specific cases, and guild restrictions might be relaxed by a town in the midst of crisis.[46] More decisive was the need for the new industrial structure to migrate to the countryside in search of the labour essential for rapid expansion, which could not well be found among communities that were nearly always rather small;[47] it was simpler to take the work to the villages where most people lived. In any case the trend was not total. In Worcestershire cloth manufacture was essentially urban, amply justifying Leland's claim that 'noe towne of England ... maketh so many cloathes as Worcester dothe'. Here, incidentally, there was a boom in building until *circa* 1520, and again after 1560, with a pause in the interim matching the levelling-off of industrial expansion and a possible concomitant slackening in immigration.[48] Almost certainly the migration of industry to the countryside was limited in practice to the clothing trade, there being no pressing need for others to follow suit if they were not developing at the same pace. All the specialised crafts, for whose wares demand was relatively inelastic, continued to flourish in towns as diverse as Leicester, Northampton, and Sudbury, in contrast to the villages and little boom towns of the Stour Valley where most people were engaged in textile manufacture.[49]

A systematic tour of the urban centres of one county is in every respect preferable to paying flying visits to an arbitrary selection. For Sussex the schedules of the twentieth of 1327,[50] which were directly assessed, should afford a more penetrating view than the standardised quotas of 1334: the wealth of six places was much the same at both dates, at six others it was higher in 1327, while only at two was it significantly lower. Growth rates of aggregate wealth give a more vivid impression of relative vitality than comparisons, though one effect of this procedure is to heighten contrasts: tax paid by Horsham and Lewes, for instance increased approximately 850 per cent from 1334 to 1524, by which reckoning all the towns in the lower half of Table 6.1, not merely the two bottom ones, lost ground.

Backgrounds were as various as the changing fortunes of these Sussex towns. In sad contrast to Chichester and Lewes, New Shoreham was now but a shadow of its former self, returning a miserable 20 taxpayers compared with 45 in 1327, 56 in 1332 and almost 100 in 1296. Ranking

Table 6.1 Wealth of Sussex towns, 1327–1524

Town	£ 1327	Rank	£ 1524	Rank	Growth %
Horsham	53	12	648	6	1,130
Lewes	124	5	1,488	2	1,100
Battle (hundred)	107	6	1,138	3	964
Chichester	217	1	1,809	1	734
Midhurst	52	13	410	8	689
Cuckfield (parish)	75	9	491	7	555
Petworth (parish)	128	4	837	4	554
East Grinstead	38	14	155	13	308
Steyning and Bramber	74	10	295	9	299
Storrington	70	11	231	11	230
Arundel	100	7	271	10	171
Hailsham (parish)	85	8	162	12	91
New Shoreham	187	3	36	14	−81

second only to Chichester in 1327,[51] its prosperity was already on the wane by 1334 when its wealth was represented as £120; its quota was slashed by two-thirds in 1433, and temporarily remitted altogether in 1445. Enemy action makes as good an explanation as any of this débâcle, but the abject poverty of its few inhabitants should rather be attributed to environmental changes, perpetuated by a possible inundation in 1509, for Camden remarked that 'the greatest part . . . is ruin'd and under water, and the commodiousness of its Port, by reason of the banks of sand cast up at the mouth of the river, wholly taken away'.[52] Nevertheless, the overall growth in urban wealth had outpaced that of the county at large, the average for these fourteen towns being 470 per cent as against 264. Horsham, which brilliantly topped the league, distancing even Lewes by a short head, Battle and Cuckfield reflect the burgeoning of the Weald, the more wooded parts in particular, as does Petworth, which had 'right welle encreasid syns the yerles of Northumberland usid litle to ly there. For now the men there make good clothe.'[53] Here, however, the fourteenth-century figures conflict with one another, for the value expressed in 1334 was £169, suggesting, in contrast to other Wealden centres, a barely fourfold growth rate. Nonetheless, its new-found prosperity was good enough to bring amenities including a piped water supply. Other, smaller Wealden towns, like Hailsham and Storrington, were trailing badly, and, in common with Ditchling and Winchelsea, were to lose their markets by the eighteenth century; East Grinstead was isolated, its hinterland poor. Arundel stagnated: 'Except for the Castle and its Earls Arundel hath nothing memorable.'[54] Perhaps it lay too close to Chichester to be able to hold on to its trade. Everything points to a few favoured towns, well spaced out, coming to dominate districts of some size, while others, established in a bygone age and in radically different circumstances, faded into obscurity. In the twelfth and thirteenth centuries markets had, as often as not, been created more in the hope of attracting trade (and yielding a profit) than to fulfil any demonstrable need. The granting as recently as 1461 of two fairs and an additional Monday market[55] cannot have been unrelated to Horsham's exceptional growth. At the eastern extremity of Sussex, Rye almost certainly vied with Chichester and Lewes in size and wealth,[56] but as a Cinque Port it was exempt from taxation, as were the much smaller towns of Hastings, Seaford and Winchelsea.

In the eastern counties similarly it was badly sited or redundant market centres that had lost ground, while two-thirds of the towns were growing at least as fast as the counties in which they were situated. In Suffolk, where overall growth was 270 per cent, Lavenham surged ahead at a phenomenal 2,496 per cent, in spite of the death of Thomas Spring, though Nayland was not far behind at just short of 200 per cent, while Hadleigh, at 1,250 per cent, was fast overhauling both.[57] In Essex the geography of the new main centres looks almost too regular to be true, with Colchester and Saffron Walden not only dominating the north-east and north-west, respectively, but also the two fastest-growing towns. They were followed by Chelmsford in the centre and the bustling river ports of Maldon and Burnham-on-Crouch in the south-east.

Location was also decisive in the homely environment of the smaller inland shires. As no town there had ever amounted to very much the question of decline hardly arises in Buckinghamshire, where all market centres registered satisfactory progress[58] – 100 per cent growth is of course a doubling of the original value (see Table 6.2). The four fastest-growing towns, all located in the Chiltern region and closely following the general trend there, included the only chartered borough, High Wycombe, which had surged ahead to take first place from Aylesbury which, situated but a short distance from the chalk escarpment, was rapidly gaining in importance thanks to its central position. The tiny borough of Wendover, at the very foot of the hills, was undoubtedly too

Table 6.2 Wealth of Buckinghamshire towns, 1334–1524[59]

Town	£ 1327	Rank	£ 1524	Rank	Growth %
Beaconsfield	50	13	511	4	922
Amersham	78	8	765	3	851
High Wycombe	180	2	1,181	1	556
Great Marlow	73	11	407	7	458
Aylesbury	190	1	1,005	2	429
Stony Stratford	166		717	9	396
Buckingham	87	7	419	6	382
Princes Risborough	75	9	317	10	320
Winslow	53	12	200	12	277
Olney	135	5	504	5	273
Ivinghoe	75	9	259	11	245
Wendover	95	6	261	13	175
Newport Pagnell	80	2	389	8	116
County	10,077		32,581		223

near it to be able to prosper, and so in place of the former tenth of £9. 10s. now paid less than £4 for the subsidy and had long ceased sending burgesses to Parliament. The stagnation of the northern district of Buckinghamshire in general extended to most of its market centres, though, with the Buckingham hundreds forming something of an exception, Buckingham town was as lively as it had ever been; nonetheless Stony Stratford, advantageously situated on the road from London to Chester, seems to some extent to have usurped the place of Newport Pagnell which, though a fair-sized place of 700–800 souls, now paid only £9. 16s. tax in place of its earlier quota of £12. Of course the military survey puts the real wealth of, for example, Amersham, Buckingham and Wycombe, much higher, though in other places it was much the same or even lower; however, the special circumstances attending the assessments of 1522 make them perhaps less appropriate than those of 1524–5 for comparison with earlier ones.

If anything is clear it is that urban decay was not the universal trend of the final two centuries of the Middle Ages. The diversity of experience revealed by these few examples invites only the cautious conclusion that, depending on individual circumstances, certain towns languished while others visibly prospered. Tax records, of course, are primarily concerned with the wealth of individuals and communities, though, handled with discretion, they are capable of bringing fresh light to bear on related problems. In Coventry, for instance, the multitude of impoverished people recorded in 1522, complemented by an almost derisory number of taxpayers two years later, firmly disposes of any doubt that the town was in the grip of a severe economic depression. Yet the record of unemployment, formed by the shortage of assessments on wages, is balanced by a solid class of affluent merchants, eighteen of whom returned three-figure assessments, a number exceeded only in bigger towns like Exeter and Norwich, and matched in few others; two other men, moreover, had £1,000 or more. Not only was wealth on this scale quite exceptional outside London, but even Norwich, twice the size of Coventry, had only one such citizen, and the great majority of provincial towns none at all.[60] The oft-repeated complaint of a dearth of substantial burgesses able and willing to shoulder the burdens of municipal office is cited as evidence of malaise.[61] Coventry, it is contended, suffered from a 'glaring shortage' because three-quarters of its taxes were paid by precisely three men;[62] but this excludes from the definition of substantial everyone worth less than £666. 13s. 4d. (1,000 marks), and not only is it impracticable to deduce social attitudes from tax returns, but it need only be recalled that thirty or forty three-figure assessments were as many as were likely to be found in the average county, a fair proportion of them belonging to town-dwellers into the bargain, and anything in excess of £500 was extremely rare. The pathology of urban decline was complex and many of the symptoms too indistinct for accurate diagnosis.

Characteristically boastful, Henry VIII's people, in the first half of his reign, complacently affected pity for the wretched subjects of other princes who did not enjoy the same advantages, yet by the time he died in 1547, they had turned to contrasting bitterly the miserable present with the happy years before 1530 when everything had started to go sour, and even more so the golden age when Henry VII had ascended the throne. However much conditions for many people may have deteriorated towards the middle of the century, threats to the farming community like enclosure and depopulation had made comparatively little impression a generation earlier when many man either owned their land or enjoyed complete security of tenure at minimal rents. But, if inflation had not yet begun to bite, change was in the air: already population growth was creating a legion of landless labourers and homeless wanderers for whom the exclusive system of landholding was too rigid to make provision.

There was gain as well as loss. Not only was the urban crisis largely a matter of adaptation and rationalisation, it is now clear that many agricultural developments were in fact improvements in husbandry.[63] This of course was not necessarily apparent to the people directly involved. When faced with the disruption of the traditional structure of their lives and work, they reacted with panic to even the most innocuous new development. Conditioned to expect to go on indefinitely growing his daily bread on a little patch of ground, the peasant smallholder failed to understand that the conversion of arable fields to pasture might be for a limited period only in a system of convertible husbandry. The cross-section of the nation may lead to the conclusion that by the 1520s agrarian change had made only limited progress with social consequences that were less than cataclysmic, but the disappearance from enclosed and engrossed villages of the core of the well-to-do landed peasants served as a warning that the likely casualties of any further change were those who got most out of the old system.

STATISTICS OF LAY PERSONAL WEALTH

TABLES A. 1–4 are summary and selective, supplementary to figures given briefly in Chapter 2.

The complete data, direct from the records, are in the tables numbered 5, to which a further introductory note is attached.

While keeping as far as possible to the original order of the sources, use has been made of the ancient hundreds, where smaller units are more convenient than the bigger ones which had been formed by the sixteenth century, also as a means of overcoming the disorderly arrangement of some certificates. Glasscock's edition of *The Lay Subsidy of 1334* serves as a gazetteer, and maps are included in several of the *Victoria County Histories* and the volumes of the English Place-Names Society. Finally, the sporadic recording of the personal wealth of the clergy, the outlines of which are summarised in Table 2.20, imposes the necessity of restricting the data presented here to the laity.

Table A.1 (a) Regional distribution of lay personal wealth

	Under £1	Under £2	£2	£3–4	£5–9	£10–19	£20–39	£40–99
(a) Musters, 1522								
Norfolk: east	1,278	786	576	530	441	267	116	60
Heathland	393	476	378	267	228	145	84	41
south	46	124	141	129	167	107	35	14
Suffolk: Babergh hundred	375	389	324	207	199	198	133	66
Rutland	338	201	170	189	224	186	93	22
Buckinghamshire: Vale	976	1,461	1,004	870	704	379	163	44
Chiltern	494	428	392	298	260	189	109	42
Berkshire: west	942	784	349	450	431	227	139	82
Gloucestershire: Cotswold	354	1	480	417	559	474	237	95
Vale	425	649	792	726	981	556	219	62
Forest	447	349	338	269	246	137	51	10
Worcestershire: north-east	605	292	381	350	335	234	87	15
Yorkshire: Staincliffe	945	562	38	26	33	1	24	4
(b) Subsidy, 1524–5								
Sussex: coastal plain		1,041	573	301	300	171	119	47
Downs		595	213	136	140	81	54	26
low Weald		1,193	693	346	462	218	181	56
high Weald		1,637	585	426	447	309	112	30
Suffolk: west		1,475	477	284	203	139	66	32
Stour Valley		1,759	648	282	341	260	124	90
west centre		795	511	263	250	150	56	23
east centre		593	1,127	393	385	277	105	25
north-east		1,383	911	491	461	317	127	39
Essex: north-west		1,457	502	360	329	248	101	24
centre		2,144	902	620	653	416	128	75
north-east		877	481	193	186	138	63	38
Saltings		1,870	1,089	683	623	451	228	132
Northamptonshire: Towcester hd.		98	64	38	37	26	9	6
Lincolnshire (Lindsey): Louthesk and Ludborough wapentakes		397	208	113	154	66	25	9

				Amount of wealth							
		Under	Under								
£100+	Total	£1	£2	£2	£3–4	£5–9	£10–19	£20–39	£40–99	£100+	Total
13	4,067	44	822	1,172	1,849	2,740	3,100	2,719	3,079	1,892	17,417
16	2,028	3	529	788	930	1,472	1,651	1,900	2,032	3,420	12,725
4	767	–	129	284	436	1,075	1,369	835	640	633	5,401
43	1,934	–	401	658	730	1,248	2,352	3,082	3,481	10,738	22,690
10	1,433	2	219	337	635	1,430	2,183	2,125	1,135	1,253	9,319
20	5,621	144	1,580	2,090	3,086	4,445	4,466	3,531	2,111	3,512	24,695
9	2,221	1	461	812	1,034	1,682	2,206	2,564	2,050	2,073	12,883
16	3,420	239	844	1,157	1,555	2,718	2,758	3,283	4343	2,906	19,803
27	2,644	–	1	982	1,467	3,565	5,677	5,438	5,050	5,345	27,525
17	4,427	7	694	1,639	2,569	6,174	6,476	4,676	3,292	2,308	27,835
4	1,851	17	384	715	942	1,550	1,557	1,107	430	666	7,368
3	2,302	20	308	771	1,269	2,164	2,753	1,973	767	483	10,509
2	1,635	362	670	76	85	183	13	510	180	300	2,379
9	2,561	–	1,068	1,169	1,007	1,819	2,072	2,866	2,541	1,666	14,207
2	1,247	–	608	431	621	844	991	1,302	1,248	210	6,260
7	3,156	–	1,211	1,406	1,185	2,728	2,480	3,976	2,614	1,580	17,180
7	3,553	–	1,758	1,193	1,494	2,835	3,946	2,757	1,505	876	16,364
17	2,693	–	1,503	992	1,015	1,228	1,637	1,627	1,568	2,726	12,296
37	3,541	–	1,831	1,315	1,006	2,127	3,132	3,069	4,539	7,166	24,190
7	2,055	–	880	1.058	928	1,539	1,857	1,309	1,174	1,063	9,808
2	2,909	–	618	2,288	1,446	2,404	3,298	2,463	1,262	566	14,345
6	3,735	–	1,532	1,812	1,732	2,902	3,809	3,070	1,795	1,533	18,185
3	3,024	–	1,524	1,009	1,245	2,094	2,973	1,766	1,291	400	12,302
9	4,947	–	2,275	1,871	2,253	3,970	5,310	3,018	3,694	1,676	24,067
14	1,990	–	943	1,001	669	1,188	1,705	1,601	1,788	2,444	11,339
44	5,120	–	2,014	2,231	2,352	3,945	5,748	5,833	7,047	7,091	36,261
–	278	–	87	130	134	223	338	206	284	–	1,402
–	972	–	397	416	382	977	787	558	472	–	3,989

Table A.1 (b) Percentage distribution of lay personal wealth

	Number of assessments							
	Under £1	Under £2	£2	£3–4	£5–9	£10–19	£20–39	£40–99
(a) Musters, 1522								
Norfolk: east	31.4	19.3	14.2	13.0	10.8	6.6	2.9	1.5
Heathland	19.4	23.5	18.6	13.2	11.2	7.2	4.1	2.0
south	6.0	16.2	18.4	16.8	21.8	14.0	4.6	1.8
Suffolk: Babergh hundred	19.4	20.1	16.8	10.7	10.3	10.2	6.9	3.4
Rutland	23.6	14.0	11.9	13.2	15.6	13.0	6.5	1.5
Buckinghamshire: Vale	17.4	26.0	17.9	15.5	12.5	6.7	2.9	0.8
Chiltern	22.2	19.3	17.7	13.4	11.7	8.5	4.9	1.9
Berkshire: west	27.5	22.9	10.2	13.2	12.6	6.6	4.1	2.4
Gloucestershire: Cotswold	13.4	–	18.1	15.9	21.1	17.9	9.0	3.6
Vale	9.6	14.7	17.9	16.4	22.2	12.6	4.9	1.4
Forest	24.2	18.8	18.3	14.5	13.3	7.4	2.8	0.5
Worcestershire: north-east	26.3	12.7	16.6	15.2	14.6	10.2	3.8	0.7
Yorkshire: Staincliffe	57.8	34.4	2.6	1.6	2.0	0.1	1.5	0.2
(b) Subsidy, 1524–5								
Sussex: coastal plain		40.5	22.4	11.8	11.7	6.7	4.7	1.8
Downs		47.7	17.1	10.9	11.2	6.5	4.3	2.1
low Weald		37.8	22.0	11.0	14.6	6.9	5.7	1.8
high Weald		46.1	16.5	11.9	12.6	8.7	3.2	0.8
Suffolk: west		54.8	17.7	10.5	7.5	5.2	2.5	1.2
Stour Valley		49.7	18.3	8.0	9.6	7.3	3.5	2.5
west centre		38.7	24.9	12.8	12.2	7.3	2.7	1.1
east centre		20.4	38.7	13.5	13.2	9.5	3.6	0.9
north-east		37.0	24.4	13.2	12.3	8.5	3.4	1.0
Essex: north-west		48.2	16.6	11.9	10.9	8.2	3.3	0.8
centre		43.3	18.2	13.2	12.5	8.4	2.6	1.5
north-east		44.1	24.2	9.7	9.4	6.9	3.2	1.9
Saltings		36.5	21.3	13.3	12.2	8.8	4.5	2.6
Northamptonshire: Towcester hd.		35.3	23.0	13.7	13.3	9.4	3.2	2.2
Lincolnshire (Lindsey): Louthesk and Ludborough wapentakes		40.8	21.4	11.6	15.8	6.8	2.6	0.9

£100+	Total	Under £1	Under £2	£2	£3–4	£5–9	£10–19	£20–39	£40–99	£100+	Total
0.3	100.0	0.3	4.7	6.7	10.6	15.7	17.8	15.6	17.7	10.9	100.0
0.8	100.0	–	4.2	6.2	7.3	11.6	13.0	14.9	16.0	26.9	100.1
0.5	100.1	–	2.4	5.3	8.1	19.9	25.3	15.5	11.8	11.7	100.0
2.2	100.0	–	1.8	2.9	3.2	5.5	10.4	13.6	15.3	47.3	100.0
0.7	100.0	–	2.4	3.6	6.8	15.3	23.4	22.8	12.2	13.5	100.0
0.4	100.1	0.6	6.3	8.4	12.4	17.8	17.9	14.1	8.5	14.1	100.1
0.4	100.0	–	3.6	6.3	8.0	13.1	17.1	19.9	15.9	16.1	100.0
0.5	100.0	1.2	4.3	5.8	7.9	13.7	13.9	16.6	21.9	14.7	100.0
1.0	100.0	–	–	3.6	5.3	13.0	20.6	19.8	18.3	19.4	100.0
0.3	100.0	–	2.5	5.9	9.2	22.2	23.3	16.9	11.7	8.3	100.0
0.2	100.0	0.4	5.2	9.7	12.8	21.0	21.2	15.0	5.8	9.0	100.0
0.1	100.2	0.2	2.9	7.3	12.1	20.6	26.2	18.8	7.3	4.6	100.0
0.1	100.3	15.2	28.2	3.2	3.6	7.7	0.5	21.4	7.6	12.6	100.0
0.4	100.0	–	7.5	8.2	7.1	12.8	14.6	20.2	17.9	11.7	100.0
0.2	100.0	–	9.7	6.9	10.0	13.5	15.8	20.8	19.9	3.4	100.0
0.2	100.0	–	7.1	8.2	6.9	15.9	14.4	23.1	15.2	9.2	100.0
0.2	100.0	–	10.7	7.3	9.1	17.3	24.1	16.9	9.2	5.4	100.0
0.6	100.0	–	12.2	8.1	8.3	10.0	13.3	13.2	12.8	22.2	100.1
1.1	100.0	–	7.6	5.4	4.2	8.8	12.9	12.7	18.8	29.6	100.0
0.3	100.0	–	9.0	10.8	9.5	15.7	18.9	13.3	12.0	10.8	100.0
0.1	99.9	–	4.3	15.9	10.1	16.8	23.0	17.2	8.8	3.9	100.0
0.2	100.0	–	8.4	10.0	9.5	16.0	21.0	16.9	9.9	8.4	100.1
0.1	100.0	–	12.4	8.2	10.1	17.0	24.2	14.4	10.5	3.3	100.1
0.2	99.9	–	9.5	7.8	9.4	16.5	22.1	12.5	15.3	7.0	100.1
0.7	100.1	–	8.3	8.8	5.9	10.5	15.0	14.1	15.8	21.6	100.0
0.9	100.1	–	5.6	6.2	6.5	10.9	15.9	16.1	19.4	19.6	100.2
–	100.1	–	6.2	9.3	9.5	15.9	24.1	14.7	20.3	–	100.
–	99.9	–	10.0	10.4	9.6	24.5	19.7	14.0	11.8	–	100.0

Table A.2 Distribution of personal wealth in Cornwall

Number of assessments

Hundred	Under £1 natives	aliens	£2	£3–4	£5–9	£10–19	£20–39	£40–99	£100+	Totals natives	all
Penwith	3 (106)	131	188	204	185	79	30	10	3	702 (805)	936
Kerrier	12 (311)	–	337	286	117	82	33	11	2	880 (1,179)	1,179
Trigg	14	9	229	188	80	74	40	8	–	633	642
West	79 (140)	44	194	248	111	125	44	23	3	827 (888)	932
East	279 (297)	–	485	559	258	172	65	14	1	1,834 (1,852)	1,852*

Amount of wealth

Hundred	Under £1	£2	£3–4	£5–9	£10–19	£20–39	£40–99	£100+	Total
Penwith	–	394	715	1,124	919	664	410	433	4,659
Kerrier	–	708	1,145	785	1,064	748	487	333	5,270
Trigg	–	469	733	548	851	876	384	–	3,861
West	–	398	973	790	1,374	985	1,209	300	6,029
East	–	978	2,119	1,790	1,974	1,476	711	100	9,148*

Percentages of native assessments (number)

Hundred	Under £1	£2	£3–4	£5–9	£10–19	£20–39	£40–99	£100+	Total
Penwith	0.4	26.7	29.1	26.4	11.3	4.3	1.4	0.4	100
Kerrier	1.4	38.2	32.5	13.3	9.3	3.8	1.3	0.2	100
Trigg	2.2	36.2	29.7	12.6	11.7	6.3	1.3	–	100
West	9.6	23.5	29.9	13.4	15.1	5.3	2.8	0.4	100
East	15.2	26.4	30.5	14.1	9.4	3.5	0.8	(0.1)	100

Percentages of native assessments (amount)

Hundred	£2	£3–4	£5–9	£10–19	£20–39	£40–99	£100+	Total
Penwith	8.5	15.3	24.1	19.8	14.2	8.8	9.3	100
Kerrier	13.4	21.7	14.9	20.2	14.2	9.3	6.3	100
Trigg	12.1	19.0	14.2	22.0	22.7	10.0	–	100
West	6.6	16.1	13.1	22.8	16.3	20.1	5.0	100
East	10.7	23.1	19.6	21.6	16.1	7.5	1.1	100

Percentages of all persons

Hundred	Under £1 natives	aliens	£2	£3–4	£5–9	£10–19	£20–39	£40–99	£100+	Total
Penwith	11.3	14.0	20.1	21.8	19.8	8.4	3.2	1.1	0.3	100.1
Kerrier	26.4	–	28.6	24.3	9.9	7.0	2.8	0.9	0.2	100.1
Trigg	2.2	1.4	35.7	29.3	12.5	11.5	6.2	1.3	–	100.1
West	15.0	4.7	20.8	26.6	11.9	13.4	4.7	2.5	0.3	99.9
East	16.0	–	26.2	30.2	13.9	9.3	3.5	0.8	(0.1)	(100.0)

* Includes one assessment at £1.

Table A.3 Examples of town wealth (lay)

	Number of assessments										Amount of wealth									
	Under £1	Under £2	£2	£3–4	£5–9	£10–19	£20–39	£40–99	£100+	Total	Under £1	Under £2	£2	£3–4	£5–9	£10–19	£20–39	£40–99	£100+	Total
Coventry (1522)	749	126	139	83	96	59	61	44	20	1,377	25	126	286	278	576	672	1,349	2,311	6,090	11,713
Exeter (1522)		457	175	27	85	68	45	33	29	919		522	333	90	508	818	1,002	1,410	4,294	8,997
Bury St Edmunds (1524)		298	125	79	51	48	26	16	8	651		298	255	282	310	575	664	738	1,093	4,215
Worcester (1525)		226	100	54	40	48	22	9	–	499										
Great Yarmouth (1522)	179	68	68	51	46	32	25	19	5	493	2	69	138	175	290	394	599	1,000	833	3,500
Leicester (1524)		175	78	61	34	30	10	13	2	403		175	156	208	207	386	220	620	700	2,672
Chichester (1525)		114	105	46	22	25	11	6	1	330		122	211	174	144	312	287	363	200	1,813
Hadleigh (1524)		114	82	20	41	15	16	14	5	307		114	164	73	238	182	377	660	753	2,561
Nottingham (1524)		135	71	35	16	24	5	8	1	295		135	143	119	103	311	105	400	100	1,416
Percentages																				
Coventry	54.4	9.2	10.1	6.0	7.0	4.3	4.4	3.2	1.5	100.1	0.2	1.1	2.4	2.4	4.9	5.7	11.5	19.7	52.0	99.9
Exeter		49.7	19.0	2.9	9.3	7.4	4.9	3.6	3.2	100.0		5.8	3.9	1.0	5.7	9.1	11.1	15.7	47.7	100.0
Bury St Edmunds		45.8	19.2	12.1	7.8	7.4	4.0	2.5	1.2	100.0		7.1	6.0	6.7	7.4	13.6	15.8	17.5	25.9	100.0
Worcester		45.3	20.0	10.8	8.0	9.6	4.4	1.8	–	99.9										
Great Yarmouth	36.3	13.8	13.8	10.4	9.3	6.5	5.1	3.9	1.0	100.0		2.0	3.9	5.0	8.3	11.3	17.1	28.6	23.8	100.0
Leicester		43.4	19.4	15.1	8.4	7.4	2.5	3.2	0.5	99.9		6.6	5.8	7.8	7.7	14.5	8.2	23.2	26.2	99.9
Chichester		34.6	31.8	13.9	6.7	7.6	3.3	1.8	0.3	100.0		6.7	11.6	9.6	7.9	17.2	15.8	20.0	11.0	100.0
Hadleigh		37.1	26.7	6.5	13.4	4.9	5.2	4.6	1.6	100.0		4.5	6.4	2.9	9.3	7.1	14.7	25.8	29.4	99.8
Nottingham		45.8	24.1	11.9	5.4	8.1	1.7	2.7	0.3	100.0		9.5	10.1	8.4	7.3	22.0	7.4	28.2	7.1	100.0

Note For Worcester, as the subsidy roll is in poor condition the figures are reproduced from A.D. Dyer, *The City of Worcester in the Sixteenth Century* (Leicester, 1971), p. 175, by kind permission of the author.

Table A.4 Industrial wealth

Number of assessments

	Under £1	Under £2	£2	£3-4	£5-9	£10-19	£20-39	£40-99	£100+	Total
SUFFOLK										
Babergh hundred										
clothing places	273	297	244	122	132	136	97	60	42	1,403
non-clothing places	102	92	80	85	67	62	36	6	1	531
Sudbury	45	37	37	23	21	26	12	11	9	221
Lavenham	23	33	33	10	12	15	13	18	12	169
Long Melford	31	25	16	9	13	14	7	4	5	124
GLOUCESTERSHIRE										
Bisley hundred	10	–	39	24	41	45	26	4	6	195
Stroud	–	–	3	–	4	–	3	–	3	13
Cirencester	6	–	9	12	16	8	16	9	4	80
Vale townships	29	92	84	47	57	33	27	10	4	383

Amount of wealth

	Under £1	Under £2	£2	£3-4	£5-9	£10-19	£20-39	£40-99	£100+	Total
SUFFOLK										
Babergh hundred										
clothing places	–	304	492	435	839	1,610	2,248	3,800	10,605	19,733
non-clothing places	–	97	166	295	409	742	834	281	133	2,957
Sudbury	–	37	73	79	139	306	270	509	1,240	2,653
Lavenham	–	35	44	35	74	176	311	1,043	5,333	7,051
Long Melford	–	27	32	32	84	173	147	217	1,333	2,045
GLOUCESTERSHIRE										
Bisley hundred	–	–	78	85	241	532	596	190	1,006	2,728
Stroud	–	–	6	–	21	–	60	–	573	660
Cirencester	–	–	18	45	97	80	378	539	800	1,957
Vale townships	–	98	172	170	345	385	643	499	600	2,912

Percentages

Number of assessments

	Under £1	Under £2	£2	£3-4	£5-9	£10-19	£20-39	£40-99	£100+	Total
Babergh hundred										
clothing places	19.5	21.2	17.4	8.7	9.4	9.7	6.9	4.3	3.0	100.1
non-clothing places	19.2	17.3	15.1	16.0	12.6	11.7	8.8	1.2	0.2	100.1
Sudbury	20.4	16.7	16.7	10.4	9.5	11.8	5.4	5.0	4.1	100.0
Lavenham	14.6	20.9	13.9	6.3	7.6	9.5	8.2	11.4	7.6	100.0
Long Melford	25.0	20.2	12.9	7.3	10.5	11.3	5.5	3.2	4.0	100.0
Bisley hundred	5.1	–	20.0	12.3	21.0	23.1	13.3	2.1	3.1	100.0
Stroud	–	–	23.1	–	30.7	–	23.1	–	23.1	100.1
Cirencester	7.5	–	11.3	15.0	20.0	10.0	20.0	11.3	5.0	100.1
Vale townships	7.6	24.0	21.9	12.3	14.9	8.6	7.1	2.6	1.0	100.0

Amount of wealth

	Under £1	Under £2	£2	£3-4	£5-9	£10-19	£20-39	£40-99	£100+	Total
Babergh hundred										
clothing places	–	1.5	2.5	2.2	4.3	8.2	11.4	16.2	53.7	100.0
non-clothing places	–	3.3	5.6	10.0	13.8	25.1	28.2	9.5	4.5	100.0
Sudbury	–	1.4	2.8	3.0	5.2	11.5	10.2	19.2	46.7	100.0
Lavenham	–	0.5	0.6	0.5	1.1	2.5	4.4	14.8	75.6	100.0
Long Melford	–	1.3	1.6	1.6	4.1	8.5	7.2	10.6	65.2	100.1
Bisley hundred	–	–	2.9	3.1	8.8	19.5	21.8	7.0	36.9	100.0
Stroud	–	–	0.9	–	3.2	–	9.1	–	86.8	100.0
Cirencester	–	–	0.9	2.3	5.0	4.1	19.3	27.5	40.9	100.0
Vale townships	–	3.4	5.9	5.8	11.9	13.2	22.1	17.1	20.6	100.0

5 FULL TABLES OF LAY ASSESSMENTS ON GOODS

As the number of separate townships is very large and many contain only a handful of assessments the figures are totalled by hundreds. By the sixteenth century it is improbable that these possessed any special significance. Nevertheless, they were active administrative units, and in several counties their returns display marked individual characteristics. The number of townships, or other divisions, in each is that shown in the return. At times two or more were combined; in much of East Sussex no divisions are shown. As, moreover, a township might not remain permanently in the same hundred, it is not in every case feasible to determine whether any are missing. Seriously defective lists are omitted.

The subsidy figures are taken from the first (1524) list as far as possible, gaps being made good from the second if it is available.

Berkshire

The section headed 'Kintbury Egle hundred' also contains Compton and Faircross hundreds and Newbury borough; from the manner in which the townships are mixed up it is clear that they were administered as a unit.

Buckinghamshire

By this time the fifteen Domesday hundreds of the north of the county had been grouped in threes. For convenience the data are rearranged according to the smaller units. The Chiltern hundreds were less intimately associated. Although treated as a single entity by the subsidy, the survey distinguishes them while apparently assessing them under a common set of rules. Simpson (Seckloe hundred) and the detached parish of Caversfield (Rowley) are missing from the survey, as is Edgcott (Lamua) from the subsidy.

Cornwall

Certificates are extant for five of the nine hundreds, each displaying strong characteristics within the basic format used throughout the county. These are seen in the use of joint, or family, assessments, and in the treatment of nil and £1 assessments, and aliens.

Lincolnshire

The parishes of Ludburgh are combined in four groups.

Norfolk

The certificates represent eleven of the thirty-four hundreds plus Great Yarmouth, one of three boroughs separately assessed for the subsidy. They fall into three broad groupings:

1 North-east: South Erpingham, West Flegg, Happing, Tunstead. In these as many men, or more, are listed as in the corresponding subsidy schedule; they may be regarded as very thorough.

2 Heathland: Brothercross, Gallow, North Greenhoe, Holt. These contain 25–30 per cent fewer names than the subsidy, the shortfall affecting mainly the poor. Nevertheless, the distribution of assessments is comparable with that in similar arable farming districts of East Anglia.

3 Blofield, East Flegg and Walsham have a very low percentage of nil and £1 assessments. Compared with the subsidy lists the last two are almost certainly deficient. Blofield contains 294 names compared with 291 in 1524; it is situated on the edge of the wood-pasture region, and its composition is analagous to that of the subsidy schedules for east-central Suffolk.

Essex

Except for one parish there is no return for Tendring hundred. An odd parish or two may be missing from a few hundreds.

Rutland

A few entries on the first folio, relating to Whissendine, Alstoe hundred, are illegible.

Suffolk

The division of the Babergh hundred muster into clothing and non-clothing townships is arbitrary. Half of Ipswich is missing, the returns for Blackborne are useless, and only parts of Lackford and Risbridge hundreds are extant.

Sussex

The return for Rushmonden hundred is useless; several others have lacunae (see SRS, lvi). Administratively, Sussex was divided into six rapes which ran diametrically across the boundaries of natural regions. In Table 3.1 the data have been rearranged according to the latter (see SAC, cxiv, 3, 26: appendix 2).

Gloucestershire

The method of handling nil and £1 assessments shows that the county was administered in three divisions for the musters. Gloucester town and the adjacent hundred of Dudstone and King's Barton are missing. Bristol, which belonged partly to Somerset, would have assessed itself.

Worcestershire

The two volumes of the survey are fragments consisting of parts of Halfshire and Oswaldslow hundreds, plus a single parish of Pershore, set out in no logical order. The traditional topography is confusing. The pragmatic solution is adopted of arranging the data according to the Domesday hundreds, with minor modifications. Came is complete; the isolated parish of Yardley (Pershore hundred) is added to it. Esch is represented by Feckenham, Hanbury and Inkberrow, to which is added Stock and Bradley, a detached part of Oswaldslow. Oswaldslow itself is represented by a few parishes to the east of Worcester, with Broughton Hackett (Esch) and Martin Hussingtree (Pershore) added. Clent was divided into two parts separated by Came. The southern one, centring on Droitwich, is complete; the northern, around Stourbridge, is fragmentary. Mitton is missing from Cresslau hundred, but Ombersley (Fishborough) in included with it.

Exeter

The survey lacks the parishes of All Hallows on the Walls, St Lawrence and St Mary Steps; the subsidy lists for St Kerrian, St Pancras and St Stephen are too defective to be used. Both returns are therefore reproduced.

Table A.5 (a) Musters, 1522

| County and hundred | Townships | Number of assessments | | | | | | | | | | Value of goods (to nearest £) | | | | | | | | | |
		Under £1	£2	£2	£3–4	£5–9	£10–19	£20–39	£40–99	£100+	Total	Under £1	£2	£2	£3–4	£5–9	£10–19	£20–39	£40–99	£100+	Total
Berkshire																					
Faircross	22	290	131	98	93	90	45	24	16	3	790	31	142	204	319	566	525	585	840	360	3,572
Newbury	1	62	61	39	24	24	10	14	10	4	248	15	65	82	81	154	121	315	587	1,013	2,433
Kintbury Egle	22	210	144	86	76	67	46	24	15	–	668	31	161	178	264	434	542	553	748	–	2,911
Compton	8	72	33	24	20	30	13	8	4	2	206	11	39	52	70	181	173	182	220	400	1,328
Lambourn	6	48	63	39	36	20	26	15	5	1	253	24	47	82	122	127	319	389	254	124	1,488
Wantage	16	116	136	97	66	63	37	21	13	–	549	50	152	206	223	390	439	495	739	–	2,694
Ganfield	10	47	73	56	41	37	11	5	5	2	277	26	78	118	147	233	134	109	305	533	1,683
Shrivenham	19	49	94	70	66	73	32	25	9	3	421	27	111	150	230	469	409	588	439	343	2,766
Faringdon	8	48	49	40	27	27	8	3	6	1	209	24	49	85	96	164	106	67	277	133	1,001
Buckinghamshire																					
Three hundreds of Hewport																					
Bunsty	18	51	114	71	52	62	26	9	3	1	389	–	127	144	184	391	310	182	187	133	1,658
Moulsoe	20	61	111	90	66	41	18	12	2	–	401	–	125	194	219	248	220	264	107	–	1,377
Secloe	12	94	125	96	69	45	26	12	1	1	469	–	134	198	250	276	283	254	67	133	1,595
Three hundreds of Buckingham																					
Lamua	11	72	115	77	76	75	35	14	3	1	468	36	128	162	287	451	408	291	120	200	2,083
Stotfold	13	55	68	52	61	44	22	5	5	2	314	22	72	112	222	271	265	112	260	413	1,749
Rowley	8	31	36	23	28	24	11	4	3	1	161	18	39	47	98	164	127	86	120	200	899
Three hundreds of Cottesloe																					
Yardley	6	73	97	59	46	55	20	6	3	3	362	–	105	127	161	358	240	131	156	333	1,611
Cottesloe	12	66	99	84	72	45	22	6	5	1	400	–	104	162	239	272	250	150	260	467	1,904
Mursley	13	28	128	75	69	51	17	12	3	2	385	–	141	158	239	306	197	272	120	200	1,633
Three hundreds of Ashendon																					
Waddesdon	10	51	33	40	44	22	18	1	1	3	213	10	35	81	138	136	210	20	40	533	1,203
Ashendon	12	79	89	53	62	46	14	7	4	2	356	24	97	111	215	296	163	155	197	400	1,658
Ichill	13	76	103	67	67	52	39	14	1	–	419	24	114	138	217	316	491	313	40	–	1,673

Three hundreds of Aylesbury																					
Stone	12	45	75	38	27	39	33	12	2	2	273	1	77	87	104	264	386	278	80	200	1,477
Aylesbury	16	147	203	134	99	80	64	41	8	1	778	5	214	274	377	551	748	831	357	300	3,657
Risborough	4	40	53	37	24	15	10	8	–	–	187	1	55	78	87	93	115	162	–	–	591
Chiltern hundreds																					
Desborough	17	188	164	149	103	100	64	38	18	2	826	1	173	309	360	648	744	911	823	340	4,309
Burnham	13	193	154	147	134	94	70	42	17	2	853	–	171	306	460	611	857	1,000	822	500	4,727
Stoke	11	113	110	96	61	66	55	29	7	5	542	–	117	197	214	428	605	653	405	1,233	3,847
Cornwall																					
East	39	279	1	485	559	258	172	65	14	1	1,834	–	1	978	2,119	1,790	1,974	1,476	711	100	9,149
West	22	79	–	194	248	111	125	44	23	3	827	–	–	378	973	790	1,374	985	1,209	300	6,029
Trigg	12	14	–	229	188	80	74	40	8	–	633	–	–	469	733	548	851	876	384	–	3,861
Kerrier	28	12	–	337	286	117	82	33	11	2	880	–	–	708	1,145	785	1,064	748	487	333	5,270
Penwith	26	3	–	188	204	185	79	30	10	3	702	1	–	394	715	1,124	919	664	410	433	4,660
Gloucestershire																					
Forest																					
Bleckisloe	8	63	69	41	31	11	7	–	–	–	291	7	78	147	144	192	117	140	–	–	825
St Briavels	14	154	100	99	76	63	16	7	2	2	618	6	112	220	348	476	732	360	300	466	3,020
Bothow	16	92	117	89	70	56	32	10	3	1	470	–	123	183	246	351	349	218	130	100	1,700
Westbury	7	51	16	26	13	27	6	–	1	–	153	–	18	53	42	169	153	140	–	100	675
Duchy	8	87	47	53	46	56	18	12	–	–	319	4	53	112	162	362	206	249	–	–	1,148
Vale																					
Tewkesbury	22	182	–	71	58	106	66	39	24	6	552	–	–	151	221	646	767	964	1,318	733	4,800
Tibaldstone	3	14	–	14	13	24	17	8	–	1	90	–	–	29	46	143	190	196	–	–	604
Deerhurst	9	26	–	27	37	32	21	5	5	1	154	–	–	56	137	209	233	100	260	100	1,095
Whitstone	16	30	55	73	111	135	89	34	8	3	538	–	61	151	388	883	1,070	789	501	375	4,218
Berkeley	42	32	267	229	170	266	156	79	10	3	1,212	7	292	477	599	1,695	1,821	1,372	539	367	7,169
Thornbury	10	23	57	74	57	79	41	14	4	–	349	–	59	152	195	505	440	307	198	–	1,876
Pucklechurch	5	25	23	35	28	42	12	4	1	–	170	–	24	73	98	252	130	93	40	–	710
Henbury	7	12	44	63	61	51	18	5	–	–	254	–	46	132	216	313	204	113	–	–	1,024

Table A.5 (a) *continued*

County and hundred	Townships	Number of assessments										Value of goods (to nearest £)									
		Under	£1	£2	£3-4	£5-9	£10-19	£20-39	£40-99	£100+	Total	Under	£1	£2	£3-4	£5-9	£10-19	£20-39	£40-99	£100+	Total
Barton near Bristol	5	7	41	32	22	27	12	5	1	–	147	–	42	66	77	160	142	107	40	–	634
Grumbalds Ash	30	74	162	174	169	219	124	26	9	4	961	–	170	352	592	1,368	1,479	615	396	733	5,705
Cotswolds																					
Rapsgate	12	2	–	9	22	30	24	12	3	1	103	–	1	18	82	202	291	300	185	120	1,198
Langtree	17	5	–	61	55	49	41	21	11	2	245	–	–	122	189	305	501	458	505	293	2,313
Bisley	13	10	–	39	24	41	45	26	4	6	195	–	–	78	85	241	532	596	190	1,006	2,728
Cheltenham	7	4	–	35	26	25	27	13	9	1	140	–	–	70	89	159	339	290	450	200	1,597
Kiftsgate	47	274	1	152	83	166	154	54	21	4	909	–	1	323	296	1,038	1,804	1,249	1,089	1,406	7,206
Westminster	8	31	–	36	35	32	15	24	3	2	178	–	–	75	122	196	172	541	207	567	1,880
Slaughter	22	11	–	52	55	66	40	25	6	–	255	–	–	104	199	416	464	572	310	–	2,065
Crowthorn	17	4	–	28	35	39	33	9	4	–	152	–	–	56	122	245	392	210	307	–	1,332
Bradley	21	1	–	20	19	39	25	17	12	1	134	–	–	40	63	261	319	380	608	140	1,811
Brightwells Barrow	15	–	–	13	33	29	51	12	11	5	153	–	–	26	114	195	643	264	580	540	2,362
Cirencester Liberty	2	6	–	12	17	20	10	19	9	5	98	–	–	24	62	161	106	454	539	1,033	2,379
Cleeve	1	6	–	23	13	23	9	5	2	1	82	–	–	46	44	146	116	124	80	100	656
Norfolk																					
Great Yarmouth borough	1	179	68	68	51	46	32	25	19	5	493	2	69	138	175	290	394	599	1,000	833	3,500
West Flagg	13	72	59	54	51	44	18	15	6	–	319	1	60	108	173	270	211	338	260	–	1,421
Tunstead	27	326	222	145	160	151	90	25	10	2	1,131	12	229	294	578	936	1,030	579	465	266	4,389
Happing	17	198	139	122	122	83	50	12	5	–	731	1	139	246	415	493	582	280	257	–	2,413
South Erpingham	39	503	298	187	146	117	77	39	20	6	1,393	28	325	386	508	751	883	923	1,097	793	5,694
North Greenhoe	14	136	131	121	79	66	50	23	16	7	629	–	143	254	270	441	566	545	802	907	3,928
Brothercross	11	60	53	36	16	22	17	7	6	2	219	–	59	69	61	129	195	180	240	320	1,253
Gallow	26	93	115	86	53	39	29	20	6	2	443	2	130	185	183	258	328	472	310	1,493	3,361
Holt	26	104	177	135	119	101	49	34	13	5	737	1	197	280	416	644	562	703	680	700	4,183

Blofield	16	21	47	51	41	61	46	21	5	1	294	–	18	103	143	391	578	484	240	133	2,120
South Walsham	13	19	50	55	52	73	39	4	4	1	297	–	54	110	170	483	513	105	190	200	1,825
East Flegg	9	6	27	35	36	33	22	10	5	2	176	–	27	71	123	201	278	246	210	300	1,456
Suffolk: Babergh																					
Clothing parishes	17	273	297	245	122	132	136	97	60	42	1,403	–	304	492	435	839	1,610	2,248	3,200	10,605	19,733
Other parishes	15	102	92	80	85	67	62	36	6	1	531	–	97	166	295	409	742	834	281	133	2,957
Rutland																					
Alstoe	12	59	38	25	42	40	50	8	1	–	253	–	43	50	132	250	500	172	60	–	1,207
Soke of Oakham	9	90	51	38	46	76	19	11	2	1	345	–	53	77	158	494	371	258	90	200	1,701
Martinsley	11	57	29	34	49	36	26	25	1	–	276	–	30	64	176	220	571	576	50	–	1,687
East	9	63	34	31	23	30	10	15	9	6	236	–	34	62	78	194	193	248	545	600	1,954
Wrandike	13	69	49	42	29	42	46	34	9	3	323	2	59	84	91	272	548	770	390	453	2,669
Worcestershire																					
Came	12	167	102	139	114	114	50	12	1	2	701	4	112	290	402	757	567	264	40	234	2,670
Esch	5	59	41	41	24	33	19	13	1	–	231	6	45	82	83	198	235	286	60	–	995
Clent (north)	7	70	25	27	21	41	26	13	3	–	226	4	27	54	74	237	316	285	120	–	1,117
Clent (south)	8	118	28	23	29	30	10	1	–	–	239	1	29	47	120	188	344	217	40	–	986
Oswaldslow	11	45	19	36	51	43	18	7	–	–	219	2	19	74	186	273	212	171	–	–	937
Cresslau	9	169	80	120	96	88	94	35	8	1	691	4	88	248	341	592	1,145	716	440	133	3,707
Coventry																					
City (1)	10	714	128	152	66	96	65	54	40	20	1,335	20	130	311	240	580	750	1,257	2,141	5,973	11,402
Foreyns	13	77	15	27	20	15	13	4	–	3	174	4	16	57	69	95	146	97	–	634	1,118
Long Compton, Warks. (1)	1	24	15	12	8	6	2	–	–	–	67	1	19	25	27	35	25	–	–	–	132
Exeter (part): Survey (1)	14	442	99	59	26	62	67	40	26	18	839	35	106	122	91	392	751	915	1,478	2,753	6,663
Subsidy (1)	14	–	289	172	51	63	52	37	26	25	715	–	313	353	183	386	624	820	1,107	3,435	7,221
Yorkshire: Staincliffe	34	945	562	38	26	33	1	24	4	2	1,635	362	670	76	85	183	13	510	180	300	2,379

Table A.5 (b) Subsidy, 1524–5

County and hundred	Townships	Number of assessments										Value of goods (to nearest £)									
		Under £1	£1	£2	£3–4	£5–9	£10–19	£20–39	£40–99	£100+	Total	Under £1	£1	£2	£3–4	£5–9	£10–19	£20–39	£40–99	£100+	Total
Essex																						
Colchester: borough	11	–	224	191	64	59	50	22	25	6	641	–	231	388	210	404	645	546	1,178	1,200	4,802
	5	–	44	28	10	14	4	4	1	–	105	–	44	56	40	94	57	100	40	–	431
Lexden	30	–	609	262	119	113	84	37	12	8	1,244	–	668	557	419	690	1,003	955	570	1,244	6,106
(Centre)																						
Chelmsford	25	–	350	192	129	99	74	21	18	–	883	–	393	404	472	639	916	520	917	–	4,261
Dunmow	26	–	481	170	118	124	93	25	20	2	1,033	–	515	356	400	769	1,271	575	1,069	225	5,180
Hinckford	41	–	731	304	200	233	147	37	14	3	1,669	–	734	628	688	1,503	1,883	845	641	721	7,643
Ongar	26	–	269	105	118	106	68	27	16	3	712	–	299	211	408	698	831	637	722	580	4,386
Witham	17	–	313	131	88	58	34	18	7	1	650	–	384	272	285	361	409	441	345	100	2,597
(West)																						
Clavering	8	–	181	55	22	25	17	8	2	–	310	–	185	111	78	145	211	183	93	–	1,006
Freshwell	10	–	161	66	45	58	46	4	2	1	383	–	162	134	153	365	522	80	116	100	1,632
Harlow	13	–	238	77	86	69	41	16	8	1	536	–	259	158	301	441	550	379	347	100	2,535
Uttlesford	34*	–	651	214	144	130	128	63	9	–	1,339	–	665	432	495	820	1,496	896	505	–	5,309
Waltham	8	–	226	90	63	47	16	10	3	1	456	–	253	174	218	323	194	228	230	200	1,820
(Saltings)																						
Barstable	34	–	398	154	118	108	85	32	16	1	912	–	431	314	408	698	1,077	912	817	100	4,757
Becontree	22	–	454	347	221	153	99	63	25	7	1,369	–	461	702	734	879	1,107	1,496	1,137	1,170	7,686
Chafford	15	–	241	127	81	66	53	18	11	2	599	–	242	258	280	422	669	455	612	217	3,155
Dengie	21	–	229	92	74	95	73	40	26	13	642	–	248	197	274	665	1,006	1,038	1,490	2,301	7,219
Rochford	20	–	245	172	77	101	62	34	31	8	730	–	297	351	273	650	838	841	1,659	1,304	6,213
Thurstable	9	–	88	76	30	27	39	22	7	8	297	–	99	157	107	172	532	584	444	1,239	3,334
Winstree	14	–	139	76	53	60	29	12	7	2	378	–	158	157	179	378	394	326	343	340	2,275
Maldon borough	4	–	76	45	29	13	11	7	9	3	193	–	75	95	97	81	125	181	545	520	1,719

Lincolnshire

Leuthesk	36	–	337	175	100	137	60	23	8	–	840	–	337	350	337	868	720	488	420	–	3,520
Ledburgh	4	–	60	33	13	17	6	2	1	–	132	–	60	66	45	109	67	70	52	–	469

Northamptonshire

Towcester	9	–	96	64	38	37	26	9	6	–	278	–	87	130	134	223	338	206	284	–	1,402

Suffolk

Lackford (part)	11	–	212	56	52	16	15	8	3	–	362	–	228	119	192	109	183	200	160	–	1,191
Risbridge (part)	20	–	414	106	62	49	30	7	3	3	674	–	489	221	218	265	354	157	165	380	2,249
Thedwastre	21	–	267	110	53	44	16	13	5	4	512	–	277	230	186	276	187	327	205	633	2,321
Thingoe	19	–	254	80	38	43	30	12	5	2	464	–	261	167	137	268	338	279	300	620	2,370
Bury St Edmunds (1)	5	–	298	125	79	51	48	26	16	8	651	–	298	255	282	310	575	664	738	1,093	4,215

Stour Valley

Labergh	32	–	1,036	329	151	191	150	75	51	25	2,008	–	1,086	665	543	1,209	1,862	1,875	2,682	5,103	15,025
Cosford	16	–	393	159	50	106	54	28	18	5	813	–	391	321	174	640	635	679	820	753	4,413
Samford	28	–	330	160	81	44	56	21	21	7	720	–	354	329	289	278	635	515	1,037	1,310	4,747

West centre

Bosmore and Claydon	28	–	248	177	104	80	57	20	13	4	703	–	285	362	358	486	686	435	608	733	3,953
Hartismere	32	–	391	240	121	121	62	23	6	1	965	–	421	500	434	748	801	583	376	100	3,963
Stow	13	–	156	94	38	49	31	13	4	2	387	–	174	196	136	305	370	291	190	230	1,892

East centre

Hoxne	24	–	165	358	145	164	95	23	4	1	955	–	181	728	538	1,036	1,187	573	210	133	4,586
Thredling	5	–	39	80	26	20	22	4	3	–	194	–	40	161	90	125	234	80	160	–	890
Loes	20	–	125	222	87	84	61	34	8	2	623	–	132	458	311	500	734	769	402	433	3,739
Carlford	18	–	82	148	54	48	35	15	7	–	389	–	82	301	203	324	376	359	370	–	2,015
Wilford	16	–	135	161	58	38	36	19	2	–	449	–	136	324	203	229	429	437	80	–	1,838
Colnes	10	–	47	158	23	31	28	11	1	–	299	–	47	316	101	190	328	245	40	–	1,267

North east

Mutford	8	–	144	70	47	36	18	8	2	–	325	–	150	143	160	223	228	207	86	–	1,197
Wangford	27	–	323	213	118	116	73	41	15	2	901	–	338	430	417	735	902	1,022	749	600	5,193
Blything	49	–	623	329	240	219	134	43	12	3	1,603	–	711	661	855	1,366	1,574	993	520	800	7,480

Table A.5 (b) *continued*

County and hundred	Townships	Number of assessments										Value of goods (to nearest £)									
		Under										Under									
		£1	£2	£2	£3–4	£5–9	£10–19	£20–39	£40–99	£100+	Total	£1	£2	£2	£3–4	£5–9	£10–19	£20–39	£40–99	£100+	Total
Dunwich borough	1	–	77	77	21	20	19	12	3	–	229	–	96	157	69	127	237	311	140	–	1,137
Plomesgate	24	–	216	232	65	70	73	23	7	1	677	–	237	421	231	451	868	537	300	133	3,178
Sussex																					
Chichester Rape																					
Aldwick	14	–	125	52	29	26	18	9	4	2	265	–	125	105	100	152	232	230	243	200	1,387
Bosham	7	–	71	32	29	19	14	6	3	1	175	–	72	64	95	113	171	145	160	100	920
Box and Stockbridge	20	–	222	89	57	47	24	18	7	4	468	–	231	182	183	285	278	479	367	733	2,738
Manhood	8	–	85	51	28	36	21	5	3	1	230	–	91	103	91	220	282	138	170	133	1,228
Westbourne	10	–	88	28	29	29	17	7	3	1	193	–	88	56	68	189	194	170	130	110	1,005
Singleton	7	–	51	35	31	17	12	6	4	1	156	–	52	71	109	100	150	130	180	–	792
Dumpford	8	–	80	54	35	34	20	5	1	1	230	–	81	109	122	199	226	104	44	460	1,345
Easebourne	11	–	131	59	31	31	13	8	3	1	277	–	131	120	106	182	134	185	140	400	1,398
Chichester city (1)	5	–	114	105	46	22	25	11	6	1	330	–	122	211	174	144	312	287	363	200	1,813
Midhurst boro'	1	–	43	34	10	2	8	6	–	–	103	–	43	68	36	13	90	160	–	–	410
Arundel Rape																					
Avisford	8	–	76	60	23	35	14	10	5	–	223	–	77	130	77	216	165	218	250	–	1,133
Poling	18	–	126	69	41	46	25	39	11	1	358	–	127	138	137	275	288	885	511	100	2,461
Bury	7	–	50	35	39	32	8	11	2	–	177	–	51	70	133	193	99	232	107	–	885
West Easewrithe	13	–	112	83	46	45	21	19	3	1	330	–	120	166	149	250	244	410	167	200	1,706
Rotherbridge	11	–	223	114	42	76	36	17	10	1	519	–	224	228	145	461	437	364	413	200	2,472
Arundel boro'	1	–	17	30	12	12	3	2	–	–	76	–	17	61	40	70	41	42	–	–	271
Bramber Rape																					
Brightford	11	–	161	82	38	37	17	17	8	1	361	–	166	168	131	237	191	388	477	200	1,958
Burbeach	6	–	27	27	11	14	4	8	2	–	93	–	28	56	37	90	40	177	90	–	518
Fishersgate	1	–	19	1	3	5	2	1	1	–	32	–	21	3	9	27	20	30	67	–	177

Tarring	3	–	60	12	8	16	12	10	–	–	118	–	60	25	29	97	134	223	–	–	568
East Easewrithe	5	–	49	39	13	25	16	11	3	–	156	–	49	79	40	149	162	237	140	–	856
Steyning	10	–	110	48	26	39	23	22	9	1	278	–	111	100	89	219	258	478	430	120	1,805
Tipnoak	3	–	53	32	12	12	12	8	1	2	132	–	55	69	42	73	143	164	40	200	786
West Grinstead	5	–	47	44	16	28	15	10	7	–	167	–	48	91	58	177	175	230	303	–	1,082
Windham	2	–	20	11	2	6	8	8	2	–	57	–	20	22	7	33	87	190	90	–	449
Bramber boro'	1	–	10	4	–	2	1	–	–	–	17	–	10	8	–	10	10	–	–	–	38
Horsham boro'	1	–	52	21	7	11	4	7	5	–	107	–	54	43	23	68	49	170	241	–	648
New Shoreham boro'	1	–	12	6	–	2	–	1	–	–	20	–	12	12	–	12	–	–	–	–	36
Steyning boro'	1	–	41	10	–	4	2	5	1	–	63	–	41	20	–	26	23	107	40	–	257
Lewes Rape																					
Fishersgate	1	–	7	20	4	8	2	1	1	–	43	–	7	40	13	40	20	20	–	–	220
Holmestrowe	(5)	–	22	16	14	14	3	4	2	–	75	–	22	32	49	82	30	95	90	–	400
Swanborough	(3)	–	29	10	2	5	3	3	–	–	52	–	29	20	6	26	30	80	–	–	191
Whalesbone	1	–	46	21	12	10	3	5	1	–	98	–	46	43	42	56	38	113	66	–	404
Younsmere	(3)	–	23	12	9	4	2	2	2	1	55	–	23	25	30	20	25	42	90	100	355
Barcombe	(3)	–	51	15	23	27	4	4	3	–	127	–	51	30	79	158	54	94	156	–	622
Buttinghill	(7)	–	139	61	47	47	21	22	3	3	343	–	142	128	124	293	240	498	178	413	2,016
Lindfield	1	–	42	13	7	16	1	1	1	–	81	–	43	26	21	88	20	20	50	–	258
Poynings	1	–	31	16	11	7	1	6	2	1	75	–	31	32	38	39	10	130	117	133	530
Streat	1	–	73	50	26	59	16	25	4	1	253	–	73	100	95	333	165	537	213	–	1,516
Lewes and Southover	2	–	141	71	38	30	9	20	3	1	313	–	141	142	144	158	208	475	120	100	1,488
Pevensey Rape																					
Alciston	(6)	–	38	18	15	13	5	2	1	–	92	–	39	37	55	90	59	50	50	–	380
Eastbourne	1	–	130	19	5	5	10	9	1	–	183	–	135	38	31	30	135	227	53	–	649
Flexborough	4	–	29	9	7	12	6	2	1	–	66	–	29	18	23	73	81	60	40	–	324
Totnore	(6)	–	30	19	11	9	10	8	1	–	88	–	30	38	37	55	124	195	40	–	519
Willingdon	(5)	–	98	13	6	20	12	3	8	–	160	–	102	26	21	122	152	63	362	–	848
Danehill Horsted	1	–	30	17	15	6	3	–	–	–	71	–	33	35	53	37	30	–	–	–	188
Danehill Sheffield	1	–	51	17	11	14	7	3	1	–	104	–	55	35	37	86	77	77	40	–	407
Dill	(3)	–	35	23	15	23	5	1	1	–	103	–	40	46	56	136	68	20	45	–	411
East Grinstead	1	–	29	8	5	10	10	–	–	–	62	–	36	18	18	61	118	–	–	–	251

Table A.5 (b) *continued*

Group headers: **Number of assessments** (Under £1, £2, £3–4, £5–9, £10–19, £20–39, £40–99, £100+, Total) and **Value of goods (to nearest £)** (Under £1, £2, £3–4, £5–9, £10–19, £20–39, £40–99, £100+, Total).

County and hundred	Townships	\<Number of assessments\> Under	£1	£2	£3–4	£5–9	£10–19	£20–39	£40–99	£100+	Total	\<Value of goods\> Under	£1	£2	£3–4	£5–9	£10–19	£20–39	£40–99	£100+	Total
Hartfield	1	—	70	31	13	12	9	6	—	1	142	—	84	63	47	78	117	130	—	133	652
Longbridge	(10)	—	91	46	20	22	12	7	8	—	206	—	96	93	70	266	157	180	418	—	1,280
Loxfield	1	—	196	78	71	72	56	13	4	—	490	—	216	160	246	476	743	326	206	—	2,373
Ringmer	1	—	112	21	22	9	12	8	3	1	188	—	130	42	89	53	162	197	150	100	923
Rotherfield	1	—	69	39	29	12	11	1	—	—	161	—	74	79	101	72	146	20	—	—	492
Shiplake	5	—	59	31	19	20	11	9	—	—	149	—	60	62	61	120	146	186	—	—	635
East Grinstead boro'	1	—	18	9	6	8	1	2	—	—	44	—	18	18	20	49	10	40	—	—	155
Hastings Rape																					
Baldslow	1	—	44	20	19	23	20	4	1	—	131	—	44	40	63	150	269	118	50	—	734
Battle	1	—	113	26	29	28	27	7	3	—	233	—	123	56	101	172	339	197	150	—	1,138
Bexhill	1	—	30	16	7	15	6	—	—	—	74	—	29	33	22	111	92	—	—	—	287
Foxearle	1	—	117	31	24	18	20	8	2	1	221	—	129	62	80	121	229	215	90	100	1,026
Goldspur	5	—	83	30	23	24	12	6	3	—	181	—	98	60	81	157	184	133	128	—	841
Gostrow	1	—	38	20	7	10	11	10	1	—	97	—	39	40	26	64	156	266	40	—	631
Guestling	1	—	39	16	8	11	4	4	3	—	85	—	39	33	29	64	49	102	200	—	516
Hawksborough	(3)	—	125	39	25	30	20	3	—	1	243	—	130	79	88	186	244	75	—	200	1,002
Henhurst	(2)	—	60	15	13	9	3	2	—	—	102	—	61	31	45	50	39	48	—	—	274
Netherfield	(4)	—	53	21	11	21	11	2	—	1	120	—	57	42	41	124	148	50	—	100	562
Ninfield	1	—	79	14	9	17	4	7	2	—	132	—	75	36	29	113	49	174	122	—	598
Robertsbridge	1	—	34	6	8	6	8	3	—	1	66	—	55	12	29	37	41	98	—	—	294
Shoyswell	(3)	—	61	19	15	13	14	4	1	1	128	—	55	39	54	92	166	104	49	110	669
Staple	1	—	50	25	15	20	23	8	3	1	145	—	50	50	55	138	314	161	144	133	1,045

272

DISTRIBUTION OF LAND

THE FIGURES are the totals of separate parcels, as recorded. No attempt has been made to indicate the number of actual owners, break down global assessments, or fill lacunae. Returns suspected of being seriously defective have been excluded, with the exception of that for the Liberty of the Duchy of Lancaster in Gloucestershire which is retained for the sake of completeness.

The recording of Crown lands is patchy. Frequently no values are given, and there is no alternative source comparable with the *Valor Ecclesiasticus*. In the Cornwall certificates a number of values are entered but struck out. They are deemed to have been correct ones which were deleted to conform with a policy of not assessing royal property; several are corroborated by a Duchy of Cornwall account from the same year (BL, Add. Charter 32897). Any missing values have been made good from this source, eked out with two ministers' accounts: PRO, SC6, Hen. VIII, 434, and Edward VI, 80.

Table B.1 Distribution of land

Group structure: **TEMPORALITIES** — Lay owners (Crown £, Resident No./£, Absentee No./£, Total £); Clergy (Secular No./£, Regular No./£, Miscell. No./£, Total £); Total Temporalities £. **SPIRITUALITIES** — Secular clergy (Resident No./£, Absentee No./£, Regulars No./£, Total £); Grand total £.

County and hundred	Crown £	Resident No.	Resident £	Absentee No.	Absentee £	Lay Total £	Secular No.	Secular £	Regular No.	Regular £	Miscell. No.	Miscell. £	Clergy Total £	Total Temporalities £	Resident No.	Resident £	Absentee No.	Absentee £	Regulars No.	Regulars £	Spirit. Total £	Grand total £
Buckinghamshire																						
Newport	174	386	388	340	1,178	1,740	7	26	47	209	19	52	287	2,027	24	256	16	231	14	126	613	2,640
Buckingham	22	64	274	137	481	777	5	11	42	229	8	62	302	1,079	20	168	16	195	3	21	334	1,413
Cottesloe	33	412	560	218	690	1,283	2	75	35	271	9	15	361	1,644	19	206	10	103	14	253	562	2,206
Ashendon	88	105	254	197	845	1,187	4	3	36	297	4	4	304	1,491	17	102	15	154	16	195	451	1,942
Aylesbury	176	327	501	243	910	1,587	7	55	29	493	5	23	571	2,158	5	46	21	249	6	129	424	2,582
Desborough	60	172	202	145	375	637	3	61	30	213	2	7	281	918	12	127	6	54	5	64	245	1,163
Burnham	50	230	418	199	866	1,334	–	–	20	82	4	10	92	1,426	6	50	9	190	6	59	299	1,725
Stoke	110	158	285	124	405	800	3	51	10	209	5	7	267	1,067	9	70	5	69	6	93	232	1,299
Cornwall																						
East	167	96	149	485	873	1,189	4	59	20	192	–	–	251	1,440	42	317	16	327	12	245	889	2,329
West	87	87	122	312	642	851	–	–	7	30	–	–	30	881	32	270	15	250	5	105	625	1,506
Trigg	18	34	81	234	400	499	2	22	5	31	–	–	53	552	22	144	5	67	4	34	245	797
Kerrier	97	88	145	602	861	1,103	10	39	8	92	2	4	135	1,238	29	290	6	81	13	238	609	1,847
Penwith	22	67	119	633	938	1,075	2	2	3	2	1	1	5	1,080	7	73	8	146	10	269	488	1,568

Berkshire																					
Faringdon	–	28	20	34	29	49	7	27	13	183	1	1	211	260	3	20	7	110	–	–	130	390
Shrivenham	3	23	40	64	373	416	8	86	18	289	1	1	375	791	6	40	7	96	3	24	160	951
Ganfield	109	11	20	27	133	262	4	2	6	77	1	–	80	342	3	38	6	66	5	73	177	519
Wantage	70	41	70	134	475	615	7	22	22	233	6	34	289	904	4	52	9	129	13	82	263	1,167
Compton	–	1	–	39	199	199	4	1	7	33	–	–	34	233	4	60	4	55	2	2	117	250
Lambourn	49	20	17	7	145	211	3	3	8	8	7	25	36	247	4	29	–	–	2	80	109	356
Kintbury Egle	44	28	34	133	376	454	2	1	23	197	2	1	199	653	1	8	2	18	4	58	84	737
Faircross	16	37	77	124	423	516	2	6	30	285	4	2	293	809	3	28	10	95	2	16	139	948
Gloucestershire																						
Cotswolds																						
Rapsgate	43	3	6	12	56	105	1	9	9	54	1	8	71	176	1	11	7	77	–	–	88	264
Langtree	8	14	26	78	247	281	1	20	16	139	4	21	180	461	–	–	11	150	1	2	152	613
Bisley	149	12	39	76	219	407	8	15	15	34	–	–	49	456	–	–	7	88	1	10	98	554
Cheltenham	–	30	53	101	117	169	3	–	2	75	2	9	86	255	1	7	7	25	1	70	102	347
Cleeve	25	7	20	34	62	107	2	56	3	28	–	–	84	191	–	–	1	25	–	–	95	286
Kiftsgate	–	38	186	61	522	708	5	26	30	718	8	46	790	1,498	17	125	20	236	10	239	600	2,098
Westminster	–	9	75	35	95	150	–	–	7	94	–	1	94	244	3	16	3	57	–	–	73	319
Slaughter	–	23	139	57	142	281	3	35	22	222	1	1	258	539	–	–	16	152	6	76	228	767
Crowthorn	–	3	58	18	161	219	1	2	19	130	3	24	156	375	–	–	10	96	2	26	122	407
Bradley	3	9	42	30	93	138	4	75	24	162	4	–	237	375	–	–	18	153	2	19	172	547
Brightwells Barrow	46	3	6	28	170	222	3	20	17	117	2	14	151	373	–	–	10	91	2	11	102	479
Cirencester Liberty	–	16	249	21	29	278	–	–	4	82	–	1	83	361	–	–	–	–	–	–	–	361

Table B.1 *continued*

County and hundred	Crown £	Lay owners Resident No.	Lay owners Resident £	Lay owners Absentee No.	Lay owners Absentee £	Lay owners Total £	Clergy Secular No.	Clergy Secular £	Clergy Regular No.	Clergy Regular £	Clergy Miscell. No.	Clergy Miscell. £	Clergy Total £	Total Temporalities £	Spir. Secular Resident No.	Spir. Secular Resident £	Spir. Secular Absentee No.	Spir. Secular Absentee £	Regulars No.	Regulars £	Spir. Total £	Grand total £
Vale																						
Tewkesbury	48	45	219	46	251	518	1	–	4	189	–	–	189	707	17	92	4	60	1	36	188	895
Tibaldstone	–	4	4	–	–	4	–	–	3	47	–	–	47	51	2	11	–	–	3	68	79	130
Deerhurst	–	1	1	39	90	91	4	93	3	136	–	–	229	320	6	45	6	81	1	12	138	458
Whitstone	92	44	131	41	287	510	3	15	6	275	1	–	291	801	–	–	8	78	6	56	134	935
Berkeley	196	114	293	30	299	788	1	3	6	104	2	21	128	916	18	121	11	196	9	58	375	1,291
Thornbury	47	5	15	21	201	263	–	–	1	67	–	–	67	330	10	59	4	60	3	58	177	507
Pucklechurch	–	7	38	5	53	91	1	110	1	32	–	–	142	233	5	28	5	53	1	–	81	314
Henbury	–	3	13	7	77	90	1	72	2	15	–	–	87	177	3	18	2	54	1	23	95	272
Barton near Bristol	–	4	12	12	59	71	2	4	3	35	1	2	41	112	2	5	1	4	4	46	55	167
Grumbalds Ash	–	41	142	91	638	780	2	16	18	280	5	24	320	1,100	24	138	27	322	–	–	460	1,560
Forest																						
Bledisloe	–	61	136	16	133	269	–	–	4	61	1	5	66	335	3	22	3	14	2	19	55	390
St Briavels	20	149	384	19	104	508	1	7	4	28	1	6	41	549	9	49	3	46	1	8	103	652
Botlow	–	92	269	29	123	392	–	–	8	110	1	6	116	508	7	34	7	60	1	34	128	636
Westbury	3	30	36	12	58	97	–	–	5	66	–	–	66	163	2	12	3	51	2	29	92	255
Duchy Liberty	2	79	105	18	74	255	–	–	4	23	–	–	23	278	1	5	4	26	3	21	52	330
Rutland																						
Alstoe	–	22	196	33	167	363	–	–	8	17	1	4	23	386	10	77	5	50	4	34	161	547
Soke of Oakham	–	17	22	23	61	83	1	5	9	55	1	7	67	150	9	47	2	20	2	52	119	269
Martinsley	–	16	103	20	79	182	–	–	4	38	–	–	38	220	13	94	3	37	–	–	131	351
East	–	23	225	16	92	317	–	–	9	50	–	–	50	367	6	46	4	77	4	17	140	507
Wrandike	–	71	153	52	114	267	3	61	7	24	4	9	94	361	10	84	6	64	1	1	149	510
Worcestershire	123	432	666	673	1,767	2,558	16	288	53	566	15	56	910	3,468	36	283	37	346	14	111	740	4,208

PROBLEMS OF INTERPRETATION

CERTAIN DIFFICULTIES encountered in the data, which have been briefly noted above, are here considered in detail, and practical solutions discussed.

DEFICIENCIES IN THE LISTINGS

At best there are three returns for every township, i.e. the muster and two subsidy schedules. Although they did not apply to exactly the same people, the intervals between the making of each were so short that any discrepancies should be of a very minor nature; nonetheless, detailed comparison shows that any single list is likely to contain only about two-thirds of the total number of persons produced by a conflation of all three. Table 5.5 shows the shortfall occurring mainly below the £2 level. Although this was natural in some ways,[1] it was much affected by administrative practice. Separate lists in Norfolk of able men, clergy and assessed laymen give too few nil assessments, and for Brothercross, Gallow and north Greenhoe hundreds the solution adopted is to count as nils able men who do not appear in the list of assessments; the subsidy rolls have many wage assessments which imply that the men in question had no taxable goods. In Sussex the grouping of the hundreds in six 'rapes' results in administrative boundaries cutting across geographical regions; thus on the arable-farming coastal plain 47.1 per cent of assessments were at 20s. on wages in Box and Stockbridge hundred (Chichester rape), but only 37.1 in Avisford hundred (Arundel rape), recovering to 45 in Brightford (Bamber rape) and as high as 59 in the liberty of the archbishop of Canterbury; physical differences between these areas were negligible. In the Cotswold division of

Gloucestershire everything below £2 in 1522 was nil and almost all of these were in Kiftsgate hundred. The subsidy is very defective,[2] but in five townships 19.4 per cent of the 314 taxpayers were assessed on wages, compared with 18.5 per cent at nil out of 227 persons in the muster; of the conflated total of 306 persons 85 (27.7 per cent) were below £2. As in the smaller hundred of Brightwells Barrow £1 assessments in the subsidy[3] come to less than 36 per cent, the sub-£2 class may not have exceeded 30–35 per cent anywhere. The hypothesis that the proportion of all assessments under £2 might have been the same as in Rutland may be demonstrated in a simple manner: leaving the numbers of higher assessments unchanged produces a significant similarity in distribution which justifies increasing the number below £2:

£	Rutland %	Cotwolds %
100 and above	0.7	0.7
40–99	1.5	2.6
20·39	6.5	6.5
10–19	13.0	12.9
5–9	15.6	15.2
3–4	13.2	11.4
2	11.9	13.1
Under £2	14.0	} 37.6
Under £1	23.6	
	100.0	100.0

In the Vale region three lists for nine places give 18.7 per cent for assessments under £2, and 26 for three where the number of wage earners in the subsidy was high, compared with 14.8 for the whole division in 1522. For twelve places in Grumbalds Ash hundred these formed 21.6 per cent in 1522, and wage earners added by the subsidy rolls, which are generally in poor shape, increases the proportion to 39.4 in the conflated total.[4]

The earlier suggestion that the additional persons covered by joint assessments in Cornwall were ones who might otherwise have been assessed at less than 52 leads to the amended figures given on page 279. The Penwith sample would be better if larger; the Kerrier one is weighted by wage earners in the subsidy which give a radically different aspect from any other hundred. In East and Trigg the proportion of poor persons remains much as in Table A.5 (a). The fact that men who had made their goods over to their fathers would have nothing to be assessed does not necessarily mean that all the extra ones were poor,

CORNWALL: effect of joint assessments (natives only)

Hundred[5]	(a) Total assessments	(b) £1 + nil assessments	% (b) of (a)	(c) Extra names	(d) Total names	(e) Total (b) + (c)	% (e) of (d)
West	140	28	20.0	10	150	38	25.3
Kerrier	374	137	36.6	67	411	204	49.6
Penwith	89	11	12.4	17	106	28	26.4

although equal shares in a £2 assessment would cover two hypothetical ones of £1.

LAND VALUES

It is impossible to tell which assessments cover property in several places unless (a) this is stipulated or (b) there is alternatively evidence, such as feodary surveys or inquisitions *post mortem*; otherwise, high values are likely to fall into this category, though the occasional small one is specifically glossed as being in all places.

It is imperative to approach instances of the omission of values with circumspection, not least in dealing with the excellent Rutland return. Here the *Valor Ecclesiasticus* makes it clear that the value assigned to the manor of Lyddington also embraced Caldecote and Stoke Dry; all three belonged to the bishop of Lincoln. The most obvious omission is the values of manors which belonged to the king, viz. Ketton, Glaston, Seaton and South Luffenham where the lord's income must have been small as he had no tenants. Allowance must be made for factors such as these in attempting to restore missing values by averaging. Here the only valid intrapolations are the figures, recorded elsewhere, for Oakham, Egleton and Langham which had recently been valued[6] following the forfeiture of the duke of Buckingham. The resultant totals are £1,999. 16s. and 66,799 acres, or 69 per cent of the area of the county, giving an average of £30.3 per thousand acres, which, in view of the quality of the return, suggests that a round £30 is a better general guide than the £32 obtained from wealthier counties.

Reapportionment of values in the Vale division of Gloucestershire is made on the following basis: the hundreds of Grumbalds Ash (excluding Chipping and Old Sodbury), Henbury (excluding Westbury-on-Trim), Pucklechurch, Deerhurst, Tewkesbury, Whitstone and Tibaldstone contain 146,996 acres valued at £4,347, i.e. £29 per thousand acres. As this looks more fully valued than the rest of the region there are grounds

279

for assuming that the true average overall was about £30, even the full £32, which give a possible aggregate £8,192 for the 256,000 acres of the region as a whole, which, assuming that Church property was assessed at full value, and allocating the increment to the laity, may be apportioned thus:

The Crown	£383	4.7%
The laity	£4,486	54.8%
The Church	£3,323	40.6%
Totals	£8,192	100.1%

At £30 per thousand acres the Church's share is marginally increased, the laity's reduced, and the Crown's becomes an even 5.0 per cent.

The area of the Cotswolds is 343,000 acres which, at £32, produces a revised total of £10,976 of which the £4,071 belonging to the Church forms 37.1 per cent and the Crown's £274 is 2.5 per cent, leaving the laity £6,631 or 60.4 per cent.

Multiplied by £32 the 223,000 acres covered by the Berkshire muster gives a total value of £7,136. Apportioned this produces:

The Crown	£292	4.1%
The laity	£4,149	58.1%
The Church	£2,695	37.8%
Totals	£7,136	100.0%

Inasmuch as fewer royal lordships are left unvalued, this result is an improvement on the Gloucestershire ones; at the same time it is to be noted that in the four richest, and presumably most accurately assessed, hundreds the church actually owned one half or more of the land.

HOW THE MUSTER CERTIFICATES WERE PREPARED

ALTHOUGH MATERIALS for making any significant additions to Goring's thorough account of the inception of the military survey[1] do not exist, a further insight may yet be gained from a brief consideration of the problems of execution revealed by the extant certificates.

Since, in the first place, none of the original commissions has been preserved, the precise requirements of the government have to be inferred from the results. Hall hinted that the fiscal element was tacked on to the basic mandate to hold musters, and, despite Polydore Vergil's insistence that the true purpose was to ascertain the material condition of the nation it looks as though initially no special emphasis was placed on assessments: significantly it was only these which had to be redone when the first returns were judged unsatisfactory, the military particulars gathered in the first phase being retained unaltered. When the looked-for results failed to materialise, a second stage had to be directed specifically to assessment, and Wolsey was obliged to take the commissioners into his confidence and admit that the assessments were preparatory to new taxation.

It is far from certain how, and in what form, the government's original directive was transmitted by the commissioners, via the chief constables of hundreds and wapentakes, to 'the constables of euery hamlet, parish and village', on whom devolved the burden of collecting the information on the ground. Transmission of orders from the centre to the lowest tiers of local administration posed a perennial problem, and it may well be that they only percolated down to this level in summary form, as seems implied by supplementary instructions sent to some subsidy commissioners.[2] As the only extant set, the instructions circulated in Essex[3] have perforce gained acceptance as a *pro forma*; in fact there is no

281

shred of evidence that identical memoranda circulated in other shires. Nor is it known how parish officers were briefed, whether orders were reproduced *verbatim*, summarised, or, as is probable in the absence of reprographic facilities, communicated orally to the constables assembled at the hundred meeting place, when misunderstandings could easily have arisen. Even if the orders were copied out in full, most constables would have needed assistance in reading them – from persons who might have been no better than marginally literate.

After listing all laymen aged sixteen and over, the Waltham constables had to furnish a certificate in writing, giving not just simple things like names but also more complete details such as

> who be owners of euery parcell of land within any town . . . with the yeerely value of euery mans land within the same townes . . . And of euery stocke and stocks of cattell, or other things that be occupied vpon any ferme . . . and who be owners of them. Also what aliants or strangers dwell in any towne . . . Item what occupation, mystery, or substance they be of. Item the value and substance of euery person being 16 yeeres and aboue . . . as well spirityall as temporall . . .

Doubtless the intention was clear enough to whoever drafted this, but some of the wording is ambiguous and likely to confuse the unlettered.

That these specifications were met in full by the Rutland and Coventry returns proves that they were not exclusive to Essex; nevertheless, the exact particulars furnished by any given certificate make it clear that within the broad design there was ample room for variation in detail.

The differing formats of each book show that the enterprise posed a problem for each administrative division to solve as best it could. In Buckinghamshire, Gloucestershire and Rutland, as well as Coventry and Exeter, the findings were embodied in a single volume. In Norfolk, unless the gatherings of a single original volume have become separated, several smaller ones were produced. One contains Great Yarmouth borough and four hundreds; a fifth, Blofield, is listed on the cover, but its certificate has strayed into a volume of the State Papers. South Erpingham has a volume to itself, and five other hundreds share two more. The survival of a certificate for just one Suffolk hundred suggests that piecemeal compilation was the rule in East Anglia. For Cornwall the returns of Kerrier, Trigg and West hundreds form one volume, while East hundred and a fragment of Penwith are bound up with the loan schedules for the whole county, the remainder of Penwith having strayed into the subsidy rolls. Here the *modus operandi* is less apparent, although the list for each hundred is written in a different hand, leaving no doubt as to its separate provenance, their present location among the miscellaneous class of the Court of Augmentations gives ground for thinking they were not the 'top copies' but duplicates retained locally. The Berkshire book is also located in the same class; although now covering only half the county, it is written in a uniform hand and could well be the remnant of a larger volume. Similarly the two Worcestershire books could be fragments of one original volume.

Irrespective of physical make-up, material for any one county generally keeps to the same plan throughout. If this was settled prior to the commencement of the survey it presumably expresses the commissioners' understanding of what was required. In some shires, however, there are signs of the final format being imposed at a later stage; major variants in what was recorded in different divisions indicate commissioners working in small groups without an agreed plan, so that in Cornwall, for instance, while many aliens were listed in Penwith they were virtually ignored in the neighbouring hundred of Kerrier.

The comprehensive Rutland certificate is tabulated throughout, with colums giving men's names, status and landlords, and the values of their lands and goods. their military rating and any equipment they happen to possess being noted in the margins; naturally the entry for a non-resident landowner is restricted to his name and the value of his property.

To reconstruct the process of compilation we can do no better than look once again at Preston,[4] as an average Midland village with a typical return, and imagine following the constable on his round, or eavesdropping as he makes out his certificate in consultation with a friendly priest from a nearby parish, for Parson Christopher Goodworth was one of a good many absentees who had not appointed a deputy. First of all they put down the name of the lord, who in this case happens to be the king, for which reason the value of the manor may not be readily ascertainable, and anyway no purpose seems to be served by giving it, as the king pays no taxes; were the lord in residence the value of his goods and chattels would be added too. They continue with the name of the steward and his fee (sometimes omitted) followed by the clergy and other landowners. Next comes the main body of the inhabitants, loosely in order of wealth, those who also have some land tending to head the list. The roll is completed by 'poor' labourers and servants who own neither land nor goods. This order is never slavishly followed, the lists abounding with examples of mistakes being rectified as the work proceeds; at Wardley the rector is forgotten until the very end. Well down the list of Cottesmore inhabitants John Walker is entered as a tenant of the prioress of St Michael, Stamford, at which point the clerk realised that in detailing absentee proprietors he had forgotten this lady, and so slipped in the value of her holding – 6s. 8d., which doubtless Walker had stated was the rent he paid. The Coventry book gives the rent paid by every householder, though strictly this was not required. Again, in the middle of Sir John Hussey's tenants at Great Casterton we find John Colley, who states that his landlord is Francis Brown, the lord of Little Casterton, but the constable either did not think to enquire the rent or forgot to make a note of it. In the Barleythorpe and Normanton sections parcels were inserted as apparent afterthoughts, though as no tenants were named they could have been vacant at the time.[5]

Not only are all particulars tabulated, but also the status of every person is precisely defined, and all absentee landlords, clerical as well as lay, distinguished by the gloss *'nil quia manet extra'* (frequently abbreviated to q.e.) in the goods column. Inhabitants are mostly described as somebody's tenant and assessed on goods. Labourers and servants, though seldom classed as tenants, and, with few exceptions, having no property of any kind, are glossed 'poor', most being further classed as young and able-bodied.

Although a single integrated list doubtless appeared to be the ideal to aim for, it was not stipulated, unless in the lost original commissions. The ambiguous wording of the working instructions seems, however, to envisage the alternative of listing each category separately. In each Cornish parish clergy, landowners and inhabitants (with their personalty) are separated, making the identification of resident landowners almost impossible. In Norfolk three lists for each hundred give, by parishes, (1) clergy assessments, (2) able men, and (3) assessments of inhabitants (with a final inadequate note of absent landowners) from all of which most nil assessments have to be deduced by elimination. The Berkshire certificate resembles the Cornish ones, with the addition of sections detailing military equipment. At Exeter the inhabitants are divided into able men and others, and here again resident landowners are hard to identify.

The Buckinghamshire musters are tabulated throughout, but although the authors must have known what they were about, it is now difficult to fathom their train of thought at some points. Instances abound where it is hard to tell whether a person is supposed to be an inhabitant or an absentee landholder. Not only are there many more landowners than in Rutland, but a much higher proportion resided in the parishes where their property lay. Two vital clues are lacking - the names of the inhabitants' landlords and, except sporadically, the gloss '*quia extra manet*'. Generally the only guidance is the grouping of absentees near the beginning of the township section, with the goods column left blank, residents having something, if only nil, in the goods column, supplemented by a military rating as appropriate. Examples of landowners without goods occur, nonetheless, in the middle of lists of inhabitants, and a good many are ambiguous.[6] Attempts at greater precision are neither systematic nor sustained: in ten parishes of the three hundreds of Newport the section commences with the subheading '*liberi tenentes extra villam*', but in several its usefulness is diminished by the absence of a further heading '*inhabitantes*', and while the latter are duly labelled at Wavendon the non-resident landowners are not. One helpful pointer, nonetheless, is the insertion among the inhabitants of Newport Pagnell and North Crawley of men who owned land but not goods. Hereabouts, as in Rutland, the mainly nucleated villages readily lend themselves to the differentiation of residents from absentees, but the hamlet settlements of the Chiltern hills required a different procedure, and it is clear that many constables went round the parish visiting one settlement or farmstead at a time, to end with a list in which both types of person are mingled indiscriminately. Much the same plan was followed in the Forest of Dean, Gloucestershire, and in Worcestershire, the return for which is not tabulated, the values of a man's land and goods being given on successive lines, making it almost impossible to judge whether he was resident or not. The use of a similar layout in the Norfolk books causes no problem since they tend to ignore non-resident landowners.

Possibly because the original commissions were less precise than the memorandum implies, the Coventry and Rutland returns alone furnish all the prescribed information, and indeed more, insofar as only the occupations of aliens were really required, for at this point the wording could be construed as applying to everyone. This, however, was the directive for the first, unsatisfactory survey, while the extant records must be taken as representing the final, revised version. By the time this point was reached the specification had been drastically reformulated, with the effect of shifting the emphasis decisively to the fiscal aspect, so that all surviving returns consist essentially of assessments supplemented by the military information that had provided the ostensible rationale of the inquest. Any additional details amount to optional extras, the Babergh hundred (Suffolk) book giving occupations, the Berkshire one the names of lords, while aliens featured prominently in the port of Great Yarmouth as well as in the maritime county of Cornwall, though the standard of registration there varied from hundred to hundred. In many respects the Staincliffe loan book represents the irreducible minimum, reproducing from the muster book a complete list of inhabitants, as opposed to the minority on whom the loan was actually levied,[7] with their assessments on land and goods – nothing more; all that is missing of a monetary nature are the assessments of absent landowners. If this was not a case of saving work by reusing the first draft of the muster book, to which further particulars were to be added later, the commissioners, conscious of close supervision by government, might have felt it safer to furnish evidence that the great majority of the population were far below the threshold of the loan.

Concerned only with names and assessments, the subsidy rolls cause no problems, except in ignoring any assets that were not taxed, though parallel muster books show that only a small minority of people owned any other significant wealth; also the differential rates conceal the actual assessments behind tax paid, which is all some rolls give. Extra details are rare, though some invaluable schedules state reasons why abatements were allowed.[8]

A NOTE ON THE SOURCES

IT IS DOUBTFUL if the survey of 1522 was carried out in all counties; in fact only twenty-nine made complete returns, and two others partial ones, several in the North failing to produce any at all.[1] Since the books had to be certified by the Star Chamber,[2] a good many must have shared the fate of other records of this court on its abolition in the seventeenth century. Prior to that event a number had been transferred to the Treasury of Receipt, and, along with other musters, are preserved among its miscellaneous books. At least one found its way into the State Papers Office, others are in the miscellaneous books of the Court of Augmentations, and a few are in municipal custody or private ownership.

There are complete certificates for Rutland (PRO, E35/55, also 54, an unfinished eighteenth-century copy),[3] Buckinghamshire (a seventeenth-century copy) lacking the entry for one parish (Bod., MS Eng. Hist. e. 187),[4] the city and county of Coventry (Coventry Record Office, A.96), and Gloucestershire, excluding the county town and the hundred of Dudstone and King's Barton.[5] Fragments of varying length include most of the city of Exeter (City Library),[6] the western half (approximately) of Berkshire (PRO,E315/464) and four of the nine hundreds of Cornwall bound up with the loan books for 1522–3 (E315/77-8), a fifth being in the subsidy rolls (E179/87/122).[7] About one-third of Worcestershire – the north east – is in two rough books (E36/35-6), which as the contents are in no clear order, might have been working notes. For Norfolk there is Great Yarmouth borough and ten of the thirty-two hundreds in several books (E36/22, 25, E101/61/16, E315/466[8]) one of which is bound into a volume of the State Papers (SP1/234, ff.19-29v), for Suffolk an excellent return for

Babergh hundred only,[9] and finally an isolated list for Long Compton parish, Warwickshire.[10] The value of a summary abstract of the Surrey certificate (Loseley MSS)[11] is inevitably limited. Supplementing these are loan books for Staincliffe wapentake in West Yorkshire, i.e. the Craven District (E179/206/116), which omits only the military aspects of the original survey, and for the City of London (E179/251/15B), which has occupations as well as assessments, but the value of other examples of this class is very limited.

The lay subsidy rolls form a class of their own in the records of the Exchequer (PRO, E179). Sets are complete for some counties, but fragmentary for others. All extant material for Buckinghamshire, Exeter, Rutland, Suffolk and Sussex has been published,[12] and the County Record Office has a complete set of transcripts for Essex.[13] The time-consuming labour required to transcribe the material of even a single county limits the use of the subsidy rolls to these and a few others I have had occasion to abstract for one purpose or another. From the separate clerical subsidy the return for Lincoln diocese has also been printed.[14] Although the condition of these records varies, only a few are quite illegible, in which respect the muster certificates pose very few problems.

ABBREVIATIONS

Ag.HR	*Agricultural History Review*
AHEW	*Agrarian History of England and Wales*
Archaeol.	Archaeological
BIHR	*Bulletin of the Institute of Historical Research*
BL	British Library
Bod.	Bodleian Library
BRS	Buckhamshire Record Society
Econ. HR	*Economic History Review*
EETS	Early English Text Society
EHD	*English Historical Documents*
EHR	*English Historical Review*
HMC	Historic Manuscripts Commission
J.	*Journal*
LP	*Letters and Papers of the Reign of Henry VIII*
LPS	*Local Population Studies*
P & P	*Past and Present*
PRO	Public Record Office
R.	Record(s)
RB	*Records of Buckinghamshire*
RO	Record Office
RRS	Rutland Record Society
SAC	*Sussex Archaeological Collections*
Soc.	Society
SRS	Sussex Record Society
Statutes	*Statutes of the Realm*
TED	*Tudor Economic Documents*
Trans.	Transactions

TRHS	*Transactions of the Royal Historical Society*
VE	*Valor Ecclesiasticus*

NB. standard abbreviations are used for the names of counties, except Gloucs. (never Glos.) for Gloucestershire

NOTES

PREFACE

1   Charles Wilson and Geoffrey Parker eds, *An Introduction to the Sources of European Economic History, 1500–1800*, Volume 1: *Western Europe* (1977), p. xxii.

INTRODUCTION

1   G.R. Elton, *Studies in Tudor and Stuart Politics and Government*, iii (Cambridge, 1983), 436; *The Lisle Letters*, ed. M. St Clair Byrne, 6 vols (Chicago, 1981).
2   Printed by John Stow, *Annals* (1631), p. 515
3   PRO, E36/55, f. 19.
4   Rapin de Thoyras, *History of England*, trans. N. Tindal (1732), i, 750.
5   See my 'English Population in the Early Sixteenth Century', *Econ. HR*, 2nd ser., xxiii (1970), 32–44.
6   Detailed in Appendix D.
7   The origins are exhaustively discussed by J.J. Goring, 'The General Proscription of 1522', *EHR*, lxxxvi (1971), 681–705, to which the present account is much indebted.
8   Edward Hall, *Chronicle: Henry VIII*, ed. C. Whibley (1904), i, 274 and *passim*; *The Anglica Historia of Polydore Vergil*, ed. D. Hay, Camden 3rd series, lxxiv (1950), 300–3.
9   W.G. Hoskins, *The Age of Plunder* (1976), pp. 22–3.
10   14 and 15 Henry VIII, c. 16, *Statutes*, iii, 230–9.
11   R.S. Schofield, 'Parliamentary Lay Taxation, 1485–1547', unpublished PhD thesis, Cambridge Univ. (1963), p. 416.

1   STATUS AND WEALTH

1   E. Dudley, *The Tree of Commonwealth* (1509), ed. D.M. Brodie (Cambridge, 1948), pp. 39–48.
2   Sir Thomas Smith, *De Republica Anglorum* (1550), ed. L.M. Alston (Cambridge, 1906), pp. 31, *et sqq*.
3   Cf. the comments of W.G. Hoskins, *The Age of Plunder* (1976), p. 56.
4   *A Discourse of the Common Weal of this Realm of England*, ed. E. Lamont (Cambridge, 1893).
5   See below, Chapter 5.
6   1 Henry VIII, c. 14, 7 Hen. VIII, c. 6, 23 Hen. VIII, c. 14, 24 Hen. VIII, c. 13: *Statutes*, iii, 8, 179–80, 342, 430–1.

7   K. Pickthorn, *Early Tudor Government: Henry VII* (1949 ed.), p. 62.
8   PRO, E179/165/112–13; E315/77–8; Wards 9/120; RRS, i, *passim*; Bod., MS Eng. Hist. e. 187; BRS, viii, *passim*; SRS, lvi, *passim*; *Suffolk in 1524, passim*.
9   T.B. Pugh, 'The Magnates, Knights and Gentry', in S.B. Chrimes, C.D. Ross and R.A. Griffiths, eds, *Fifteenth Century England, 1399–1509* (1972), pp. 97–100.
10   Sir Thomas Smith, loc. cit.
11   A.R. Wagner, *Heralds and Heraldry in the Middle Ages* (1956), pp. 79–80.
12   R.B. Smith, *Land and Politics in the England of Henry VIII* (Oxford, 1970), p. 86.
13   17 Richard II, c. 2; William Harrison, *The Description of England* (1577), ed. G. Edelen (Ithaca, NY, 1968), p. 117.
14   *Discourse of the Common Weal*, p. 82.
15   C. Phythian-Adams, *Desolation of a City* (Cambridge, 1979), p. 12; W.G. Hoskins, *Provincial England* (1963), p. 70.
16   RRS, i, 26, 110.
17   H. Ellis. 'Inventory of Goods &c . . . taken 1549', *SAC*. xiii (1861), 128–9.
18   Sir Thomas Smith, op. cit., p. 46.
19   A. Everitt, 'Farm Labourers', *AHEW, iv (1967), 422 et sqq*.
20   V.H.T. Skipp, 'Economic and Social Change in the Forest of Arden, 1530–1649', in J. Thirsk, ed., *Land, Church and People* (Reading, 1970), p. 70.
21   W.G. Hoskins, *Essays in Leicestershire History* (Liverpool, 1950), p. 151, idem, *The Age of Plunder*, pp. 56–7.
22   RRS, i, 24, 32, 63, 75–8, 109, 114–17; HMC Report, *Hastings*, i, 254; *RB*, xiii (1934–40), 282; Bod., MS Eng. hist. 187, ff. 94v–95, 96v.
23   Sir Thomas Smith, loc. cit.; T. Starkey, *A Dialogue between Reginald Pole and Thomas Lupset*, ed. K.M. Burton (1948), p. 81.
24   J.J. Goring, 'Military Obligations of the English People, 1511–1558', unpublished PhD thesis, London Univ. (1955), pp. 145–6. The usual method of raising soldiers was for the king to call on lords and gentlemen. The recipient of a commission looked among his household servants, secondly his tenants. The Rutland survey distinguishes both categories. The superior status of these 'servants' and 'retainers' clearly marks them as key personnel.
25   RRS, i. 76
26   T. Smith, loc. cit.
27   See my 'John Carter of Denham, Yeoman', *RB*, xvi, part 2 (1955–6), 83–95.
28   J. Cornwall, 'The Squire of Conisholme', in C.W. Chalklin and M.A. Havinden, eds, *Rural Change and Urban Growth, 1500–1800* (1974), pp. 32–53.
29   RRS, i, 60, 63–5; Lincoln Archives Office, Inv. 11/76; Worcestershire RO, 008.7/65/1554.
30   *LP*, iv, 2002.
31   My 'Early Tudor Gentry', *Econ. HR*, 2nd ser., xvii (1965), 467–9; M.S. Holgate, ed., *Sussex Inquisitions*, SRS, xxxiii (1927), no. 20; W.D. Peckham, ed., *The White Act Book*, ibid., lii (1952), no. 51.
32   PRO, E179/206/116.
33   R.B. Smith, op. cit., p. 88.
34   See Ch. 4 below.
35   Hoskins, *Provincial England*, pp. 78–81.
36   Phythian-Adams, op. cit., *passim*.
37   Coventry RO, A. 96, ff. 6, 48v, 71.
38   *Tudor Exeter*, ed. M.M. Rowe, Devon and Cornwall Rec. Soc., n.s. 22 (1977), pp. 7, 26.
39   PRO, E179/251/15B.
40   Coventry RO, A.96, f. 87v; Phythian-Adams, op. cit., p. 116.
41   Coventry CRO, A96, f. 48v.
42   W.T. McCaffrey, *Exeter, 1540–1640* (Cambridge, Mass., 1956), pp. 246 *et sqq*; W.G. Hoskins, *Old Devon* (Pan ed, 1971), pp. 75–6.

43 Coventry CRO, A96.

44 Bod., MS Eng. Hist. e. 187, f. 60v; *LP*, iv, 1136.

45 B. McClenaghan, *The Springs of Lavenham and the Suffolk Cloth Trade in the Fifteenth and Sixteenth Centuries* (Ipswich, 1924), *passim*.

46 BL, MS Harl. 304, f. 75; also S.T. Bindoff, *Ket's Rebellion* (1949), *passim*.

47 Hall, i, 287.

48 Arguably the effect of inflation made £50 the equivalent of £40 earlier on.

49 For a case study see Cornwall in Chalklin and Havinden, eds, pp. 32–53.

50 J.F. Willard, *Parliamentary Taxes on Personal Property 1290–1332* (1934), p. 7.

51 L. Stone, *The Crisis of the Aristocracy, 1558–1641* (1965), p. 284.

52 *The Lisle Letters*, ed. M. St Clair Byrne (Chicago, 1981) i, 23.

53 J.F. Pound, 'The Social and Trade Structure of Norwich', 1525–1575', in P. Clark, ed., *The Early Modern Town* (1976), p. 131; W.T.McCaffrey, op. cit., *passim*.

54 J. Thirsk, 'Industries in the Countryside', in F.J. Fisher, ed., *Essays in the Economic and Social History of Tudor and Stuart England* (1961).

55 PRO, E315/464, ff. 106–11.

56 W.R.D. Jones, *The Tudor Commonwealth, 1529–1559* (1970), p. 101, concludes that any rigid sociological pattern has little relevance for sixteenth-century England.

2 THE STRUCTURE OF PERSONAL WEALTH

1 *LP*, iii, 2959.

2 Percentages ranged from nearly 40 in the Cottesloe hundreds to barely 6 in the Buckinghamshire hundreds.

3 SRS, lvi, 59, and see Appendix C.

4 *AHEW*, iv, 44.

5 *TED*, i, 1, 5, 86.

6 J. Spratt, 'Agrarian Conditions in Norfolk and Suffolk, 1600–1650', unpub. MA thesis, London Univ. (1935), pp. 104–6; J. Cornwall, 'The Agrarian History of Sussex. 1560–1640', unpub. thesis, London Univ. (1953), p. 80.

7 *AHEW*, iv, 53–4; E. Kerridge, *The Agricultural Revolution* (1967), pp. 126–8; R.J. Hammond, 'The Economic and Social Background of Ket's Rebellion', unpub. MA thesis, London Univ. (1933), p. 100; Cornwall, thesis, pp. 230–48; *LP*, xvii, *passim*.

8 Daniel Defoe, *A Tour Through England and Wales* (1724–6), Everyman ed. (1928), i, 291, 298.

9 *AHEW*, iv, 53–4. Per capita wealth was exceptional in Dengie hundred, on the Blackwater estuary, and wages were uniformly high in Becontree, the hundred closest to London.

10 *AHEW*, iv, 66.

11 R.H. Hilton, *The Decline of Serfdom in Medieval England* (1969), pp. 47–51, and see further Appendix C.

12 SRS, lvi, *passim*; PRO, E179/108/154; see also J. Cornwall in *SAC*, cxiv, 2–9.

13 D. MacCulloch, 'Kett's Rebellion in Context', *Past and Present*, no. 84 (Aug. 1979), pp. 40–1.

14 Over 52 per cent of people in Faircross hundred (including Newbury) had less than £2.

15 *AHEW*, iv, 45–6; R.J. Hammond, 'The Economic and Social Background of Ket's Rebellion', unpub. MA thesis, London Univ. (1933), pp. 47–8.

16 *LP*, iii, 2444, iv, 2972.

17 J. Leland, *Itinerary*, ed. L.T. Smith (1907), ii, 113; Kerridge, op. cit., pp. 56–9; *AHEW*, iv, 49–70, 1; J. Fitzherbert, *The Boke of Serueyeng and Improuementes* (1523), f. 49v.

18 Cf. *Jacobean Household Inventories*, ed. F.G. Emmison, Beds. Historical Record Society, xx (1938), *Household and Farm Inventories in Oxfordshire, 1550–1763*, ed. M. Havinden (1965), *passim*; *AHEW*, iv, 49.

19   M.W. Beresford, *The Lost Villages of England* (1954), *passim*.

20   *TED*, iii, 55–6.

21   Robert Reyce, *Suffolk in the XVIIth Century: The Breviary of Suffolk . . . 1618* ed. F. Hervey (1902), p. 29.

22   The level of wealth, £40 per 1,000 acres, was barely half that in the rest of Suffolk, the average of little more than £3 per head compares with £4–£6 in other parts; 60 per cent of the inhabitants of Risbridge hundred were labourers, according to the fragmentary data.

23   *AHEW*, iv, 46–9, cf. also Table 2.6, below.

24   See Appendix A for figures.

25   See Appendix C.

26   That this practice was probably widespread is indicated by the subsidy act firstly fixing 40s. as the threshold for the rate of 6d. in the pound on goods; the realisation that this might exempt many people doubtless prompted adding the poll tax of 4d. on wage earners as a makeweight.

27   Kerridge, *Agricultural Revolution*, pp. 65, 127–8; *AHEW*, iv, 64–71.

28   *The Chorography of Suffolk*, ed. D. MacCulloch, Suffolk Record Soc., xix (Ipswich, 1976), 19.

29   Reyce, *The Breviary of Suffolk*, p. 26.

30   Suffolk Rec. Soc., xix, 20.

31   Less than 20 per cent on the clay, 34.6 per cent in borderline places, 40 per cent in the whole hundred where twenty-two places were on the sandlings and only two on clay. In Plomesgate 24.1 per cent in fourteen sandlings places and 24.5 in others. Weighted by clay villages, Loes figures give 26.2 per cent in five sandlings ones, similar to 28 in Wilford at the southern tip of the sandlings.

32   John Norden, *The Surveyor's dialogue* (1607), p. 19; Arthur Young, *General View of the Agriculture of Suffolk* (1813), pp. 3, 125; *AHEW*, iv, 43; J. Thirsk, *English Peasant Farming* (1957), pp. 54–7.

33   N. Scarfe, *The Suffolk Landscape* (1972), pp. 36–43.

34   Young, op. cit., frontispiece and p. 4.

35   McClenaghan, *The Springs of Lavenham*, pp. 29–30; *Suffolk in 1524*, ed. S.H.A. H[ervey], Suffolk Green Books, x (Woodbridge, 1910), *passim*.

36   F. Hull, 'Agriculture and Rural Society in Essex, 1560–1640', unpub. PhD thesis, London Univ. (1950), *passim*; PRO,E179/108/150.

37   See my 'Farming in Sussex, 1560–1640', *SAC*. xcii (1954), 67–81. Exclusive of £1 assessments the chalk regions averaged £8.66, the Weald vale £8.15, the high Weald £7.67: J. Cornwall in *SAC*, cxiv, 4–5.

38   Thirsk in Fisher, ed. (1961), pp. 70 *et sqq*; A. Everitt, 'Farm Labourers', n *AHEW*, iv, (1967), 425–9.

39   Goods below 40s. in value were not positively exempted from tax, but simply not mentioned in the Act.

40   E. Kerridge, *Agrarian Problems in the Sixteenth Century and After* (1969), p. 52.

41   Goods, 890, wages (including 'labourers'). 829; in Blything hundred only: goods, 309, wages, 286, land 281.

42   Leland, ii, 64.

43   Cresslau hundred: it is helpful to regroup the disorderly contents of the muster according to the ancient hundreds.

44   Oswaldslow hundred.

45   V.H.T. Skipp, *Medieval Yardley* (1970), pp. 89–97; idem in Thirsk, ed. (1970), pp. 89–92; idem, Crisis and Development (1978), *passim*.

46   PRO, E.36/35, pp. 123–40; Leland, ii, 92–3.

47   Cf. Hull, thesis, maps, 1,5,6.

48   Cf. Schofield in *Econ. HR*, 2nd ser. xvii (1965), 504.

49   PRO, Wards 9/129, f. 98; Lincoln Archives Office, inv. 2/54; PRO, E179/138/478.

50 Thirsk, *English Peasant Farming*, p. 83.

51 Ibid., pp. 54–5.

52 In other counties, men initially classed as poor were often uprated, presumably after inheriting the property of deceased parents who dropped out of the lists. In cases of variable assessment it is assumed that the higher is the more realistic.

53 See Appendix C.

54 Kerridge, *Agricultural Revolution*, p. 64.

55 Leland, i, 129; T. Fuller, *Worthies of England* (1662), quoted by E. Lipson, *Economic History of England*, ii, 270–1; P.J. Bowden, *The Wool Trade in Tudor and Stuart England* (1962), pp. 30, 58; G.D. Ramsay, *The Wiltshire Woollen Industry in the Sixteenth and Seventeenth Centuries* (Oxford, 1943), p. 7.

56 Beresford, op. cit., *passim*.

57 Hawling returned 11 men in 1522 and 16 in 1525, indicating probably 55 and 80 persons respectively; in 1563 there were 13 households, equal (at 4½ persons apiece) to less than 60 persons all told. Batsford had 7 men in 1522, 6 in 1525, i.e. 30–35 people, and 6 households, say 27 persons, in 1563.

58 R.E. Prothero, Lord Ernle, *English Farming Past and Present*, 2nd ed. (1917), p. 151.

59 See G. Haigh, *The History of Winchcombe Abbey* [1947], *passim*.

60 See Appendix C.

61 Hoskins, *Essays in Leicestershire History*, P. 129.

62 Kerridge, *Agricultural Revolution*, p. 109.

63 Hoskins, *Age of Plunder*, p. 24. The loans of course ignored assessments below £5; muster certificates survive for only a few counties, Rutland's being one of the few complete ones.

64 In 1515 Rutland ranked twenty-second. Gloucestershire sixth, Berkshire tenth and Buckinghamshire seventeenth: Schofield, loc. cit. In 1524 Rutland ranked twenty-fourth on tax paid: after Exchequer enrolled accounts, PRO, E314/41.

65 Hall, i, 274, 277.

66 BL, Cott. MSS, Cleo. Fvi, ff. 250–6, quoted by Goring in *EHR*, lxxxvi, 687.

67 *Suffolk in 1524, passim*; the last subsidy referred to may be that of 1515, but this is not certain, since individual assessments were not recorded.

68 PRO, E179/202/167, 171, 212/107, 206/140; *Taxation in Salford Hundred*, ed. J. Tait, Chetham Soc., n.s. 83 (1924), *passim*; R.B. Smith, op. cit., pp. 264–6.

69 PRO, E179/212/107; Leland, i, 51.

70 PRO, E179/116, ff. 24, 36, 37v.

71 *AHEW*, iv, 19–25; Kerridge, *Agricultural Revolution*, pp. 161–4; J. Porter, 'Waste Land Reclamation in the Sixteenth and Seventeenth Centuries: The Case of South-eastern Bowland', *Trans. Historic Society of Lancashire and Cheshire*, cxxvii (1978), 11–23.

72 Lincoln Archives Office, Inventories, 2/54, 10/30, 140, 179.

73 E.g. in 1542, see *LP*, xvii, *passim*.

74 6 Henry VIII, c. 3, *Statutes*, iii, 124.

75 PRO, E179/200/137; Hoskins, *Old Devon*, p. 195.

76 PRO, E179/206/116, ff. 5v, 11, 53v.

77 A stray 20s. at Landrake near Saltash could easily be a clerical error.

78 See Appendix A.2; no returns are extant for Powder, Pydar, Lesnewth and Stratton hundreds.

79 See J. Cornwall in *SAC*, cxiv, 2; seventy-nine more aliens were listed in Cinque Port towns which were exempt from subsidy.

80 Leland, i, 178.

81 PRO, E179/87/126; Hoskins, *Old Devon*, p. 105.

82 PRO, E179/87/231–2.

83 Richard Carew, *Survey of Cornwall* (1600), ed. J. Tonkin (1769), pp. 61, 118; C. Henderson, *Essays in Cornish History* (1935), p. 19.

84 J. Hatcher, 'A Diversified Economy: Later Medieval Cornwall', *Econ. HR*, 2nd ser., xxii (1969), 221–6.

85 Carew, op. cit., p. 34.

86 Ibid., p. 119.

87 See Appendix C.

88 PRO, E315/77, pp. 144; cf. also examples in the Berkshire certificate, PRO, E315/464; several wage earners at Hambleton, Rutland, were, however, listed as sons of husbandmen: RRS, i, 67–9; see also Hoskins, *Essays in Leicestershire History*, p. 129.

89 Leland, i, *passim*.

90 Leland, v, 19.

91 Cf. *AHEW*, iv, 478; P. Clark and P. Slack, *English Towns in Transition* (Oxford, 1976), p. 1, settle for an arbitrary minimum of 'six or seven hundred'.

92 Leland, i, 22.

93 See further Appendix A; it is unnecessary to clutter these pages with statistics conveniently available in print: Hoskins, *Age of Plunder*, *passim*; W.T. MacCaffrey, *Exeter, 1540–1640*, 2nd ed. (Cambridge, Mass., 1975), p. 248; P. Clark, ed., *The Early Modern Town* (1976), p. 131.

94 See further my 'The People of Rutland in 1522', *Trans. Leics. Archaeol. Soc.*, xxxvii (1963), 18–23.

95 Cf. Clark and Slack, op. cit., pp. 2–7

96 Hoskins, *Age of Plunder*, p. 13, Suffolk statistics p. 45.

97 Lord Leconfield, *Petworth Manor in the Seventeenth Century* (1954), *passim*; C. Gill, *History of Birmingham*, i (1952), 32; *VCH, Lancashire*, iii, 6–9; *The Book of John Towe*, ed. W.H. Godfrey, SRS, xxxiv (1928), 120; *VCH, Bucks.*, iii, 8.

98 Henderson, *Essays in Cornish History*, p. 9.

99 More than one-third of the men listed in St Ives, Marazion and Penzance and one in eight at Helston were of foreign origin: PRO, E315/77–8, *passim*.

100 Cf. A.L. Rowse, *Tudor Cornwall* (1941), pp. 87–8.

101 *VCH, Sussex*, ii, 256–7; Cornwall in *SAC*, cxiv, 18–19.

102 Ramsay, op. cit., p. 7.

103 C. Platt, *The English Medieval Town* (1976), pp. 75 *et sqq*; for the sixteenth century see also *AHEW*, iv, 490–502.

104 A.D. Dyer, *The City of Worcester in the Sixteenth Century* (Leicester, 1971), p. 69.

105 D. Charman, 'Wealth and Trade in Leicester in the Early Sixteenth Century', *Trans. Leics. Archaeol. Soc.*, xxv (1949), 85–90; D.M. Palliser, *Tudor York* (Oxford, 1980), pp. 190–2; cf. also MacCaffrey, op. cit., pp. 162–4; A.D. Dyer in *Northamptonshire Past and Present*, vi, 2 (1980), 73-80.

106 W. Harrison, *The Description of England* (1577), ed. G. Edelen (Ithaca, NY, 1968), p. 248.

107 Ramsay, op. cit., p. 18; fulling mills, needing to be beside suitable watercourses, were frequently located in the countryside as well.

108 Carew, op. cit., p. 181.

109 *The Description of the City of Exeter*, by John Vowell, alias Hooker, ed. W.J. Harte et al., Devon and Cornwall Rec. Soc., (1919), p. 68; BL, MS Harl. 1576, ff. 251–9; my *Revolt of the Peasantry, 1549* (1977), pp. 56–8, 137–9.

110 F. Braudel, *Capitalism and Material Life, 1400–1800*, trans. M. Kochan, Fontana ed. (1974), pp. 76–80.

111 After W.D. Peckham, 'The Valuation of Chichester Cathedral, 1535', *SAC*, xcii (1954), 155–77; *Tudor Exeter*, ed. M.M. Rowe, Devon and Cornwall Rec. Soc., n.s. 22 (1977), pp. 7–23; both clerical and lay assessments are imperfect; SRS, lvi, *passim*.

112 Cf. A.L. Beier, 'The Social Problems of an Elizabethan County Town: Warwick, 1580–90', in P. Clark, ed., *County Towns in Pre-industrial England* (Leicester, 1981), pp. 46–79.

113 Ibid. Beier, however, points out that the paupers and vagrants were most thoroughly recorded in towns of the first rank.

114 *RRS*, i, 76–81; Cornwall in *SAC*, cxiv, 8–9; the wages of the vicars choral, four of whom were laymen, were £2. 12s. 8d. apiece: Peckham in *SAC*, xcii, 170.

115 *Suffolk in 1524*, pp. 248–58; PRO, E315/464, ff. 102v–103v. 106v–112.
116 Henderson, *Essays in Cornish History*, pp. 27–8; E315/78, pp. 74–119.
117 Though small, Bodmin and Helston make good examples.
118 Quarter sessions were peripatetic until *c.* 1700, when they made Aylesbury, the most central town, their headquarters: *Calendar of Buckinghamshire Sessions Records*, ed. W. le Hardy, i (Aylesbury, 1933), *passim*.
119 PRO, SC 12/98/28; Lipson, iii, 459.
120 Charman in *Trans. Leics. Archaeol. Soc.* xxv, 72–4, 94.
121 A.D. Dyer, op. cit., p. 175, estimates about 2,500.
122 Data for Blackborne, Lackford and Risbridge hundreds are defective.
123 For an alternative analysis see Hoskins, *Age of Plunder*, p. 40.
124 I.e. John Bricknoll, whose subsidy assessment was scaled up from £200 in 1522: *Tudor Exeter*, pp. 18, 38; as the muster is defective I have followed MacCaffrey's analysis of the subsidy figures: op. cit., p. 248.
125 PRO, E179/192/30.
126 Hoskins, loc. cit.
127 Phythian-Adams, op. cit., *passim*.
128 J.F. Pound, 'The Social and Trade Structure of Norwich, 1525–1575', *Past and Present*, 34 (1966), pp. 49–69; idem, ed., *The Norwich Census of the Poor, 1570*, Norfolk Rec. Soc., xl (Norwich, 1971), *passim*.
129 Hoskins, *Age of Plunder*, p. 41.
130 D. Knowles, *The Religious Orders in England*, iii (Cambridge, 1959), p. 249.
131 Compton, Faircross, Kintbury Eagle and Lambourn. These form the most obvious hinterland for the town; though lying close to the county boundary, much of its commerce may well have originated in Hampshire.
132 PRO, E315/464, *passim*.
133 PRO, E179/251/15B.
134 See Hoskins, *Age of Plunder*, pp. 37–8. He kindly acknowledges my count of the number of assessments; I am glad to return the compliment by adopting his estimate of the £0–£4 group.
135 See Appendix C for details.
136 Pound, *The Norwich Census of the Poor, 1570*, 107. His estimate for 1525 of upwards of 12,000 in P. Clark, ed., *The Early Modern Town*, p. 129, appears to be based on rather generous multipliers.
137 Ibid., p. 38, based on Table 3.1, the estimate for the £0–£4 group is Hoskins's own.
138 Hoskins, *Age of Plunder*, p. 13.
139 G. Unwin, *Industrial Organisation in the Sixteenth and Seventeenth Centuries* (1904), p. 44.
140 S.L. Thrupp, *The Merchant Class of Medieval London* (Ann Arbor, Michigan, pbked, 1962), p. 46.
141 John Stow, *The Survey of London* (Everyman ed., 1912), pp. 196, 478.
142 Ibid., pp. 102–3; *LP*, iv, part ii, p. 1235.
143 Thrupp, op. cit., p. 43.
144 Stow, *Survey*, pp. 102, 468.
145 Thrupp, op. cit., p. 46; in the early sixteenth century the tailors' yeomanry still consisted of journeymen: G. Unwin, *The Gilds and Companies of London* (4th ed., 1963), p. 228.
146 Thrupp, op. cit., p. 104.
147 Ibid., pp. 88 *et sqq.* Many men were made to pay more than their initial assessments.
148 He also owned real estate valued at £42 p.a. A fishmonger assessed at £115 claimed debts of £143. 13*s.* 4*d.*; debts could well account for a substantial number of men being entered at nil.
149 Thrupp, op. cit., p. 110.
150 Ibid., p. 46; *TED*, i, 102–7.
151 Thrupp, op. cit., p. 43.

152   Shakespeare, *Merchant of Venice*, Act I, sc. 1.
153   H.R. Schubert, *History of the British Iron and Steel Industry to 1775* (1957), pp. 162–3.
154   Stow, *Survey*, pp. 100–5, 466.
155   In Rutland everyone listed as a tradesman by one return was entered as a farmer or labourer in the other.
156   *The Courts of the Archdeaconry of Buckingham, 1483–1523*, ed. E.M. elvey, BRS, xix (1975), 380–4.
157   Hoskins, *Age of Plunder*, p. 94.
158   BL, MS Lansd. 74; L.A. Clarkson, 'The Leather Crafts in Tudor and Stuart England', *Ag. HR*, xiv, (1966) 1, 24–6; E. Searle, *Lordship and Community* (Toronto, 1974), pp. 301–12.
159   After G. Schanz, *Englisches Handelspolitik gegen Ende des Mittelalters* (Leipzig, 1882), ii, 113.
160   *Abstracts of Sussex Wills*, R.G. Rice, SRS, xli–xliv (1941–5), *passim*.
161   Further examples in Appendix A.5.
162   The subsidy lists 2,008 persons, 74 more than the muster, in which those below £2 seem seriously under-represented, yet adding the difference to the muster total cannot raise the labouring element to as much as 42 per cent.
163   McClenaghan, op. cit., p. 78. In 1524 Mrs Spring had £1,000 and Bridget £333. 6s. 8d. in goods; the son must have inherited some personalty too.
164   *Suffolk in 1524*, p. 1.
165   Leland, i, 143.
166   Hall, ii, 42–3.
167   Wealth of clothiers, 1522

	£7,500
Deduct loans @ 10%	750
	6,750
Deduct Spring (3200 − 320)	2,880
	3,870
Deduct subsidy, 1524 @ 5%	194
	3,676
Deduct ditto, 1525 @ 5%	184
Remaining	3,492

Trading profits for these years cannot be estimated.
168   E.M. Carus-Wilson and O. Coleman, *England's Export Trade, 1275–1547* (Oxford, 1963), pp. 115–16.
169   H.A.L. Fisher, *The History of England from the Accession of Henry VII to the Death of Henry VIII, 1485–1547, Political History of England*, v (1906), pp. 254–6.
170   McClenaghan, op. cit., p. 26.
171   *Suffolk in 1524, passim; Suffolk in 1568*, ed. S.H.A. H[ervey], Suffolk Green Books, xii (Woodbridge, 1909), *passim*.
172   PRO, E179/108/154; E. Power, *Medieval People* (Pelican ed., 1937), pp. 174–5.
173   PRO, E179/108/163; *VCH, Essex*, ii, 381–5.
174   *VCH, Berkshire*, i, 387, iv, 321; Leland, i, 123, 199.
175   *VCH, Berkshire*, i, 389, ii, 213.
176   Lipson, ii, 25n, 27; at Blackwell Hall, London, Berkshire cloth was traded in the 'Reading Room'.

177   G.D. Ramsay, 'The Distribution of the Cloth Industry in 1561–2', *EHR*, lvii (1942), 361–9.
178   Lipson, iii, 311; *VCH, Berkshire*, iv, 441.
179   Ramsay, op. cit., pp. 31–7.
180   PRO, E315/464, ff. 199v–212v; *VCH, Berkshire, passim*; Defoe, *Tour*, i, 291.
181   E.M. Carus-Wilson, 'Evidence of Industrial Growth on Some Fifteenth-Century Manors', *Econ. HR*, 2nd ser., xvi (1959).
182   Perhaps three or four dozen unlisted servants should be allowed for.
183   Alderley, Berkeley, Dursley, Thornbury, Tortworth, Wickwar, Wotton-under-Edge, and Chipping Sodbury, from occupations given in the muster, *passim*; Leland, i, *passim*.
184   Leland, i, 95–6; muster, *passim*.
185   Leland, i, 100–1; muster, pp. 77–80, 368–71.
186   PRO, E179/113/213; Carus-Wilson, loc. cit.
187   PRO, E179/197/151.
188   Leland, ii, 91; Dyer, *City of Worcester, passim*.
189   Leland, ii, 87, 95; PRO, E 36/35, 84–103, E36/35, 29–33.
190   25 Henry VIII, c. 18, *Statutes*, iii, 349; C. Dyer, *Lords and Peasants in a Changing Society* (Cambridge, 1980), p. 345; K.P. Buchanan, 'Studies in the Localisation of Seventeenth-Century Worcestershire Industries', *Trans. Worcs. Archaeol. Soc.*, xviii (n.s.) (1941), 35–7.
191   Ramsay in *EHR*, lvii, 361–9; SRS, lvi, *passim*. Textile workers made just over 7 per cent of wills, 1525–60: SRS, xli–xliv, *passim*.
192   Leland, *passim*.
193   Ibid., ii, 92–3; muster, pp. 444–5. Two-thirds of the men of Clipsham, Rutland, also noted for quarries, were labourers: RRS, i, 72, 117–18.
194   Leland, ii, 92.
195   BL, MS Harl. 6252, ff. 20, 22.
196   Carew, op. cit., p. 52; Leland, i, 210, 319, 324.
197   Leland, i, 94.
198   Ibid., i, 191, 326–30.
199   *LP*, xiv, 652, East: Calstoke, Lewanick, Northill, Rillaton, Stoke Climsland, Menheniot (Henderson MSS, xx, 28) = 445 men, £2,122, average £4.8, hundred av. £5.2. West: Cardinham, Liskeard, St Cleer, St Neot, Warleggan = 335 men, £3,532, av. £7.5, hundred av. £7.3. Trigg: Blisland, Bodmin = 98 men, £1,238, av. £6.3, hundred av. £6.1.
200   Carew, op. cit., p. 371.
201   PRO, E179/87/140.
202   Carew, op. cit., pp. 58–9; A.L. Rowse, *Tudor Cornwall*, pp. 64–5.
203   R.G. Fitzgerald-Uniacke, 'The Barhams, Shoesmiths of Wadhurst', *SAC*, lvi (1914), 100–60; E. Straker, *Wealden Iron* (1931), pp. 270, 278–9; SRS, lvi, 124–5.
204   L.F. Salzman, *English Industries in the Middle Ages* (Oxford, 1923), pp. 21, *et sqq*; Schubert, *History of the British Iron and Steel Industry to 1775*, pp. 160 *et sqq*; Ellis in *SAC*, xiii, 126–9; *Sidney Ironworks Accounts*, ed. D.W. Crossley, Camden 4th ser., 15 (1975), p. 25n.
205   Leland, ii, 94.
206   Schubert, loc. cit.; S. Smiles, *Industrial Biography* (1863), quoted by M. Campbell, *The English Yeoman* (New Haven, Conn., 1942), p. 163.
207   SRS, lvi, *passim*; Schubert, op. cit., pp. 166–83; Straker, op. cit., *passim*, who does not mention John Levett's (*ob.* 1535) tenancy of Strumlet furnace and forge; *Dictionary of National Biography*, s.n. Sackville.
208   SRS, lvi, *passim*; Schubert, op. cit., pp. 166–8; Straker, op. cit., p. 247; *Sidney Accounts*, p. 43.
209   Cf. Appendix A.1.
210   *Sidney Accounts*, pp. 43–7; SRS, lvi, *passim*: John Rabet of Brightling (goods £12) carried stone, John Stonstret of Robertsbridge (£12) carted sow iron, William Goldsmith, who dug stone, was perhaps related to a Rotherfield servant, and Cogger, a mason, to

three Ticehurst men taxed at £4–£10. John Sawnder, cleaned the pond, and William Henley, four days work, belonged to smallholding or labouring families.

211 Schubert, op. cit., pp. 23–5.
212 I. Blanchard, 'Labour Productivity and Work Psychology in the English Mining Industry, 1400–1600', *Econ. HR*, 2nd ser., xxxi (1978), 1–24.
213 *Sidney Accounts*, pp. 23–5.
214 Carew, op. cit., p. 61.
215 Blanchard, loc. cit.
216 See Cornwall in *SAC*, cxiv, 22: few aliens were actually defined as French, and some two-thirds were in the towns.
217 Schubert, loc. cit.
218 Carew, op. cit., p. 61.
219 Blanchard, loc. cit.; W. Harrison, op. cit., pp. 131–2, though he imputes intemperance to the lower orders generally; for the St Monday custom see L.J. Mayes, *The History of Chairmaking in High Wycombe* (1960), pp. 47–8.
220 *Sidney Accounts, passim*; D.W. Crossley, 'Ralph Hogge's Ironwork Accounts, 1576–81', *SAC*, cxii (1974), 55–97; Searle, op. cit., p. 443; SRS, lvi, 154.
221 *Sidney Accounts, passim*; *VCH, Sussex*, ii, 235–8.
222 *TED*, i, 231–8.
223 G. Hammersley, 'The Charcoal Iron Industry and its Fuel', *Econ. HR*, 2nd ser., xxvi (1973), 593–613.
224 Leland, ii, 94.
225 Buchanan in *Trans. Worcs. Arch. Soc.*, n.s. xviii, 35–49; Skipp in Thirsk, ed. (1970), p. 109; idem, *Medieval Yardley, passim*; PRO, E36/35, pp. 49–55; Clarkson in *Agric. HR*, xiv, 25–39.
226 Leland, ii, 96–7; the importance of the metal trades should not be underestimated solely on the basis of conflicting evidence, cf. Gill, loc. cit.
227 H.C. Darby, ed., *A New Historical Geography of England before 1600* (Cambridge, 1973), *passim*.
228 M. Bowker, *The Secular Clergy of the Diocese of Lincoln, 1495–1520* (Cambridge, 1968), p. 105n; temporary vacancies, however, do not adequately account for all the gaps.
229 RRS, i, 73; *VCH, Rutland*, 160.
230 Coventry RO, A96, f. 91, 92v; Knowles, op. cit., iii, 314.
231 Bod., MS Eng. Hist. e.187, f. 55; *Valor Ecclesiasticus*, ii, 246–7.
232 RRS, i, 76; *VCH, Rutland*, i, 161–2; in 1535 the income was £12. 12s. 11d. cf. Anthony Trollope, *The Warden*, for a fictitious picture of the misappropriation of charitable endowments in a later age.
233 PRO, E301/39; K.L. Wood-Legh, *Perpetual Chantries in Britain* (Cambridge, 1965), pp. 186 *et sqq*, 275; the Gloucs. muster does not mention the chaplains of two chantries at Tetbury.
234 PRO, E301/38, no. 2; RRS, i, 58; *A Subsidy Collected in the Diocese of Lincoln in 1526*, ed. H. Salter, Oxford Historical Society, lxiii (Oxford, 1913), 146.
235 Bod., MS Eng. Hist. e.187, f. 57v; Ashleyworth has the extraordinary figure of £26: Gloucs. muster, p. 398.
236 RRS, i, 35, 71.
237 H.F. Westlake, *The Parish Gilds of Medieval England* (1919), pp. 30, 38–44, 60–2.
238 Ibid., p. 38; *Suffolk in 1524, passim*.
239 Coventry RO, A96, ff. 92–5; PRO, E36/25, p. 230.
240 Westlake, op. cit., p. 91; PRO, E179/81/31, E315/77, pp. 74–83.
241 Excluding Babergh hundred, Suffolk, for which the data are incomplete.
242 I am indebted to Dr J.F. Pound for a preview of his forthcoming study of the Norfolk clergy which generally confirms this conclusion.
243 Cf. Bowker, loc. cit; for the sharp division between the beneficed and unbeneficed,

see F. Heal, 'Economic Problems of the Clergy' in F. Heal and R. O'Day. eds, *Church and Society in England: Henry VIII to James I* (1977), p. 102.

244   Cf. Bowker, loc. cit.

245   Bod., MS Eng. Hist. e.187, ff. 6–7.

246   Ibid., ff. 1v, 174; one of the Norfolk assessments is in fact only £97.

247   B.R. Mitchell and P. Deane, eds, *Abstract of British Historical Statistics* (Cambridge, 1971), p. 485.

248   BRS, xix, 350–2; Chaucer, *Canterbury Tales*: General Prologue, 11. 480–2; Bod., MS Eng. Hist. e. 187, f. 85; a man of the same name was also curate of Quarrendon with £6 in goods (ibid., f. 54v) though the possession of two households would be unusual for a man of this standing.

249   BRS, xix, 348.

250   Bod., MS Eng. Hist. e. 187, ff. 1b, 24, 117; PRO, E36/35, f. 94; E36/36, f. 29; E36/25, f. 11; E315/466, ff. 4, 33v.

251   PRO, E179/87/122.

252   Bod., MS Eng. Hist. e. 187, f. 6; Coventry RO, A96, ff. 98–100.

253   Bod., MS Eng. Hist. e. 187, f. 111v.

254   See also I. Luxton, 'The Reformation and Popular Culture', in Heal and O'Day, eds, p. 164.

255   Tennyson, *Audley Court*; the dramatis personae above are of course from Shakespeare.

3   LANDOWNING

1   Bod., MS Eng. Hist. e. 187, *passim*; *VCH, Bucks.*, iii, 74–5; the reference to Doddershall looks to be completely out of date: ibid., iii, 96.

2   RRS, i, 52, 59, 72; Bod., MS Eng. Hist. e. 187, *passim*; H. Miller, 'Subsidy Assessments of the Peerage in the Sixteenth Century', *BIHR*, xxviii (1955), 19.

3   RRS, i, 61, 97–8.

4   Oxford Historical Soc., lxiii, 145.

5   J. Cornwall, 'The Squire of Conisholme', in C.W. Chalkin and M.A. Havinden, eds, (1974), *Rural Change and Urban Growth, 1500–1800* (1974), pp. 43–6.

6   Bod., MS Eng. Hist. e. 187, f. 53; other places are Chilton, Middle Claydon, Ellesborough, Northall, Wendover and Wingrave, ibid., *passim*.

7   PRO, E36/35, f. 49; E315/464, *passim*; Gloucs. muster, p. 258; see also below, p. 117.

8   RRS, i, 72, 74.

9   Ibid., 53–5.

10   Bod., MS Eng. Hist. e. 187, ff. 52, 81, 98v, 162, 182; PRO, E36/36, ff. 39, 43.

11   PRO, E36/25, f. 164; E101/61/16; *VCH, Rutland*, ii, 246; Bod., MS Eng. Hist. e. 187, f. 11v.

12   E. Kerridge, 'The Movement of Rent, 1540–1640', *Econ. HR*, 2nd ser., vi (1953), 16–34; and see below, p. 104.

13   Fitzherbert, *Boke of Serueyeng*, cap. xlj.

14   PRO, Wards 9/129, f. 52v; Bod., MS Eng. Hist. e. 187, ff. 129v–134; BRS, viii, 20; *VCH, Bucks.*, iii, 83, 232; Gloucs. muster, p. 430.

15   PRO, Wards 9/129, f. 78v: total £102. 18s. 4d.; RRS, i, 41; *VCH, Rutland*, ii, 282.

16   Gloucs. muster, p. 493; I. Gray, 'A Gloucestershire Postscript to the "Domesday of Inclosures"', *Bristol and Gloucestershire Arch. Soc. Trans.*, xcvii (1979), 77.

17   Bod., MS Eng. Hist. e. 187, ff. 54, 80, 100.

18   Coventry RO, A96, *passim*.

19   A. Savine, *English Monasteries on the Eve of the Dissolution* (Oxford, 1909), pp. 105–7; *Calendar of Frere MSS: Hundred of Holt*, ed. B. Cozens-Hardy, Norfolk Rec. Soc., i (1931), 12–38.

20 *VCH, Gloucestershire*, viii, 103, x, 25, 167; M.W. Beresford, 'Glebe Terriers and Open-Field Buckinghamshire', *RB*, xv (1948–52), 283–98, xvi (1953–9), 5–28.

21 PRO, E36/36, f. 50; Bod., MS Eng. Hist. e. 187, f. 78.

22 Cf. Haigh, *History of Winchcombe Abbey* [1947], pp. 32–4, 146.

23 RRS, i, 37; PRO, E315/464, f. 61v; Gloucs. muster, pp. 275, 285.

24 Bod., MS Eng. Hist. e. 187, ff. 4, 11, 42.

25 PRO, E36/35, pp. 70, 94, 96, 126, E36/36, p. 47.

26 PRO, E36/35, pp. 10, 24, E36/36, p. 56.

27 PRO, E36/35, p. 10; C. Dyer, *Lords and Peasants in a Changing Society* (Cambridge, 1980), p. 157.

28 RRS, i, 29; PRO, E36/35, p. 56; Dyer, op. cit., p. 159.

29 PRO, E101/61/16; E36/35, p. 36.

30 PRO, E301/39; RRS, i, 72; F.C. and P.E. Morgan, 'The Survey of Chantries, Hospitals, Colleges, Free Chapels, etc. in Worcestershire . . . in 1546', *Trans. Worcs. Arch. Soc.*, 3rd ser., iv (1974), 75–80; for further examples see *Sussex Chantry Records*, ed. J.E. Ray, SRS, xxxvi, *passim*.

31 Bod., MS Eng. Hist. e. 187, ff. 104v, 160 *et sqq*; PRO, E36/53, p. 61, E36/36, pp. 5, 59.

32 *VCH, Bucks.*, iii, 7–11; *Dictionary of National Biography*, s.n. Pole.

33 Coventry RO, A06, f. 58v; Bod., MS Eng. Hist. e. 187, ff. 132v, 135v.

34 Birmingham Reference Library, 504, 916.

35 Gray in *Bristol and Gloucestershire Arch. Soc. Trans.*, xcvii, 75–80. Meon does not have a separate section and only a dozen or so inhabitants were registered at Quinton: Gloucs. muster, p. 670.

36 Bucks. RO, D/A/W(E), 2, f. 150, D/A/W(E), 3, f. 62v; BRS, xix, no. 345; Bod., MS Eng. Hist. e. 187, ff. 53r–v, 67v, 189v.

37 SRS, xxxiv, 117–18.

38 C. Rawcliffe, *The Staffords, Earls and Dukes of Buckingham, 1394–1521* (Cambridge, 1978), pp. 61–4; Kerridge, loc. cit., in *Econ. HR*, 2nd ser., vi.

39 Kerridge, loc. cit.; G. Batho, 'Landlords in England: (A) The Crown,' *AHEW*, iv, 265–8; J. Youings, 'Landlords in England: (B) The Church', ibid., 311 *et sqq*.

40 PRO, SC 11/852, SC12/18/76.

41 *A Discourse of the Common Weal of this Realm of England*, ed. E. Lamont (Cambridge, 1893), pp. 19, 41.

42 I.S. Leadam, 'The Security of Copyholders in the Fifteenth and Sixteenth Centuries', *EHR*, viii (1889), 684–96; R.H. Tawney, *The Agrarian Problem in the Sixteenth Century* (1912), pp. 287–301; E. Kerridge, *Agrarian Problems in the Sixteenth Century and After* (1969), pp. 65–93; C. Dyer, *Lords and Peasants*, pp. 294–7.

43 SRS, xxxiv, 77.

44 Kerridge, *Agrarian Problems*, pp. 36–40.

45 SRS, xxxiv, 92.

46 PRO, LR2/188, ff. 119–25.

47 With the possible exception of John Martyn, who was mustered as a labourer; however, he was probably the son of Robert, who owned land valued at 10*s*., and related to Thomas, whose land was worth 12*s*.

48 *VCH, Bucks.*, iii, 412.

49 A.C. Chibnall, *Sherington: Fiefs and Fields of a Buckinghamshire Village* (Cambridge, 1965), *passim*.

50 H. Hall, *Society in the Elizabethan Age* (1886), pp. 155–6.

51 Kerridge, *Agrarian Problems*, pp. 45–53; Tawney, *Agrarian Problem*, pp. 80, 127; SRS, xxxiv, 83.

52 W.G. Hoskins, *The Midland Peasant* (1957), p. 125; *TED*, i, 35; see also C. Dyer, op. cit., pp. 313–14.

53 PRO, LR2/188, ff. 13–21v; *VCH, Bucks.*, ii, 284.

54 PRO, LR2/188, ff. 23–34, 39–42, 243–50.
55 PRO, E315/393, ff. 33–40v, 48v.
56 PRO, LR2/187–8, *passim*.
57 Tawney, *Agrarian Problem*, p. 25; J. Cornwall, 'The Agrarian History of Sussex, 1560–1640', unpub. thesis, London Univ. (1953), p. 297.
58 PRO, SC2/205/53; Cf. C. Dyer, loc. cit.; V.H.T. Skipp, *Crisis and Development, 1580–1674* (Cambridge, 1978) p. 41.
59 Birmingham Reference Library, 346761.
60 Ibid., 347026–74; C. Dyer, op. cit., p. 233.
61 R. Crowley, *Select Works*, ed. J.M. Cooper, EETS (1872), pp. 166–7; C. Dyer, loc. cit.
62 Skipp, loc. cit.
63 R.J. Hammond, 'The Economic and Social Background of Ket's Rebellion', unpublished MA thesis, London Univ. (1933), *passim*; Cornwall, thesis, *passim*; Kerridge, *Agrarian Problems*, *passim*.
64 C.J. Harrison, 'Elizabethan Village Surveys: A Comment', *Ag. HR*, xxvii (1979), 82–9.
65 Aylesbury: Bucks. County Museum, MS 8/48.
66 Harrison, *Ag. HR*, xxvii, 87.
67 Crowley, loc. cit., and p. 40; Thomas Lever, *Sermons*, ed. E. Arber (1870), p. 129.
68 *Nottinghamshire Household Inventories*, ed. P.A. Kennedy, Thornton Soc. Record Series, xxii (1963), 89; see also *Jacobean Household Inventories*, ed. F.G. Emmison, Bedfordshire Historical Rec. Soc., xx (1938), *passim*.
69 *LP*, ii, part 2, 2935, 3551–2; *VCH, Rutland*, ii, 93; RRS, i, 39–41, 63.
70 RRS, i, 46.
71 Landowners who can be matched with residents assessed on goods are excluded.
72 Tawney, *Agrarian Problem*, p. 25.
73 PRO, E315/77, pp. 105, 213–14; E315/78, pp. 97, 104–7; E179/87/122.
74 R. Carew, *Survey of Cornwall* (1769), p. 118. The returns do not confirm his assertion that men took their names from their lands. Use of the patronymic seems to have been familiar and everyday, and so occurs largely in the lists of inhabitants; legal requirements would have dictated the use of normal surnames in lists of landowners.
75 H.L. Gray, *English Field Systems* (Cambridge, Mass., 1915), pp. 263–8. His statement that runrig had almost disappeared by the sixteenth century, in conjunction with the absence of direct allusion, may indicate that any form of partible inheritance was also in process of extinction.
76 A further result may be Carew's observation, loc. cit., that most Cornish gentlemen 'can better vaunt their pedigree than their livelihood'.
77 M. Coate, 'The Vyvyan Family of Trelowarren', *TRHS*, 4th ser., xxxii (1950), 113.
78 J.L. Vivian, *Visitations of Cornwall* (1981), pp. 5, 178; the Glyn girls married Richard Coode of Morval, Gilbert Beckett of Menheniot, and William Godolphin of Godolphin.
79 PRO, E179/87/122.
80 Ibid.
81 Ibid.
82 Carew, op. cit., p. 179.
83 In Penwith ten owners had the initial D. None had more than one holding there, and none can be conclusively traced within the hundred. Three are 'heirs'. John Jack Davye had an 8s. holding in St Ives: John Davyes lived in Penzance, St Buryan and St Just, but there is no clear link with any of them. There may be a connexion between Roger Dewyn, who owned land worth £1 in Gwinear, the heir of Dewyn, owner of 1s. 11d. in St Buryan, and the Dewyns of Landwenack in Kerrier hundred, but this is conjectural only. John Dewyn of Landwenack held sundry small parcels in Kerrier; he was assessed jointly with his son Roger. All 'heirs' could of course have been women married to local men: PRO, E179/87/122, E315/77.

84   Ibid. His subsidy assessment was £20: PRO, E179/87/126.
85   PRO, E179/87/131, E315/77; his inquisition *post mortem* notes lands in twelve more parishes: PRO, C142/68/5.
86   PRO, E179/78, p. 276.
87   A.E. Bland, P.A. Brown and R.H. Tawney, eds, *English Economic History: Select Documents* (1914), pp. 249–50.
88   *Discourse of the Common Weal*, p. 19.
89   Global estimates can be broken down only with the aid of feodary surveys which give complete statements of the values of estates. The more common inquisitions *post mortem* are inadequate because a separate one was made in every county where the deceased owned property, and not all have been preserved. As the number of proven global sums is not large the cumulative effect on county aggregates may not be all that serious, especially since they are offset by lacunae.
90   Originally computed by Professor Hoskins, to whom I am indebted.
91   An earlier estimate of £32 for Rutland (*Trans. Leics. Arch. Soc.*, xxxvii, 26 n. 9), based on townships for which the returns appeared complete, embodied assumptions which must now be regarded as premature, and was too freely reconstructed. It is now clear that the bishop of Lincoln's assessment under Liddington comprehended Caldecote and Stoke Dry (*VE*, iv, 305), also that church stocks are erroneously entered as land values.
   The revised computation is based on thirty-three townships which appear to suffer from no major lacunae – an aggregate for the deserted village of Gunthorpe can just be made out – together with seven Crown lordships for which the missing values can be offset, viz. Ketton, Glaston, South Luffenham and Seaton where the Crown's income must have been negligible as it had no tenants, and Egleton, Langham and Oakham which had just been valued following the forfeiture of the duke of Buckingham (PRO, E36/150, f. 63v). No other intrapolations have been made. The resultant totals are £1,999. 16s. and 66,799 acres, giving £30.3 per 1,000 acres.
92   *Suffolk in 1524*, p. 24: Sir William Waldegrave's subsidy assessment was £266. 13s. 4d.; for Thomas Spring see B. McClenaghan, *The Springs of Lavenham* (Ipswich, 1924).
93   See Appendix B for recorded figures. Data for Crown property in Berkshire is incomplete. £725 seems a reasonable estimate for the nineteen Crown lordships in Rutland: the Buckingham valor gives £196 for three. Values for two royal manors in Worcestershire are got from PRO, SC12/18/61, and *VCH, Worcestershire*, iii, 76. Thornbury (Gloucestershire Vale), a Buckingham lordship, was valued at £239 in 1521 (*LP*, iii, 1286), but has not been added as it is not clear whether it referred to that place alone.
94   Hundreds of Grumbalds Ash (less Chipping and Old Sodbury), Henbury (less Westbury-on-Trim), Pucklechurch, Deerhurst, Tewkesbury, Whitstone and Tibaldstone.
95   Many Dean lordships, including the whole of the Liberty of the Duchy of Lancaster, belonged to the Crown and so were not assessed; consequently a large part of the district, including the Liberty, has to be excluded from the calculation.
96   *LP*, iii, 2959.
97   BL, Cott. MSS, Cleo. E iv, 458–74; Savine, *English Monasteries*, p. 78.
98   Simon Fish, *A Supplication for the Beggars* (1528), EHD, v, 670.
99   *LP*, iii, 76.
100   *VCH, Rutland*, i, 159–60.
101   Figures based on *Valor Ecclesiasticus, passim*; see also D. Knowles, *The Religious Orders in England*, iii, *The Tudor Age* (Cambridge, 1959), *passim*; J. Gairdner, *The English Church in the Sixteenth Century, from the Accession of Henry VII to the Death of Mary* (1902), *passim*.
102   F.C. Dietz, *English Government Finance, 1485–1558* (Urbana, Ill., 1920), ch. II and *passim*. This has been criticised and corrected by B.P. Wolffe, *The Crown Lands, 1461–1536* (1970), pp. 76–88. See also idem, *The Royal Demesne in English History* (1971), *passim*.

103 Wolffe, *The Crown Lands*, pp. 84–5.
104 Ibid., pp. 179–80.
105 *VCH, Rutland*, i, 135–6, 166–7.
106 PRO, E36/181, and see supra, p. 122.
107 PRO, SC6/Edw. VI, no. 80. Insofar as they can be compared, the values given here show some advance on those of 1522; however, they are the only figures available.
108 *VCH, Worcs.*, iii, 76; PRO, SC12/18/61.
109 Kerridge in *Econ. HR*, 2nd ser., vi, 30–3.
110 *LP*, iii, 1287–8, 2382, 3162; Dietz, op. cit., pp. 89–90; Wolffe, loc. cit.
111 Savine, *English Monasteries*, pp. 76–88.
112 Goring in *EHR*, lxxxvi, 693.
113 Fitzherbert, *Boke of Serueyeng*, *passim*.
114 RRS, i, 65–6; PRO, E301/39, no. 1; *VCH, Rutland*, i, 163.
115 Coined by A.L. Rowse, *The England of Elizabeth* (1950), p. 325.
116 PRO, E36/35–6; Gloucs. muster, *passim*; C. Dyer, *Lords and Peasants*, *passim*. The survey gives no value for Westbury-on-Trim and there is no entry in *VE*; presumably most of the profits went to the wealthy college there which had been founded by a previous bishop: C. Dyer, op. cit., p. 154 and *passim*.
117 *VE, passim*; see C. Dyer, op. cit., pp. 193–5, for the spiritualities of Worcester; these included two rectories, but they were accounted for by estate officials on the same basis as temporalities.
118 P. Heath, *The English Parish Clergy on the Eve of the Reformation* (1969), p. 173; for a less gloomy view see Heal in F. Heal and R. O'Day, eds, *Church and Society in England: Henry VIII to James I* (1977), *passim*.
119 M. Bowker, *The Secular Clergy in the Diocese of Lincoln, 1495–1520* (Cambridge, 1968), pp. 140–1.
120 RRS, i, 25, 45; Oxford Hist. Soc., lxiii, 145, 147; *VE*, iv, 343–4.
121 Heath, op. cit., p. 22.
122 PRO, E101/61/16; *VCH, Norfolk*, ii, 250.
123 Coventry RO, A96, ff. 97v–100.
124 PRO, E179/108/176; Bod., MS Eng. Hist. e. 189, f. 33. A separate column for prelates would contain few entries.
125 1. Edward VI, c. 14, *Statutes*, iv, 24; G.R. Elton, *The Tudor Constitution* (Cambridge, 1965), pp. 382–5; H.F. Westlake, *The Parish Gilds of Medieval England* (1919), pp. 60–1.
126 Bod., MS Eng. Hist. e. 189, *passim*; PRO, E36/35, f. 34; Gloucs. muster, p. 284.
127 RRS, i, 72; PRO, E36/35, pp. 3, 94; Bod., MS Eng. Hist. e. 189, *passim*.
128 Heath, op. cit., pp. 50–6.
129 Bowker, op. cit., pp. 73, 94.
130 *VCH, Rutland*, ii, p. xl.
131 RRS, i, *passim*; Oxford Hist. Soc., lxiii, 143–8.
132 Bowker, op. cit., p. 45.
133 Joan Wake, *The Brudenells of Deene* (2nd ed., 1954), p. 27.
134 Bowker, op. cit., p. 73.
135 Ibid., p. 70.
136 *Leicestershire and Rutland Notes and Queries*, iii (1895), 225–6; Oxford Hist. Soc., lxiii, 145.
137 Bowker, op. cit., p. 107.
138 F. Rose-Troup, *The Western Rebellion of 1549* (1914), *passim*.
139 Knowles, op. cit., pp. 248, 273; G.A.J. Hodgett, *Tudor Lincolnshire* (Lincoln, 1975), p. 17; *VCH, Sussex*, ii, 97; Savine, *English Monasteries*, pp. 270–88.
140 Savine, *English Monasteries*, pp. 77, 98; Knowles, op. cit., pp. 247–8.
141 Savine, *English Monasteries*, p. 99; Knowles, loc. cit.
142 PRO, E315, f. 47; Gloucs. muster, p. 26; Bod., MS Eng. Hist. e. 189, ff. 187v; *VE*, iv, 243, 248.

143   RRS, i, 76, 79; Bod., MS Eng. Hist. e. 187, ff. 22, 47v, 75; Haigh, op. cit., p. 190.
144   VE. iv, 241–53; Bod., MS Eng. Hist. e. 187, passim.
145   Bod., MS Eng. Hist. e. 189, ff. 53, 59; BRS, viii, 42; PRO, E315, ff. 99, 131.
146   T.B. Pugh, 'The Magnates, Knights and Gentry', in S.B. Chrimes, C.D. Ross and R.A. Griffiths, eds, Fifteenth-Century England (1972), p. 96.
147   Discourse of the Common Weal, p. 81.
148   E. Dudley, The Tree of Commonwealth (1509), ed. D.M. Brodie (Cambridge, 1948), pp. 44, 105–6; Sir Thomas Smith, De Republica Anglorum (1550), ed. L.M. Alston (Cambridge, 1906), p. 37.
149   L. Stone, The Crisis of the Aristocracy (Oxford, 1965), p. 53.
150   Ibid., pp. 756–8; P. Ramsey, Tudor Economic Problems (1963), p. 121. The minimum was 43 in 1509 and the maximum 82 in 1559.
151   Buckingham's lands were valued at £196. 7s.: PRO, E36/181; Lord Zouche had £12. 4s. 4d., Lord Scrope £4, and Lord Mountjoy £18. 5s., plus an unstated amount in Market Overton. The total is £230. 16s. 4d. out of about £1,530 in lay ownership.
152   Bod., MS Eng. Hist. e. 189, passim; RRS, i, passim; PRO, E315/464, f. 56v and passim.
153   See H. Miller, in BIHR, xxviii; for distribution of peerage wealth in 1559 see Stone, op. cit., p. 760.
154   R. Virgo, 'The Recovery of the Howards in East Anglia, 1485 to 1529', in E.W. Ives, R.J. Knecht and J.J. Scarisbrick, eds, Wealth and Power in Tudor England (1977), p. 18.
155   Miller in BIHR, xxvii, 29–30; LP, iii, 1287–8; J.M.W. Bean, The Estates of the Percy Family, 1416–1537 (1958), passim.
156   H.L. Gray, 'Incomes from Land in England in 1436', EHR, xlix (1934), 614–18, criticised by T.B. Pugh and C.D. Ross, 'The English Baronage and the Income Tax of 1436', BIHR, xxvii (1953), 1–28.
157   My Revolt of the Peasantry, 1549 (1977), passim.
158   PRO, E359/41; I.S. Leadam, The Domesday of Inclosures, 1517–18 (1897), i, 210.
159   LP, iv, 2972; Dictionary of National Biography, passim; G. Anstruther, Vaux of Harrowden (Newport, 1953), pp. 18–19, 25–6.
160   SRS, lvi, 8; LP, iv, 1936.
161   PRO, Wards 9/129, ff. 58, 78v, 231, Wards 9/131, f. 272v; E36/55, f. 6v; BRS, viii, 87.
162   LP, iii, 2667, 3282; G. Lipscombe, History and Antiquities of the County of Buckingham (1845), iii, 530.
163   Chibnall, Sherington, pp. 160–1; The Book of Bartholomew Bolney, ed. M. Clough, SRS, lxiii (1953), p. xxx.
164   PRO, E179/150/207.
165   T. Smith, op. cit., p. 42.
166   RRS, i, 50, 75.
167   Babergh muster, pp. 1–18; PRO, E36/25, ff. 11–37; E315/77, ff. 38–42; E315/464, ff. 106v–112; E179/206/116, ff. 3–5v; Bod., MS Eng. Hist. e. 189, ff. 140–144v; Gloucs. muster. pp. 450–5, 469–87; Coventry RO, A96, passim; RRS, i, 35v–38v.
168   The land of Sir Edward Digby of Stoke Dry is not valued and there is no assessment for Sir William Hussey's manor of Stretton.
169   RRS, i, 33–5, 51–3, 55–7.
170   Ibid., i, 64, 75.
171   Resident owners of several parcels are assigned to the region in which they lived. Absentee estates are assigned to the region in which they were predominantly situated, though William Tracy (£150) is counted as a Vale landowner as Toddington (£105), though part of the Cotswold hundred of Kiftsgate, is situated near Tewkesbury. Three

peers, holding £52, £110 and £141, respectively, are excluded because their estates are more or less evenly distributed.

172 Gloucs. muster, p. 294; RRS, i, 30, 33, 86.

173 Cleeve, which straddles the escarpment, belongs more to the Vale, but administratively was treated as a Cotswold hundred.

174 Gloucs. muster, pp. 347, 354, 581.

175 Quoted by Thirsk, *AHEW*, iv, 71.

4 THE COMMON WEAL

1 A.C. Chibnall, *Sherington* (Cambridge, 1965), *passim*.

2 W.G. Hoskins, *Essays in Leicestershire History* (Liverpool, 1950), pp. 133, 147.

3 Ibid., p. 130; J. Cornwall, 'The Squire of Conisholme', in C.W. Chalklin and M.A. Havinden, eds, *Rural Change and Urban Growth, 1500–1800* (1974), pp. 39–40; R.G. Rice, 'The Household Goods, etc, of Sir John Gage at West Firle', *SAC*, xlv (1902), 114–27; *Lincoln Wills*, ed. C.W. Foster, Lincoln Rec. Soc., x (1918), 50–2; Lincoln Archives Office, Inventories, 10/130, 140.179, 11/26, 61; H. Hall, *Society in the Elizabethan Age* (1886), pp. 149–53.

4 PRO, E179/180/187; *LP*, xvii, 719.

5 E. Kerridge, *Agrarian Problems in the Sixteenth Century and After* (1969), pp. 65–93.

6 Ibid., p. 82.

7 PRO, Req. 2/10/68; this case was noted by Leadam, *EHR*, viii, as early as 1889; see also my 'The Ecclesden Outrage', *SAC*, cxiii (1975), 7–15, for a full account.

8 R.W. Ambler and M. Watkinson, 'The Agrarian Problem in Sixteenth Century Lincolnshire: Two Cases from the Court of Star Chamber', *Lincolnshire History and Archaeology*, xi (1976), 13, 15; J. Sheail, 'The Regional Distribution of Wealth in England as indicated by the Lay Subsidy Returns of 1524/5', unpublished PhD thesis, London Univ. (1968), ii, 64; *Lay Subsidy of 1334*, p. 173.

9 Ambler and Watkinson, loc. cit.

10 *TED*, i, 29–39 where the case is misleadingly titled, 'Enclosure of Commons and oppression of copyholders'.

11 H.E. Craster, *A History of Northumberland*, ix (1909), 122–4, 194. Joshua Delavale, the source of the story, seems to have gone out of his way to represent his cousin's actions in the worst light; the background was overlooked by Tawney, *The Agrarian Problem in the Sixteenth Century* (1912), pp. 257–8.

12 J. Porter, 'Waste Land Reclamation in the Sixteenth and Seventeenth Centuries: The Case of South-eastern Bowland', *Trans Hist. Soc. of Lancashire and Cheshire*, cxxvii, (1978), 7–23, esp. p. 20.

13 E. Kerridge, 'The Movement of Rent, 1540–1640', *Econ. HR*, 2nd ser., vi (1953), 18; *The Book of John Rowe*, ed. W.H. Godfrey, SRS, xxxiv (1928), 221–2, 224.

14 Kerridge, loc. cit.

15 Kerridge, *Agrarian Problems*, pp. 38–40; *The Buckhurst Terrier, 1597–1598*, ed. E. Straker, SRS, xxxix (1933), 75.

16 T. Blore, *The History and Antiquities of the County of Rutland* (Stamford, 1811), p. 179.

17 For references see J. Cornwall, 'The Agrarian History of Sussex, 1560–1640', unpub. thesis, London Univ. (1953), p. 175.

18 PRO, SC2/206/48–9; Hove Public Library, Clymping and Ford court rolls; BL, Add. MS 28421.

19 Kerridge, in *Econ. HR*, 2nd ser., vi (1953), 16–34.

20 *EHD*, v, 272.

21 Kerridge, art. cit., pp. 24–5, 34; he maintains that Wiltshire was typical, and, in a

postscript to the 1962 reprint (in Carus-Wilson, ed., *Essays in Economic History*, ii, 236) adds, 'the Herbert rent index . . . is the best ever likely to become available' and 'may be taken as generally applicable to lowland England'. The evidence supporting this is not indicated.

22 F. Hull, 'Agriculture and Rural Society in Essex, 1560–1640', unpub. PhD thesis, London Univ. (1951), pp. 338, 347–50, 353–4.

23 J. Cornwall, thesis, loc. cit.

24 J. Spratt, 'Agrarian Conditions in Norfolk and Suffolk, 1600–1650', unpub. MA thesis, London Univ. (1935), pp. 114–16.

25 A. Simpson, *The Wealth of the Gentry, 1540–1640* (Cambridge, 1961), pp. 79, 207; P. Rutledge, 'Sir Thomas Knyvett and his North Norfolk Manors, 1577–1591', *Norfolk Archaeology*, xxii (1961), 346.

26 *The Chorography of Suffolk*, ed. D. McCulloch, Suffolk Record Soc., xix (1976), *passim*.

27 V.H.T. Skipp, 'Economic and Social Change in The Forest of Arden, 1530–1649', in J. Thirsk, ed., *Land, Church and People* (Reading, 1970), p. 106; idem, *Crisis and Development 1580–1674* (Cambridge, 1978), p. 68.

28 C. Dyer, 'A Redistribution of Incomes in Fifteenth Century England', *Past and Present*, no. 39 (1968), 11–33; idem, *Lords and Peasants in a Changing Society* (Cambridge, 1980), pp. 186, 279–80, 288–90.

29 B.J. Harries, 'Landlords and Tenants in England in the Later Middle Ages: the Buckingham Estates', in R.H. Hilton, ed., *Peasants, Knights and Heretics* (Cambridge, 1976). This, however, has been criticised as misleading by C. Rawcliffe, *The Staffords, Earls and Dukes of Buckingham, 1394–1521* (Cambridge, 1978), p. 62.

30 *Chorography of Suffolk*, p. 32.

31 Simpson, op. cit., pp. 28, 84–5, 207.

32 Ibid., pp. 143–6, 152, 196–202, 214–15.

33 Ibid., pp. 28, 199.

34 *A Discourse of the Common Weal of this Realm of England*, ed. E. Lamont (Cambridge, 1893), pp. 38–9.

35 Birmingham Reference Library, 34756–61, 346957–63, 347038–57; Aylesbury, Bucks. County Museum, 8/48; PRO, LR2/187–8, *passim*, SC2/205/50; BL, Add. MS 5701, f. 130; Chibnall, op. cit., *Sherington*, p. 181; D.G. Hey, *An English Rural Community: Myddle under the Tudors and Stuarts* (Leicester, 1974), pp. 70–83; Lord Leconfield, *Petworth Manor in the Seventeenth Century* (Oxford, 1954), pp. 17–21.

36 PRO, SC2/205/53, SC11/647, SC12/3/57; SRS, xxxiv, 56–62; Cornwall in *SAC*, cxiv, 12–14; J.H. Mee, *Bourne in the Past* (Hove, 1913), p. 62.

37 D.M. Palliser, *Tudor York* (Oxford, 1980), p. 136.

38 *The Anglica Historia of Polydore Vergil, A.D. 1485–1537*, ed. D. Hay, Camden Soc., 3rd ser., lxxiv (1950), 301.

39 Sir Thomas More, *Utopia*, in *Complete Works*, ed. E. Surtz and J.H. Hexter (New Haven, Conn., 1965), iv, 66–71.

40 22 Henry VIII, c. 12, 1531: *Statutes*, iii, 328.

41 J.J. Scarisbrick, 'Cardinal Wolsey and the Common Weal', in E.W. Ives, R.J. Knecht and J.J. Scarisbrick, eds, pp. 45–67, *Wealth and Power in Tudor England* (1977), see esp. pp. 63–4.

42 Gregory King's tables, 1688, in C. Whitworth, ed., *Political and Commercial Works of Charles Davenant* (1761), ii, 184, reprinted in J. Thirsk and J.P. Cooper, eds, *Seventeenth Century Economic Documents* (Oxford, 1972), pp. 780–1. I have taken the categories 'lesser freeholders' and 'farmers' for purposes of comparison.

43 *Discourse of the Common Weal*, pp. 49–50. Significantly it is the Doctor, in the role of moderator, who intrapolates this caveat.

44 More, ed. cit., iv. 66–7; T. Starkey, *A Dialogue between Reginald Pole and Thomas Lupset*, ed. K.M. Burton (1948), p. 89.

45 Starkey, op. cit., p. 79; More, ed. cit., iv, 62–3; Edmund Dudley, *The Tree of Commonwealth* (1509), ed. D.M. Brodie (Cambridge, 1948), p. 48; W. Harrison, pp. 134–5.

46 BL, MS Harl. 304, f. 75ff; S.T. Bindoff, *Ket's Rebellion* (1949), after R.J. Hammond, 'The Economic and Social Background of Ket's Rebellion', unpublished MA thesis, London Univ. (1933); *TED*, i, 29030; W. Harrison, op. cit., p. 296.

47 Robert Crowley, 'The Waie to Wealth', *Select Works of Robert Crowley*, ed. J.M. Cooper, EETS (1872), p. 132; *TED*, iii, 337–41.

48 Henry Brinkelowe, *The Complaynt of Roderyck Mors*, ed. J.M. Cooper, EETS (1874), chs ii, iv.

49 Starkey, op. cit., p. 62.

50 *Discourse of the Common Weal*, p. 92.

51 More, loc. cit.; Brinkelowe, op. cit. chs iv, xx; Hugh Latimer, *Sermons*, ed. G.E. Corrie, Parker Society (Cambridge, 1844), p. 249.

52 W.R.D. Jones, *The Tudor Commonwealth, 1529–1559* (1970), appears to overlook this fundamental point.

53 *EHD*, v. 941.

54 2 & 3 Philip & Mary; c. 11, Statutes, iv, i, 286; 5 Elizabeth I, c. 4, ibid., iv, i, 414–22; 31 Eliz. I, c. 7, ibid., iv, ii, 804; 30 Eliz. I, c. 2, ibid., iv, i, 893; *TED*, i, 353; J.E. Thorold Rogers, *Six Centuries of Work and Wages* (1884), p. 398; R.H. Tawney, 'The Assessment of Wages in England by the Justices of the Peace' (1913) in W.E. Minchinton, ed., *Wage Regulation in Pre-industrial England* (Newton Abbot, 1972), p. 65; *Documents in English Economic History: England from 1000 to 1760* ed. B.W. Clapp, H.E.S. Fisher and A.R.J. Jurica (1977), p. 503.

55 But see H.R. Trevor-Roper, *Religion, the Reformation and Social Change* (1972), as to the conservative aspiration of the reformers.

56 Buckinghamshire RO, D/A/W, various items; BRS, xix, *passim*.

57 Hoskins, *Essays in Leicestershire History*, p. 135.

58 Bucks. RO, D/A/Wf/1, no. 26; Hoskins, *Essays in Leicestershire History*, pp. 146–8.

59 Bucks. RO, D./.A/W (E), 1523–7, f. 24v: inventory value, £6. 4s. 4d., assessment, 1522, £6. 13s. 4d.; 1524, £2.

60 Bucks. RO, D/A/W (E), 1523–7, f. 157v; BRS, viii, 14.

61 Bucks. RO, D/A/W (E), 1523–7, f. 5v.

62 RRS, i, 50, 90; SRS, lvi, 84.

63 BRS, viii, 1–10.

64 Sheail in *Trans. Inst. Brit. Geographers* (March 1972), p. 123.

65 PRO, E179/155/132.

66 BRS, xix, 348.

67 H.A.L. Fisher, *The History of England from the Accession of Henry VII to the Death of Henry VIII, 1485–1547 (Political History of England,* vol. v, 1906), pp. 208–10, 293.

68 Thomas Smyth of Gayton, Northants, was cut from £27. 8s. to £16 after endowing his sons Richard and John, who make their first appearance in 1525 assessed at £7 and £5 respectively.

69 C. Howell, 'Peasant Inheritance Customs in the Midlands, 1280–1700', in J. Goody, J. Thirsk and E.P. Thompson, eds, *Family and Inheritance* (Cambridge, 1976), pp. 145–6.

70 Sussex Archaeological Trust, Aber. 129–32; *SRS*, xxxiv, 56–62.

71 See above, p. 160.

72 Latimer, *Sermons*, p. 101.

73 M.W. Beresford, *The Lost Villages of England* (1954), p. 81.

74 Hoskins, *Essays in Leicestershire History, passim.*

75 A population of approximately 2½ million would probably have contained upwards of half a million households.

76 F. Aydelotte, *Elizabethan Rogues and Vagabonds* (1913), p. 146.

77   W. Harrison, loc. cit.

78   Cf. M. Postan, 'Village Livestock in the Thirteenth Century', *Econ. HR*, 2nd ser., xv (1962), 219–49. E. Kerridge, *The Agricultural Revolution* (1967; New York 1968), *passim*, shows that numbers were increased by new techniques. For an example in the 1520s see Cornwall in Chalklin and Havinden, eds, pp. 40–4.

79   P. Bowden in *AHEW*, iv, 657 *et seq.*

80   Latimer, *Sermons*, p. 240; see also Thirsk in *AHEW*, iv, 192–3.

81   *Chorography of Suffolk*, p. 19; E. Kerridge, 'The Agrarian Development of Wiltshire, 1540–1640', unpub. thesis, London Univ. (1951), *passim.*

82   A. MacFarlane, *The Origins of English Individualism* (Oxford, 1978), *passim*; this interesting thesis, that an English peasantry never existed, either disregards or summarily dismisses much important recent work.

83   Goody, Thirsk and Thompson, eds, op. cit., pp. 113–18.

84   Bucks. RO, D/A/W, various items.

85   MacFarlane, op. cit., pp. 18, 26, 29–30.

86   *The Italian Relation*, ed. C.A. Sneyd, Camden, o.s., xxxvii (1847), 10.

87   Starkey, op. cit., p. 87.

88   C.M. Hoare, 'The Last of Bondmen in a Norfolk Manor', *Norfolk Archaeology*, xix (1917), 9–11; A. Savine, 'Bondmen under the Tudors', *TRHS*, n.s., xvii (1903), 270.

89   Hoare, op. cit., pp. 12–16; Savine, op. cit., pp. 281–6; PRO, E36/150, ff. 4v, 9v, E36/157, f. 180.

90   Truro Museum, Henderson MSS, x, 263, xxi, 54.

91   C. Dyer in *Past and Present*, no. 39, pp. 19–20; I.S. Leadam in *EHR*, viii (1889), 684–96; Tawney, *Agrarian Problem*, p. 330; *LP*, xii, part 1, 163.

92   Crowley, op. cit., p. 144, Lever, *Sermons*, p. 106; W. Tyndale, *Doctrinal Treatises*, ed. H. Walter, Parker Soc. (1848), pp. 201–2.

93   Latimer, *Sermons*, loc. cit.; Aydelotte, loc. cit.

94   I. Blanchard, 'Population Change, Enclosure and the early Tudor Economy', *Econ. HR*, 2nd ser., xxiii (1970), 439; *Discourse of the Common Weal*, p.xlviii; Tawney, *Agrarian Problem*, pp. 325, 341.

95   Starkey, op. cit., p. 57; *TED*, iii, 320–1.

96   Blanchard in *Econ. HR*, 2nd ser., xxiii, 442; F.J. Fisher, 'Commercial Trends in Sixteenth-Century England', in *Essays in Economic History*, ed. Carus-Wilson, i, 155; *TED*, ii, 184.

97   Crowley, op. cit., pp. 142–4.

98   Brinkelowe, op. cit., p. 49. John Haryngton's *Oceana* (1656) proposed an equalisation of wealth by limiting the acreage allowable to each man, so as to remove the cause of civil strife: quoted by C.H. Wilson, *England's Apprenticeship* (1965), p. 109.

99   39 Elizabeth I, c. 2, 1598: *Statutes*, iv, 893.

100   M.L. Bush, *The Government Policy of Protector Somerset* (1975), p. 60; *TED*, iii, d55, 314; cf. also ibid., iii, 20.

101   Crowley, loc. cit.

102   *Discourse of the Common Weal, passim.*

103   Cf. claims by e.g., dockers, to new types of job as of right, also the espousal for tactical purposes of worthy causes such as those of lower-paid workers and old-age pensioners.

104   E.A. Wrigley and R.S. Schofield, *The Population History of England, 1541–1871* (Cambridge, 1981), pp. 208–9; Cornwall in *Econ. HR*, 2nd ser., xxii (1970), 32–44; T.H. Hollingsworth, *Historical Demography* (1969), pp. 375–88: his projection (p. 384) of 1.56 million, *c.* 1421, merits serious consideration.

105   Beresford, *Lost Villages*, p. 210 and *passim*; see *Nonarum Inquisitiones* (Record Commission, 1807), *passim*, for cultivation of poor soils abandoned before 1341.

106   Gregory King's tables, in *Seventeenth-Century Economic Documents*, pp. 780–1; some servants would of course have been included in great households.

107 Fisher in Carus-Wilson, ed. i, 159–60; P. Ramsey, *Tudor Economic Problems* (1963), p. 25.

108 *EHD*, v, 282–7.

109 Blanchard in *Econ. HR*, 2nd ser., xxiii, 437–42; *TED*, iii, 328–9.

110 I.S. Leadam, *The Domesday of Inclosures, 1517–18*, 2 vols (1897) *passim*; *TED*, i, 44–6; E. Kerridge, 'The Returns of the Inquisitions of Depopulation', *EHR*, lxx (1955), 212–28, warns against using the returns of 1517 as statistical proof of large-scale enclosure and depopulation.

111 W. Harrison, p. 217; *TED*, i, 174; cf. C. Dyer, *Lords and Peasants*, pp. 241, 312.

112 Tawney, *The Agrarian Problem*, pp. 253–65; the argument in general is unconvincing, the example cited on p. 256 not necessarily supporting the conclusion drawn from it.

113 Blanchard in *Econ. HR*, 2nd ser., xxiii, 340; SRS, xxxiv, 48–65, 334.

114 G.H. Kenyon, 'Petworth Town and Trades, 1610–1760', *SAC* (1958–61), xcvi, 35–107, xcviii, 71–117, xcix, 102–48.

115 *Seventeenth-Century Economic Documents*, pp. 761–98; initially (p. 768) King estimated 400,000 farmers. P. Mathias, 'The Social Structure in the Eighteenth Century: A Calculation by Joseph Massie', *Econ. HR*, 2nd ser., x (1957), 30–45, derives 350,000 farmers from King, 1688, and 365,000 for 1760. It should also be noted that King's methods and conclusions have been sharply criticised by G.S. Holmes, 'Gregory King and the Social Structure in Pre-industrial England', *TRHS*, 5th ser., xxvii (1977), 41–68.

116 Cornwall in *Econ. HR*, 2nd ser., xxiiii, 32–44.

117 See Table 1.2 above.

118 Wrigley and Schofield, loc. cit.

119 J. Thirsk, *English Peasant Farming* (1957), *passim*.

120 W.G. Hoskins, *Provincial England* (1963), *passim*. Less than 2¼ per cent of Bedfordshire was absorbed into bigger units in thirty years up to 1607: after J. Godber, *History of Bedfordshire* (1969), p. 180.

121 M. Spufford, *Contrasting Communities* (Cambridge, 1973), *passim*.

122 Hey, op. cit., pp. 85–142; Chibnall, *Sherington, passim*; Leconfield, *Petworth Manor*, pp. 45–7.

123 Skipp, *Crisis and Development*, pp. 79–80; Spufford, loc. cit.

124 McCulloch in *Past and Present*, no. 64, p. 37; see generally my *Revolt of the Peasantry, 1549* (1977), *passim*.

125 Lever, *Sermons*, p. 129; Crowley, loc. cit., goes into comparable detail; also, e.g., *TED*, iii, 57, 61.

126 Disregarding the gentry as normally affluent and the poor as mostly landless, half the landholders had £10 or more in goods, and half the landless £3 or less, averaging, £15 and £6.9, respectively, in Rutland.

127 Twelve out of 117; most had one tenant only, though one wealthy yeoman had four; seventeen men were listed as their tenants.

128 Men with incomes from land totalled 115 and their goods aggregated £1,494, mean £13; 110 others recorded as landowners in the muster had goods aggregating £441, mean £4: BRS, viii, 1–10, xvii, 66–114. Assessments on goods from the muster are preferred as being the more realistic ones.

129 *Parliamentary Surveys of the County of Sussex*, ed. J.R. Daniel-Tyssen (Lewes, 1878), pp. 156–7; A.E. Bland, P.A. Brown and R.H. Tawney, eds, *English Economic History: Select Documents* (1914), p. 243; SRS, xxxiv, 88, 91, 204, 210, 233; Leconfield, *Petworth*, p. 10. B. Harvey, *Westminster Abbey and its Estates in the Middle Ages* (Oxford, 1977), pp. 307–11, noting the leasing of customary land, pertinently suggests that the right of demise might well have been defined in the tenants' copies, and that, as subsistence farmers, many in the fifteenth century might not have wished to sublet; a more competitive arrangement in the sixteenth might well have changed their attitude.

130 *TED*, ii, 160–7.

131 G.R. Batho in *AHEW*, iv, 301–6.

5   THE LABOURING CLASS AND THE POOR

1   Both W. Hasbach's pioneering *A History of the English Agricultural Labourer* (1908) and G.E. Fussell's *The English Rural Labourer* (1949) commence effectively from the close of the sixteenth century; A. Everitt's 'Farm Labourers', *AHEW*, iv, 396–465, is primarily descriptive.

2   R.H. Tawney, *Religion and the Rise of Capitalism*, Pelican ed. (Harmondsworth, 1938), p. 22.

3   This has been shown to have been observed in practice by E.A. Wrigley, 'Family Limitation in Pre-industrial England', *Econ. HR*, 2nd ser., xix (1966), 87.

4   6 Henry VIII, c. 3, *Statutes*, iii, 124; 5 Eliz. I, c. 4, ibid., iv (1), 414–22; *TED*, i, 336, 340, 345–6; West Sussex RO, Quarter Sessions Rolls, 1606 *et. sqq.*

5   E.g. SRS, lvi, 74: the heading 'The howshold seruants of the Lord la Warr in yerely wages' is followed by the names of two gentlemen who were big landowners and a man worth £20 in goods.

6   *TED*, i, 344–6; West Sussex RO, Quarter Sessions rolls; *A Discourse of the Common Weal of This Realm of England*, ed. E. Lamont (Cambridge, 1893), pp. 49–50; W.G. Hoskins, *The Midland Peasant* (1957), p. 171; Everitt, loc. cit.

7   *TED*, i, 138, 336.

8   *EHD*, v, 995.

9   J. Thirsk, *English Peasant Farming* (1957), pp. 41, 74, 83, 98, 149; W.G. Hoskins, *Old Devon* (1966; Pan ed., 1971), p. 195; idem, *Essays in Leicestershire History* (Liverpool 1950), pp. 129–30.

10   See supra, pp. 32–6.

11   J. Sheail, 'The Regional Distribution of Wealth in England as indicated by the Lay Subsidy Returns of 1524/5', unpub. PhD thesis, London Univ. (1968), *passim*.

12   6 Henry VIII, c. 3, *Statutes*, iii, 124.

13   PRO, E179/87/126–36.

14   The actual figures are 133 on annual wages and 380 on day wages. Twenty-five entries are simply 'wages', but 'servant' is added in seven cases. It is assumed, though by no means certain, that the remaining eighteen imply day rates.

15   Gregory King's tables, 1688, reprinted in J. Thirsk and J.P. Cooper, eds, *Seventeenth Century Economic Documents* (Oxford, 1972), pp. 780–1. I take the 764,000 families of labouring people and cottagers as equivalent to labourers. For servants the 511,586 families which 'increase the wealth of the kingdom' is multiplied by 4 (which is the average household multiplier indicated) giving 2,046,744 persons; the difference between this and the total number of persons comprised by these families, i.e. 2,675,520, may be regarded as servants, 600,000 in round numbers, of which half, say, are assumed to have been males, i.e. 300,000. Very roughly, therefore, servants amounted to 28.3 per cent of all wage earners. Keith Thomas in 'The Levellers and the Franchise', in G.E. Aylmer, ed., *The Interregnum: The Quest for Settlement, 1646–1660*, (1972), pp. 70–3, reaches substantially this conclusion. I am in agreement with his criticism of C.B. Macpherson's estimate of 130,000 male in-servants in *The Political Theory of Possessive Individualism* (Oxford, 1962), pp. 282–6.

16   In Compton, Faircross and Kintbury Eagle hundreds - 547 inhabitants, of which servants number 125 (36.4 per cent) and labourers 11; nil and £1 assessments total 254, but only 88 were servants, of whom the remaining 37 had goods of from £2 to £13. 6s. 8d. Similar headings occur in Winstree and Witham hundreds, Essex extended to 'Laborers ernynge by the yere 20s in Hinckford: PRO, E179/108/154, 176.

17   The problem is fully examined with reference to the Levellers' programme, 1647–9, by Thomas, op. cit., pp. 70–8.

18   E. Lipson, *The Economic History of England*, i (12th ed.), 468, *et sqq.*; ii (6th ed.), cv, 13 *et sqq.*

19   *Tudor Exeter*, ed. M.M. Rowe, Devon and Cornwall Rec. Soc, n.s. 22 (1977), p. 7.

20 R.H. Tawney, *The Agrarian Problem in the Sixteenth Century* (1912), pp. 99–100.
21 R. Carew, *Survey of Cornwall*, ed. J. Tonkin (1769), pp. 185–6; D.C. Coleman, 'Labour in the English Economy in the Seventeenth Century', *Econ. HR*, 2nd ser., viii (1956), 290–5; Everitt in *AHEW*, iv, 296–400.
22 *Discourse of the Common Weal*, loc. cit.
23 E. Hall, *Chronicle: Henry VIII*, ed. C. Whibley (1904), ii, 54; see also *LP*, iv, 1235; J.S. Brewer, *The Reign of Henry VIII* (1884), ii, 53–4.
24 31 Elizabeth I, c. 7, *Statutes*, iv, part i, 304–5.
25 Thirsk, op. cit., *passim*, and in *AHEW*, iv, ch. I, *passim*; Everitt in *AHEW*, iv, 441.
26 *TED*, i, 178.
27 Cf. the Statute of Artificers.
28 Everitt in *AHEW*, iv, 400–6, 417–18.
29 Cf. P. Laslett, *The World We Have Lost*, 2nd ed. (1971), *passim*.
30 Due possibly to the shortage of good farming land, the percentage of £1 assessments is a relatively high 47.2, with 656 wage assessments, inclusive of persons taxed on profits: *SAC*, cxiv, 26.
31 *VCH, Gloucestershire*, ii, 219 (for the equipment of a free miner), 221–3.
32 Everitt in *AHEW*, iv, 419–20.
33 Hoskins, *Essays in Leicestershire History*, p. 129.
34 E. Kerridge, *Agrarian Problems in the Sixteenth Century and After* (1969), p. 37.
35 G.R. Corner, 'On the Custom of Borough English as existing in the County of Sussex', *SAC*, vi (1953), 164–7; E.E. Barker, 'Some Woolavington and Wonworth Leases', ibid., xciv (1956), 48–69.
36 R.H. Hilton, *The English Peasantry in the Later Middle Ages* (Oxford, 1975), p. 13; note especially, p. 11, his reservations as to Laslett's theory of a one-class society.
37 The total is given as forty-eight in *Trans. Leics. Arch. Soc.*, xxxvii, 24, but it now seems that two identifications in different lists were premature.
38 The 1525 list omits occupations and bases all £1 assessments on goods.
39 See my 'Evidence of Population Mobility in the Seventeenth Century', *BIHR*, xl (1967), 143–52, and H. Hanley, 'Population Mobility in Buckinghamshire, 1578–1583', *LPS*, 15 (Autumn, 1975), pp. 33–9.
40 The inner ring comprises Burley, Whitwell, Edith Weston, Lyndon, Manton, Normanton and Egleton; the outer ring, Oakham, Ashwell, Cottesmore, Exton, North Luffenham, Pilton, Wing, Preston, Ridlington, Brooke, Braunston, and Empingham.
41 P. Clark has shown that servants were a highly mobile type, though labourers were less so: 'The Migrant in Kentish Towns, 1580–1640', in P. Clark and P. Slack, eds, *Crisis and Order in English Towns, 1500–1700* (1972).
42 The situation was much the same in Berkshire, where indeed listing labourers are servants separately from householders does not clarify problems of identification.
43 See above, p. 172.
44 Sir Edmund Dudley, *The Tree of Commonwealth* (1509), ed. D.M. Brodie (Cambridge, 1948), p. 48; T. Starkey, *A Dialogue between Reginald Pole and Thomas Lupset*, ed. K.M. Burton (1948), pp. 79–80.
45 Sir Thomas Smith, *De Republica Anglorum* (1550), ed. L.M. Alston (Cambridge, 1906), p. 42.
46 A rare, somewhat ambiguous comment occurs in Starkey, *Dialogue*, p. 87.
47 Hilton, *English Peasantry*, pp. 31–6; Hoskins, *Essays in Leicestershire History*, pp. 198–9; E. Powell, *The Rising in East Anglia* (1896), *passim*; C. Oman, *The Great Revolt of 1381* (1898), pp. 169, *et sqq*: the structure of the Essex Poll Tax lists printed here suggests, however, that *laborarii* were akin to French *laboureurs*, who corresponded to English husbandmen.
48 W.D. Cooper, 'Participation of Sussex in Cade's Rising, 1450', *Sussex Arch. Coll.*, xviii (1866), 23–30.
49 P. Stubbes, *Anatomy of Abuses in England in Shakespeare's Youth*, part II, ed. F.J. Furnivall, New Shakespeare Soc. (1882), pp. 44–5.

50 M.W. Beresford, *The Lost Villages of England* (1954) p. 210; C. Dyer, *Lords and Peasants in a Changing Society* (Cambridge, 1980), pp. 244–63

51 J.C. Russell, *British Medieval Population* (Albuquerque, NM, 1948), pp. 270–81; T.H. Hollingsworth, *Historical Demography* (1969), pp. 380–8: his suggestion that the population might have sunk to a very low level during the fifteenth century is well worth consideration.

52 *The Italian Relation*, ed. C.A. Sneyd, Camden Soc., xxxvii (1847), 10.

53 I. Blanchard, 'Population Change and the Early Tudor Economy', *Econ. HR*, 2nd ser., xxiii; Beresford, op. cit., p. 146.

54 P. Laslett, 'Mean Household in England since the Sixteenth Century', in Laslett ed., *Household and Family in Past Time* (Cambridge, 1972), pp. 125–58: his sample, conceded as not fully representative (p. 128), contains only five cases from pre-1650, three of them from sizeable towns; he also admits (p. 134) his results are maxima.

55 In King's tables 62 per cent of families were below mean size. In the 1520s the religious totalled nearly 10,000: A.G. Dickens, *The English Reformation*, Fontana ed. (1967), p. 80; the number of seculars probably exceeded the 10,000 estimated by King in 1688.

56 It is within Hoskins' estimate: *The Age of Plunder* (1976), p. 5. A closer approximation to 2.3 million may be had by (1) rounding labouring families down to 155,000, or (2) using multipliers of 5 and 3½, on the general grounds that as yet inflation had hardly eroded wage earners' standard of living and fewer were wage-dependent than later on. Also much of the commercial and professional superstructure of King's day may reflect a more developed economy which enabled a higher proportion of households to employ servants.

57 E.H. Phelps Brown and S.V. Hopkins, 'Seven Centuries of the Prices of Consumables compared with Builders' Wage Rates', *Economica*, n.s., xxiii (1956), 296–314.

58 E.A. Wrigley, *Population and History* (1969), p. 78.

59 Ibid., p. 75; F.J. Fisher, 'Influenza and Inflation in Tudor England', *Econ. HR*, 2nd ser., xviii (1966), 127. From a sample of the few extant parish registers I estimate a 10 per cent decrease in these years.

60 *TED*, i, 74; supra, p. 000.

61 *TED*, i, 20; see also Cornwall in *SAC*, cxiii, 7–15.

62 *Hoskins, The Midland Peasant*, p. 142.

63 Blanchard in *Econ. HR*, 2nd ser., xxiii, 442.

64 Clearly defined by Clement Armstrong in 1535–6: *TED*, iii, 115–29.

65 Sir Thomas More, *Utopia*, in *Complete Works*, ed. E. Surtz and J.H. Hexter (New Haven, Conn., 1965), iv *TED*, iii, 19; W. Harrison, *Description of England* (1587), ed. G. Edelen (Ithaca, NY, 1968), p. 183.

66 E. Kerridge, 'The Returns of the Commissions of Depopulation' in *EHR*, lxx (1955).

67 A.F. Pollard, *Wolsey* (1929), Fontana ed. (1965), p. 86.

68 Cf. the limitation of Protector Somerset's interest in depopulation, 1548–9, to its effect on the state's resources: M.L. Bush, *The Government Policy of Protector Somerset* (1975), *passim*; however, J.J. Scarisbrick, 'Cardinal Wolsey and The Common Weal', in E.W. Ives, R.J. Knecht and J.J. Scarisbrick, eds, *Wealth and Power in Tudor England* (1977), pp. 45–67, argues that Wolsey's aim was agrarian reform.

69 Cf. Cornwall in *Econ. HR*, 2nd ser., xxiii, 43–4; Hollingsworth, op. cit., pp. 375–88.

70 *EHD*, v, 1023–4.

71 27 Henry VIII, c. 25, 1536, *Statutes*, iii, 558–60; 18 Eliz. I, c. 3, 1576, *Statutes*, iv, 1, 610 *et sqq.*

72 22 Henry VII, c. 12, 1531, *Statutes*, iii, 328–9.

73 G.R. Elton, *Studies in Tudor and Stuart Politics and Government* (Cambridge, 1974), ii, 37–54; cf. also idem, *Reform and Renewal* (Cambridge, 1973), pp. 99–100.

74 A.E. Bland, P.A. Brown and R.H. Tawney, eds, *English Economic History: Select Documents* (1914), p. 366; J.F. Pound, *Poverty and Vagrancy in Tudor England* (1971), p. 103.

75 *TED*, ii, 339, 341.

76 Everitt in *AHEW*, iv, 409–12; C. Hill, *The World Turned Upside Down* (1972), ch. 3 and *passim*; *TED*, i, 73; the Chiltern woodlands were a centre of Lollardy: John Foxe, *Acts and Monuments*, ed. G. Townsend and S.R. Cattley (1837), iv, 221–40.

77 Cornwall in *Econ. HR*, 2nd ser., xxiii, 42–4.

78 11 Henry VII, c. 2, 1495; 19 Henry VII, c. 12, 1503–4; 22 Henry VIII, c. 12, 1531; 27 Henry VIII, c. 25, 1536; 1 Edward VI, c. 3, 1547; *Statutes*, ii–iii, *passim*; relevant excerpts in *EHD*, v, 1023–32.

79 W.K. Jordan, *Edward VI: The Young King* (1968), p. 177.

80 Pound, op. cit., pp. 40–3. His argument that constables were reluctant to enforce the law is, however, based on the analogy that much later some were said to be unwilling to apprehend thieves and so bring them to the gallows. It is also arguable that this law was irrelevant to the problem. For a full discussion see C.S.L. Davies, 'Slavery and Protector Somerset: The Vagrancy Act of 1547', *Econ. HR*, 2nd ser., xix (1966), 610–13.

81 18 Elizabeth I, c. 3, *Statutes* iv (1), 610–13.

82 W. Harrison, op. cit., p. 20; Elton, *Reform and Renewal*, pp. 99–100.

83 *TED*, i, 143.

84 P.A. Slack, 'Vagrants and Vagrancy in England, 1598–1664', *Econ. HR*, 2nd ser., xxvii (1974), 367.

85 A.L. Beier, 'Vagrants and the Social Order in Elizabethan England', *Past and Present*, 64 (Aug. 1973), pp. 7–27; D.C. Coleman in *Econ. HR*, 2nd ser., viii (1956), 291–5; E.E. Rich, 'The Population of Elizabethan England', ibid., 2nd ser., ii (1950), 260; for long-distance migrancy see P. Clark in Clark and Slack, eds, op. cit., p. 13, and Slack, art. cit., pp. 368–9.

86 Slack, art. cit., p. 367.

87 *Calendar of State Papers Domestic, 1547–1580*, p. 308.

88 Slack, art. cit., p. 465.

89 Coleman, loc. cit.

90 Starkey, op. cit., pp. 80–1; 'A Treatise concerninge the Staple and the Commodities of this Realme', *TED*, iii, 90–104; 'Howe to reforme the realme in settyng them to werke and to restore tillage', ibid., iii, 115–29.

91 *Discourse of the Common Weal*, p. 15.

92 Thirsk and Cooper, eds, *Seventeenth Century Economic Documents*, p. 753.

93 J.F. Pound, *The Norwich Census of the Poor, 1570*, pp. 7–16.

94 Cf. A.L. Beier, 'The Social Problems of an Elizabethan County Town: Warwick, 1580–90', in P. Clark, ed., *County Towns in Pre-industrial England* (Leicester, 1981), pp. 46–85.

95 E. Lipson, *Economic History of England*, iii, 548 and *passim*; *Statutes*, iii, 656, iv (1), 7–8.

96 Coleman in *Econ. HR*, 2nd ser., viii, 303; cf. also *Statutes*, iv (1), 610–13; *TED*, ii, 340.

97 See the abundant records of quarter sessions, especially following the act 11 William III, c. 18, *Statutes*, vii, 607–8, which transferred to the county the cost of removals across its boundaries, e.g. *Buckinghamshire Sessions Records*, ed. W. Le Hardy, 6 vols (Aylesbury, 1933–59), *passim*.

98 No allowance need be made for personnel legitimately deleted because there could easily have been others who were never recorded at all.

99 Also in the Newport hundreds, Bucks., although the relevant personnel are largely concentrated in the subsidy, leaving the muster short.

100 Some muster lists are very little longer, some much shorter, as in the Newport hundreds, Bucks., and even at places such as Clipsham and Empingham in the otherwise meticulously compiled Rutland volume.

101   A.J. and R.H. Tawney in *Econ. HR*, v (1934–5), 47–63. 19,400 men were mustered, aged 16–60 (see L. Boynton, *The Elizabethan Militia, 1558–1638* (1971), p. 16) compared with approximately 30,000 male communicants, aged 16–60+ (BL, MS Harl. 594, ff. 225–255v) of whom at least 10 per cent might have been too old for service (cf. K.J. Allison, 'An Elizabethan Village "Census"', *BIHR*, xxxvi (1963), 91–103. The count of communicants excludes a handful of parishes which belonged to Bristol diocese. Deducting 1,060 from the 10,600 'absentees' leaves just over 9,500 not accounted, and allowing for the unfit leaves, say, 6,000–8,000 who were untraceable as a result of removal.

102   C.I. Hammer, jr, 'The Mobility of Skilled Labour in Late Medieval England: Some Oxford Evidence', *Viertel Jahrschrift fur Sozial - und Wirtschaftgeschichte*, lxiii, 2 (1976), 198.

103   PRO, E179/155/131–2; P. Laslett and 'J. Harrison, 'Clayworth and Cogenhoe', in H.E. Bell and R.L. Ollard, eds, *Historical Essays, 1600–1750* (1963), pp. 174–7.

104   Consistent with a crude mortality rate of 20–30 per cent; cf. D.V. Glass and D.E.C. Eversley, eds, *Population in History* (1965), p. 404.

105   Slack in *Econ. HR*, 2nd ser., xxvii, 369.

106   *Remotus* was used to justify the exemption of three Rutland men from the loan, who were duly taxed in the same places; others registered in 1522 and 1525 were excluded in 1524, including two Hambleton labourers who would have had fewer ties than the occupants of farms: PRO, E179/165/266A; RRS, i, *passim*.

107   In the whole of East hundred, from which these examples are taken, 63 persons were classed as poor, of whom 15 were tenants; 39, including just over half the tenants, occur in one list only: RRS, i, 33–43, 96–102.

108   At Great Waldingfield, Suff., 44 out of 51 men were householders, 13 having under £2 in goods; although 17 householders were listed only once, five sub-£2 men turned up twice; five out of seven non-householders were omitted from the subsidy: Babergh muster, pp. 48–54, *Suffolk in 1524*, pp. 16–17.

109   D.M. Palliser, *Tudor York* (Oxford, 1980), pp. 214–15; Slack, art. cit., p. 365; C.G. Cruickshank, *Army Royal* (1969), p. 41.

110   *TED*, ii, 317; A.L. Beier, 'Social Problems in Elizabethan London' *Journal of Interdisciplinary History*, ix (1979), 208, stressed the role of bad housing, overcrowding, etc., in a rapidly urbanising area in bringing about vagrancy.

111   Hollingsworth, op. cit., pp. 49–52, shows by a theoretical calculation that each of the three Hambleton lists could form a complete roster of adult males on the day it was made. Taking no account of nominal composition and the numerous changes, this remains no more than a suggestive mathematical *jeu*, though serving as a warning that attempts to rectify supposed defects can be carried too far.

112   Beier in *Past and Present*, 64, pp. 5–14.

113   BRS, viii, 70–89; RRS, i, 101, 104.

114   Richard Gough, *The History of Myddle*, ed. D.G. Hey (Harmondsworth, 1981), p. 72.

6   NEW PERSPECTIVES

1   C. Phythian-Adams, 'Urban Decay in Late Medieval England', in P. Abrams and E.A. Wrigley, eds, *Towns in Societies* (Cambridge, 1978), p. 163.

2   R.H. Tawney, *The Agrarian Problem in the Sixteenth Century* (1912), p. vii.

3   Ibid., *passim*.

4   Cornwall in *Econ. HR*, 2nd ser., xv and xxiii, and *Trans. Leics. Arch. Soc.*, xxxvii.

5   PRO, E36/55, ff. 25v, 26, also E179/165/119.

6   RRS, i, 38–9, 86; *VCH, Rutland*, 1, 221.

7   H. Latimer, *Sermons*, ed. G.E. Corrie (Cambridge 1844), p. 100.

8   Sir Thomas More, *Utopia, in Complete Works*, ed. E. Surtz and J.H. Hexter (New Haven, Conn., 1965), iv, 66–7.

9   M.W. Beresford, *The Lost Villages of England* (1954); Gloucs. muster, pp. 685–7.

10 Bod., MS Eng. Hist. e. 187: f. 165, Caldecote, 173, Cotman End, 179, Great Woolstone.

11 Accepted, though not specifically endorsed by Tawney, op. cit., p. 7.

12 SRS, lvi, 27.

13 *The Domesday of Inclosures, 1517–18*, ed. I.S. Leadam (1897), i, 158–214, ii, 572–9; see also *VCH, Bucks.*, ii, 115.

14 Kerridge in *EHR*, lxx, 212, but cf. also Scarisbrick's recent analysis of the subsequent prosecutions, in E.W. Ives, R.J. Knecht and J.J. Scarisbrick, eds, *Wealth and Power in Tudor England* (1977), pp. 55–67.

15 Beresford, op. cit., p. 298. Traces of Eckney cum Petsoe, which was still reckoned a separate parish in 1563, can be found under Emberton; Petsoe, recently acquired by Lincoln College, Oxford, being valued at £14: Bod., MS Eng. Hist. e. 187, ff. 183v, 184; A.C. Chibnall, *Beyond Sherington* (Chichester, 1979), pp. 224–5; Beresford, op. cit., p. 343.

16 BRS, viii, 57; Beresford, op. cit., p. 342.

17 BRS, viii, 37. Greville was not listed in Gloucestershire where he was a JP and had been accused of enclosing: I. Gray, 'A Gloucestershire Postscript to the "Domesday of Inclosures"', *Bristol and Gloucestershire Arch. Soc. Trans.*, xcvii (1979), 77.

18 Ibid., viii, 57; Bod., MS Eng. Hist. e. 187, ff. 54v, 47v; BL, MS Harl. 618, f. 29; J. Leland, *Itinerary*, ed. L. Toulmin Smith (1907), ii, 110; *VCH, Bucks.*, ii, 115.

19 I.S. Leadam, *The Domesday of Inclosures, 1517–18* (1897) i, 207–8; Bod., MS Eng. Hist. e. 187, f. 75; BRS, viii, 39; BL, MS Harl. 618, f. 31.

20 Bod. MS Eng. Hist. e. 187, f. 54v; BRS, viii, 40, 43, xiv, 104; *VCH, Bucks.*, ii, 74; Beresford, op. cit., p. 164; BL, MS Harl. 618, *passim*.

21 Bod. MS Eng. Hist. e. 187, ff. 60v, 61; BRS, viii, 38; Beresford, op. cit., p. 132; *VCH, Bucks.*, iv, 54–5.

22 Bod., MS Eng. Hist. e. 187, f. 92v; there were twenty-four families in 1563; Beresford, op. cit., p. 314: his assertion that abandonment was total must be an exaggeration.

23 Bod., MS Eng. Hist. e. 187, ff. 170–1; BRS, viii, 73; Kerridge in *EHR*, lxx, 214.

24 *A Discourse of the Common Weal of this Realm of England*, ed. E. Lamont (Cambridge, 1893), p. 48; K.J. Allison, 'Flock Management in the Sixteenth and Seventeenth Centuries', *Econ. HR*, 2nd ser., xi (1958), 110.

25 The latest statements by the two leading protagonists are: C. Phythian-Adams, 'Urban Decay in Late Medieval England', in P. Abrams and E.A. Wrigley, eds, *Towns in Societies* (Cambridge, 1978), and A.R. Bridbury, 'English Provincial Towns in the Later Middle Ages', *Econ. HR*, 2nd ser., xxxiv (1981); see also Phythian-Adams, *Desolation of a City* (Cambridge, 1979), Bridbury, *Economic Growth: England in the Later Middle Ages*, 2nd ed. (Hassocks, 1975), A. Dyer, 'Growth and Decay in English Towns, 1500–1700', S.H. Rigby, 'Urban Decline in Later Medieval England: Some Problems in Interpreting the Statistical Data,' both in *Urban History Yearbook* (1979); R.B. Dobson, 'Urban Decline in Late Medieval England', *TRHS*, 5th ser., xxvii (1977), offers a balanced assessment.

26 *The Three Earliest Subsidies for the County of Sussex*, ed. W. Hudson, SRS, x (1909).

27 Only the Coventry muster records out-of-town income, otherwise landholdings have to be pieced together from the returns for rural parishes.

28 E.g. Coventry, and Cirencester and Tewkesbury: Gloucs. muster, pp. 276–84, 469–87.

29 Bod., MS Eng. Hist. e. 187, ff. 25–6, 140–144v; BRS, viii, 2; L.J. Ashford, *History of the Borough of High Wycombe from its origins to 1880* (1960), p. 115; RRS, i, 76–9.

30 See Phythian-Adams' undeveloped suggestion in Abrams and Wrigley, eds, p. 161.

31 *Lay Subsidy of 1334*, ed. R.E. Glasscock, Records of Social and Economic History, n.s., ii (1975) p. xvi; R.S. Schofield, 'Parliamentary Lay Taxation, 1485–1547', unpub. PhD thesis, Cambridge Univ. (1963), p. 416.

32 32 Henry VIII, c. 18, 27 Henry VIII, c. 1, 33 Henry VIII, c. 36, 35 Henry VIII, c. 4: *Statutes*, iii, *passim*, esp. p. 768.

33   W.G. Hoskins, *The Age of Plunder* (1976), p. 13.

34   E. Lipson, *Economic History of England*, i, 207: tax paid rose only from £52 to £57 compared with from £1,341 to £2,392 for the whole county.

35   After PRO, E314/14; BL MS Harl. 618, f. 2; J.W.F. Hill, *Tudor and Stuart Lincoln* (Cambridge, 1956), *passim*. Figures for houses are subject to qualification, see Bridbury in *Econ. HR*, 2nd ser., xxxiv, 8–10.

36   PRO, E314/14; BL, MS Harl. 618, f. 2; Schofield in *Econ. HR*, 2nd ser., xviii, 483–510; G.A.J. Hodgett, *Tudor Lincolnshire* (Lincoln, 1975), pp. 83–7; Leland, ii, 114, 181–2.

37   PRO, E314/14; BL, MS Harl. 594, ff. 162, 162v.

38   J.D. Mackie, *The Earlier Tudors* (Oxford, 1952), p. 204; Leland, ii, 77, 82.

39   William Camden, *Britannia*, ed. E. Gibson (1695), p. 20, 164, 175; J. Dallaway, *History of the Western Rapes of Sussex* (2 vols, 1815–32), i, 152; W.H. Godfrey, 'The Parish Churches of Lewes in the Fourteenth Century', *SAC*, lxviii (1927) 175; SRS, xxxiv, 97; Leland, i, 271; D.M. Palliser, *Tudor York* (Oxford, 1980), p. 51.

40   C. Platt, *The English Medieval Town* (1976), pp. 182–3; Palliser, op. cit., pp. 205–6; Phythian-Adams, *Desolation of a City*, *passim*.

41   Charman in *Trans. Leics. Arch. Soc.*, xxv; Palliser, op. cit., pp. 208–11.

42   Lipson, i, 216; W. McL. Homan, 'The Marshes between Hythe and Pett', *SAC*, lxxix (1938), 210; cf. Leland, *passim*.

43   W.G. Rimmer, 'The Evolution of Leeds', in P. Clark, ed., *The Early Modern Town* (1976), pp. 273–8.

44   *Statutes*, iv, 244, my italics.

45   Ashford, op. cit., p. 92.

46   Lipson, i, 415–6; Rimmer, loc. cit; Palliser, op. cit., p. 212; Phythian-Adams, *Desolation of a City*, pp. 45–6.

47   Lipson, i, 307.

48   A.D. Dyer, *The City of Worcester in the Sixteenth Century* (Leicester, 1971), pp. 95, 102.

49   Charman, loc. cit.; A.D. Dyer in *Northants Past and Present*, vi, 2 (1980), *passim*; Babergh muster, *passim*.

50   SRS, x, *passim*.

51   Strictly Eastbourne ranked second, but the town was not distinguished from the rural parts of the eponymous hundred.

52   SRS, x, *passim*; G.D. Johnston, 'The Possible Encroachment in 1509', *Sussex Notes and Queries*, xiii (1951), 155–6; Camden, *Britannia*, p. 173.

54   Camden, *Britannia*, p. 170.

55   Dallaway, op. cit., ii, part 2, p. 334.

56   L.A. Vidler, *A New History of Rye* (Hove, 1934), pp. 47, 60.

57   The rates are based on tax quotas - measured by actual wealth, Lavenham's was 3,344 per cent.

58   Only two very small market centres, hardly more than villages, cannot be examined.

59   The county total for 1524 is completed by muster data for the Aylesbury hundreds, it appearing that the assessments were almost identical. Aylesbury town poses the problem that the subsidy (1525) has 202 names, the muster only 143, and even with many assessments scaled down total wealth was somewhat higher; the muster is also used for Princes Risborough and Sendover. In 1334 the two 'sides' of Stony Stratford were not distinguished from Calverton and Wolverton parishes, respectively, hence it has to be treated here in the same way for 1524; the ranking in parenthesis is based on the valuation of the town alone in 1522, i.e. £356. Colnbrook, which lay partly in Horton and partly in Langley Marish, has not been dealt with.

60   See Hoskins in *TRHS*, 5th ser., vi, 6–7 for the major provincial towns generally.

61   Palliser, op. cit., p. 204.

62   Phythian-Adams, *Desolation of a City*, p. 47.

63   E. Kerridge, *Agrarian Problems in the Sixteenth Century and After* (1969), *passim*.

APPENDIX C
PROBLEMS OF INTERPRETATION

1 See Chapter 5.
2 PRO, E179/113/301.
3 PRO, E179/113/213.
4 PRO, E179/113/199, 200.
5 Restricted to places for which there is at least one subsidy return; West hundred: Boconnoc, Lansalvoys, St Veep, Warleggan; Kerrier: Cury, Lavale, Helston, Mylor, St Antony, Stithians; Penwith: Gwythian, Ludgvan, Phillack.
6 PRO, E36/150, f. 63v.

APPENDIX D
HOW THE MUSTER CERTIFICATES WERE PREPARED

1 J.J. Goring, 'Military Obligations of the English People, 1511–1558', unpublished PhD thesis, London Univ. (1955).
2 Cf. L.F. Salzman, 'Early Taxation in Sussex', *SAC*, xcix (1961), 61: *LP*, iv, 122.
3 Stow, *Annals*; see also Introduction, above.
4 RRS, i, 60–1, reproduced on pp. 232–3 above.
5 Ibid., *passim*.
6 In more than one case the decision how to classify an entry is basically a hunch.
7 Only 64 out of more than 1,600 were liable for the loan.
8 PRO, E179/155/131; BRS,viii, 1–10.

APPENDIX E
A NOTE ON THE SOURCES

1 *LP*, iii, 3683.
2 Ibid.
3 *The County Community in the Reign of Henry VIII*, ed. J. Cornwall, RRS, i (Oakham, 1980).
4 *The Certificate of musters for Buckinghamshire in 1522*, ed. A.C. Chibnall, Royal Commission on Historical MSS, JP 18, BRS, 17 (1973).
5 Berkeley Estates Trustees, to whom I am obliged for making a microfilm available per the Keeper of Western MSS, Bodleian Library.
6 *Tudor Exeter: Tax Assessments, 1489–1595*, ed. M.M. Rowe, Devon and Cornwall Record Society, 22 (Exeter, 1977), pp. 7–33.
7 H.M. Whitley, ed., 'A Valuation of the Lands and Goods of the Inhabitants of Penwith, temp. Henry VIII', *Journal of the Royal Institution of Cornwall*, ix (2) (1887), 222–70.
8 Viz. *North greenhoe*, ed. M. Dale, Norfolk Record Society, i (1931), 42–68.
9 Lincoln Archives Office, Anc. 16/2 (modern transcript in Suffolk RO, Ipswich), ed. John Pound, *The Military Survey of 1522 for Babergh Hundred*, SRS, xxviii (1986).
10 *LP*, iii, 3685; the return for Knightlow hundred (Wars. RO, HR, 65) became available too late to be used in the present work.
11 'Abstract of the Original Returns of the Commissioners for Musters and the Loan in Surrey', *Surrey Archaeological Collections*, xxx (1917), 13–30.
12 *Subsidy Roll for the County of Buckingham, anno 1524*, ed. A.C. Chibnall and A.V. Woodman, BRS, 8 (1950). Exeter, see n. 6. Rutland, see n. 3. *Suffolk in 1524*, ed. S.H.A. H[ervey], Suffolk Green Books, x (Woodbridge, 1910). *The Lay Subsidy Rolls for the County of Sussex, 1524–25*, ed. J. Cornwall, SRS, 56 (1957).
13 To be published shortly, ed. by the present writer, in Essex Historical Documents.
14 Ed. H.E. Salter, Oxford Historical Society, lxiii (1909).

SELECT BIBLIOGRAPHY

Abrams, P. and Wrigley E.A., *Towns in Societies*, Cambridge, 1978.

Alison, K.J., 'Flock Management in the Sixteenth and Seventeenth Centuries', *Econ. HR*, 2nd ser., xi, 1958.

Ambler, R.W. and Watkinson, M., 'The Agrarian Problem in Sixteenth Century Lincolnshire: Two Cases from the Court of Star Chamber', *Lincolnshire History and Archaeology*, xi, 1976.

Ault, W.O., *Open Field Farming in Medieval England*, 1972.

Bean, J.M.W., *The Estates of the Percy Family, 1416–1537*, 1958.

Beier, A.L., 'Vagrants and the Social Order in Elizabethan England', *Past and Present*, 64, lxiv, Aug. 1974.

Beier, A.L., 'Social Problems in Elizabethan London', *Journal of Interdisciplinary History*, ix, 1979.

Beier, A.L. 'The Social Problems of an Elizabethan County Town: Warwick, 1580–90', in P. Clark, ed., *County Towns in Pre-industrial England*, Leicester, 1981.

Beresford, M.W., 'Glebe Terriers and Open-field Buckinghamshire', *Records of Buckinghamshire*, xvi, 1953–9.

Beresford, M.W., *The Lost Villages of England*, 1954.

Blanchard, I., 'Population Change, Enclosure and the Early Tudor Economy', *Econ. HR*, 2nd ser., xxiii, 1970.

Blanchard, I., 'Labour Productivity and Work Psychology in the English Mining Industry, 1400–1600', *Econ. HR*, 2nd ser., xxxi, 1978.

Bland, A.E., Brown, P.A. and Tawney, R.H., eds, *English Economic History: Select Documents*, 1914.

Blore, T. *The History and Antiquities of The County of Rutland*, Stamford, 1811.

Book of Bartholomew Bolney The, ed. M. Clough, Sussex Record Society, lxiii, 1964.

Book of John Rowe, The, ed. W.H. Godfrey, Sussex Record Society, xxxiv, 1928.

Bowden, P.J., *The Wood Trade in Tudor and Stuart England*, 1962.

Bowker, M., *The Secular Clergy in the Diocese of Lincoln, 1495–1520*. Cambridge, 1968.

Boynton, L., *The Elizabethan Militia, 1558–1638*, Newton Abbot, 1971.

Braudel, F., *Capitalism and Material Life, 1400–1800*, trans. M. Kochan, Fontana ed., 1974.

Brenner, Y.S., 'The Inflation of Prices in Early Sixteenth Century England', *Econ. HR*, 2nd ser., xiv, 1961.

Brewer, J.S., *The Reign of Henry VIII*, 2 vols, 1884.

Bridbury, A.R., *Economic Growth: England in the Later Middle Ages*, 2nd ed., Hassocks, 1975.

Bridbury, A.R., *England and the Salt Trade in the Later Middle Ages*, Oxford, 1955.

Bridbury, A.R., 'English Provincial Towns in the Later Middle Ages', *Econ. HR*, 2nd ser., xxiv, 1981.

Brinkelowe, H., *The Complaynt of Roderyck Mors*, ed. J.M. Cooper, EETS, 1874.

Brown, E., Phelps, H. and Hopkins S.V., 'Seven Centuries of the Prices of Consumables Compared with Builders' Wage Rates', *Economica*, n.s., 1956.

Buchanan, K.P., 'Studies in the Localisation of Seventeenth-Century Worcestershire Industries', *Trans. Worcs. Archaeological Society*, xviii, n.s., 1941.

Buckingham, Courts of the Archdeaconry of, 1483–1523, ed. E.M. Elvey, Buckinghamshire Record Society, xix, 1975.

Buckhurst Terrier, The 1597–1598, ed. E. Straker, Sussex Record Society, xxxix, 1933.

Camden, W., *Britannia*, ed. E. Gibson, 1695.

Carew, R. *Survey of Cornwall*, ed. J. Tonkin, 1769.

Carus-Wilson, E., 'Evidence of Industrial Growth on some Fifteenth-Century Manors', *Econ. HR*, 2nd ser., xvi, 1959–60.

Carus-Wilson, E., ed., *Essays in Economic History*, 3 vols, 1954–62.

Carus-Wilson, E., and Coleman, O., *England's Export Trade, 1275–1547*, Oxford, 1963.

Charman, D., 'Wealth and Trade in Leicester in the Early Sixteenth Century', *Trans. Leics. Archaeological Soc.*, xxv, 1949.

Chibnall, A.C., *Beyond Sherington*, Chichester, 1979.

Chorography of Suffolk, The, ed. D. McCulloch, Suffolk Record Society, xix, 1976.

Clapp, B.W., Fisher, H.E.S. and Jurica, A.R.J., eds, *Documents in English Economic History*, 2 vols, 1977.

Clark, P., ed., *The Early Modern Town*, 1976.

Clark, P. and Slack, P.A., *English Towns in Transition, 1500–1700*, Oxford, 1976.

Clark, P. and Slack, P.A., eds, *Crisis and Order in English Towns, 1500–1700*, 1972.

Clarkson, L.A., 'The Leather Crafts in Tudor and Stuart England', *Ag. HR*, xiv, 1, 1966.

Coate, M., 'The Vyvyan Family of Trelowarren', *TRHS*, 4th ser., xxxii, 1950.

Coleman, D.C., *The Economy of England, 1450–1750*, Oxford, 1977.

Coleman, D.C., *Industry in Tudor and Stuart England*, 1975.

Coleman, D.C., 'Labour in the English Economy in the Seventeenth Century', *Econ. HR*, 2nd ser., viii, 1956.

Coleman, D.C., and John, A.H., eds, *Trade, Government and Economy in Pre-Industrial England*, 1976.

Cooper, J.P., 'Social Distribution of Land and Men in England, 1436–1700', *Econ. HR*, 2nd ser., xx, 1967.

Craster, H.E., *A History of Northumberland*, ix, 1909.

Crossley, D.W., 'Ralph Hogge's Ironworks Accounts, 1576–81', *SAC*, cxii, 1974.

Crowley, Robert, *Select Works*, ed. J.M. Cooper, EETS, 1872.

Cruickshank, C.G., *Army Royal*, Oxford, 1969.

Cruickshank, C.G., *Elizabeth's Army*, 2nd ed, Oxford, 1966.

Dallaway, J., *History of the Western Rapes of Sussex*, 2 vols, 1815–32.

Darby, H.C., ed., *A New Historical Geography of England before 1600*, Cambridge, 1973; paperback ed., 1976.

Defoe, Daniel, *A Tour Through England and Wales (1724–6)*, Everyman's ed., ed. G.D.H. Cole, 2 vols, 1928; 1950.

Dickens, A.G., *The English Reformation*, Fontana ed., 1967.

Dietz, F.C., *English Government Finance, 1485–1558*, Urbana, Ill., 1920.

Discourse of the Common Weal of this Realm of England, A, Ed. E. Lamont, Cambridge, 1893.

Dobson, R.B., 'Urban Decline in Late Medieval England', TRHS, 5th ser, xxvii, 1977.

Dodgson, R.A. and Butlin, R.A., eds, *An Historical Geography of England and Wales*, 1978.

Dudley, Edmund, *The Tree of Commonwealth* (1509), ed. D.M. Brodie, Cambridge, 1948.

Dyer, A.D., *The City of Worcester in the Sixteenth Century*, Leicester, 1971.

Dyer, A.D., 'Northampton in 1524', *Northamptonshire Past And Present*, vi, 2, 1980.

Dyer, A.D., 'Growth and Decay in English Towns, 1500–1700', *Urban History Yearbook*, 1979.

Dyer, D., *Lords and Peasants in a Changing Society*, Cambridge, 1980.

Elton, G.R., *Reform and Reformation: England, 1509–1558*, 1977.

Elton, G.R., *Reform and Renewal*, Cambridge, 1973.

Elton, G.R., *Studies in Tudor and Stuart Politics and Government*, 2 vols, Cambridge, 1974; vol. iii, 1983.

Elton, G.R., *The Tudor Constitution*, Cambridge, 1965.

Elton, G.R., *The Tudor Revolution in Government*, Cambridge, 1953.

Emmison, F.G., *Jacobean Household Inventories*, Bedfordshire Historical Record Society, xx, 1928.

English Historical Documents, vol. v. *1485–1558*, ed. C.H. Williams, 1967.

Ernle, G.W. Lord Prothero *English Farming, Past and Present*, 2nd ed, 1917.

Finberg, H.P.R., ed., *Gloucestershire Studies*, Leicester, 1957.

Finch, M.E., *The Wealth of Five Northamptonshire Families, 1540–1640*, Northamptonshire Record Society, xix, 1956.

Fisher, F.J., 'Commercial Trends in Sixteenth-Century England', *Econ. HR*, x, 1940.

Fisher, F.J., ed., *Essays in the Economic and Social History of Tudor and Stuart England*, 1961.

Fisher, H.A.L., *The History of England from the Accession of Henry VII to the Death of Henry VII (Political History of England*, vol. v) *1485–1547*, 1906.

Fitzherbert, J., *The Boke of Serueyeng and Improuementes*, London, 1523.

Fitzherbert, J., *The Book of Husbandry by Master Fitzherbert*, ed. W.W. Skeat, English Dialect Society, 1882.

Floud, R., ed., *Essays in Quantitative Economic History*, Oxford, 1974.

Foxe, J., *Acts and Monuments*, ed. G. Townsend and S.R. Cattley, 1837.

Gairdner, J., *The English Church in the Sixteenth Century, from the Accession of Henry VIII to the Death of Mary*, 1902.

Glass, D.V. and Eversley, D.E.C., eds, *Population in History*, 1965.

Goody, J., Thirsk, J. and Thompson, E.P., eds, *Family and Inheritance*, Cambridge, 1976.

Goring, J.J., 'The General Proscription of 1522', *EHR*, lxxxvi, 1971.

Goring, J.J., 'Military Obligations of the English People, 1511–1558, unpublished PhD thesis, London University, 1955.

Gray, H.L., *English Field Systems*, Cambridge, Mass., 1915.

Gray, H.L., 'Incomes from Land in England in 1436, *EHR*, xlix, 1934.

Haigh, G., *History of Winchcombe Abbey* [1947].

Hall, E., *Chronicle: Henry VIII*, ed. C. Whibley, 2 vols, 1904.

Hall, H., *Society in the Elizabethan Age*, 1886.

Hammer, C.I., jr., 'The Mobility of Skilled Labour in Late Medieval England: Some Oxford Evidence, *Viertel Jahrschrift fur Sozial- und Wirtschaftgesichte*, lxiii, 2, 1976.

Hammersley, G., 'The Charcoal Iron Industry and its Fuel, 1540–1750', *Econ. HR*, xxvi, 1973.

Hammond, R.J., 'The Economic and Social Background of Ket's Rebellion', unpublished MA thesis, London Univ., 1933.

Hanley, H.A., 'Population Mobility in Buckinghamshire, 1578–1583', *LPS* 15, Autumn 1973.

Harries, B.J., 'Landlords and Tenants in England in the Later Middle Ages: The Buckingham Estates', in R.H. Hilton, ed., *Peasants, Knights and Heretics*, Cambridge, 1976.

Harrison, C.G., 'Elizabethan Village Surveys: A Comment', *Ag. HR*, xxvii, 1979.

Harrison, W., *The Description of England* (1577), ed. G. Edelen, Ithaca, NY, 1968.

Harvey, B.F., *Westminster Abbey and its Estates in the Middle Ages*, Oxford, 1972.

Hatcher, J., 'A Diversified Economy: Later Medieval Cornwall', *Econ. HR*, 2nd ser., xxii, 1969.

Havinden, M., *Household and Farm Inventories in Oxfordshire, 1550–1763, 1965*.

Heal, F., and O'Day, R. eds, *Church and Society in England: Henry VIII to James I*, Problems in Focus series, 1977.

Heath, P., *The English Parish Clergy on the Eve of the Reformation*, 1969.

Henderson, C., Essay in Cornish History, Oxford, 1935.

Hexter, J.H., *Reappraisals in History*, 1962.

Hey, D.G., *An English Rural Community: Myddle under the Tudors and Stuarts*, Leicester, 1974.

Hill, J.W.F., *Tudor and Stuart Lincoln*, Cambridge, 1956.

Hilton, R.H., *The Decline of Serfdom in Medieval England*, 1969.
Hilton, R.H., *The English Peasantry in the Later Middle Ages*, Oxford, 1975.
Hilton, R.H., ed., *Peasants, Knights and Heretics*, Cambridge, 1976.
Hoare, C.M., 'The Last of Bondmen on a Norfolk Manor', *Norfolk Archaeology*, xxx, 1947.
Hodgett, G.A.J., *Tudor Lincolnshire*, History of Lincolnshire, vi, Lincoln, 1975.
Hollingsworth, T.H., *Historical Demography*, 1969.
Hooker, alias Vowell, John, *The Description of the City of Exeter*, ed. W. Schopp, W.J. Harter and H. Tapley-Soper, 1919.
Hoskins, W.G., *The Age of Plunder*, 1976.
Hoskins, W.G., *Essays in Leicestershire History*, Liverpool, 1950.
Hoskins, W.G., 'Harvest Fluctuations and English Economic History', *Ag. HR*, xii, 1964.
Hoskins, W.G., *The Midland Peasant*, 1957.
Hoskins, W.G., *Old Devon*, 1966; Pan ed., 1971.
Hoskins, W.G., *Provincial England* 1963.
Howell, C., 'Stability and Change, 1300–1700: The Socio-Economic Context of the Self-Perpetuation Family Farm in England', *Journal of Peasant Studies*, ii, 1973.
Howell, C., 'Peasant Inheritance Customs in the Midlands, 1280–1700', in Goody, J., Thirsk, J. and Thompson, E.P., eds, *Family and Inheritance*, Cambridge, 1976.
Hughes, P.L. and Larkin, J.D., *Tudor Royal Proclamations*, 2 vols, 1964.
Hull, F., 'Agriculture and Rural Society in Essex, 1560–1640', unpublished PhD thesis, London Univ., 1951.

Italian Relation, The, ed, C.A. Sneyd, Camden Soc., xxxvii, 1847.
Ives, E.C., Knecht, R.J. and Scarisbrick, J.J., eds, *Wealth and Power in Tudor England*, 1977.

Jones, W.R.D., *The Tudor Commonwealth, 1529–1559*, 1970.
Jones, W.R.D., 'Land and People at Leighton Buzzard in the Later Fifteenth Century', *Econ. HR*, 2nd ser., xxv, 1972.
Jordan, W.K., *The Charities of Rural England*, 1961.
Jordan, W.K., *Edward VI: The Young King*, 1968.
Jordan, W.K., *Philanthropy in England, 1480–1660*, 1950.

Kelsall, R.K., *Wage Regulation under the Statute of Artificers*, 1938.
Kenyon, G.H., 'Petworth Town and Trades, 1610–1750, part 1', *Sussex Archaeological Collections*, xcvi, 1958.
Kerridge, E., 'The Agrarian Development of Wiltshire, 1540–1640', unpublished PhD thesis, London Univ., 1951.
Kerridge, E., *Agrarian Problems in the Sixteenth Century and After*, 1969.
Kerridge, E., *The Agricultural Revolution*, 1967; New York, 1968.
Kerridge, E., 'The Returns of the Inquisitions of Depopulation', *EHR*, lxx, 1955.
Kerridge, E., 'The Movement of Rent, 1540–1640', *Econ. HR*, 2nd ser., vi, 1953.
Knowles, D., *The Religious Orders in England*, iii, *The Tudor Age*, Cambridge, 1959.

Laslett, R., ed., *Household and Family in Past Times*, Cambridge, 1972.
Laslett, P., *The World We Have Lost*, 1965; 2nd ed., 1971.
Laslett, P. and Harrison, J., 'Clayworth and Cogenhoe', in Bell, H.E. and Ollard, R.L., eds, *Historical Essays, 1600–1750, presented to David Ogg*, 1963.
Latimer, H., *Sermons of Hugh Latimer*, ed. E.G. Corrie, Cambridge, 1844.
Lay Subsidy of 1334, ed. R.E. Glasscock, Records of Social and Economic History, new series, ii, 1975.
Leadam, I.S., *The Domesday of Inclosures, 1517–18*, 2 vols, 1897.
Leadam, I.S., 'The Security of Copyholders in the Fifteenth and Sixteenth Centuries', *EHR*, viii, 1889.
Leconfield, Lord, *Petworth Manor in the Seventeenth Century*, Oxford, 1954.
Leconfield, Lord, *Sutton and Duncton Manors*, Oxford, 1956.
Leland, John, *Itinerary*, ed. L. Toulmin Smith, 5 vols, 1907.
Letters and Papers of the Reign of Henry VIII, ed. J.S. Brewer et al.
Lever, Thomas, *Sermons*, ed. E. Arber, English Reprints, 1870.
Lincoln, Subsidy, 1526, in the Diocese of, ed. H.E. Salter, Oxford Historical Soc. lxiii, 1913.
Lipscombe, G., *History and Antiquities of the County of Buckingham*, 4 vols, 1845.
Lipson, E., *Economic History of England*, 3 vols, several editions.
Lisle Letters, The, ed. M. St Clair Byrne, 7 vols, Chicago, 1981.

McCaffrey, W.T., *Exeter, 1540–1640*, 1956; 2nd ed., Cambridge, Mass. 1975.
McClenaghan, B., *The Springs of Lavenham and the Suffolk Cloth Trade in the Sixteenth and Seventeenth Centuries*, Ipswich, 1924.
MacFarlane, A., *The Origins of English Individualism: The Family, Property and Social Transition*, Oxford, 1978.
Mackie, J.D., *The Earlier Tudors, 1485–1558*, Oxford, 1952.
Mathias, P., 'The Size of Farms in the Eighteenth Century', *Econ. HR*, 2nd ser., xiv, 1962.
Mathias, P., 'The Social Structure in the Eighteenth Century: A Calculation by Joseph Massie', *Econ. HR*, 2nd ser., x, 1957.
Mee, J.H., *Bourne in the Past*, Howe, 1913.
Miller, H., 'Subsidy Assessments of the Peerage in the Sixteenth Century', *BIHR*, xxviii, 1955.
Minchinton, W.E., ed. *Wage Regulation in Pre-Industrial England*, Newton Abbot, 1972.
Mitchell, B.R. and Deane, P., *Abstract of British Historical Statistics*, Cambridge, 1971.
Moore, J.S., *The Goods and Chattels of our Forefathers, 1539–1884*, Chichester, 1976.
More, T., *The Complete Works of Thomas More*, ed. E. Surtz and J.H. Hexter, 8 vols, New Haven, Conn., 1965.

Norden, John, *The Surveyor's dialogue*, 1607.

Outhwaite, R.B., *Inflation in Tudor and Stuart England*, 1968.

Palliser, D.M., *Tudor York*, Oxford, 1980.
Parker, L.A., 'The Agrarian Revolution in Cotesbach, 1501–1612', *Trans. Leicestershire Archaeological Soc.*, xxiv, 1948.

Parliamentary Surveys of the County of Sussex, ed. J.R. Daniel-Tyssen, Lewes, 1878.

Patten, J. *English Towns, 1500–1700*, 1878.

Pythian-Adams, C., *Desolation of a City: Coventry in the Urban Crisis in the Late Middle Ages*, Cambridge, 1979.

Pythian-Adams, C., 'Urban Decay in Late Medieval England', in Abrams and Wrigley, eds, 1978.

Pickthorn, K., *Early Tudor Government: Henry VII*, Cambridge, 1929.

Pickthorn, K., *Early Tudor Government: Henry VIII*, Cambridge, 1934.

Platt, C., *The English Medieval Town*, 1976.

Pollard, A.F., *Henry VIII*, 1902.

Pollard, A.F., *Wolsey*, 1929; Fontana ed., 1965.

Porter, J., 'Waste Land Reclamation in the Sixteenth and Seventeenth Centuries: The Case of South-Eastern Bowland', *Trans. Historic Society of Lancashire and Cheshire*, cxxvii, 1978.

Postan, M.M., 'Evidence of Declining Population in the Later Middle Ages', *Econ. HR*, 2nd ser., ii, 1950.

Pound, J.F., *Poverty and Vagrancy in Tudor England*, 1971.

Pugh, T.B., 'The Magnates, Knights and Gentry', in Chrimes, S.B., Ross, C.D. and Griffiths, R.A., eds, *Fifteenth Century England, 1399–1509*, 1972.

Ramsay, G.E., 'The Distribution of the Cloth Industry in 1561–2', *EHR*, lvii, 1942.

Ramsay, G.E., *The Wiltshire Woollen Industry in the Sixteenth and Seventeenth Centuries*, Oxford, 1943.

Ramsey, P., *Tudor Economic Problems*, 1963.

Rawcliffe, C., *The Staffords, Earls and Dukes of Buckingham, 1394–1521*, Cambridge, 1978.

Reyce, Robert, *Suffolk in the XVIIth Century: The Breviary of Suffolk by R.R.* (1618), ed. F. Hervey, 1902.

Rigby, S.H., 'Urban Decline in Later Medieval England: Some Problems in Interpreting the Statistical Data', *Urban History Yearbook*, 1979.

Rimmer, W.G., 'The Evolution of Leeds', in P. Clark, ed., *The Early Modern Town*, 1976.

Roberts, B.K., 'A Study of Medieval Colonization in the Forest of Arden', *Ag. HR*, xvi, 1968.

Rogers, J.E.T., *A History of Agriculture and Prices*, Oxford, 1886–99.

Rogers, J.E.T., *Six Centuries of Work and Wages*, 1884.

Rowse, A.L., *The England of Elizabeth: The Structure of Society*, 1950.

Rowse, A.L., *Tudor Cornwall*, 1941.

Russell, J.C., *British Medieval Population*, Albuquerque, NM, 1948.

Rutledge, P., 'Sir Thomas Knyvett and his North Norfolk Manors, 1577–1591', *Norfolk Archaeology*, xxii, 1961.

Salzman, L.F., 'Early Taxation in Sussex', *SAC*, xcix, 1961.

Savine, A., 'Bondmen under the Tudors', *TRHS*, new series, xvii, 1903.

Savine, A., *English Monasteries on the Eve of the Dissolution*, Oxford Studies in Legal and Social History, 1909.

Scarfe, N., *The Suffolk Landscape*, 1972.

Scarisbrick, J.J., *Henry VIII*, Pelican ed., 1971.
Scarisbrick, J.J., 'Cardinal Wolsey and the Common Weal', in Ives, Knecht and Scarisbrick, eds, 1977.
Schanz, G., *Englische Handelspolitik gegen Ende des Mittelalters*, 2 vols, Leipzig, 1882.
Schofield, R.S., 'Parliamentary Lay Taxation, 1485–1547', unpublished PhD thesis, Cambridge Univ., 1963.
Schofield, R.S., 'The Regional Distribution of Wealth in England, 1334–1641', *Econ. HR*, 2nd ser., xvii, 1965.
Schubert, H.R., *History of the British Iron and Steel Industry to 1775*, 1957.
Searle, E., *Lordship and Community: Battle Abbey and its Banlieu, 1066–1538*, Toronto, 1974.
Sheail, J., 'The Regional Distribution of Wealth in England as indicated by the Lay Subsidy Returns of 1524/5', unpub. PhD thesis, London Univ., 1968.
Sidney Ironworks Accounts, 1541–1573, ed. D.W. Crossley, Camden 4th series, 15, 1975.
Simpson, A., *The Wealth of the Gentry, 1540–1640*, East Anglian Studies, Cambridge, 1961.
Skipp, V.H.T., *Crisis and Development, 1580–1674*, Cambridge, 1978.
Skipp, V.H.T., *Medieval Yardley*, 1970.
Skipp, V.H.T., 'Economic and Social Change in the Forest of Arden, 1530–1649', in Thirsk, J., ed., *Land, Church and People*, Reading, 1970.
Slack, P.A., 'Vagrants and Vagrancy in England, 1598–1664', *Econ. HR*, 2nd ser., xxvii, 1974.
Smith, R.B., *Land and Politics in the England of Henry VIII: The West Riding of Yorkshire, 1530–46*, Oxford, 1970.
Smith, Sir Thomas, *De Republica Anglorum* (1550), ed. L.M. Alston, Cambridge, 1906.
Spratt, J., 'Agrarian Conditions in Suffolk and Norfolk, 1600–1650', unpublished MA Thesis, London Univ., 1935.
Spufford, M.E., *Contrasting Communities*, Cambridge, 1973.
Starkey, T., *A Dialogue between Reginald Pole and Thomas Lupset*, ed. K.M. Burton, 1948.
Stone, L., *The Crisis of the Aristocracy, 1558–1641*, Oxford, 1965.
Stow, John, *Annals*, 1631.
Stow, John, *The Survey of London* (1598), ed. H.B. Wheatley, Everyman ed., 1912.
Straker, E., *Wealden Iron*, 1931.
Suffolk in 1524, ed. S.G.A. H[ervey], Suffolk Green Books, x Woodbridge, 1910.
Sussex Inquisitions, ed. M.S. Holgate, SRS, xxxiii, 1927.

Tawney, R.H., *The Agrarian Problem in the Sixteenth Century*, 1912.
Tawney, R.H., 'The Rise of the Gentry, 1558–1640', *Econ, HR*, xi, 1941.
Tawney, R.H., and Power, E., eds, *Tudor Economic Documents*, 3 vols, 1924.
Thirsk, J., *English Peasant Farming*, 1957.
Thirsk, J., 'Industries in the Countryside', in Fisher, ed., 1961.
Thirsk, J. and Cooper, J.P., eds, *Seventeenth Century Economic Documents*, Oxford, 1972; paperback, ed., 1974.

Thomas, J.H., *Town Government in the Sixteenth Century*, 1933.
Thrupp, S.L., *The Merchant Class of Medieval London*, Ann Arbor, Mich., pbk 1962.
Trevor-Roper, H.R., *The Gentry, 1540–1640*, 1953.

Unwin, G., *The Gilds and Companies of London*, 1908; 4th ed., 1963.
Unwin, G., *Industrial Organization in the Sixteenth and Seventeenth Centuries*, 1904.

'The Valuation of Chichester Cathedral, 1535', *SAC*, 92, 1954.
Vergil, Polydore, *The Anglica Historia of Polydore Vergil, A.D. 1485–1537*, ed D. Hay, Camden 3rd series, lxxiv, 1950.
Victoria County Histories, as cited.

Wake, J., *The Brudenells of Deene*, 2nd ed., 1954.
Westlake, H.F., *The Parish Gilds of Medieval England*, 1919.
White Act Book of Chichester Cathedral, The, ed. W.D. Peckham, SRS, 52, 1954.
Will and Inventories from the Register of the Commissary of Bury St Edmunds and the Archdeaconry of Suffolk, ed. S. Tymms, Camden Soc., xlix, 1850.
Willard, J.F., *Parliamentary Taxes on Personal Property, 1290–1332*, 1934.
Wilson, C.H., *England's Apprenticeship, 1603–1763*, 1965.
Wiltshire, Two Sixteenth-Century Taxation Lists for, ed. G.D. Ramsay, Wiltshire Archaeological Soc., Record Branch, x, Devizes, 1954.
Wolffe, B.P., *The Crown Lands, 1461–1536*, 1970.
Wolffe, B.P., *The Royal Demesne in English History*, 1971.
Wood-Legh, K.L., *Perpetual Chantries in Britain*, Cambridge, 1965.
Woodward, D., 'The Background to the Statute of Artificers: The Genesis of Labour Policy, 1558–1563', *Econ. HR*, 2nd ser., xxxiii, 1980.
Woodward, G.W.O., *The Dissolution of the Monasteries*, 1966.
Wrigley, E.A., *Population and History*, 1969.
Wright, J., *History of Rutland*, 1684.

Yelling, J.A., *Common Fields and Enclosure in England, 1450–1850*, 1977.
Youings, J., *The Dissolution of the Monasteries*, 1971.
Young, Arthur, *General View of the Agriculture of Suffolk*, 1813.

Index

Note Since little is gained by indexing passing references to unimportant persons and places, the only personal names included are those of historical figures, chiefly contemporary commentators, also, apart from those of a few major towns, only the names of places which are examined in sufficient detail to rank as subjects; the names of each county means in addition '. . . and places therein'.